PIMLICO

OF THE PEOPLE, BY THE PEOPLE

Roger Osborne's work has provided a range of innovative insights into our views of the past, and how they inform the present. His previous books include *The Floating Egg: Episodes in the Making of Geology*, *The Deprat Affair: Ambition, Revenge and Deceit in French Indo-China*, *The Dreamer of the Calle San Salvador: Visions of Sedition and Sacrilege in Sixteenth-Century Spain* and *Civilization: A New History of the Western World*. He lives in Scarborough.

Also by Roger Osborne

The Floating Egg:
Episodes in the Making of Geology

The Deprat Affair:
Ambition, Revenge and Deceit in French Indo-China

The Dreamer of the Calle de San Salvador:
Visions of Sedition and Sacrilege in Sixteenth-Century Spain

Civilization:
A New History of the Western World

The Art of Persuasion
(play)

As Co-Author

The Atlas of Earth History
The Atlas of Evolution

OF THE PEOPLE, BY THE PEOPLE

A New History of Democracy

————

ROGER OSBORNE

PIMLICO

Published by Pimlico 2012

2 4 6 8 10 9 7 5 3 1

First published in Great Britain in 2011 by
The Bodley Head

Pimlico
Random House, 20 Vauxhall Bridge Road,
London SW1V 2SA

www.vintage-books.co.uk

Addresses for companies within The Random House Group Limited can be found at:
www.randomhouse.co.uk/offices.htm

The Random House Group Limited Reg. No. 954009

A CIP catalogue record for this book
is available from the British Library

ISBN 9781845950620

The Random House Group Limited supports The Forest Stewardship Council (FSC®), the
leading international forest certification organisation. Our books carrying the FSC label are
printed on FSC® certified paper. FSC is the only forest certification scheme endorsed by
the leading environmental organisations, including Greenpeace. Our paper procurement
policy can be found at www.randomhouse.co.uk/environment

Typeset by Palimpsest Book Production Limited, Falkirk, Stirlingshire
Printed and bound by CPI Group (UK) Ltd, Croydon, CR0 4YY

CONTENTS

Prologue

I

CHAPTER 1: Athens and the Ancient World
The Involved Citizen

7

CHAPTER 2: Parliaments and Things
The Represented Citizen

29

CHAPTER 3: Medieval Towns and City Republics
The Burgher-Citizen

46

CHAPTER 4: Democracy in the High Alps
The Communal Citizen

68

CHAPTER 5: The English Revolution
The Subject-Citizen

75

CHAPTER 6: Democracy in America
The Citizen-Elector

98

CHAPTER 7: France, 1789–95
The Citizen-Activist

118

CHAPTER 8: Republics in Latin America
The Subdued Citizen
142

CHAPTER 9: Europe in the Nineteenth Century
The Denied Citizen
157

CHAPTER 10: Embrace and Retreat
The Idealised Citizen
178

CHAPTER 11: India
The Independent Citizen
205

CHAPTER 12: The Postwar West
The Consumer-Citizen
219

CHAPTER 13: Democracy and Decolonisation
The Exploited Citizen
239

CHAPTER 14: The Collapse of Communism in Europe
The Citizen Triumphant
255

CHAPTER 15: Democracy since 1989
The Informed Citizen
276

Notes
291

References and Further Reading
299

Picture Credits
309

Index
311

PROLOGUE

Let's be clear from the beginning: democracy is humanity's finest achievement. Championed, idealised, misused, abused, distorted, parodied and ridiculed it might be; courted by unfaithful lovers, glad-handed by false friends and skinned by unscrupulous allies it undoubtedly has been; but democracy as a way of living and a system of government is the avenue by which modern humans can fulfil their need to construct lives of real meaning. More than all the paintings and sculptures on earth, more than all poems, plays and novels, and more than every scientific and technological invention put together, democracy shows humanity at its most creative and innovative; democracy is a continual, collective enterprise that binds us together while allowing us to live individually. While it endures there is hope, without democracy the world is bereft.

If we're looking for a way of thinking about democracy, then change is a good starting point. In 2009 Barack Obama ran his campaign for the US presidency under the slogan 'Change We Need'; in 2010 David Cameron asked the British people to 'Vote For Change', while future coalition partners the Liberal Democrats promised 'Change That Works For You'. Though our leaders may not like it, the best way to achieve change is by voting them out of office. The ultimate sanction against any government is to throw them out, and democracy's great asset is that it allows this to happen peacefully. Those choreographed moments of transition in front of the Capitol building, when the new president takes the oath of office watched by his defeated predecessor, or the outgoing British prime minister appearing in Downing Street to tell the world that he (it still is almost always a he) is looking forward to spending more time with his family, are the essential rituals of democracy – the equivalent of the public funeral where death is marked so that life can go on. They, and similar scenes in Paris, Berlin, Delhi, Tokyo and Santiago, are formal expressions of the agreement of our rulers to govern only with the consent of the people – and when that consent is withdrawn, they must go.

Peaceful transitions of power, ruling by consent, free and fair elections, universal suffrage – these are all elements of democracy, yet when we try to pin down exactly what democracy is, we find ourselves chasing rainbows. The problem is that every time we get near to a definition, or compile a list of conditions that any democracy must fulfil, we find examples of fully functioning democracies that do not comply, or of societies that are not regarded as democratic but nevertheless fulfil *some* of the criteria. Moreover, every democracy that has ever existed has been different from every other and the more we find out about democracies, the more we realise that any definition will always remain beyond us.

One reason for this elusiveness is that, despite being an apparently Western invention, democracy falls foul of one central intellectual tradition of the West. Ever since Plato, Western thinkers have made it their task to consider the world conceptually. They have set about constructing ideas such as justice, truth and goodness believing that within them lies the route to wisdom, knowledge and understanding. Along with other descriptive terms such as 'civilisation', democracy has had the misfortune to be allocated the status of a concept[1] which then needs to defined, analysed and contested in order for us to gain some kind of greater understanding about the world. This impulse is understandable; if we could define the essential nature of democracy, if we could draw up a manual, then we could apply the 'democracy blueprint' to any society on earth. But in fact democracy is rooted in the converse tradition of the West, one which has emerged in parallel and in rebuke to the world of abstract concepts, and is instead based on practical experience and continual human interaction. Democracy, despite the efforts of philosophers and political scientists, thumbs its nose at theory, rolls up its sleeves and gets on with the task in hand. Democracy does not seek its own perfection, and at times when its adherents do so – through rigid constitutions or immutable laws – they often hasten its demise. Instead it remains in a continual state of adaptation. The truth that there is no blueprint for democracy may dismay some scholars and policy advisers, but it should fill the rest of us with joy.

In newspapers, TV and radio programmes, in everyday conversations as well as in books and scholarly journals, the meaning of democracy is endlessly argued over. And sooner or later we realise that the never-ending nature of this discussion holds the clue to its own resolution. Democracy is ever changing, ever adapting and impossible to formulate, precisely because its major function is to sustain societies where change and adaptation can freely occur. Democracies – both the institutions of government and the practice of governing democratically – exist in a symbiotic relationship with the society in which they are embedded. Where societies resist change, democratic politics cannot operate; where democratic institutions and practices are set in stone, society ossifies.

This elusive and adaptive nature may be a cause for celebration but it leaves open the question of how to write a history of democracy – and of what to include and what to exclude. But here too an answer awaits us. Instead of striving to produce a definitive history of democracy, we should contribute to democracy itself by showing different aspects of its past, revealing the complexity, diversity and creativity that has underlain its fleeting existence. The aim of this book therefore is not to tie up loose ends or to tuck the subject neatly away, but to provide a stimulating historical framework that will help to inform our thinking about democracy and about the way our societies are governed.

With that in mind, this book will take the reader on a journey beginning in the crowded marketplaces of ancient Athens and Rome where we see not only the foundation of active democracy, but the building of the multiplicity of institutions needed to support it. The ancient world also introduces us to a functioning republic: a state without a monarch where the people are sovereign. From the Mediterranean we travel to the great tribal gatherings of the Norse people that show a sophisticated understanding of participation in power; and from there to the parliaments of medieval Europe which introduced political representation, and to the burgeoning cities of the Netherlands and Italy where civic loyalty and the practical needs of government brought about the foundation of the modern state.

The next stopping point is sixteenth-century Graubünden in the high Alps, the first truly democratic state of modern times, which held up democracy as the highest expression of communal life. From there we travel to a church hall in Putney where common soldiers, fresh from the battlefields of the English Civil War and with vernacular Bibles in hand, argued for the right of every man to have a say in government. Across the Atlantic we see how the practice of democracy came to America, rooted in the church gatherings, town meetings and beliefs of its immigrant settlers. France in the 1790s provides the greatest contradictions on our journey – the French Revolution combined a passionate belief in equality and democracy with political violence. The new democracies in nineteenth-century South and Central America reveal how government is embedded in the cultural history of society, and how difficult it is to overcome entrenched interests.

The tumultuous nineteenth century in Europe shows how political reforms were originally brought in precisely to keep democracy at bay, before democratic government was forced into reality by the power of industrialised labour and through political expediency. In the early twentieth century we will see democracy springing up across the globe, before suffering a worldwide and catastrophic retreat in the 1930s. The post-1945 period offers differing fortunes in the stories of India and other ex-colonies, while in the 1950s democracy in the United States faced its greatest challenge from inside. In 1989 European communism collapsed, leaving a world in which democracy became the passport to membership of the international community. At the end of our journey we inspect the conditions for democracy in China, due to become the biggest economic power in the world, before looking finally at the changing face of democracy in Western societies.

Not all of the societies we will examine tick all the boxes of a full democracy. But in each of these times and places we witness the development of democratic practices (such as ballots) or institutions (such as parliaments) that came to be adopted later as essential ingredients of a democracy. Societies develop solutions to their own unique problems, some of which are then available to political activists and reformers elsewhere, eager to adapt them again to their own circumstances.

Before embarking on this historical journey, there is one more point to bear in mind. A chronological narrative seems to imply development and this can lead us to false assumptions. First, that democracies have learned from what has gone before. In fact almost every democracy has had to create democratic institutions and practices in its own way. We have come to believe that, for example, Thomas Jefferson devised the American Constitution based on his knowledge of classical Athens and Rome; but, as we shall see in Chapter 6, American democracy was far more influenced by the practice of town ballots which its citizens had brought with them from Britain, and by the governance of Puritan churches, than by the ancient world. The second false assumption would be that development means improvement. This stands even less scrutiny. Ancient Athens was in many ways the most highly developed democracy that has ever existed, while in recent times democracy has been subject to continual bouts of decline, retrenchment and burgeoning. Our story shows that *democracies* exist at different times, but *democracy* does not necessarily improve over time.

Democracy is always under siege. Yet it is our defence, not just against an overpowering state but against the power of entrenched privilege and of corporate and individual wealth. Democracy is not a dry intellectual concept, it is a set of beliefs and assumptions embedded in our culture – and it is something worth fighting for. However imperfectly, democracy attempts to solve the great dilemma of human life: how to flourish as an individual while existing as part of a community. With all that in mind, let us embark on an imperfect history of an indefinable subject.

ATHENS AND THE ANCIENT WORLD

The Involved Citizen

Walking towards the city from Eleusis you might notice an increase in the number of your fellow travellers. Go through the Sacred Gate, where the Eridanos river flows into the city and the walls tower over you, and then head south-east along the Panathenaic Way, towards the agora and the heart of the city. Men have come from all over Attica, some making a day-long journey, and the open space of the agora is getting more and more crowded. The traders are struggling to do business as men gather in groups, talking and arguing. Here they are surrounded by monuments to the glory of their city – temples where they can thank the gods for their good fortune, commemorations of fallen heroes and public buildings where the business of government goes on.

What a grand city this is. To the south-east lies the hill of the Acropolis, crowned by the recently built Parthenon temple; directly south is the Areopagus, the meeting place of the council of nobles; to the west is a hillside topped by the temple of Hephaestus. Around the agora itself are the Bouleuterion, the meeting place of the Council of 500; two law courts with a third under construction; the mint with its weights-and-measures officials at hand; the Strategeion, the meeting house for the generals; the Tholos, the official residence for the council leader; and a series of *stoas* or roofed 'porches' used for worship and teaching. Crowding in too are temples to Apollo and Aphrodite and the altar to the twelve great gods of Greece. Finally, standing within the agora on the west side are the statues of the heroes after whom the ten groups within the city-state, or polis, are named.[1] This is the year of the archonship of Lysimachus – 436–5 BC – and Athens is at the summit of its power and prestige.

Suddenly the agora starts to empty as men make their way up the hill towards the Pnyx, the vast amphitheatre carved out of the side of the Hill of the Nymphs. As a citizen it is your right and duty to join them in the citizens' assembly, or *ekklesia*, held every ten days throughout the year. Clerks with ropes dipped in red paint will sweep the agora to discourage citizens from lingering. The business of the assembly will have been prepared by the Council of 500, on which each citizen sits in turn for one year. The 500 members sit on benches facing the 6,000 or so in the assembly, arranged on the tiered rows carved out of the bare rock. But before the business can begin a sacrifice is made to one of the gods: Athenians believe their democracy has been granted to them as a divine favour. Then citizens take turns to stand on a small stage to address the assembly before votes are taken, either by a show of hands or by dropping pebbles into different urns. The assembly is not divided into parties (it is illegal to collude) and each citizen votes for himself; the decisions are recorded and filed in the city archives. The meetings are respectful but occasionally they can get rowdy. Taxation and public works are debated and passionate speeches from leading figures present the assembly with the choice of war or peace. The assembly has to decide whether to accept peace offers from the city's enemies, whether to sanction invasions and naval expeditions, whether to be a peaceful neighbour or an aggressive power. As the day's business ends the citizens file out, making their way home to resume their livings as farmers, traders, craftsmen and sailors.

We have just witnessed democracy in action, but the open meetings were only one part of the framework of democracy in ancient Athens. Early on in this first fully recorded democracy, the citizens of Athens had realised that for their will to be properly refined, articulated and acted on, a host of institutions had to be created to support the assembly of the people. Firstly, the Areopagus, or council of nobles, scrutinised any measures passed by the assembly. After 460 BC this function was handed to the jury courts, which then had a political and judicial function. The jurors' political powers were underpinned by a further measure. Under Athenian law any citizen could challenge a measure passed by the assembly on the grounds that it was unlawful or, more controversially, if it was unfair.

Jury courts and citizens' rights supported and regulated the power of the assembly, but at the heart of Athenian democracy was the Council of 500, drawn from every part of the polis through a complex system of lots. This body both elected officials to serve for one year, and examined their performance. These officials oversaw building programmes, street cleaning, festivals, processions, and weights and measures; they served as jurors, civil and military magistrates and, last but not least, *strategoi* or generals. Athenians were acutely aware of the danger that their democracy could be undermined by those intent on accruing personal power, so in addition to monitoring their officials they introduced the famous system of ostracism in order to rid themselves of the politically overambitious.[2]

A key element in this complex system was openness. In most other societies in the ancient world crucial decisions were taken in private, citizens could be punished without recourse to public appeal, and trials took place behind closed doors. Though we do not know every detail of life in ancient Athens, it is clear that major decisions about high-level policy were taken after public discussion, while every citizen had the right to face his accusers and be tried in public. The concept of an open society became popular among philosophers in the twentieth century,[3] but Athens was fusing the practice of democracy and transparency 2,500 years earlier.

The culture that gave us the word democracy (*demos* = people; *kratos* = rule) provides evidence of its practical workings over a period of roughly 200 years, longer than almost any modern democracy: the city-state of Athens was a democracy from around 507–323 BC. That evidence is fragmentary but compelling, giving us a convincing picture of a sophisticated and fully functioning political system. Although many other societies would to some degree have been ruled through consensus and consultation before that time, Athens is the first fully fledged democracy that we know about. How and why did democracy arise in this particular time and place?

The Greeks of the fifth and fourth centuries BC saw themselves as the descendants of immigrants. Their myths told of cities being founded by the benevolence of the gods of Olympus but there is historical evidence that the peoples who occupied the Greek peninsula and islands came from the north, in the same twelfth-century BC migrations that saw others push westwards into mainland Europe. This is many centuries before the classical period, but cultural attitudes run deep and long – the central historical myth of the Greeks was the siege of Troy, an event now dated to the eleventh century BC but endlessly retold seven centuries later.

The sense of being an immigrant people is important for several reasons. Migrant societies display a large degree of social mobility; often they resist hierarchies and live without kings, princes or aristocrats. This may be because social power is connected with ownership of land, while moving to new territories dissolves social structures based on deference and allows the possibility of a more egalitarian culture and society. In certain times and places these connections are discernible, but in most others the opportunity for immigrants to maintain an egalitarian society is quashed by the rapid assumption of power by small groups. The achievement of the Athenians, as we shall see, was to develop a system that would preserve the fundamental structure of their society.

The centuries from 1000 to 650 BC, known to historians as the Dark Ages of Greece, are almost a closed book with little or no historical and archaeological evidence from the region. However, some finds show that alphabetic writing made its way into the Greek world between 800 and 750 BC. The Phoenician alphabet was extended and developed by the Greeks and two finds from the late eighth century BC – Nestor's cup from southern Italy and the Dipylon vase from Athens – both carry long inscriptions written in recognisable alphabetic Greek.

By this time Greek city-states were becoming more prosperous through trade, agriculture, mining and the manufacture of metals. Some of these cities began to set up colonies along the shores of the Black Sea and the Mediterranean. Eretria, Chalcis, Corinth and Rhodes were notable colonisers, founding settlements as far west as Neapolis (Naples), Massilia (Marseilles) and Saguntum (Sagunto in Spain). Athens was not at the forefront of these developments, and it is likely that its size and geography worked against it. At that time the city-state was more like a collection of farms, with settlements spreading across the 4,000 square kilometres of the Attican plain, rather than a tightly defined centre-with-catchment such as Corinth or Thebes. The first recorded political event in Athens was the unsuccessful attempt by a man named Cylon to seize power in 632 BC. This is evidence that the polis of Athens had come into existence as a political entity.

We know that customary laws in Athens and Attica at this time were based around the use of land. In a system known as *hektemoriori*, farmers paid one-sixth of their produce as rent to landowners. These had probably acquired the land as settlement of debts in a process that began to change Attica from a society of small farmers into a hierarchy of wealthy landowners and tenant farmers. Yet the process of *hektemoriori* began to break down in the late seventh century BC when many subsistence farmers who were unable to pay their rent became the possessions of the landowners. This system of debt bondage became so widespread in Athens that, as Aristotle commented 200 years later, 'the many became the slaves of the few'.

In the seventh century BC the polis of Athens was governed through the sharing and rotation of power among the leading families. In this oligarchy a set of three leaders, or archons, were chosen by their fellow nobles. According to Aristotle, the archons were first selected for life and later for a ten-year period of office. Once he served his term, each archon would sit on the Areopagus for life. This system served the nobility well, but the rest of the population had no voice in the government. While this was not unusual in human history, what happened next seems unique. Some time around 600 BC Athenians decided to ask an eminent citizen named Solon to draw up a set of laws to govern their polis. These laws were intended to solve the problems caused by debt bondage and make Athens a more harmonious society. But why should the wealthy ruling class have agreed to this? Why did Athens not become a polarised society of wealthy landowners and enslaved subsistence farmers? We can only guess from the little evidence we have, but some facts may help us to understand why Athens eventually became a democracy.

It appears that the polis was not as prosperous as its neighbours and the ruling class may have felt this keenly. They were unable to wring more wealth out of their lands and, in terms of trade, they had become suppliers of commodities to other wealthier cities. They may have felt the need to remedy this stagnation. In addition, after the attempted coup by Cylon, the ruling families would have feared that any one of them could raise enough support among the citizens to stage a takeover of power. As well as this, the defence of the polis depended on a volunteer army drawn from the ranks of farmers and artisans and, when banded together, the poor farmers had more military power than the rulers.

There may also have been cultural reasons for this unusual move. If we look at societies in the ancient world we see a variety of ways of allowing, restraining, delegating and acknowledging power, all of them much more subtle and sophisticated than simple labels like empire, monarchy, clan, tribe, tyranny and oligarchy suggest. The farmers, fishers and traders of Attica may well have entered into the humiliation of debt bondage while retaining a strong belief in old customs and practices that gave justice, access to power and dignity to all members of their society. Once the effective enslavement of the farmers reached epidemic levels, the ruling class could have faced a social revolution.

Such underlying reasons are obviously crucial to understanding how Athenian democracy arose, but unfortunately they are interpretations based on conjecture. In later history, democracy frequently emerged from a crisis of political leadership. It is frustrating that at the birth of the world's first recorded democracy we do not have any hard information about the circumstances that brought it about. Indeed much of the evidence that we do have on the development of Athenian democracy is historically unreliable. The earliest sources for almost all the political reforms in Athens date from after the late fifth century, two centuries after Solon; the major surviving descriptive work, Aristotle's *Constitution of Athens*, was written around 350 BC. These later texts are not merely likely to show the inaccuracies of passing time, but assumptions and deliberate distortions have probably been included for contemporary political purposes. What follows here, therefore, is a qualified approximation of the development of democracy in Athens. 4

Although Solon's measures, adopted from around 580 BC, were largely economic their effects were highly political. Debts incurred under the system of land rents were abolished and all the land that had been taken from tenant farmers was returned. A ban on exports of foods – except olive oil, which Athens produced in surplus – was brought in, and weights and measures were standardised with those of Corinth, the principal trading city of the region. In addition, skilled workers from elsewhere were encouraged to settle in Attica.

Solon divided the citizens of Athens into four property classes – probably a formal recognition of the existing situation – and gave members of the top three classes a chance to participate in the government of the polis. Members of the highest class (the *pentacosiomedimni*), now including those with wealth as well as the nobility, were qualified to be archons, to be chosen by lot. The Areopagus, comprised of former archons, was made the guardian of the constitution and laws. The next two classes – the *hippeis* (with property bringing in 300 measures) and the *zeugitae* (200 measures) – qualified to be members of the assembly or *boule*, now formally called the Council of 400. This body was to be made up of a hundred members from each of the four ancient tribes, or *phylae*, of Athens; they also qualified for various administrative posts. Citizens of the lowest order, the *thetes*, had the right to sit in the citizens' assembly – the *ekklesia* which we have seen working on a hillside in Athens – though the powers of this body were not originally as great as they would become later. *Thetes* over the age of thirty could sit as jurors in the special courts (*dikasteria*), a position that enabled them to restrain the power of the wealthy. (Those Athenian residents below the *thetes* – women, foreigners and slaves – did not qualify as citizens.) These four institutions – the high council, the council of 400, the citizens' assembly, and the jury courts – were to be the cornerstones of Athenian democracy in the fifth and fourth centuries BC; by participating in them the citizens of Athens governed their polis.

Solon left Athens immediately after his reforms were adopted, in order, according to Herodotus, to 'avoid the necessity of repealing any of the laws he had made';[5] Aristotle tells us that he got tired of criticism from all sides. The wide sharing of power that Solon had intended lasted only for a couple of decades until, in 546 BC, authority was seized by a single ruler named Peisistratus. Nevertheless, to Athenians Solon became a semi-mythic figure: the founder of their freedoms and of their method of government.

The events that ushered in the golden age of Athenian democracy are mired in family feuds and political double-dealing. The tyrannical Hippias, son of Peisistratus, was removed from power in 510 BC by an alliance of the powerful Alkmaeonid family and the rulers of neighbouring Sparta. The leader of this family was Cleisthenes, who retained control in the face of rebellions from other noble families by turning for help to the lower orders – Attica's farmers, fishers, craftsmen and traders. We don't know the motives for his revival of democracy: he may have been keen to reward his power base among the ordinary citizens of Athens; he may, when forced into exile, have seen democratic styles of government elsewhere and decided to emulate them; or it may be that Cleisthenes was just one player in a wider movement for political reform.

Whatever the exact events, Cleisthenes has a strong claim to be the founder of Athenian democracy. He drew up reforms of the city's political institutions that gave substantial power to the citizens, both individually and collectively, and had the political influence to push them through. Cleisthenes understood that to restore the Athenians' ancient rights as free citizens, Solon's constitution would not be enough; further reforms were needed.

Firstly, and most radically, Cleisthenes abolished the four ancient tribes of Athens. These dated back to the times when the polis was a disparate collection of settlements, and reflected loyalties based on kinship networks and location; it is likely that the territory of Athens had originally been roughly divided into four spheres of influence. Cleisthenes saw these tribes as a major source of power, through systems of patronage and deference, for the leading families. In their place he brought in ten new tribes, organised so that the membership of each equally represented districts, or *demes*, on the coast, in the countryside and in the city. This not only dissolved the old power bases, but brought people from different parts of the polis into contact with each other, reinforcing a sense of communal identity. This political redistribution lasted, with minor alterations, for 700 years. We need to remember that the *phylae* were vertical divisions of society, containing members from every class, while the classes themselves – the *pentacosiomedimni, hippeis, zeugitae* and *thetes* – were horizontal divisions based on wealth.

Solon's Council of 400 was now transformed into the Council of

500, with fifty members from each tribe selected annually by lot, in a system that ensured that each *deme* was represented, and that every citizen served on the council in rotation. The *demes* themselves became self-governing for civil matters and membership became a badge of pride, with each citizen asked to add the name of his *deme* to his given name in place of his inherited name. The *ekklesia* too was given more powers and met more regularly. Public officials, who held their positions for a year – the *strategoi* were the sole exception and could remain in post indefinitely – were assessed at the end of their term by members of the council, with punishments meted out for those who had not served the polis well.

Citizens were not allowed to serve on the Council of 500 for two consecutive years, and were restricted to two terms in total; finding enough councilmen was therefore a continual problem. We should remember too that the *demes* had to be administered, so citizens were engaged in an onerous amount of civic duties. While the excitement of a reformed political system would probably have motivated citizens at the beginning, how was their involvement sustained over time? Why were Athenian citizens prepared to give such a big portion of their lives to the government of their polis? One reason must have been that politics was the place where citizens could feel both valued and equal to each other. Moreover, the polis was not a separate entity: the political sphere – the meetings, the debates, the votes – was the place where citizens protected their way of life, and where their common identity was found and celebrated.

There was also a strong military element in the administration of the polis. Athens had to have an effective fighting force and each tribe was required to supply a hoplite regiment, a force of well-armoured heavy infantry, with their own equipment. From 501 BC a board of ten *strategoi* was elected annually, though each general could always stand for re-election. The commitment to the defence of the polis and the ethos of military service doubtless contributed to the citizens' sense of political involvement.

Cleisthenes is a fascinating figure for anyone interested in the practice of politics. His reforms show the eternal paradox of democracy – that the mechanics of the democratic system must periodically change in order to preserve its essential qualities. In order to restore the customary ways of sharing power, Cleisthenes was prepared to be utterly radical. The four tribes of Athens had been the social bedrock of society for as long as anyone could remember, but Cleisthenes believed they were a barrier to the distribution of authority; as long as the four tribes existed the great families could control the polis from behind the scenes. Sweeping them away was perhaps the most extraordinary event in the political history of Athens – social engineering on a grand scale that could only have been brought about by someone who was welcomed as a liberator.

Cleisthenes introduced his reforms around 507 BC and during the next thirty years Athens underwent a series of critical events. The city was on the verge of being destroyed yet, in a remarkably short time, emerged as the wealthiest and most powerful state in a region that had become a crossroads of the Eurasian world. In 490 BC a huge Persian fleet carrying around 25,000 foot soldiers and 800 cavalry landed at Marathon on the coast of Attica. Greek cities on the Ionian coast and islands had already fallen to the Persians. The Athenian assembly met and decided that they should confront the invaders rather than stay behind the city's walls and sit out a siege. An army of around 10,000 Athenians set out to Marathon where they camped in a location overlooking a narrow section of the road to Athens. After a few hours of stalemate, elements of the Persian army began to reboard their ships, presumably to find a better place to launch an attack. Of the ten *strategoi*, five wanted to attack the Persians before they escaped, while the other five advocated a withdrawal to Athens. The leading general or *polemarch*, Callimachus, had the casting vote: as a result the Athenians attacked and inflicted a crushing defeat on the Persian army. They knew that their surprise victory was brought about both by the ten *strategoi* and by the bravery of the citizen army; it was, in short, not just a victory for Athens, but for democracy.

Ten years later the Persian fleet returned led by the emperor Xerxes. This time, in a bold strategy that required the co-operation of the whole population, the Athenian people abandoned the city and found refuge on the nearby island of Salamis. Athens was taken and burned, but the Athenian fleet then lured the Persian navy into the straits of Salamis, where it was destroyed. The triumphant Athenians returned and began to rebuild their city.

The victories at Marathon and Salamis convinced Athenian citizens that their democratic method of government gave their polis special strength. The victory at Salamis also showed the importance of sea power – and while the army was substantially manned by hoplites from the middle two classes (*hippeis* and *zeugitae*), the navy consisted of oarsmen drawn from the *thetes*, the lowest class of citizen. After Salamis the power and self-confidence of the *thetes* began to alter the nature of Athenian democracy.

By the 460s BC a major political divide began to emerge in Athens. While conservatives supported the continuing power of the Areopagus, radical democrats saw it as an obstacle to democracy. In 461 BC Cimon, the leader of the conservative faction, led a force of hoplites to help the rulers of Sparta to suppress a rebellion among their own people, a controversial expedition opposed by the radical faction. While Cimon was away the radicals struck. Led by Ephialtes, they pushed a measure through the people's assembly that transferred the powers of the Areopagus to the Council of 500 and the jury courts, leaving the council of nobles with the single right to try homicide cases. With 4,000 hoplites away, the measures were passed by a majority of *thetes*. When Cimon returned from Sparta and tried to get them reversed, he was ostracised.

Historians have called the reforms of 461 BC a revolution – a seizure of authority by the people and a transformation from a system where the wealthy still wielded power to a system based on equality.[6] Whatever we want to call them, the changes certainly demonstrated the fluidity of Athenian politics. Cleisthenes had devised a structure based on fairness, but any structure is vulnerable to exploitation and it seems likely that many citizens objected to the way the Aeropagus used its power. Thus the mechanisms of democracy had to be changed.

In 460 BC Ephialtes was murdered, possibly by political rivals, leaving his acolyte Pericles as the leading force in the radical democracy camp. Pericles would dominate the golden age of Athens and Athenian politics for the next thirty years, shaping domestic and foreign policy. Pericles was not a head of state or even the leader of a party: he was a citizen in a radical democracy who used his position as *strategos* – a post he held from 443 BC to his death in 429 BC – his personal leverage, wealth and political skills to influence his fellow citizens at a time when the polis became the primary power of the Hellenic world.

From 460 to 430 BC Athens followed an expansionary foreign policy, using revenue from its silver mines and taxes on its allies to build up a navy that dominated the Aegean – a vital seaway in the burgeoning trade between the Black Sea and the Mediterranean. Its allies in the Delian League – formed after the defeat of Persia at Salamis – became, in effect, client states in what has been called a sophisticated protection racket. The term 'league' is deceptive since Athens, in much the same way that Persia had tried, forced almost every city-state in the Aegean to become its ally and pay tribute; the league has more accurately been called the Athenian Empire. Its trading network aimed to bring prosperity to all its members, but any who tried to break the dominance of Athens or refused to pay taxes for 'protection' were severely punished.

The prosperity of the mid fifth century BC provided the funds for great public projects. In 459 BC the Athenians built two walls linking the city with the port of Piraeus, creating a single defendable space with access to the sea. The 'long' walls each extended for seven kilometres, giving a total circumference of twenty-six kilometres. The construction of the Parthenon on the Acropolis, the traditional site for Athenian temples, was begun in 447 BC, followed by a series of other buildings, each showing extraordinary innovation in architecture, sculpture and painting. Athens was by then the centre of the Greek world with poets, musicians, dramatists and artists of all kinds flocking to the city for work and inspiration. The regular festivals and processions were spectacular affairs with every form of entertainment from bawdy comedy and song to the tragedies of Euripides and Sophocles.

As a democracy, Athens was open to internal criticism. The dramatist Aristophanes, for one, liked to remind its citizens of the dangers of demagoguery. In his play *The Knights*, the character Demosthenes tells of how Paphlagon, 'a low-down lying swine', had learned how to handle Demos, the People: 'He took him in hand, like a worn-out shoe, And oiled him and soaked him and softened him up.'[7] Aristophanes also provides the only existing view of Athenian democracy from the perspective of the common citizen. At the beginning of *The Archanians* – first performed at the Lenaea festival in 425 BC – Dicaeopolis complains: 'there's a regular meeting of the assembly fixed for sunrise and here's the Pnyx deserted, while the people chatter in the Agora and run up and down dodging the vermilion rope . . . So now I've come absolutely prepared to shout, interrupt, abuse the speakers, if anyone speaks about anything but peace.'[8] Yet while early in the fifth century BC writers like Aeschylus in his play *The Suppliants* (463 BC) promoted the democratic way of life, later dramatists began to focus on the problematic relationship between the polis and the individual: in Sophocles' *Antigone* (442 BC), for example, the heroine breaks the city's laws in an act of personal moral courage.

Democracy assumes that the voice and opinions of the ordinary citizen deserve to be heard; we might believe this to be a continual assumption in human history, but it is exceptional. During the fifth century BC, Athenians showed a growing interest in the understanding of humanity. Sculptors and painters – we have tragically lost almost every painting from this time – began to depict people in highly realistic rather than stylised ways, as objects worthy of study. While previously stories of the gods and heroes had satisfied Greek audiences, the invention of theatre came out of the need to show individuals struggling with the complexities of their own lives. The writing of history too began as an exploration of why people act as they do, while Western philosophy originated in Athens from the need to address questions left unanswered by other forms of cultural expression, such as how to live the good life, how to act justly and how to balance the demands of freedom and order.

The end of Athens' dominance of the Greek world came with the Peloponnesian War, which began in 431 BC and lasted, with a seven-year interval, to 404 BC. The war tore the Hellenic world apart. At different times during the conflict the Athenian assembly showed itself capable of savagery (ordering the massacre of the people of Mytilene in 428 BC) and mercy (rescinding the same order); recklessness (ordering the fleet on a disastrous mission to Sicily in 415 BC) and dereliction of responsibility (the execution of six Athenian generals after the loss of ships and men in a storm at Arginusae in 406 BC).

The war is known about in more detail than any other in the ancient world because of the account written by the Athenian Thucydides, one of the earliest surviving examples of historical writing. Its most famous passage is a speech by Pericles, known as the Oration over the Athenian War Dead. It is a passionate celebration of a free society: 'Our constitution does not copy the laws of neighbouring states; we are rather a pattern to others than imitators ourselves. Its administration favours the many instead of the few; this is why it is called a democracy.' After defining Athens as a democracy, Pericles extolled the virtues of an equal society: 'If we look to the laws, they afford equal justice to all in their private differences . . . advancement in public life falls to reputation for capacity, class considerations not being allowed to interfere with merit; nor again does poverty bar the way, if a man is able to serve the state, he is not hindered by the obscurity of his condition.'⁹ Pericles celebrated the openness of his city, which welcomed foreigners to observe its way of life, and forged a connection between democracy, fairness, justice, openness and freedom that chimes with current Western ideals. Though this was a piece of propaganda in the midst of war, it would be the last public celebration of democracy for 2,000 years.

Despite Pericles' glowing words, there is little doubt that war and the pursuit of glory had a damaging effect on Athenian democracy. It allowed the *strategoi* to maintain control over the city's policies without much recourse to democratic procedures, and to persuade the assembly of the necessity of malign decisions in the pursuit of victory. In one notorious example Athenians negotiated with the city of Melos in 415 BC in an attempt to persuade them to give up their neutrality. When the leaders of Melos refused, the city was captured, its men massacred and its women and children sold into slavery. A group of citizens were then sent from Athens to repopulate Melos – and run it as a democracy.

After the defeat of Athens in 404 BC, the city underwent a short period of brutal rule by the so-called Thirty Tyrants who were supported by its enemy Sparta. Yet when democratic leaders who had been forced into exile mounted a rebellion in 403 BC, Sparta changed sides and supported the restoration of democracy. While the power of Athens declined in the fourth century, democratic processes nevertheless continued to control the institutions of government, the legal system, public finances and foreign policy. The most notable evidence of their endurance comes from the surviving speeches and writings of the lawyer and statesman Demosthenes (384–22 BC), which earned him the reputation of being one of the great orators of the ancient world. His defence of democracy still rings true in the modern world: 'There is one safeguard known generally to the wise, which is an advantage and security to all, but especially to democracies as against despots – suspicion.'[10] Democracy continued in Athens until 323 BC when the polis was subsumed into the vast empire created by the Macedonian king, Philip, and his son Alexander.

Earlier in this chapter we asked how and why democracy arose and was sustained in this particular time and place. The answer to 'How?' lies in the history I have tried to elucidate; the answer to 'Why?' risks obscuring the achievement of Athens by glib explanations. It seems that though other ancient Greek and Mediterranean cities probably had elements of democracy, Athens was a historical fluke. A particular set of circumstances occurred in one place and at one time: a diffuse territory; a divided oligarchy; a relatively powerful class of small farmer-soldiers; a power vacuum; a culture of self-dependence and power sharing; silver mines as a source of prosperity; outside threats that brought the people together; a culture shared with other cities that allowed the immigration of talented people from across the Greek world – the list goes on, but can never provide a definitive recipe for a democratic society. We can only marvel at the historical fact of Athenian democracy and the miraculous preservation of documents and artefacts that tell its story.[11]

As well as providing a prime example of a functioning democracy, ancient Greece gave birth to the theory of politics. Previously societies had operated through complex relations of kinship and deference, and through the allowance and restraint of authority using embedded sets of customs and rituals. Democracy in Athens gave birth to a new kind of politics in which the conflicts in society were both brought out into the open – and debated in the council and the assembly – and contained within those forums. This was such a breathtaking innovation in human affairs that it took decades for Greek writers to begin to comprehend its significance. Political theory, in other words, lagged behind practice. It is important for us to understand what Greek thinkers wrote about democracy, because their pronouncements would provide a lasting legacy. Yet we might be surprised to learn that the democracy which seems such a marvel to us was not viewed that way by contemporaries with the most profound influence.

The central question posed by Greek thinkers was: how can a society achieve both freedom and order? If, for example, everyone was free to report for military service only when they wanted, how could the city reliably defend itself; if people could choose not to educate their children, how would the future society function; if citizens could vote how they liked, how could anyone guarantee that the decisions would be good for society?

The response to these questions came in two quite different forms. The most influential of all Greek writers, Plato and Aristotle, approached the problem through rational enquiry and observation. Plato was born to a noble Athenian family who were implicated in the Rule of the Thirty at the end of the fifth century BC, and was a follower of Socrates, who was sentenced to death by a democratic jury court in 399 BC. While the work of Socrates was never written down, Plato composed an extraordinary series of works with his teacher as the central figure; these dialogues would form the foundations of Western philosophy. Plato's pupil Aristotle arrived in Athens around 366 BC to study at the academy set up by his mentor before founding the Lyceum.

Plato sought to isolate abstract concepts, such as justice and goodness, before imagining a society where these ideals could flourish. His political theory resolved any possible conflict between the needs of the polis and the needs of the individual – between order and freedom – by closing the distance between them. The individual was expected to become part of a highly structured system that prescribed not only government, but also the bringing up of children, religion, culture and every aspect of life. If the polis and the individual are as one, internal conflict and the messy business of politics disappear. In Plato's perfect society, described in *The Republic*, all difficulties are solved by an all-encompassing system of just government devised and run by rational men with everyone living by a strict set of rules.[12]

Aristotle, on the other hand, looked at the different forms of government in the ancient world, categorising and analysing them. He was impressed by democracy's claims to give every citizen a voice and to restrain the power of tyrants. But his rational approach led him back to the question of how giving power to the majority could guarantee that the outcome would be good for society. Aristotle's answer was to restrict citizenship to those who could be deemed to be virtuous. They comprised those with a good education, since knowledge helped to instil virtue, and a certain amount of wealth – Aristotle had argued elsewhere that succeeding in the world was a sign of virtue. This small section of society would then govern in the name of all and, being wise and virtuous, would make decisions that were good for society. While acknowledging democracy's claim that it brings liberty and equality, Aristotle described it as the rule of the poor; this led to him being cited later by those who opposed democracy as the rule of the ignorant masses. Though their approaches were different Aristotle followed Plato in devising a polis in which internal conflict was eliminated. The politics of democratic Athens, which drew conflict into the open and contained it within the forums of the public assemblies, would, in both Plato's and Aristotle's ideal societies, disappear.

The other principal strand of Greek political thinking took an entirely different view. Protagoras and Democritus looked at Athens and saw that, through circumstance and the efforts of its people, it had managed to hold freedom and order together. Protagoras (485–415 BC) was a teacher from Thrace who believed that theoretical concepts could not be separated from practical experience. You can only arrive at understanding through observing how people behave in real life – hence his famous phrase 'Man is the measure of all things'. Protagoras argued that the political community does not and should not eliminate conflict between the polis and the individual, or between different people or interest groups; instead it needs to accept conflict and resolve it through openness and argument. This resolution, though, is never final – and as conflicts inevitably arise, politics will always be necessary. But how does politics resolve the problem of freedom and order? According to Protagoras the citizens of a democracy exercise power by collective expression and create order through collective self-restraint – acknowledging that their interests are communal rather than personal. The reward for this self-restraint exists in the real world: it gives man the highest form of self-realisation through interacting in government with people from different classes and backgrounds, and makes possible his autonomy, freedom and excellence.

Like Protagoras, Democritus (460–370 BC) revelled in the practical workings of democracy. Democritus also came from Thrace and became a prominent figure in Athens. The fact that such a renowned thinker found no place in the writings of Plato or Aristotle has led some historians to sniff a conspiracy – perhaps Democritus was such a formidable philosopher that neither of his rivals wanted his ideas to be preserved or promoted. We know about his thought mainly through references by other writers.[13]

Democritus argued that we should not be spending time rationalising an ideal future, but instead try to rub along with the present. He understood that humans were both good and bad: 'There is no device in the present shape of society to stop the wrongdoing of officials, however thoroughly good they may be.' So the task of the polis was to oversee and reward its public officials, as they undertook the hard grind of public life that is crucial to the well-being of society. Never an ideological democrat, the thrust of Democritus' work is that the messiness and confusion of political life should be managed not eliminated.[14]

The final thinker in this vein is Thucydides, historian of the Peloponnesian War. History writing involves selection and interpretation, but by laying out the actual events of his times Thucydides was explicitly seeking an alternative to the theoretical approaches of his contemporaries, as well as a break with the mythic storytelling of the past. He examined the relative power of states and of factions within states, taking note of their strategic interests and the calculations they make in deciding when to go to war and when to sue for peace. In his world the competing claims of states and individuals, their fears, ambitions, greed, humility and generosity are the stuff of politics. And when politics fails to acknowledge and resolve human conflict, the result is war and oppression.

Though Athenian democracy was brought to an end by the conquests of Philip and Alexander of Macedonia, it was the rise of Rome that decisively altered the ancient Mediterranean world. Alexander had created a vast empire that stretched as far east as India. Rome took control of much of this Hellenistic Empire from 215 to 148 BC as well as making conquests to the north, west and south. In the process Rome came under such influence from Greek culture that, in the east at least, what emerged was a Graeco-Roman culture.

Roman political history introduces the other key political concept that we have inherited from the ancient world: the res publica or republic. A republic is a state in which supreme power rests in the hands of the people – they are sovereign. This has come to mean a state without a monarch, but its real meaning runs deeper and carries the sense that, whatever structures of government are devised, the people are the ultimate authority. This is not the same as a democracy; nevertheless, the modern intertwining of republic and democracy make an investigation of the Roman Republic an essential part of the history of democracy. Unfortunately, as with Athenian democracy, the origins of the republic are available to us only through myth and the writings of much later, and notoriously unreliable, Roman historians. These have been sifted and supplemented by archaeological evidence to give us a patchy record.[15]

It is believed that the Roman Republic was founded around 509 BC (roughly the same time as Cleisthenes' reforms in Athens), with the expulsion of the last king by a combination of powerful families led by Lucius Junius Brutus. It seems that the city-state of Rome already had a senate made up of men from noble and ancient families and possibly a popular assembly, though both were subject to the king. Brutus revived and expanded the senate and after 509 BC Rome was ruled by two consuls, chosen annually from the ranks of senators. This would have made the city an effective oligarchy, but early on in the life of the republic the plebeian lower orders staged a rebellion against the patrician senate. The price of peace was the granting of certain rights to all citizens of Rome. The plebeian assembly gained formal status as well as the right to elect officials, known as tribunes, who had the power to protect the rights of plebeians by, for example, intervening in legal cases and vetoing laws.

The relations between the patrician families who dominated the senate, the aspiring merchant classes who wanted more power, and the mass of citizens, led to the continual development of the unwritten constitution of the Roman Republic. In this brief history we can only take a snapshot of the workings of Roman politics at a particular time, so let us look at the late republic around 150 BC.

By that time the city of Rome was home to over one million people, a huge population that was not equalled in the modern world until the Industrial Revolution. The city was full of multi-storey tenements, crammed with people eking a living, and always in danger from fire. Of the more than one million inhabitants 200,000 were full citizens and 300,000 slaves; the rest were free people with limited rights, women, who had the same legal protection as citizens but no voting rights, and groups with citizen status such as non-Roman Italians. In contrast to Athens, Rome was generous with its citizenship often granting foreigners full rights. Within the citizenry there were seven classifications according to wealth, and these were originally used to decide on the level of military service. Movement between these classes, and in particular entry into the senate, became more frequent during the late republic: by the first century BC plebeian citizens such as Crassus, Pompey and Cicero became powerful figures, effectively ennobling their families in the process.

The Roman Republic, with all its political complexities, was ruled by an elite. Entry into that elite may have become easier as the centuries passed, but the sovereignty of the people that is implied by the term republic was more or less disregarded. There were some areas, though, where the ordinary citizens of Rome could exercise power. Indeed the political system was able to function because contact between the different levels of society was maintained in a variety of ways. Men of power and prestige were expected to be patrons of men of lower status, to offer protection and education in return for service; this relationship was multiplied many times leading to chains of connections between citizens at different levels of society. In addition all men with political ambitions, from whatever class, had to undertake military duties that would bring them into prolonged contact with their fellow citizens from other classes. Personal relationships built in military service would often last a lifetime.

There were other areas in which contact was made across the classes. First, it was essential for any ambitious politician to be elected to a series of magistracies, and while these elections were manipulated, any candidate who antagonised voters was in danger. When Scipio Nasica ran for the administrative post of aedile, he joked with voters that a labourer's hands were so hard he must walk on them; viewed as someone who insulted the poor, Nasica consequently lost the election.[16] In addition, the ancient post of tribune retained some of its original meaning as a guardian of the people's interests: those who filled it on their way up the slippery pole had to be available at all times to all their fellow citizens. Last but not least, while movement between the classes was restricted, the senate nevertheless understood the need to renew itself through the inclusion in its ranks of powerful and talented men from the lower orders. It made sense to bring those with commercial or social power into the political process.

The Roman Republic eventually collapsed when the powers of the elite became virtually uncheckable. While politics had always contained an element of competition, in the late republic the difference between winning and losing power became a matter of life and death and so politicians began to rely on violence and political manoeuvring to get to the top. In addition Rome had annexed so much territory that distant provincial governors did as they pleased, becoming fabulously wealthy and powerful. Power became attached to successful generals like Julius Caesar and Gnaeus Pompeius, resulting in civil wars fought over loyalty to one leader or another. Suetonius, writing a century later, around 120 AD, is scathing about Caesar's corruption of the republic: 'The rest of his words and deeds . . . outweigh all his excellent qualities . . . he not only appropriated excessive honours, such as the consulship every year, the dictatorship for life, and the censorship, but also the title of emperor.'[17] Julius Caesar is an early example of a leader retaining a constitutional structure while occupying all the important positions himself – a pattern that many have followed. In 44 BC his grandiloquence provoked a group of conspirators who were desperate to save the republic from becoming a monarchy. But Caesar's assassination brought about another power struggle that ended in 27 BC when Octavian was named by the senate Augustus, or 'the revered one'. The Roman Republic gave way to the Roman Empire.

The influence of the Roman Republic on later political history has been immense. Italian cities from the twelfth century began to appoint consuls and later to call themselves republics in a deliberate echo of the Roman past. The United States named its upper chamber of government the Senate, and put its Congress on Capitol Hill (one of the seven hills of Rome). While Napoleon dressed as a Roman emperor for his coronation in 1804, it was Republican Rome that had inspired the revolutionaries of 1789. For good or ill, nineteenth-century European leaders saw the model of a wise senate of great men as their inheritance and talked of a Great Chain of History, in which the responsibility of civilisation had been passed from Rome to themselves.

When the educated and powerful of western Europe rediscovered the ancient world they admired its rationality, republicanism and the rule of the patrician classes. With the notable exception of the United States, democracy was drowned out.

PARLIAMENTS AND THINGS

The Represented Citizen

We strictly require you to cause two knights from the aforesaid county, two citizens from each city in the same county, two burgesses from each borough, of those who are especially discreet and capable of labouring, *to be elected* [my italics] without delay, and to cause them to come to us at the aforesaid time and place.

Edward I to the sheriff of Northamptonshire, 1295[1]

We are used to the historical truism that no functioning democracy existed between the conquest of Athens by Macedonia in 323 BC and the declaration of independence by the United States in 1776 – an interval of some 2,100 years. But neither Athenian nor American democracy came out of nowhere. In each case existing customs and practices, structures and assumptions were brought together to form a coherent and enduring system of government. The next chapters look at times and places where elements of democracy – assemblies, representative parliaments, voting systems, equality before the law – were established and practised, argued for and developed, including one European state that was a functioning democracy 200 years before the United States. In this chapter we will examine what historical evidence there is for democratic practices and structures in the distant past, before looking at the development of medieval parliaments and town government. Fitting elements of democracy into a clear historical chronology is a difficult process when the evidence is fragmentary; the best we can do is show that certain practices existed in certain times and places.

Any beginnings lie outside recorded history. Social anthropologists have examined non-literate societies with sophisticated ways of not only sharing power but conducting trials, making communal decisions and meting out fair punishments with the aim of maintaining social cohesion. But we cannot assume that these kinds of arrangements have existed everywhere and throughout human history – Claude Lévi-Strauss has pointed out that those who we call 'primitive' peoples are likely to be as far removed from the original condition of humanity as ourselves, albeit in a different direction. Nevertheless, it is reasonable to assume that communal systems of organisation on a small interpersonal scale have existed from the earliest times; working together – one of the root elements of democracy – has always been part of human society.[2]

Ancient Athens was part of a trading world centred on the Levant and the Mesopotamian valley. We know that there were assemblies in ancient Mesopotamia and in the cities of Phoenicia, which covered roughly the area of present-day Lebanon with satellite ports along the North African coast, including Carthage. Phoenician traders of the first millennium BC were in continual contact with the Greeks bringing with them, among other things, a rudimentary alphabet. While the ancient world was generally dominated by empires, they were not so omnipotent as we often believe; cities were frequently left to govern themselves as long as they paid taxes to their distant rulers. Empires were not democracies but Herodotus tells of how Darius, emperor of Persia, seized power around 522 BC only after a long discussion between his fellow conspirators over the best form of government. One of them made a passionate plea for a republican democracy: 'I think . . . that the time has passed for any one man among us to have absolute power . . . I propose that we do away with the monarchy, and raise the people to power; for the state and the people are synonymous.'[3] While democracy was debated in Persia, there are estimates that up to half of the 200 or so cities in ancient Greece had a form of democracy at some point in their history, many existing before democracy took hold in Athens. And after the collapse of the Athenian Empire around 400 BC, bodies such as the Arcadian and Aeolian leagues operated on broadly democratic principles with cities sending delegates to joint assemblies.

As we have seen in the previous chapter, the Greek world was transformed in the fourth century BC by the conquests of Alexander the Great. The Hellenistic culture was taken across western Asia as far as India and south to Egypt, and endured largely intact through the takeover by Rome until the Arab conquest of the eighth century AD. Within this vast region assemblies almost certainly had an important role in the government of individual cities. A recent historian tells us that 'Cassandreia had a council (*boule*) and Thessalonica had both a council and an assembly (*ecclesia*). An assembly is also attested for Philippi and Amphipolis, and it seems highly likely that all the cities [of Macedonia] . . . possessed both institutions.'[4] In these and other cases power was negotiated between the city institutions and the imperial governor throughout the Roman period.

While the Roman Empire dominated the Mediterranean world and western Europe until the fifth century AD, the political arrangements of European peoples outside its borders are known principally from the work of Roman writers. Writing around the end of the first century AD, Tacitus describes how the German chiefs consulted the whole tribe (though probably only the adult males) before important decisions were taken:

> About minor matters the chiefs deliberate, about the more important the whole tribe. Yet even when the final decision rests with the people, the affair is always thoroughly discussed by the chiefs . . . Silence is proclaimed by the priests, who have on these occasions the right of keeping order. Then the king or the chief, according to age, birth, distinction in war, or eloquence, is heard, more because he has influence to persuade than because he has power to command. If his sentiments displease them, they reject them with murmurs; if they are satisfied, they brandish their spears. The most complimentary form of assent is to express approbation with their spears.[5]

We cannot say how widespread this practice was, but written documents mentioning assemblies in northern Europe have been preserved from the ninth century onwards. In Scandinavia formal assemblies carried the name ding or ting or thing. The Legend of Asgar, recorded in the ninth century, tells of the Ding meeting at Birka on the Swedish island of Björkö; similar events seem to have taken place in Denmark at around this time. Much more is known about the Althing in Iceland. Recorded as beginning in 930, this assembly of thirty-six clan chiefs met annually beneath the Lögberg or Law Rock at Thingvelir and elected a speaker, appointed judges and passed laws; majority voting was introduced in 1130. The meeting was preceded by the Farthings, assemblies of the four quarters of the island. Later medieval Nordic societies followed the patterns of local assemblies: the Swedish lands had twelve regions or provinces each with its own ding; Denmark had three landlings, while Norway had lögthings. The tynwald on the Isle of Man and the logting on the Faeroes are recorded from similar times although the existence of all these assemblies undoubtedly stretched back in time.[6]

There is further evidence for assemblies meeting in different parts of Europe before the turn of the first millennium but it is difficult to know whether these were gatherings of nobles selected by the monarch, or representatives of local communities. Anglo-Saxon witans were certainly gatherings of the most powerful people in the realm summoned by their kings, but whether those people were representative of certain groups, such as the clergy or the nobility, or regions is hard to discover. While the existence of such assemblies indicates that kings needed to keep powerful nobles onside, there is no evidence of widespread participation in government, or indeed in the choosing of government. Regular assemblies were often held at significant religious times (Easter or Whitsun) so that ecclesiastical and secular matters were combined. Called variously synods, conventus or witanegemots, 116 were held in England between the Viking and Norman invasions (851–1066). William the Conqueror was declared king at one of these assemblies, which continued to meet throughout his reign, and under him attendance was made mandatory. As evidence of similar meetings being held across Europe at that time accumulates, we need to examine in more detail how the continent was transformed in the early Middle Ages.

The slow disintegration of the Roman Empire had left a series of shifting territories ruled over by local clan leaders, dynastic rulers, counts, Roman patrons, bishops and various other authorities. Within these territories there would have been forms of local government, but for several centuries Europe conducted itself without substantial large-scale organisation or trade. Yet in the eighth century a change in the heart of Europe marked the beginning of a new kind of political organisation.

By then the Franks held sway over most of present-day France, Belgium, and western and southern Germany. The Frankish lands remained a loose realm with its nominal centre in Aachen, until a palace revolution saw the Martel family take power in 737. While previously the nobility had scraped a living from the land and attended a court whose prime concern was hunting, Charles Martel introduced a new system of landownership, society and government. Martel brought the Frankish lands into the legal control of the nobility, the monarchy and the church, with some areas being left as common ground, or as hunting forests. Portions of these lands were then enfeoffed, that is they were granted to farmers and peasants in return for work or military service. Many of these arrangements were set down in writing and became legally enforceable; they effectively tied the whole society, from villein to king, into one vast system. This feudal pyramid served to draw wealth out of villages and peasant holdings and send it upwards to the lords and the monarch. Charles Martel's grandson, Charlemagne, used it to fuel his military ambitions, expanding the Frankish kingdom to take in the whole of mainland western Europe – apart from southern Italy and the Iberian peninsula – where he established feudalism and Latin Christianity.

By the eleventh century Charlemagne's realm had been broken up, but the cultural unity of much of Europe would be reinstated by an extraordinary people, the Normans. Descendants of Viking invaders who had settled an area of northern France in the ninth century, the Normans marked their independence from the French king and began a period of expansion and expedition. In the eleventh and twelfth centuries Norman knights successfully invaded England, Sicily, southern Italy and parts of the Byzantine Empire; in combination with Frankish knights, their military superiority enabled them even to attempt the conquest of the Levant. By the end of the twelfth century Norman and Frankish nobles, together with Visigoth magnates in Iberia, had adopted the same culture and often intermarried; as a

distinct group they comprised the ruling elite of every corner of
western Europe from England to Sicily. The feudal system that had
taken root in the Frankish heartland in the ninth century had now
been exported to almost every part of the continent.[7]

It is therefore not surprising that subsequent political developments
throughout Europe showed certain similarities. In the feudal system,
and its marriage with local customs, the king was not a supreme
leader but the most important of a collection of nobles. He would
reward these barons for their services, but they retained a degree of
independence including the loyalty of their own troops. The feudal
system meant that the monarch's place was at the centre of a system
of exchange; he was bound to his fellow nobles through a series of
legal obligations in the same way that they were bound to him. But
the king was more than just *primus inter pares*; he was at the same
time a symbol of the unity of the realm, the guarantor of justice and
defender of the common good. He secured his place on the throne
through recognition by foreign powers, through military victories over
his rivals, and by having direct control of a large swathe of territory.
He benefited further from the feudal custom that estates without
heirs automatically reverted to the monarch.

Recognition by the Pope was vital for the medieval monarch.
Western Europe was a deeply religious society and the church had
immense political as well as spiritual power; thus a king or prince was
seen as 'a particularly distinguished child of the Church'.[8] In return
for recognition by the Pope, the sovereign was expected to rule
according to Christian principles, to defend the servants of the Church,
observe feast days, give succour to the poor, and ensure that his knights
and subjects gave respect to the priests in his kingdom. Rather than
being all-powerful, then, medieval kings needed to negotiate power
within a strict set of limitations imposed by their barons, powerful
neighbours and the church.

Each monarch relied on his council, a small inner circle of advisers.
In addition his court comprised a substantial group of nobles, some
favoured by the monarch and invited to court, others being so powerful
that they could insist on their presence. The monarch's court and
council would, particularly in summer, travel around the realm occasionally holding meetings that were attended by members of the lower

nobility, the clergy and, as we shall see later in more detail, representatives of the towns. In France and England these special meetings were called parliaments (they had other names but it will be clearer if we use just one), so that parliament was originally an occasion rather than an institution.

From the late twelfth century regular formal meetings of the king, his council and court with regional representatives were becoming established in the kingdoms of Castile, Aragon and England. The early development of parliaments in Spain is explained by some as evidence of Islamic influence.[9] In 1188, in an address to the first ever Cortes in the city of Léon, Alfonso IX promised that 'I shall not make war or peace or any treaty without the counsel of the bishops, nobles and good men'.[10] The term 'cortes' describes both a city council and the city where a king keeps his court; the three estates that attended were the nobility, the clergy and the towns – acknowledgement that the latter lay outside the feudal system.

By the thirteenth century parliaments in the Spanish realms were being supported by written statutes. The famous *Siete partidas* (literally 'Seven Chapters', originally known as the *Book of Laws*), completed and issued by Alfonso X of Castile in 1265, declared that a prince was forbidden to issue new laws without the consent of 'the people'; what this meant was clarified in the Cortes of Barcelona in 1283, which stated that 'if we [princes] or our successors should wish to make any general constitution or statute in Catalonia, we will do this with the approbation and consent of the prelates, barons, knights and citizens of Catalonia.'[11]

The Spanish kings may have gone further than their northern counterparts in promising not to act without the consent of their parliament, but feudal lords were flexing their muscles elsewhere. In 1258 supporters of Simon de Montfort presented Henry III of England with the Provisions of Oxford, which included the requirement to hold a parliament three times a year to discuss 'the common needs of the Realm'; this is one of the earliest uses of the word parliament in this context. A subsequent letter from the king in 1261 to the sheriffs of Norfolk and Suffolk ordered knights from each county to come to Windsor on the feast of St Matthew: 'we command you on your part to give strict orders to those knights from your bailiwick . . . avoiding all excuse they must come to us at Windsor on the said day to have a colloquium with us on the aforesaid matters [i.e. the needs of the realm].' Simon de Montfort defeated the king in battle in 1264 and the first formal English Parliament met at Westminster Hall in January 1265. This Parliament had extensive powers over the king, but lasted only until the defeat of de Montfort the following year. Nevertheless, the notion of a formal assembly lived on and was permanently established in the reign of Henry's successor, Edward I.[12] A first-hand account of the so-called Good Parliament of 1376, written by Thomas Walsingham, shows power being exercised against Edward III, first by the elected Speaker, Peter de la Mare, and then by Parliament which refused extra funds, telling the king he must 'live off his own' income.[13]

In the Holy Roman Empire, where the emperor was elected by the princes of seven German states, assemblies attended by the emperor and his full retinue were held within the individual realms, and there is evidence that membership of these gatherings expanded from the nobility and bishops to include other social classes. These were known variously as colloquia, conventions or diets. In 1119 Emperor Henry V declared that important measures could not be passed without a colloquium of the princes of the empire; in 1159 Frederick Barbarossa announced that princes and wise men had to be consulted on all serious matters. An imperial diet held at Roncaglia the previous year considered the limits of imperial power and the autonomy of individual states. This meeting began with a council, where the emperor discussed the issues with his advisers; it then moved to an imperial court where the legality of the proposed measures was argued; and finally a parliament or grand council of representatives from all parts of the empire subscribed to the decisions taken. In 1274 Rudolf of Habsburg summoned a 'general court' with the words of the Justinian Codex, the principal source of Roman law: 'what concerns all must be approved by all'. Edward I of England used the same passage to summon clergy to Parliament in 1295, giving classical authority to the word of a medieval Christian king.

The Capetian dynasty had gained control of the western empire (the territory of most of present-day France) through an election held on the death of the childless Louis V in 987. Owing their succession to the approval of his fellow nobles and bishops, the Capetian monarchs were nominally obliged to hold assemblies of the powerful members of their realm; more pressingly they also needed help with finances and with the administration of the vast territory of West Francia. The Paris assembly of 1059 comprised bishops and nobles, but also many knights and 'greater and lesser people'. By the twelfth century the summons to attend assemblies in France was also extended to certain towns or communes, known as *bonnes villes*. An assembly of 1173 was called a *magnum concilium* or great council, comprising not only the secular and church nobility but also the 'clergy and people of the kingdom of France'.[14] In 1302, in a measure that was to have significant effects later in the history of France, King Philip summoned a body known as the Estates General, comprising separate bodies representing the nobility, clergy and commoners: 'They shall be present in Paris to treat and to deliberate on these matters: to hear, to receive and to do all and singular and to offer assent.'

Over the next 200 years parliaments continued to be called in the German states, France, England and Spain, as well as in Poland, Hungary, Denmark, Sweden, Scotland and the Netherlands, many of these remaining in place until the political upheavals of the late eighteenth century. In Hungary, as elsewhere, the divisions between the 'estates' in society were reflected in the parliament; here, in order to break any deadlocks between them it was decreed that 'the decision was to be made *per sententiam sanioris partis*, that is "of the wiser and more powerful part of the nation".'[15]

The evidence for parliaments in medieval Europe, serving a variety of functions, is widespread. In some cases they were electoral bodies that chose the king; in 1295, for example, the parliament of Sicily elected Frederick III in preference to his older brother. In others, such as the English House of Lords, they acted as courts, trying particularly important cases including those involving their fellow peers. More frequently, however, parliaments fulfilled the twin functions of counsel and consent, including approval of taxation. Counsel consisted of advice from regional power brokers and expert minds, while consent was agreement to measures that monarchs wished to enact. The king was expected to run his court, his jurisdiction and his armed retinue out of the earnings from his feudal holdings, but his duties and responsibilities were extensive and, particularly in times of war, he required additional income. Inflicting taxes was essential, which explains why

attendance at parliament was often compulsory – and why, given
that the burden of taxation fell mainly on the members of parliament,
some were reluctant to attend. In addition, by gaining its consent
the king could use parliament to associate the principal people in the
kingdom with any contentious measures he wished to take, especially
those involving religious matters or military campaigns. This association gradually evolved into the accepted custom that parliament
was the legislative body of the kingdom; though the monarch could
issue decrees, it was parliament that enacted laws, which the king
could then enforce through the courts.

The other side of this relationship was that parliaments, even in
their earliest manifestations, were able to force monarchs to sign
measures that gave greater rights to the nobility and even occasionally
to ordinary subjects. The parliaments that emerged in late medieval
Europe differed from the earlier Anglo-Saxon witans and the tings of
the north in their procedures and their powers to restrain the monarch,
but they were built on the same cultural assumptions as their predecessors. Once summoned, parliaments asserted what their members saw
as ancient rights to make laws that bound the monarchy, and to hold
the king and his council to account. In return for granting taxes to
the monarch, parliaments wanted a say in whether the kingdom should
go to war, or adopt certain religious practices, appoint particular
ministers, sign treaties with its rivals, as well as deciding the extent
of royal forests, judicial procedures and punishments and the treatment of peasants. Members of parliaments didn't always get their way
in these matters, but they established themselves as an independent
voice.

To what degree, then, were these medieval parliaments representative
of the population? And if they were representative, how was this
brought about? One element of representation was the network of
nobles – princes, dukes, margraves, earls, bishops, barons and counts
– who were appointed to be sheriffs of counties, or heads of other
units of local administration. However, while this gave an invaluable
regional dimension to any gathering, it was assumed then, and for
much subsequent European history, that through birthright and
natural authority these men were able to speak and decide matters
for the whole population. Parliaments summoned by kings would

include a broad selection of the nobility and some members from the burgeoning merchant classes, but they did not include peasants. But if the lack of the lowest orders lessened any claims of equal parliamentary representation, there were countervailing forces: it is in the urban centres outside the feudal system that the most interesting developments of democratic practices took place.

We have already seen that medieval parliaments often included representatives of towns, sitting alongside dukes, counts and bishops. In much of medieval Europe there was a ready-made legal instrument for ensuring that members of parliaments from towns had full powers to represent the interests of their constituencies. The term *plena potestas* (literally 'full powers') was originally used in canon law to allow a representative to speak on behalf of a client in legal disputes over church property, but during the thirteenth century this piece of Roman law became part of constitutional practice in different parts of Europe. Pope Innocent III insisted on the possession of *plena potestas* for delegates from six cities in the Papal States in 1200; Frederick II used the term in 1231; and a writ of summons to the English Parliament of 1268 contained the phrase, which was regularly used from 1294 onwards. Around the same time, Philip IV of France insisted that representatives or proctors have these powers, and not plead the need to consult their constituents further. Roman law as outlined in the Justinian Codex did not specify the procedure by which to gain *plena potestas*, but anyone claiming to represent the interests of a town had to ensure that his position was fully supported. Before we investigate the methods used for selecting and approving representatives, we need to look briefly at the context in which towns became so politically important.

In the eleventh and twelfth centuries, just as Europe was becoming a continent of feudal monarchies, a network of trading towns emerged hosting artisans, labourers, masons, clergy and merchants. One effect of feudalism was to give a noble family authority over an area of countryside; it was in their interests to make this a safe place, where people could travel and where the count could collect road and river tolls. This measure of security helped to stimulate trade between towns and to make them into centres of prosperity. Hundreds of charters were granted to towns across Europe from the twelfth century onwards, giving them rights to hold markets, providing their traders with favourable terms over incomers, and granting rights to levy duties on goods. Improvements in agriculture helped the population of Europe to grow markedly, and increasing prosperity created ever more towns.

Towns were a new type of community in medieval Europe.[16] That they lay outside the feudal system was made specific by the use of the word 'free' – that is, free from feudal obligations – in their charters: 'Wherefore we will and firmly enjoin that the town of Wells shall be a free borough, and that all its men and their heirs shall be free burgesses for ever.'[17] The commerce of towns required flexible systems and methods of administration, authority and government if it was to work effectively and give the social and economic results that the inhabitants and the wider realm required. Their special requirements meant that a high level of self-government was necessary simply in order to function – a distant landlord was not sufficiently interested in keeping streets clear, organising fresh water supplies and drainage, deciding on planning matters, caring for the sick, organising festivities, patrolling the streets or repairing the town walls, so townspeople did all this and much more for themselves.

Towns grew organically and their internal administration and government varied, but nearly everywhere governance was character-ised by the need for widely based consent, which in turn involved participation by a significant proportion of the population. This certainly did not mean fully fledged democracy, but the practice of electing candidates for official positions became widespread. Evidence of these votes can be found in town archives across Europe, showing that a continuing culture and habit of elections was widespread throughout late medieval times. The electorate was restricted to those citizens – often called burgesses, burghers or bourgeoisie – who fulfilled certain conditions such as owning property, or paying a certain amount of tax. In English towns of several thousand inhabitants these were counted in the tens rather than hundreds. Nevertheless, elections and the declaration of results were often made into ceremonial occasions, such as Mayor Making, which involved all citizens.[18]

Having agreed that officials and representatives should be elected, the electorate then had to decide how they were to cast their votes. In some places public methods such as acclamation (shouting 'yea' for your preferred candidate), a show of hands or asking people to move to one side of a room were used, but the introduction of the ballot or secret vote dates back to at least the fourteenth century. In Lancaster in 1362, for example, the voters for the mayoral candidates were instructed to 'give their voices privily and secretly every one by himself'. In Norwich in 1415, they were told to go to the polling officer and give 'secretly' the name of the person they had chosen. The records of the Court of Aldermen in the City of London in 1526 show that two gilt boxes with the words 'Yea' and 'Nay' inscribed on them were to be used in elections, and in 1532 a single box was used 'and by putting in of white or black peas the matter is to take effect or not'. This so-called 'bean ballot' was thought to have been an invention of New England settlers in the seventeenth century, but it seems that they brought the custom with them from England.

At Lymington in 1577, three candidates stood for mayor; 'to prevent animosities' each burgess was given three bullets of different colours (bullet is synonymous with ballot, both meaning 'small ball'). In 1689 at Barnstaple another method was used: two pots, each with the name of a candidate, were placed on a table. A voter was given one ball, he put a hand into each pot before 'letting his ball fall secretly into which pott he list'. In 1656 the following notice was issued at Winchester:

It is ordained and established by this assembly that there be forthwith provided one hundred bullets, of colours red and white, in equal proportion, and that the said bullets be kept in a fit box to be provided for that purpose. And that at all such public assemblies and meetings one of the said bullets be delivered to each citizen then present . . . and that, instead of such open and public vote, each citizen put privately into said box the bullet for or against the person or purpose then in question at such nomination or election, according to the dictates of his conscience.[19]

Written ballots were a later invention. In Pontefract's 1607 charter, each burgess was instructed to write the name of his preferred mayoral candidate on a scroll of paper, which was then placed in a bag. Once the votes were counted the scrolls were publicly destroyed, so that handwriting could not be traced. These examples from English towns were repeated elsewhere in Europe.

Nevertheless, given the restrictions on the size of the electorate and qualifications of class and wealth, in what sense could town governments, or the parliaments to which towns sent their mayors and burgesses, be said to be representative? The English early fourteenth-century manual *Modus tenendi parliamentum* ('The Procedures of Parliament') put forward the belief that, while barons and bishops spoke for themselves, the lesser nobility, together with the representatives of the boroughs and the lesser clergy, spoke for England. Notwithstanding this contemporary view, there are problems with seeing this kind of 'assumed' representation as a development towards democracy. While tradespeople in some towns might have some say in the appointment of their representatives, the peasants who made up the majority of the population of Europe, as well as almost all women, had no voice at all. In addition, the king had no constitutional impulsion to take much notice of parliament; whether he did depended on the relative strength of each side. Parliament's ability to exercise its authority was therefore largely dictated by the political and military power of the monarch. Astute monarchs kept their parliaments sweet but also under control by, for instance, calling different representatives each time they met.

Those who attended parliament were able to offer counsel on matters of interest to the peasantry but the lack of direct representation and therefore of accountability resulted, from time to time, in catastrophic misjudgement by kings and their advisers. In the late fourteenth century, with the Black Death cutting the rural labour force and encouraging peasants to demand better pay and freedom from serfdom, regimes across the continent tried to face down the peasants by capping wages. The result was a series of rebellions, ranging from Flanders in 1323–8 and Estonia in 1343–5 to the Jacquarie rebellion in France in 1356–8, and the Peasants' Revolt in England in 1381, which came within a whisker of unseating the king. A spate of later rebellions came in the early sixteenth century, including the Peasants' War of 1524–6 which swept through the heart of the Holy Roman Empire. All these uprisings are characterised by the demands of labouring people to be treated fairly and to have their voices heard by their rulers.

For several centuries, therefore, two impulses of government with limited representation coexisted. The first was the king's need to have

a representative parliament through which he could communicate
with his realm, and from which he could gain counsel and consent.
The second was the need for an administration of the commercial
towns that were crucial to the prosperity of the kingdom – an administration that had to involve a representative element to work effectively. Yet these two elements never quite came together, principally
because monarchs and their courts became stronger at the expense
of their parliaments as the medieval period came to an end. The
reasons for this have been hotly debated but the central factors seem
to be the changes in weapons technology and tax-gathering. The
development of powerful artillery put an end to the defensive power
of castles and walled towns, giving monarchs the ability to control
the whole territory of their realms. Improved tax-gathering increased
their hold on power.

Despite this, and despite the lack of representation of the mass of
the population, medieval parliaments were able to codify one other
essential element of democracy: the basic rights of the citizen. In 1215
English knights had forced King John to recognise limitations on his
own power by signing Magna Carta, which outlined the rights of the
wider citizenry. Its best-known clause is a protection against arbitrary
force:

> No free man shall be seized or imprisoned, or stripped of his rights or
> possessions, or outlawed or exiled, or deprived of his standing in any
> other way, nor will we proceed with force against him, or send others
> to do so, except by the lawful judgement of his equals or by the law
> of the land.[20]

There is further evidence of the rights of citizens in the Establishments
of King Louis, a compilation of customary law promulgated in France
from 1272–3, which gave subjects the protection of trial by their peers
when accused by the king. In 1265 the king of Aragon appointed a
justicia mayor to settle disputes between the crown and its subjects.
This officer was from the lesser nobility and could not be removed
except by vote of the parliament.

Throughout the medieval period, different elements of democracy
emerged in formal institutions and practices at different times.
Representative parliaments were one of these, but we also need to

look at how organisations outside the reach of government often arranged their affairs in ways that we would recognise as at least partially democratic. The Third Lateran Council of 1179 instituted by Pope Alexander III, for example, laid down rules for the election of each pope. The *Licet de evitanda* decree brought the three orders of cardinals – bishops, priests and deacons – into a single college, and made them solely responsible for the election. The crucial provision was that each should be free to make his own choice.

Ecumenical councils or convocations, comprising the leader of the church and the senior bishops or cardinals, were the supreme religious law-making bodies, with the convocations themselves electing their leader. Synods with wider representation originated as advisory assemblies but in some churches became policy-making bodies overseeing finances and property. Different orders of monks and nuns established rules based on rough principles of equality where the senior members of the order had to carry out the same offices and rituals of penance as those lower down. Abbots and abbesses were frequently elected; the ceremonial book of the San Zaccaria convent in Venice describes an election process for the abbess where each nun announced their choice aloud in the hearing of the rest of the convent.

In the secular world, urban tradespeople joined together in guilds in order to protect their common interests. Originally set up as charities to help members of particular trades, they later became more overtly political. Along with other associations, such as neighbourhood companies, guilds were based on democratic principles so that, although membership was restricted, all members had the same status. Trade associations known as *hanses* worked to promote the interests of one city's traders in another territory – the Flemish *hanse* of London, for example, regulated trade between Flanders and England. All of these bodies showed the enduring need for people to share, delegate and restrain power in order for society to function.

In this chapter we have seen how documentary evidence of representation emerged in Europe from the late twelfth century onwards. While this representation was worked out roughly at best, it was an intrinsic part of the process of government. In towns, in trade and religious associations, a good proportion of the population were witness to some kind of election, even if they did not take part themselves.

Yet we should not brush aside too easily the crucial divide between those who were represented and those who were not. It is too easy to assume a beneficial progression that begins with medieval representation and ends with modern democracy. In European culture from medieval times to the nineteenth and even twentieth centuries, it was assumed that people of high social status were qualified and indeed obliged to speak for the lower orders; to represent if not their views, then their best interests. Thus representation, which ought to be a development towards democracy, can turn out to be a substitute, a halfway measure that is used to prevent the further involvement of the population. In Britain, for example, once Parliament took over the levers of power from the monarch in the late seventeenth century, representative government flourished but democracy was suppressed. While representation is necessary to a large-scale democracy, it can also be used to hold it at bay.

MEDIEVAL TOWNS AND CITY REPUBLICS

The Burgher-Citizen

In 1520 the artist Albrecht Dürer left his home in Nuremburg to spend a year in the Netherlands. In his diary he described a procession through the city of Antwerp on the feast of the Assumption:

> the whole town of every craft and rank was assembled, each dressed in his best according to his rank. And all ranks and guilds had their signs, by which they might be known . . . There were the Goldsmiths, the Painters, the Masons, the Borderers, the Sculptors, the Joiners, the Carpenters, the Sailors, the Fishermen, the Butchers, the Leatherers, the Clothmakers, the Bakers, the Tailors, the Cordwainers – indeed workmen of all kinds and many craftsmen and dealers who work for their livelihood. Likewise the shopkeepers and merchants and their assistants were there.[1]

The procession was accompanied by musicians and contained a group of clerics, as well as a series of floats and tableaux depicting biblical scenes, together with children dressed in the costumes of many lands – it took more than two hours to pass Dürer's house. Here was a medieval city made wealthy by trade, enjoying itself, paying respect to its traditions – social, religious and commercial – and celebrating its existence. The sense of civic pride and identity in medieval and early modern towns, and the sheer vibrancy of life in these self-contained vessels of humanity, were an essential element in their desire for self-government.

Towns in most parts of Europe fell within the realm of a monarch who carried ultimate power, but there were exceptions which give us insights into methods of representation and the need for greater participation in government that we began to see in the last chapter. Two areas of Europe are of particular interest here: the Low Countries and the north of Italy.

Around the turn of the first millennium the soggy marshland that bordered the Ijsselmeer near the edge of the North Sea was disregarded by the feudal nobility. Regularly flooded, full of dangerous and bewildering creeks, this was a land of fishers and a few cattle farmers, a place that was difficult to settle and cultivate. But, as European trade burgeoned, this near-wasteland became a crossroads, a crucial link from the North Sea and the Baltic to the heart of Europe via the Ijssel, Rhine, Waal and Meuse rivers.

By the late eleventh century the people of the area began to build dykes to hold back seawater and complex systems of locks for regulating tides and river levels. These were prodigious feats of engineering combining confidence, ambition and sheer muscle. Dams and locks allowed the marshes to be drained for pastoral use while providing navigable channels for shipping; sophisticated sets of sluices allowed water levels to be controlled, giving the precious gift of predictability to farmers and traders.

The dykes built by these medieval villagers were simply enormous; one dyke dammed the whole south side of the Ijsselmeer from the Gooi across the mouth of the Amstel nearly to Haarlem – a distance of around forty kilometres. The engineering works required large-scale planning and co-ordination, but they were not undertaken by feudal masters; they were organised by local farmers, fishers and traders to protect their land and their trade. For them water was an eternal resource and an eternal problem, and dealing with its vagaries was a matter of survival. They could not rely on some higher authority to come to their aid; they had, literally, to roll up their sleeves and get on with it.

Once built, the dyke and lock systems required administration and continual repair. By the twelfth century an administrative system of dyke managers (*dijkgraven*) and landowners (*ingelanden*) was in place. A recent historian of Amsterdam, Geert Mak, argues that this home-grown necessity made the Dutch 'tend towards decentralisation and a rough kind of democracy, [that] was to form the basis of the administrative tradition which, in the end, would determine Dutch political culture for centuries to come'.[2]

Amsterdam first appears in written records in 1275, and here we are presented with a crucial paradox in the history of democracy. The coming together to solve communal problems, such as in the medieval Netherlands, lies outside of documentary history. There was no need to write down agreements or political structures when the issue at hand was dealt with harmoniously; we can assume that people in these situations acted through consensus, participation and a need for all to have a voice. On the other hand, written records often arrive in these communities with the coming of an outside formal authority, which is invariably hostile to the widespread sharing of power. The presence of informal or undocumented democratic practices then needs to be discerned between the lines of these formal records.

In the declaration of 1275, Count Floris of Holland granted freedom from taxation 'to the people abiding near the Amsteldam' (the city is named after the dam across the Amstel river). At this time the count had nominal authority over the county of Holland, an entity within the Holy Roman Empire; his grant to the local people was significant since the bridges and locks under his control charged tolls. While this may have been an act of selfless generosity it is more likely to have been an acknowledgement of political reality. Though not yet the inhabitants of a defined city, the people of the Amstel dam were a recognisable group with the power to negotiate with their overlord.

Geert Mak describes Amsterdam as 'a country by itself, a small nation inside a large one' – a statement that rings true for many medieval towns and cities.[3] By 1296, when the van Aemstel family led a rebellion against the Count of Holland, the city had walls and a castle of sorts. These were torn down when the uprising failed (and only rediscovered in the twentieth century), but by 1305 the citizens of Amsterdam were formally recognised by the Bishop of Utrecht as having rights beyond the authority of the local church administration, the Count of Holland, or the van Aemstels.

No one gives up power without a reason. The placing of the city and its people outside the authority of church, emperor and nobility was another recognition of political reality. The instruments of authority that had grown up under the system that wove together feudalism and the Catholic Church could not cope with the new world of urban commerce. New skills, new levels of experience and hard-won expertise were needed which they simply could not supply. In the countryside feudal knights could rule over their estates with impunity and the hierarchical system produced enough surplus to keep the system working; but running a town required the co-operation of its citizens. In the social, political and mercantile economy a single absolute authority would serve only to oppress the diverse and spontaneous activity that gave the town its purpose. Recognition of this fact did not come easily, and for centuries different powers tried to muscle in on Amsterdam and other towns and cities with more or less success. But even when it was not in explicit control, the shared power of the citizenry has been an important element in the governance of European towns from medieval times onwards.

Events to the south of Amsterdam pushed the politics of the region further in the direction of self-government. By the late twelfth century, the cities of Flanders had grown rich on the wool trade. Ghent, Bruges, Kortrijk, Hesdin and Béthune were among the wealthiest towns in Europe but the trade and government of the cities were in the hands of a few patrician families supported by the French king, Philip IV. The artisans of Flanders had sympathetic allies in the form of local counts who contested the French claim of jurisdiction over Flanders. In 1302 the situation ignited when the textile workers of Ghent went on strike over taxes. When threatened with violent punishment by the ruling nobility, they grouped together under their trade banners – there is evidence that artisans were already organised into militias – though it was unlawful to assemble without permission. Ten thousand workers descended on the Friday market and proceeded to drive the city's nobles through the streets; most escaped to the citadel at Gravensteen where, after a brief siege, they surrendered and were forced to swear loyalty to the common people. The French governor prepared to take on the workers in Bruges, the French army seizing the city on 17 May 1302; but the rebels went into hiding and the following morning, using the bell for matins as a signal, they cut the throats of 120 Frenchmen together with scores of their own nobility. Then, on 11 July, the Flemish artisans defeated the French nobility at the so-called Battle of the Golden Spurs. The victory, in which the vaunted French cavalry became bogged down in the marshy ground, served as a symbol of Flemish independence and was a springboard for a change in the politics of the Low Countries. In the wealthy wool towns of Flanders, guilds now began to flex their muscles, seeking not just protection from taxes but a voice in government – in Liège, for example, from 1303 half the seats on the city's council were reserved for guilds. The gains of the guilds were never permanently established, with the nobility, the church and foreign armies all vying for power, but they became a notable element in the political power struggles of Flemish towns.

A 1305 charter decreed that Amsterdam be run by councillors and a sheriff. The councillors, who were elected from among the eligible citizens (known as burgesses), were able to pass laws and mete out justice, and to allow or disallow citizenship. The charter echoed similar documents drawn up in the twelfth, thirteenth and fourteenth centuries for towns across Europe, from Bristol (1155) to Mainz (1244), Rouen (1150), Gdansk (1235) and Lübeck (1143). Whether these were granted by monarchs, counts or bishops depended on the dominant local power at the time, but all gave protection of the rights of the citizens and traders.[4] A charter would, for example, forbid anyone from trading more than forty days in any year in a town unless he was a citizen, and would give the burgesses the right to elect a mayor and council – and even to make themselves self-governing, as happened in Mainz and Rouen.

By the fifteenth century Amsterdam was an important trading centre run by four burgomasters, a sheriff, seven magistrates (later expanded to nine) and a town council. The council of thirty-six, which represented all the citizens but was mostly drawn from the wealthy merchants, elected the burgomasters who ran the city for their year of office. The whole council was consulted on major decisions, for example whether to support other cities' military exploits, such as the 1398 Dutch expedition against the Frisians.

In Amsterdam and across Europe the late medieval period saw the emergence of a new type of European. Neither noble nor cleric, artisan nor peasant, the urban merchant did not rely on ancient lineage to make his mark on the world. Money began to dominate society and the merchants of Amsterdam knew their own worth; some even traded money itself and became immensely rich and politically powerful by doing so. These men and their families were the burgesses or bourgeoisie of the new towns of Europe, in whose charters, including that of Amsterdam, the status of a burgess was distinct. Qualification required a certain period of residence, an amount of property or taxable income, and the approval of your fellows. Approval depended on both piety and connections, and the council of Amsterdam had the ultimate power to decide who could be allowed into this special circle. The boundary of the polity, the line around that privileged group of citizenry, was carefully controlled.

We know some detail of the government of these towns through the writings of Ludovico Guicciardini, a Florentine whose *Description of the city of Antwerp* was first published in 1567. According to Guicciardini, the city was nominally ruled by the Duke of Brabant as margrave (or local representative) of the Holy Roman Empire. But he notes that the city has 'great privileges of such a character, obtained and granted from time immemorial, that it now rules and governs itself, as if autonomous, almost like a free city and republic, while always respecting the rights and suzerainty of the Prince'.[5] This sentence sums up the position of towns and cities throughout Europe – left to run their own affairs so long as they respected the authority of an external power.

Two other elements in urban society added to the development of democratic institutions and practices – defence and religion. The control of military force was the ultimate political power and Amsterdam was in the peculiar, but by no means unique, position of having to arrange its own defence while being nominally part of an empire. Armed companies and militia groups emerged with the solemn duty to defend the city. These self-organising units were common in European cities (we shall see more of this in Italy later in this chapter). Beginning as groups of neighbours who banded together to defend themselves, they became formal societies or brotherhoods of artisans. City authorities tried to regulate them but they had the potential, as we have already seen in Ghent, to take power for themselves.[6] But defence was mostly a unifying factor among townspeople across Europe, their sense of common interest reinforced by the great walls that surrounded them. In medieval towns self-defence and defence of the community meant much the same thing: everyone was involved in everyone else's well-being. The gates of

Amsterdam and a thousand other towns were shut and locked every night, and the keys ceremonially presented to the mayor or burgomaster, who then oversaw the reopening at sunrise.

The fact that religion played a part in the development of town governments is hardly surprising. Medieval Europe was a Christian society; its inhabitants viewed every aspect of their lives through the prism of their faith. From the 1520s the Reformation divided Europe into Catholic and Protestant states, intensified religious belief and made religion a potent political force. This divide cut right through the Low Countries and in the late sixteenth century plunged the small states into a war against their Catholic Habsburg ruler, Philip II of Spain. Philip's dream was to re-establish the Catholic faith across Europe; one major obstacle was Protestant England, the other was the Calvinist provinces of the Low Countries. Philip saw that if he could subdue the Dutch Calvinists and bring them back to the Catholic faith, the region would be an ideal launch pad for an invasion of England.

The religious dimension of the Dutch Revolt of 1568–1609 is central to the history of democracy. Protestantism in northern Europe encompassed a series of different practices and interpretations of the Christian faith. Nevertheless, all Protestants believed in the importance of the faith and the conscience of the individual believer. This removed the status of the church hierarchy, since priests and bishops would be an unnecessary encumbrance to the relation between believer and God. Instead the church became its members, and the organisation and administration of the church a process of debate and agreement among believers.

The view that modern democracy is the product of a Protestant culture must be heavily qualified by the events in Catholic Italy (see below); however, the role of Calvinists and other Nonconformist groups stands further examination. Martin Luther, the original theologian of the Reformation, had stressed the need for piety and a return to the simple ways of the early Christian Church. But Jean Calvin's teachings had much more resonance for the burghers of the sixteenth century, and were widely adopted by the urban people of the Low Countries as well as in Scotland and among growing numbers of the English. A brief look at the background to Calvin's work will help to show how his influence was quite different from Luther's.

Calvin was a pastor in France who broke with the Catholic Church around 1530 and fled to Switzerland. In 1536 he published *The Institutes of the Christian Religion* and was then invited to work for the Protestant church in Geneva. The city had gained its independence from the dukes of Savoy in 1530, forming a treaty with the nearby cities of Bern and Fribourg. After a dispute that led to his expulsion, Calvin was invited back to Geneva by the city council in 1541. His influence turned Geneva into an effective Protestant theocracy, with religious refugees and scholars flooding to the city from the surrounding Catholic countries. Calvin and his supporters made the city the centre of a continent-wide movement by encouraging the translation and printing of hundreds of Protestant texts that were banned elsewhere in Europe, as well as training pastors to spread the ideas of the Reformation.

Like Luther, Calvin believed in predestination: that the fate of each of us is mapped out before we are born and, moreover, that the distance between God and the individual is so great that no amount of good behaviour will have any influence with an omnipotent deity. Working hard, serving your community, behaving piously, gaining respect were not ways to bring about salvation, but they were *possible* indications that you could be among those chosen by God. Calvinists were in a continual state of unknowing about their destiny, and therefore rigorous in their pursuit of Christian duty. For the self-sufficient, pious, undemonstrative traders of northern Europe, the encouragement to good behaviour, sobriety and neighbourliness struck a deep chord. Calvin also provided the apparatus – the theology, prayer books, liturgy and pastors – through which his vision could be realised.

Along with their Dutch cousins from Haarlem, Leiden and elsewhere, the Calvinist Amsterdammers believed that the word of God stood above the orders of emperors and kings. The historian of Amsterdam Hajo Brugmans wrote that 'Calvinism has its roots in the free city [of Geneva] and has never betrayed this beginning. It has originated among a citizenship freed from noble authority and has never denied its birth.'[7] Calvinism, the product of a free city, was welcomed in the free cities of the Low Countries.

Calvinist religious culture – in which only God had the right to rule over men – manifested itself in politics in different ways. The sixteenth century had seen the strengthening of national monarchies in most of western Europe, including Spain, France, England, Scotland

and Sweden. The Habsburg-ruled Holy Roman Empire was an exception, and once the Dutch provinces threw off the rule of the Habsburgs they had to decide how they would govern themselves. In 1588 the United Provinces, as they became known, declared themselves to be an independent republic – the first since ancient times that embraced a nation rather than a city-state. It was a revolutionary move, and one that was unwelcome in the courts of Europe's monarchs.

The religious and social tolerance of the Dutch Republic spread the influence of its politics well beyond its own shores. Nonconformists of all kinds escaped persecution in their own countries by travelling to the United Provinces. John Locke fled there in 1683 under suspicion of involvement in a plot against the English king; René Descartes lived in different cities in the republic from 1628 to 1649, during which time he wrote most of his major works; and it was a congregation of English exiles in Leiden that organised the historic *Mayflower* voyage of 1621. The *Mayflower* provides a direct link between the Dutch Republic and the early history of the United States, whose name is an echo of the United Provinces; in 1643 settlers in North America called themselves the United Colonies of New England and, as we shall see in Chapter 6, their religious sensibilities would be a major element in the political life of the colonies.

The principal religion of the provinces also had an impact on politics elsewhere. Calvinism was a major factor during the English Revolution, as soldiers of the New Model Army carried Geneva Bibles containing marginal notes that approved the removal of tyrants. The connection of the Dutch Republic with Britain was firmly established in 1688 when the English Parliament invited William of Orange, Statdholder of five of the United Provinces, to be king of England and Ireland. (During his reign he also became king of Scotland, and the countries were united within the kingdom of Great Britain.) In the United Provinces, William was a prince appointed to the post of stadtholder by the councils of the different provinces, and given command of the army – in fact he won his position through his military prowess in wars against the French and English. He was therefore quite used to the constitutional arrangements that the English Parliament devised (see Chapter 4); the workings of the Dutch Republic certainly informed the British political system that emerged after 1688.

The Republic of the United Provinces emerged out of a culture of autonomy and fairness, an urban realm of hard business and a religious sensibility that placed the individual within a community of the faithful; this was a message that spread around the Protestant world.

Outside the Netherlands, the medieval cities that showed the most interesting developments in self-government were in northern Italy. The dazzling innovations in painting, architecture and sculpture that mark the Italian Renaissance have dominated our views of the history of Italian cities, but the great artistic and cultural achievements of the fifteenth century arose not from the patronage of the Medici, Sforza and Gonzaga families, but from the social and political changes that took place over the preceding centuries.

What, then, was special about cities like Venice, Florence, Padua, Milan, Genoa, Urbino, Siena, Pisa and Verona? Firstly, the lack of an external controlling authority – emperor, king or pope – gave these cities the need and opportunity to run their own affairs; secondly, the wealth generated by trade, manufacture and commerce was greater in this region than any other (though Flanders was its equal for a time), and this gave Italian cities both the resources to protect themselves and to project their power into the surrounding area. Wherever the twin factors of weak external authority and prosperity appeared in Europe, city self-government flourished. From the mid eleventh century onwards cities that lay on the boundaries of powerful realms – in Lorraine, Burgundy, the lower Rhine, Swabia, the Danube, Toulouse and Languedoc, Marseilles, Provence, and the Rhone corridor – all developed muscular forms of self-government, but it was in the north of Italy that city government was most developed and where it had the greatest lasting influence. During the late medieval period Italian cities developed a political model that replaced the feudal state: based on trade and commerce rather than enfeoffment, it would lay the foundation of modern Western politics.

By the twelfth century, northern Italy was at the southern end of Europe's golden trading arc, a zone of rich agricultural land, manufactories, trading routes and burgeoning markets running from the coasts of Britain and the Baltic, through the Low Countries and the Rhine corridor, through Champagne, Franche-Comté and the Rhône, and across the Alps to Lombardy and Tuscany, and in particular to Venice and Genoa with their access to the Mediterranean and the riches of the East. Since the disintegration of the Roman Empire the north of Italy had been either a battleground between external powers or a neglected part of an empire; in the words of one historian, Italy in the eleventh and early twelfth centuries was a place of 'political wreckage and confused authority'.[8] Lombardy and Tuscany were nominally ruled by the German king and Holy Roman Emperor, in whose absence feudal lords, counts and bishops tried to cling to powers granted by custom and practice. But their world was rapidly changing.

After centuries of stagnation, the total European population increased from around thirty-five million in 1000 to seventy-three million in 1340 on the eve of the Black Death.[9] This growth was made possible by the clearance and drainage of ever more land, which consequently became a highly desirable commodity. Feudal arrangements began to alter as land could be exchanged for cash or political support rather than fealty and service. The key here was the growing commercial cash economy which allowed nobles to move into cities rather than remaining on their estates. This was the time of a widely unheralded commercial revolution, in which Italy led the way. Venetian, Florentine, Milanese and Genoese bankers began to issue bills of exchange that could be passed on as legal tender and redeemed across a growing network of European markets. For centuries wealth and power had been reckoned through the ownership or control of land; now wealth began to be counted in money which could be used to buy goods across the whole continent.

Added to these new commercial realities were the confusions of power. Dating back to the time of Charlemagne the feudal unit of jurisdiction was a count's *contado* or county, while the church, a powerful political as well as religious force, was organised through diocese and parishes. The *contado* and the bishop's diocese were often coincident, but not always: in Siena, for example, some parishes in the *contado* belonged to two dioceses. Even within the secular realm, authority was confused with different families claiming rights to the same territory through noble titles granted by different princes. The church, being an owner of land and property, needed to protect itself against the aggressions of local nobility and often did this by appealing to the authority of the emperor. In documents dating from as early as 843 the Bishop of Arezzo was granted temporal authority over his diocese by the emperor in preference to the local count. In 1055 the emperor granted lands to the church of Siena with the following instructions: 'Further, we desire and command that the bishop shall have a right to the public services resting upon the aforenamed possessions of his church, without interference from any archbishop, bishop, duke, margrave, count, viscount, or any other person of our realm.'[10]

Thus a bishop was often the feudal as well as the religious lord of his diocesan lands, making him an alternative ruler within the *contado*. But bishops might be granted powers by the emperor, while others were favoured by the Pope. What mattered of course was power on the ground, and this was increasingly concentrated in the rapidly growing cities. The question was: who would control that power?

The first steps to develop formal political structures out of the competing interests of church, counts, princes and the emperor came in the 1080s. In that decade six major cities in Italy – Pisa, Lucca, Milan, Parma, Rome and Pavia – organised themselves as communes. Men of social rank and property, exasperated at the lack of stable authority, formed sworn associations in which they pledged loyalty to each other and declared themselves to be the governing authority. In the next seventy or so years Piacenza, Asti, Arezzo, Genoa, Como, Verona, Bologna, Siena and Florence also became communes. The Jewish traveller Benjamin of Tudela noted that 'They possess neither king nor prince to govern them, but only the judges appointed by themselves.'[11] These were exclusive oligarchies within which offices, sometimes called consulates in a deliberate echo of Rome, were rotated. There are hints of popular assemblies in the early phase of the communes: consuls in Pisa, for example, claimed that their authority derived from 'the entire people of Pisa in public gathering, by a cry of Fiat, Fiat', while in Cremona in 1120 knights who were granted lands swore an oath in front of the people 'and the whole parliament'.[12]

However, public assemblies seem to have been rapidly overtaken by councils which served the commune in different ways. Their size varied but there are indications of impressive levels of participation. The great council of Verona in 1254 had 1,285 members, while the council of Modena in 1306 numbered 1,600. In Pisa in 1162 there were ninety-one official posts in the commune, including watchmen and overseers of streets and drainage, but also valuers, assayers of currency, and accounts inspectors. In 1257 Siena had 860 official posts. Methods of election to councils were as various as those we encountered in Chapter 2, including drawing lots, two-stage indirect elections, and elections by outgoing officials – and sometimes combinations of all three.

While Italian and other European towns may have lain within the realm of kings or emperors, these were distant figures who showed no interest in the problems that had to be solved at the basic levels of urban living. For town dwellers the church was a major element in all aspects of life, and church structures were physical as well as human. *Boni homines* or 'trusty men' were elected by parish associations to maintain the fabric of the parish church,[13] and this system extended out into other communal essentials like water supply and public hygiene, and to informal courts where disputes between neighbours could be settled. Much of this self-generated activity is hidden from historians, but it starts to become visible during the eleventh century as *boni homines* began signing agreements with feudal landlords, sitting in courts and holding meetings with neighbouring parishes. The occupations of those named as *boni homines* in Florence include smiths, tailors and bell-founders, indicating members of the artisan class. A document dating from 1124 refers to *boni homines* from Siena accompanying their bishop on a journey to Rome to plead with the Pope in a dispute with the neighbouring city of Arezzo. The following year a governing body of consuls and the *boni homines* were operating in parallel in Siena. We are beginning to see the meeting of power from above and power from below.

The position of the Italian cities and their ruling communes took a dramatic turn when the German emperor Frederick Barbarossa decided to enforce his power over his Italic kingdom. Before then emperors had granted occasional rights to cities – Henry IV agreed in 1081 to build no castle within six miles of Lucca, to withdraw his jurisdiction from Pisa and not to appoint any new marquis in Tuscany without the agreement of the people of Pisa. These concessions had been made in response to occasional rebellions which Barbarossa was now determined to quell. From 1155 onwards he led six expeditions to Italy, but in 1176 the cities of Lombardy led by Milan defeated his forces at Legnano. The conflict staggered on for another seven years before Frederick acknowledged his inability to impose his will on Italy. The treaty of Constance, signed in 1183, in which he was forced to confirm the right of the Lombardy cities to elect officials and conduct their own affairs, has been called 'a notable milestone in the history of democracy'.[14] In fact it was an acknowledgement of a changed reality: the emperor no longer held any authority, nor posed any real threat to the cities of Lombardy. From 1183 until the French invasion of 1494, these cities were effectively independent states.

The independent cities of northern Italy were a collection rather than a collective – they had common interests but were also in competition. The subsequent centuries saw them engaged in conflicts with their own nobility and with neighbouring cities, each trying to extend the area under its direct control. The archives in Siena record a succession of victories by the city over neighbouring nobility in the twelfth and early thirteenth centuries, while the major conflict of the thirteenth century was that between Siena and Florence over disputed territory.

This firm control over a *contado*, giving form to a self-contained city-state, was peculiar to Italy. Nevertheless, self-contained communities – defined under Roman law as a *universitas* or 'whole' – outside Italy also began to govern themselves. In 1182 Beaumont-en-Argonne in the Ardennes adopted a law which gave the town the right to elect a mayor and officials for the administration of justice and other affairs, and this was used as a model by around 500 towns and villages in the region. In 1212 the merchants and nobility of Marseilles organised themselves into an association called the confraternity of the Holy Spirit; by 1218 the town was minting its own coins and by 1220 it had won the right from the counts of Provence to govern its own affairs. The government of Marseilles could make treaties with other cities, one of which, with the city of Nice, contained this declaration: 'Through God . . . we have won the liberty of our city, decorated our republic, increased the profit and right of our city and, through Him, we preserve the peace of our city.'[15]

By 1200 a ruling class had emerged in Italy comprising those lesser feudal lords who held lands near a city and lived within its walls as citizens, and the burghers who made money from trade and money exchange. Wealth and social distinction became entwined as nobles became traders, while merchants and bankers put their money into land. But what was it like to live in an Italian city at that time?

To take just one example, Siena had 30,000 inhabitants living in a city that was just 1.2km across. Most houses were made of wood and mud, many with brick frontages on to the streets. By 1200 the cathedral or duomo was undergoing construction (organised by the city's masons' guild) and a university was founded in 1240. There was clear social inequality, as shown by the massive stone buildings and towers of the wealthy families and the cramped spaces of the poor. Streets that look so picturesque today were narrow and winding, starting out as pathways between buildings before becoming thoroughfares. Construction was the major industry of medieval towns, employing countless labourers and skilled craftsmen, while textiles were the engine of European trade. Siena was known for the quality of its wool cloth, its craftsmen using techniques learned from the east to produce sumptuous dyed and embroidered cloth. The textile trade involved a number of skilled craftsmen, from spinners and dyers to weavers and fullers, and their workshops were surrounded by a variety of urban trades – butchers and bakers, silversmiths and stonemasons, notaries and bankers. Like every medieval town in Europe, Siena was also home to a large number of clerics – mendicant friars and nuns of different orders, priests, curates and deacons – and contained religious houses and hospitals, friaries and parish churches.

The eleventh-century communes gave each Italian city a strong identity but their initial domination by a few wealthy families did not hold. Membership of the council was severely restricted and while citizens were defined by property, taxes and military service, this did not give them rights of representation. The commune existed to give a stable authority to the elite but as the cities grew the artisans, professionals and merchants became more powerful and lost patience with the exclusivity of city politics.

An impending political crisis can be traced from as early as 1150, when Italian consuls began to be replaced by councils that were headed by an official known as a *podestà*. By 1200 these were in place in Padua, Milan, Florence, Pisa, Siena and Arezzo. In Genoa in 1190 records showed that 'Civil discords and hateful conspiracies and divisions had arisen in the city . . . So the wise men and councillors of the city met and decided that . . . the consulate of the commune should come to an end and . . . that they should have a *podestà*.'[16]

This curious post was the equivalent of the modern chief executive, who was brought in from elsewhere (the first one in Siena came from Lucca) to run the city's affairs and to act as adjudicator in political and legal disputes. The *podestàs* became professional politicians, who brought with them a retinue of jurists, lawyers and clerks. Twenty *podestàs* are known to have held office in at least six towns each; the Milanese William of Pusterla was chosen as *podestà* in no less than nine cities, completing sixteen periods of duty, including four in Bologna. The *podestàs* were a sign that consensus within the communes had broken down and outside agents had to be brought in to keep the peace, but from 1200 this too was failing as the powerful families began using armed servants as private militias, marking off parts of the city as their own territory and building huge military-style towers within the city walls.

As the cities grew dangerous and unstable, everyone from bankers to silversmiths to butchers saw the urgent need to attain political power in order to protect their own interests. Trade guilds, which acted as trade unions, welfare organisations and social fraternities started to become political bodies. Guilds splintered and multiplied; by the early thirteenth century most cities had 30 to 40, while Venice reached a total of 142. In the 1380s Cremona had 8,000 guild members and Bologna 9,000. At the same time, citizens formed armed neighbourhood associations to protect themselves against the threat of violence from the nobility who controlled the city. These neighbourhood companies were named for saints or districts, or carried symbolic names like star, sailor, horse, lion or dragon. An artisan, shopkeeper or trader therefore had two organisations to look after his interests: the neighbourhood company and the guild, which reflected a rough form of democracy driven by practical needs. By the time of Dürer's visit to Antwerp in 1520, the guilds and associations had taken on ceremonial functions, but they had been born out of communal necessity.

Initially the guilds and neighbourhood companies worked together loosely, but the aggression of the nobility in the commune regimes forced them to become a more formal movement. This movement, which emerged in every major city in the north of Italy in the thirteenth century, has become known as the Popolo, and is of central importance to the history of representative government. From around 1200 to 1500 in almost every north Italian city, therefore, power was

divided, shared, contested and transferred between different authorities
– the nobility, the church, the councils, the *podestàs* and the Popolo.

This complex, shifting picture makes the political history of the
period seem confusing and chaotic, yet the underlying landscape is
actually a consistent, continual negotiation of power, authority and
influence between an elite group of wealthy families and a wider
power base of artisans, professionals and traders. The Popolo was
formed to protect its members' interests, and it often did this by
remaining separate from the commune or the formal city council,
retaining its own militia, taxation, elected officials and courts. At other
times the Popolo took power, and there were takeovers in Bologna
in 1228 and Florence in 1244. In Padua in 1293 the trade guilds agreed
to form 'a single body, society, brotherhood or league to maintain and
conserve the city of Padua and its district in a peaceful state as a
commune, free from the domination of any tyrant'.[17] Even when it
was not formally in control of a city, the government of that city was
aware of the need to acquire the Popolo's consent. Often this was
done by granting seats on the council: in 1212 in Milan and 1222 in
Piacenza, half of all offices were given to members of the Popolo. In
Siena the Popolo assumed control of the commune from 1257 to 1262;
thereafter its formal power waxed and waned, though it remained a
powerful political element within the city.

The Popolo's main motives for acquiring power were twofold.
Firstly it sought to abolish the tax privileges of the nobility, together
with the high rates of interest earned by families who lent money to
the commune. In Florence in 1224 a twelve-man commission (which
excluded the nobility and clergy) looked into fiscal affairs. They found
that city squares and walls had mysteriously ended up being privately
owned, and taxes levied by the nobility had disappeared into their
own pockets. In Siena the Popolo appointed officials known as *popu-
lares* to assess tax, and they were urged in a council debate to 'aim to
the best of their ability at equality for all' and that 'all those who have
rich purses should be assessed in full.'[18]

The second major motivation for the Popolo was reform of the
legal system. In most cities there were parallel and competing judicial
authorities, with courts having different and often overlapping jurisdictions while using a variety of legal codes – church law, imperial law,
customary law and Roman law. The guilds had assumed authority

over legal affairs that affected their members and their trade, and so when the Popolo gained power they insisted on the right to join the legislature and to partake in the judiciary. Cities tried to deal with these confusions by rewriting their statutes, as in 1293 in Florence, where it was recognised that the different legal codes 'are superfluous, some are obscure, some contradict each other and others resemble each other; ambiguities and differences arise daily'. Laws promulgated by the *podestà*, the captain of the Popolo (a position first recorded in Parma in 1244, then in Florence and Piacenza in 1250), and by other bodies were to be harmonised.[19]

While all these authorities could adjudicate, the power to enforce laws was the key, and here the Popolo were able to compete effectively against the militias of the wealthy. In Siena the Popolo regime managed to pass laws that gave immunity for acts of revenge carried out by its members on the orders of its own council – making them an effective arm of the state. In 1262 a decree stated that 'there should be [armed] companies of those subordinate to the Popolo and its sworn members; all those who belong [to the Popolo] should be compelled to join [the companies].'[20] The tensions created by an effective state within a state occasionally exploded into conflict, as happened in Piacenza where the nobility were expelled in 1090 after fierce street fighting.

Elsewhere the Popolo brought in formal powers against the nobility. In Bologna in 1252 associations of families were abolished, the carrying of side-arms in the city prohibited and defensive towers demolished; in Florence in 1293 anyone 'who has not worked in craft with his own hands' could not represent craftsmen on the general council. Noble families in Bologna in 1282 were forced to put up monetary guarantees of their good behaviour, and between 1293 and 1295 around seventy-three of the great families were exiled. Laws were brought in to limit the height of towers and to outlaw feuding between noble families, while some decrees showed a general distrust of the nobility, for example at Modena, where 'In any accusation concerning damage, the oath of a powerful man is not to be believed, nor that of their sons of squires.'[21]

For many decades the political intervention of the Popolo was regarded as a chaotic episode from which Italian cities were rescued by the great families of the Renaissance. The picture we see now is different. Today historians argue that the Popolo was the crucial element in the extraordinary cultural innovations of the period, and that 'popular government' was more widespread and long-lasting than had been previously realised. The cities had first gained the right to self-government by declaring themselves to be independent communes; the achievement of the Popolo movement was to build on this by dramatically widening participation in government.[22] A culture of participation meant more than just a competition for power between different social groups. The guilds that were at the heart of the Popolo were run and organised by their members, each of whom had the same status. In Bergamo, Popolo members swore to 'see that . . . all the offices and honours of the commune . . . should be chosen in the interest of the community and not in favour of any party or parties'.[23] The commune, the *podestàs*, the *magnati* (council of 'great men') and the Popolo – each of these groups represented different social classes, and working in parallel they introduced systems of representation and participation that were tried, adapted and refined. While they were often in political conflict, the bottom-up requirements of the Popolo complemented the top-down rule of the communes, and the two came together in an embrace of a republican ideal of government – a revolutionary practice in a continent of kings and emperors, and a link to the Roman past.

The rise of the Popolo movement across Italy was symptom and cause of an extraordinary upsurge of self-confidence among urban citizens. The burgeoning cities gave ordinary people work, independence, status, the companionship of colleagues, involvement through the guilds in politics and in the commissioning of great public works, and a stake in the future. The artisans of the late medieval city were transformed into the artists of the Renaissance, signalling a change, we are often told, from a world of oppressive faith and feudalism to a world where humanity discovered rationality and became fascinated by itself. The truth is that the change had happened much earlier. The Popolo movement brought about a new interest in the common citizen, allowing Giotto the extraordinary innovation of putting real people in his paintings of biblical scenes as early as 1310; it established the principle that cities were not to be divided among the wealthy but that streets, piazzas, churches and town halls should be public spaces available to all; and it revived the republican belief that every citizen who had a stake in their city and was called upon to defend it, should have a voice in its government. Social interactions changed from elaborate deference to the informality of equals. The Popolo opened schools that taught secular subjects; it expanded the practice of time-served apprenticeships; and by creating new councils and offices it enlarged the political community so that more people took responsibility for the fate of their city.

The era of overt Popolo government in Italy came to an end in the fourteenth century. Wealthy traders sought to further their ambitions by making alliances with the great families and the political influence of the guilds was diminished. And because the guild-based Popolo had excluded the lower orders, it lacked a wide power base. The Popolo of Padua in 1277, for example, barred 'sailors, gardeners, agricultural labourers, landless men and herdsmen' from attending elections.[24] Throughout the period of republican regimes, the notion of 'the people' was used to gild a city's reputation but the truth was that the cities' populations were highly unequal in terms of wealth and access to power. Nevertheless, the Popolo was based on the participation of thousands of citizens who had previously been excluded from political life. It is now regarded as an essential and transforming movement whose influence lasted beyond its demise, introducing a form of government in Italian cities which, in the words of one historian, was 'broadly based [and] in which a significant proportion of male citizens from various social groups could participate in the governing councils, and would be eligible to hold elective political and administrative offices'.[25]

By the fourteenth century the larger cities were beginning to dominate the north of Italy. Giovanni Villani lived in Florence in the 1330s and described a city of more than 90,000 people, including 25,000 men ready to bear arms and 30,000 working in the cloth trade, making fine fabrics out of English wool. He counted 600 notaries and 100 pharmacies, as well as 146 furnaces for metal crafts. Villani also noted the presence of a wide range of officials and magistrates: 'These were the *podestà*, the captain, the defender of the people and the guilds; the executor of the Ordinances of Justice; [of which] the captain of the guard and defender of the people . . . had more authority than the others '. It seems that even after the demise of the Popolo jurisdiction was still contested and that being a 'defender of the people' was a badge of office.[26]

Most cities in fourteenth- and fifteenth-century Italy, the period of the high Renaissance, were now governed by a mixture of popular government and oligarchy. In Siena as late as the 1440s there were several hundred citizens qualified to sit and vote in the main legislative assembly. Some outsiders thought the popular element of the city's government debasing. Master Valesio, a Portuguese resident, complained in 1451 that the city was ruled by 'grocers, tanners, shoemakers and peasants' who were a *reggimento di merda* – a government of shit.[27]

Siena followed the pattern of other cities during the fifteenth century as a small group of families fought between themselves, creating rival factions and seeking popular support. The emergence of a single figure powerful enough, through political and military manoeuvring, to control the city had begun in the fourteenth century and continued until the French invasions of 1494. This figure became the 'Renaissance prince' immortalised by Machiavelli and embodied by Ludovico Gonzaga of Mantua, the Bentovoglio family of Bologna, the Medici of Florence, Francesco and Ludovico Sforza of Milan, and most typically Cesare Borgia. By the 1520s the cities of Italy had lost their de facto independence, and became elements in a power struggle between the empire, France, Spain and the papacy that was to divide the country for the next three centuries. Europe became a continent of powerful national monarchies; the power of cities everywhere declined, and with it the extent of popular government.

Ironically the Italian cities helped to give birth to the political system that swept away their power. The centralised nation state was made possible by new military technology that allowed monarchs to control large territories, but it was sustained by a tax-gathering bureaucracy that was born in the commercial revolution fostered in the banking houses and town halls of Italy. The modern state became a highly centralising system, giving the possibility of total power to one individual or a small group. The history of democracy now became a struggle to gain control of the state.

Nevertheless, the assertion of the rule of the people as a way of participating and taking pride in urban life is a notable marker in the history of politics; for a few centuries the towns and cities of Europe regarded popular government as a cause for celebration and emulation. The later thinkers of the Italian Renaissance, such as Leonardo

Bruni, contended that cities can only be great once their people are free, and this means free from monarchs, princes and tyrants. The participation of hundreds, and sometimes thousands, of citizens in the government and administrations of their communities, their willingness to face down the power of inherited and accumulated wealth, and their belief in res publica make the Italian cities worthy of note in the history of democracy.

4

DEMOCRACY IN THE HIGH ALPS

The Communal Citizen

Towns and cities may have provided the catalyst for more participation in government, but Europe's first democracy since Athens arrived in the unlikely setting of the high Alps. In 1499 a territory in the present-day Swiss canton of Graubünden (also previously known as Grisons, Old Upper Rhaetia, or Valtellina) seceded from the Holy Roman Empire and declared itself to be a free state.[1] Five years later it formally constituted itself as a sovereign state and in 1524 an Act of Union made it a federated republic. In some ways this simply confirmed the political reality since the inhabitants of the territory were experienced at running their own domestic affairs – the declaration speaks of a 'renewal of our understandings and treaties' – but the declaration of sovereignty by the leaders and citizens of Graubünden was a bold act of self-assertion. Independence lasted until the Napoleonic era, when it became part of Switzerland; during this time Graubünden became the first society in modern history to declare itself a democracy.

Graubünden was a territory of over 7,000 square kilometres with a population in modern times of around 150,000. Its inhabitants have always been diverse, including Germans, Romance speakers and Italians, Catholics and Protestants; it has been described as Switzerland in miniature. Throughout its history its economy and workforce has principally been agricultural, working the fields and pastures of the high Alps. Villages and hamlets were dotted around the mountain valleys, with a few towns built on trade and commerce. The free state lay on routes between the south of Germany and the Venetian Republic, a location of strategic and commercial value.

The citizens of Graubünden were in a similar position to those of the Italian cities of the twelfth century, where the lack of an over-arching, involved authority was combined with the pressing practical needs of a community. While nominally within both the realms of different dukes and counts and the territory of the Holy Roman Empire, in reality they were left to fend for themselves. The free state was a confederation of fifty or so communes, each with its own set of rules and methods of decision-making. Made up of neighbourhoods or villages, the communes were essentially political units that ran their own internal affairs, including judicial courts. Each sent a delegate to the Bundestag, or federal assembly, and it was the communes them-selves – their mechanisms and methods of working – that had the biggest influence on the structures of the state.

Equality between the communes was the basic organising principle, so that officers were selected for the highest positions by each commune in turn. A document from 1542 states: 'Concerning the offices in the Valtellina, it is established that henceforth they should be distributed equally to each commune according to the number, and that each commune should be able to select someone as officer, when and how it suits the commune.'[2] In fact, the officials appointed to run the state at different levels had little power to make policy or take strategic decisions – that was done by the people through a system of referendums. The officials' duty was to prepare the ques-tions that were put before the people, a process which made Graubünden into, effectively, a direct democracy.

The referendum in Graubünden, where such a procedure is thought to have been invented, was different from those we have come to know in recent times. Rather than being a method for individual citizens to approve or veto policies proposed by executive govern-ments, it was used to forge consensus among the population. The communes acted as electoral colleges, so that each citizen voted within his commune. This was then delegated to the level of the village or neighbourhood, so that each village needed to come to a collective view. Although this could be arrived at by a simple majority, the aim of the process was to arrive at a consensus within each community.[3]

Consensus was an essential element in the system because many of the issues that were voted on concerned communal activities, in particular management of land and construction. The historian Randolph Head gives an example of how this worked in practice:

> On the morning of the common labour, the call was made with three different signals of the village bells. By the third signal, everyone [one person from each house] had to assemble in the village square equipped with shovels, picks and hatchets. The four village heads counted those present – absences were punished with a fine – and led them to an area where the roads needed to be repaired.[4]

With regard to the political process this meant that if, for example, a vote was taken to build a road, then the voters were committing themselves to carrying out the work. As one historian has written: 'Those who willed it built it, and their labour was regarded as an expression of commonality for which no compensation was required.'[5]

Decisions taken in villages and neighbourhoods were part of a national system of policymaking but they were also the foundation of the government of each locality. There were regular assemblies in each commune, usually held after church on Sundays. Those attending were not just the heads of households and they were often required to carry a knife or sword to show their military credentials; at special gatherings held to protest against decisions taken elsewhere, members would raise military standards.

In the early seventeenth century, Giovanni Battista Padavino, the Venetian ambassador to Graubünden, described how local assemblies were asked to approve or veto the decisions taken by officials:

> In taking the vote of the people, everyone who is fit to carry a sword being entitled to have his say, they use various methods . . . In some places the decisions are made by the largest number of heads, in others by estates or parishes, or by clans as in Chur [the main town]. But the general custom is to call the people on Sunday, and the magistrates . . . publicly read the content of the letters written by the presidents [of the groups of communes, or leagues], after which everyone then has to give his opinion; [the magistrate] then announces that those who desire to accept the matters that have been proposed should raise

their hands, and then they count how many are raised, and which ones remain down to indicate the contrary opinion.[6]

Similar assemblies chose the representatives of each community. There were no ballots or secret votes – open and public displays of opinion were part of the accepted culture of the communes and of the federal assemblies. In each of these, every adult male had an equal say.

There was incessant arguing between the communes about who had jurisdiction over what, and where federal meetings should be held. These disputes were taken as a sign of weakness by contemporary outsiders and by historians. Today political disputes seem like the necessary offspring of a participatory system – the nature of democratic politics is to make debate public, voicing disagreements so that they can be resolved. Yet for those seeking order in the past this seemed disorderly.

Graubünden comprised three leagues, twenty-six higher jurisdictions, forty-nine communes and 227 autonomous neighbourhoods.[7] The state structures did not replicate those of the commune or the village, but they sprang from the same ways of thinking. The rural communes had established ways of respecting family independence, while at the same time maintaining collective social and economic discipline. Out of this communal way of life came long experience of the exercise of political authority. When they came together to form a state, the communes were thus able to draw on the habits, practices and culture that had guided the life of their villages. The functioning democratic state allowed local principles to operate on a national level.

While its system of government sprang from practical needs, Graubünden grew into a politically sophisticated society with citizens taking great pride in their democratic undertaking. This became clear in the 1620s, as the Holy Roman Empire became a battleground between the fiercely Catholic Ferdinand (who assumed the imperial throne in 1619), supported by Spain, and a league of Protestant states led by Christian IV of Denmark. The resulting Thirty Years War devastated the German lands at the heart of the empire. Remarkably, Graubünden's Catholic and Protestant citizens continued to live alongside each other. Feeling their existence at a strategic crossroads between Austria and Italy under threat, the people of Graubünden tried to find allies by arguing the case for their independence and their method of government. The *Graubündnerische Handlungen*, published in 1618, stated: 'The form of our government is democratic; and the election and removal of all kinds of magistrates, judges and officers, both here in our free and ruling lands and in those lands subject us, lies with our common man.'[8]

This is an historic use of the term 'democratic'. The word rarely appears in German before the seventeenth century and in Latin texts was generally used as an example of bad government. In their arguments the citizens of Graubünden were able to call on a century of national communal politics, rather than political theory, to tell the rest of Europe how it might think about notions of political authority and legitimacy.

Two important historical points emerge from the *Graubündnerische Handlungen* and other documents published in defence of the free state. Firstly, in Graubünden peasants are seen as political actors; previously in European history they had been politically invisible, only occasionally rebelling in defence of ancient customs. The documents from Graubünden show them actively involved in creating and developing a state and taking on political authority.

The second point is the power and persistence of communal ideas and practice at this time. From the sixteenth to the eighteenth centuries we see the gradual emergence of the self-styled rational individual, with certain rights and obligations. The aim of liberal political theory and practice became the building of a state that could adequately accommodate the needs of this educated European gentleman of the Enlightenment. In its emphasis on the communal, Graubünden was, in contrast, a medieval political culture existing in the early modern world.

The main difference between the Graubünden practice and the later tradition lies in the medieval idea of the common good or *Gemeinnutz*. In contrast to the liberal notion of the individual with free choice, the Graubünden citizen swore an oath to his commune that defined the relationship between the individual and the community. Later ideas of individual virtue, or natural liberty, were not part of the thinking here. In Graubünden the right of a citizen to dissent in the name of justice was granted to them by God, not by natural or civic right, and only because of their participation in the community.

The change from the medieval to the modern political world was from a divinely ordered cosmos to a series of sovereign states. Graubünden cuts across this transformation. It contains seeds of a voluntary social contract, yet is based on a medieval understanding of communal life. The fact that everyone had their divinely ordained place in life, for example, means that the idea of social mobility was absent. The notion of *Gemeinarbeit* or common work, for which no payment was made, is a development from feudalism, where service is provided to the commune rather than the feudal lord. And, while modern democratic thinking is based on the human potential to flourish under liberty, the medieval world view was pessimistic: the Graubünden documents reflect the teachings of St Augustine in their views of the sinfulness of man, which needs to be kept in check, and the destructiveness of human greed.

This notion of self-restraint did not always operate successfully at a communal level. The lack of authority given to governing bodies did allow acts of communal violence and revenge to take place with little restraint by, for example, a strong independent judiciary. Where the people are entirely sovereign, with insufficient checks on their powers, they do as they please; this could mean that a village acted collectively in breaking its own laws. After an incident in 1735 in which a man was accused of treason, his house sacked and his supporters stoned, a villager commented that there was no need to try him before 'the proper authorities': 'We ourselves are the authorities.'[9]

Graubünden therefore presents us with a political culture that goes beyond the formal structures of assemblies and communal decision-making. This culture includes the assumptions and expectations, actions and reflexes of people living in a political community. They act self-consciously through voting, debating, standing for election; but also unself-consciously in the ways they react to situations and difficulties, gather together to solve problems or to debate issues that are important to their lives. In other words, they have become used to living in a culture where their opinions and contributions are valued, but only within a communal setting.

Two political principles underpinned this unique society. First, that in any assembly, a majority of those present gave legitimacy to a decision; when decisions were transmitted up to the federal assemblies they were often called 'majorities'. This concept has remained a cornerstone of democracy. The second principle was that so-called 'political goods' were divided equally among the members of the commune and between the communes. Positions were allocated in rotation so that responsibility and power were shared, in turn, among everyone. This way of conducting democratic politics has been abandoned in the modern world, and it connects Graubünden more strongly to Athens than to the present day and, while the concept of individual liberty is missing, the democracy in Graubünden echoes Democritus' argument that the polis flourishes because citizens exercise self-restraint, and the reward is a flourishing of life beyond the capacity of the individual.

While democracy existed in a tiny corner of Europe, elsewhere the continent was dominated by states ruled by powerful monarchs. Our next three chapters look at the series of revolutions aimed at limiting the power of kings and, to a degree, giving citizens a voice in government. We begin with the English Revolution.

THE ENGLISH REVOLUTION

The Subject-Citizen

Early modern Europe saw the development of a new kind of state where monarchs took a much firmer grip on the territories they controlled. For centuries kingdoms had been based on loyalty to a ruler but, thanks in large part to improvements in weapons and the development of tax-gathering, they now became controlled areas – maps began to appear showing how Europe was divided up between these realms. The age of loosely governed empires and autonomous cities gave way to the age of centralised states and the emergence of nations.[1]

In this new world order, which developed between roughly 1500 and 1700, there seemed no place for the kind of participatory government described in the last chapter. The citizen instead became a subject, granted rights only through the generosity of the monarch within whose divinely conceived realm he happened to live. New dynasties, from the Tudors and Stuarts of England to the Habsburgs of Spain and Austria, the Bourbons of France, the Vasa of Sweden and Poland, and the Romanovs of Russia, successfully married the notion of royalty as a divine status with the development of a centralised state, with the monarch as its head. The story of modern democracy is of a long and bitter struggle to change the nature of the state.

The control exercised by monarchs was a fitful process. The nobility who had held power under the old feudal system fought to reassert their rights, but in this Europe-wide power struggle any notion of democracy or participatory government seemed to disappear. Yet it did not vanish entirely. In the seventeenth century the kingdoms of the British Isles were ruled by Stuart kings, and here the inability of successive monarchs to guide and control the state brought other political forces to the fore. And it was in England that the application of democratic principles to a national state was first put forward. This was no abstract theorising but a practical plan for government proposed, in the midst of a national crisis, by a group of soldiers representing the English army. The opportunity came in the power vacuum that followed the civil wars in England, Scotland and Ireland. How those wars came about, and how the population became so politicised that democracy was a real possibility, are essential episodes in our story.

In 1603 James VI, king of Scotland, inherited the English throne as James I from the childless Elizabeth Tudor. He also became king of Ireland. James was a Protestant from a Catholic family, and a believer in the divine right of kings: in 1597 in *The True Law of Free Monarchies*, he wrote that kings arose 'before any estates or ranks of men, before any parliaments were holden, or laws made, and by them was the land distributed, which at first was wholly theirs. And so it follows of necessity that kings were the authors and makers of the laws, and not the laws of the kings'.[2] Yet the realities on the ground did not make for autocratic rule and James was perceptive enough to manage his reign adequately, though without distinction.

His room for action was limited as the two central elements of the modern state – the army and taxation – were outside his control. Despite Elizabeth's success in increasing England's prestige, the country had no standing army but a collection of county militias each loyal to its local nobility, while any taxes had to be approved by Parliament – and it was on Members of Parliament that taxation fell most heavily. The balance of power between monarch and Parliament, the centre and the regions, the crown and the nobility was therefore crucial. Elizabeth did not bequeath a subservient Parliament to James but a class of nobles used to being flattered, cajoled and rewarded. In the early seventeenth century the English Parliament was a mixture of royal lackeys and independent-minded men with a complex relationship with the monarch.

We have seen why the king needed Parliament but the English

parliamentarians needed the monarch too, and were prepared to tolerate a weak and wayward king for two reasons. First, a weak king would not interfere in their affairs and would be beholden to them for financial and military support. Second, the monarchy brought stability and unity to the country; this was of incalculable value to the nobility, who benefited from a loyal and settled population. In France, Russia and Spain the monarchy began to dominate the nobility and drove into being a powerful, centralised state that was identical with the person of the king. In the British Isles this did not happen, and instead a precarious balance was reached.

Relations broke down early in James' reign when Parliament showed reluctance to vote through taxes for what it considered unnecessary expenditure. As a result the Crown ran up huge debts which Parliament refused to pay. In 1610 James dismissed Parliament, and when it was recalled in 1614 it lasted only eight weeks. From then on James fed the expenses of his court by selling earldoms and trading monopolies rather than seeking taxes. These frosty relations between king and Parliament set the tone for the rule of James' son Charles I, the most disastrous in English history.

If finance froze relations between Parliament and king, religion heated it to an incendiary level. James had won favour with the nobility and the people through his repudiation of Catholicism but Charles, who succeeded to the throne in 1625, could not bring himself to follow suit. Machiavelli's advice had been that the successful prince is unprincipled in a constructive way; he makes himself into the embodiment of the state in order to win the rewards that the state can offer. Charles did not do this and paid the price.

In common with his father, Charles saw Parliament as a necessary evil. Unlike his father, however, the new king had a taste for military adventure. Loyalty to his extended family prompted an attempt to influence the Thirty Years War by declaring war on Spain but Parliament sanctioned only £140,000, an insufficient sum for the king's ambitions. A disastrous military campaign and further signs of Charles' profligacy led parliament to pass the Petition of Right in 1628, which barred the king from certain acts without the consent of Parliament, including the right to levy taxes, imprison anyone without trial, billet troops in civilian homes or subject his people to martial law. In response Charles dismissed Parliament and declared a period of Personal Rule

– in effect he made himself dictator. While Parliament's hostility to taxes such as the notorious Ship Money led to continual confrontations, religion became the major division between the king and his subjects.

The Reformation of the sixteenth century, while it divided the continent into opposing camps, had also invigorated the Christian community. Protestants in particular were continually engaged in debates about the meaning of their faith and their relationship with God. Within English Protestantism a schism had begun to appear between those known since as Reformed Protestants and the highest officials of the Anglican Church (including the king) who embraced a form of Anglo-Catholicism. Vital theological differences pitted a hierarchical church, which believed in the importance of ritual, the divine authority of its bishops and the special status of the monarch, against a firm belief in the primacy of the individual conscience and the importance of a Christian life. While the Anglican Church had grown out of Henry VIII's desire to split from Rome, Reformed Protestantism had its roots in the Calvinist theology that had spread with electrifying effect across northern Europe.

New methods of printing made multiple copies of the Geneva Bible available in English across England and Scotland from around 1614. Appearing before the King James Version, the Geneva Bible quickly found favour among believers. Its forceful language, its annotations and study guides gave readers a confident command of the scriptures that were the basis of their faith. Annotations included political interpretations of biblical stories, showing for instance that the scriptures gave believers the authority to remove unjust rulers.

The Bible confirmed to the Reformed Protestants that their interpretation of the faith was true to the word of God, and that Catholicism was a perversion of Christianity. Their concern, which became a furious accusation, was that the bishops and many priests of the Anglican Church were Catholics by another name. When in 1633 Charles appointed William Laud Archbishop of Canterbury, people who criticised Laud for quasi-Catholic behaviour were arrested while all subjects were required to attend Anglican services. Charles' French wife Henrietta Maria was openly Catholic and both her influence over the royal children and her circle of Catholic courtiers were viewed with hostility and suspicion. At the same time, Catholic and Protestant soldiers were butchering each other (and millions of civilians) across vast areas of Middle Europe in the Thirty Years War. In the 1630s, printed pamphlets reached England and Scotland telling of Protestants being massacred in Bohemia and the Rhine Palatinate.

None of this made internal conflict inevitable, but Charles was bent on quashing all religious dissent. In 1637 the king decided that the Anglican liturgy, with a new prayer book compiled by William Laud, should be used in all three kingdoms of England, Scotland and Ireland (the countries were separate entities, though all three were ruled by Charles). In response the Scottish National Covenant was formed as a 'loyal protest', asserting that any change should first be agreed by all three parliaments and General Assemblies of the church. Charles raised an army to pacify the Scots but his expedition failed. To assert his authority over the covenanters Charles needed to raise money. A Great Council of the English nobility was summoned in York but the noble lords advised the king to seek a truce and recall Parliament. The period of Personal Rule was over.

The new Parliament, which assembled on 3 November 1640, contained a majority of members who wanted to curb the powers of the king, though no one foresaw armed conflict between Parliament and monarch. The Long Parliament, as it became known, had both the king's chief minister, the Earl of Strafford, and Archbishop Laud arrested for treason, and passed a law that Parliament could not be dissolved except by itself. Charles staked his reputation on being able to save Strafford, who nevertheless was impeached and executed in May 1641. Laud was condemned to death and finally beheaded in January 1645. The king was now isolated with only the tottering prestige of his position to call on.

The events that precipitated military conflict took place in Ireland. In 1641 Irish Catholics, fearing an invasion by Scots Covenanters and troops of the newly vigorous English Parliament, rebelled against the state authorities and claimed royal approval for their actions. Distrustful of Charles' Catholic sympathies, the English Parliament refused to grant him the money or troops to quell the rebellion, while pamphlets describing Catholic atrocities against Irish Protestants stoked an already feverish atmosphere. Rumours that Parliament intended to impeach his Catholic queen provoked Charles into action; on 4 January 1642 he arrived at the House of Commons carrying an arrest warrant for five leading Members of Parliament, alleging high treason. The entry of a monarch into the Commons chamber was an unmistakable challenge to Parliament; the arrest never happened as the MPs had been forewarned – in Charles' famous words, spoken from the Speaker's chair, 'I see the birds have flown.' By this act Charles made himself an enemy of Parliament and London became a dangerous place for the king. After several months in which both sides appealed to the people for support, in August 1642 he raised his standard at Nottingham castle and declared war on Parliament.

Parliamentary armies rapidly gained the upper hand over the royalist forces, but they failed to finish the war quickly. By the end of 1644 Parliament controlled 70 per cent of the territory of England, but while victory at the battle of Marston Moor near York in July 1644 had given them command of the north, the south was still frustrating their victory. Suspicions began to grow about the motivation of the parliamentary army's noble commanders, and this was to bring a fundamental split in the parliamentary cause. The Earl of Manchester, who led the Eastern Army in which Oliver Cromwell, Member of Parliament for Cambridge, served, began to question the point of fighting on instead of negotiating. The Earl of Essex had, in September 1644, been forced through his own incompetence to surrender to royalist forces in Cornwall. The second battle of Newbury in October 1644, where the parliamentary forces were led by Manchester, was, frustratingly for Parliament, inconclusive. It seemed that some peers of the realm were not sufficiently intent on pursuing a crushing victory – rather they were hoping that the king would come to terms.

These frustrations divided the House of Commons into a Presbyterian faction, keen to ally with the Scots and negotiate with the king, and a radical faction known as the War Party who saw decisive victory as the first aim. In April 1645 the radical group passed the Self-Denying Ordinance in which all MPs had to decide between military and parliamentary duties, and all English peers, being members of the House of Lords, had to give up military command. The southern parliamentary troops were then merged into one force called the New Model Army, led by Sir Thomas Fairfax with Oliver Cromwell second in command. The New Model Army immediately began a series of decisive victories culminating in the destruction of the royal army at Naseby in June 1645, which ended any chance of royalist recovery. Finally, on 5 May 1646, Charles surrendered to the Scots army at Southwell in Nottinghamshire. In February of the following year Parliament raised the money to buy the king from the Scots, preparing the ground for one of the most extraordinary years in English political history.

In order to understand the events of 1647 we need to look in more detail at the New Model Army and the influence of a particular political group, the Levellers. Though ostensibly a simple reorganisation of Parliament's forces, the New Model Army was a profound departure. This was a highly professional army with officers promoted through battle experience rather than family connections, and a fully motivated rank and file. The soldiers and officers were overwhelmingly Reformed Protestants for whom religious faith was the foundation of their existence. The vernacular Bibles that many soldiers carried showed that God's message was not simply obedience to authority, and more and more of them, influenced by radical writings, saw the world as, in the words of the Leveller Gerard Winstanley, 'a common treasury for all'.[3]

The Reformation had also revealed something quite new and astonishing. People had long believed that only great men – kings, princes, popes, archbishops and dukes – could alter the course of history, but the Reformation had been brought about by Martin Luther, a German monk, and consolidated by Jean Calvin, a French pastor. And though the Anglican Church had been instituted by the king of England, in Scotland John Knox, a simple clergyman, led the Protestant reforms that swept away Queen Mary. Moreover, the previous belief that an aristocrat was worth more to an army than seven common men had been ground into the bloody mud of Naseby by the New Model Army.

The Leveller movement was given its descriptive name in November 1647, though it had emerged in the autumn of 1645. Marchamont Needham wrote of the word as 'a most apt title for such a despicable and desperate knot to be known by . . . so that every jack shall be a gentleman and every Gentleman a Jack'.[4] The movement developed as the defeat of the Royalist army began to be inevitable, and ended once Cromwell and the Rump Parliament assumed control in 1649. The Levellers therefore existed in a power vacuum, when no ultimate authority had a monopoly on political power or military force.

The philosophy of the Levellers was based on their religious beliefs, yet was secular: they did not hold that political rights should be only for the godly but for saints and sinners alike, and they argued for the separation of church and state because each individual should have the right to choose his or her religion. The Levellers wanted equality in an age of deference to the high-born. For them, the oppression of the English had begun with the Norman Conquest, but they did not simply want the 'Norman yoke' removed and the pre-Conquest rights of Englishmen restored. The Leveller Richard Overton argued that 'the laws of this nation are unworthy [of] a free nation and deserve from first to last to be considered and seriously debated and reduced to an agreement with common equity and right reason, which ought to be the form and life of every government'.[5] Overton and his colleague William Walwyn wanted to promote the 'universal rules of common equity and justice.' Levellers had a set of principles and even a manifesto but they did not stand for election themselves; instead they set out rules by which the political process should be run.

This desire for political equality came through the experience of war as well as their religious views. The conflict had brought together men from a diverse set of backgrounds. The New Model Army, in particular, was drawn from volunteers who could advance through ability, and they mostly came from urban centres, particularly London with its fluid, self-reliant population; here equality was a practical reality and many of the people were 'masterless men' in an expanding commercial society (the capital had grown from around 200,000 to 350,000 inhabitants since 1600) that had little place for deference to authority.

More important still, for the first time in western history a political movement had access to that invaluable machine: the printing press. The fact that the Levellers were able to use the printed word to distribute their beliefs and arguments makes them arguably the founders of modern democracy, speaking not only to their immediate circle or the educated elite, but to the common people (at least those who could read, or knew someone who could). John Milton wrote: 'For books are not absolutely dead things but do contain a potency of life in them to be as active as that soul whose progeny they are.' It was the combination of the meritocratic New Model Army with the activism of the Levellers that brought England to the brink of democracy.

The spring of 1647 saw the country in a strange and novel situation. The Scots army had withdrawn peaceably north of the border, the king was under house arrest and the Parliamentary armies in unquestionable control. What should or could happen next was dictated by two major issues. Firstly the king, while in an apparently hopeless position, refused to negotiate with Parliament on any fundamental issue, insisting on his right to be brought to London to re-occupy the throne. The longer the king delayed, the more unpopular the parliamentary government became – taxes, the impact of its armies (often billeted in people's houses) and the strictures of its county committees all turned the country against them. The second issue was the New Model Army, now the dominant force in England. By 1647 Parliament owed £2.8 million to its soldiers. The House of Lords blocked payment to the troops explicitly in order to force the disbanding of the New Model Army; the army refused, demanding not only back pay but an indemnity against future charges of treason if the king were restored to the throne.

Consequently in early 1647 there were army mutinies throughout England and Wales. Soldiers seized their officers, excisemen, county committee members and other government officials, often holding them to ransom; more frequently troops refused to move quarters in defiance of orders. By the spring this discontented soldiery was encamped in the counties of Oxford, Warwick, Leicester, Buckingham, Hertford and Northampton awaiting developments in London.

On both these issues – the king and the army – the House of Commons remained bitterly divided between Presbyterians, eager to come to agreement with the king and dismiss the army, and radicals now known as Independents. The latter included senior officers of the New Model Army such as Oliver Cromwell and his son-in-law Henry Ireton, who wanted the army compensated in full and the king forced to accept a restricted role in the government of the country. The relative power of each side waxed and waned throughout this crucial year, with first one then the other gaining the upper hand in Parliament. Each of them also made alliances with supporters in the country – the Presbyterians with the Scots and the London militias, the Independents with groups such as the Levellers, who had adherents inside and outside the army. The crucial alliance, though, was between the Independents and the New Model Army since, on the ground, it was the force of 21,000 armed men ringed around London that controlled the kingdom. For many soldiers and officers Presbyterianism, an ostensibly Calvinist religion, had now become the creed of the established order – a feeling intensified by the attempted enforcement of a Presbyterian Covenant on all soldiers. Most soldiers were tolerant of different sects and believed that the state should not interfere with personal faith.

The atmosphere in the capital over the summer of 1647 was febrile with Parliament divided, the king under arrest, the army refusing to move and discontented soldiers from disbanded royalist and parliamentary regiments roaming the streets. Yet the political mood was beginning to shift. The king was becoming a sympathetic figure to many, while stories of sectarian soldiers violently disrupting Presbyterian services were widespread. On the other side, Parliament's continual refusal to settle the arrears and the matter of indemnity politicised the army – the soldiers believed they could win their cause only by replacing Parliament.

The rank and file of the army now began a process that we can legitimately describe as the creation of a democratic institution. The eight cavalry regiments based in East Anglia elected two representatives as commissioners and, writing to Fairfax on 28 April, they gave reasons for the troops' refusal to go to Ireland where a Catholic rebellion was brewing, seeing this as 'a design to ruin and break this army in pieces'. They also gave warning that they expected their officers to stand with them, and that any who did not would be 'a traitor to his country and an enemy to his army'.[6] In addition to previous grievances over pay and indemnity, they demanded that Members of Parliament who had criticised the army be punished.

In early May other regiments followed the East Anglian cavalry and elected agitators to represent them. This system was formalised by the appointment of equal numbers of soldier representatives and officers to the General Council of the Army, which first met in July 1647. Each regiment had its own council of agitators, who then chose from between them two representatives for the army council. For common soldiers to have a legitimate voice in the highest councils of the army was unheard of, but was agreed under the Solemn Engagement of the Army in early June 1647. Here we encounter two of the key elements of democracy: firstly, the recognition that the ordinary soldier had a right for his voice to be heard; and secondly, that the process of electing representatives to speak on the men's behalf was a legitimate and effective way of having their opinions and concerns transmitted. The wider implications were not lost on the soldiers, who understood that their democratic army stood in notable contrast to a Parliament comprised of the wealthy and the unelected who had simply assumed the right to represent their fellow countrymen.

Many of the agitators and officer representatives in the New Model Army were rewarded with promotion, while Presbyterian officers were pushed out. Nevertheless, while the army held power in the land the conservative Presbyterians held a majority in Parliament. The shifts in power were given a dramatic jolt by the seizure of the king on 1 June 1647 by a cavalry troop commanded by Cornet George Joyce, probably acting on secret orders from Oliver Cromwell. It seems likely that the Independents discovered a plot by Presbyterians in Parliament to take the king to Scotland and have him return at the head of a Scots army, and had acted to prevent this. The next decisive step was taken on 14 June when the army's Council of War, headed by Fairfax, declared that they were not a mercenary army hired to do the bidding of the state, but were 'called forth and conjured by several declarations of Parliament to the defence of our own and the people's just rights and liberties'.[7] This made the army an overtly political force.

The seizure of the king put the troops fully in control of events. The majority in Parliament now abandoned the Presbyterian leadership and sought accommodation with the New Model Army. Regiments mustered at Newmarket on 4 and 5 June at an event that increased their sense of unity and the belief that their destiny – and the country's – was in their own hands. At the Council of the Army on 16 July senior officers put forward a document for the government of the kingdom, known as the 'Heads of the Proposals'. Drawn up by Henry Ireton, it gave notable concessions to the king including restoring control of the army to him after ten years, permitting bishops to remain, and allowing the Common Prayer Book to be used, though not to be mandatory. The king refused to consider the proposals;

nevertheless on 2 August the document was published as the army's blueprint for the future of the kingdom.

Meanwhile on 26 July a crowd of Presbyterian and royalist supporters made a last throw of the dice: they invaded the Houses of Parliament calling for the restoration of the king and the reappointment of the old Presbyterian council to oversee the London militia. The Commons held out against the crowd for five hours, before a group of apprentices broke in and forced MPs to resolve that the king be brought to London. The incident gave the army a pretext for the occupation of the capital. Fifty-seven Independent MPs fled to the safety of Fairfax's headquarters, while the remaining Members declared that his command did not extend to the London militias. On 28 July, Fairfax announced that the army would be marching on the city in order to escort the MPs to their seats and to restore the freedom of Parliament.

There were some attempts to rally the people of London but when, on 4 August, 4,000 New Model Army troops entered Southwark, the reality of the situation hit home. By the following day London was secure and Fairfax was able to escort the Speaker and Independent MPs back to Parliament. On 7 August a parade of twenty regiments was held in Hyde Park, followed by an organised walk in which unarmed troops went through every street in London. Having shown themselves to be the saviours and not the enemies of the people, the troops left the city for encampments nearby. Senior officers set up a headquarters at Putney, five miles from Westminster.

In spite of this victory over the Presbyterians, the morale of the army and its popularity with the people began to wane. The people wanted freedom from taxation and the burdens of quartering the army; the army wanted full compensation – but paying off the troops was no longer enough to defuse the growing crisis: the politicised army wanted political change. No one could see a solution to the country's problems that did not involve the king, and Charles was well aware that he was indispensable. It was in his interests, or so he thought, to prolong all negotiations while hoping for help to arrive from France or Scotland. As summer turned to autumn, Parliament and the army were desperate for a solution.

In early October negotiations with the king were reopened by the army, offering more favourable terms and allowing him to form a council of royalist supporters at Hampton Court.[8] On 9 October the

Leveller-inspired document 'The Case of the Armie Truly Stated' was published, and presented to Fairfax at the General Council of the Army on 18 October. Although first greeted with hostility as a subversive tract, the council resolved that the document should be debated at the General Council meeting on 28 October, with the proposers and their civilian supporters invited to attend.

This, then, was the background to one of the most celebrated episodes in the history of democracy – the Putney Debates.[9] The 'Heads of the Proposals' remained the official army blueprint for the future of the kingdom, while a document known as 'An Agreement of the People', which was in effect a distillation of 'The Case of the Armie', became the focus of discussion in the Church of St Mary the Virgin, Putney.

Cromwell chaired the opening debate on 28 October in the absence of Fairfax, who was ill. The principal speaker for the senior army command was Henry Ireton, who had drafted the 'Heads of the Proposals'. The other side was represented by Colonel Edward Sexby, a Leveller and elected agitator, Robert Everard, a so-called New Agent also representing his regiment, and Colonel Thomas Rainborough, an old adversary of Cromwell.[10] The agitators also brought the civilians John Wildman and Maximilian Petty. Edward Sexby introduced the delegates in support of 'The Case of the Armie' and began with a spirited attack on the king and on all those who sought accommodation with him, including parliament and, implicitly at least, Cromwell and Ireton:

> The cause of our misery is upon two things. We sought to satisfy all men, and it was well; but in going about to do it we have dissatisfied all men. We have laboured to please a king and, I think, except we go about to cut all our throats, we shall not please him; and we have gone to support a house of rotten studs – I mean parliament, which consists of a company of rotten members.

The remainder of the first day was taken up with procedural matters, and it seems that Cromwell was keen to drag matters out as long as possible, while the agitators were eager to come to an agreement.

On the second day, 29 October, Robert Everard read out the

'Agreement of the People'. It contained four proposals and the first is worth quoting in full:

> That the people of England, being at this day very unequally distributed by counties, cities and boroughs for the election of their deputies in parliament, ought to be more indifferently proportioned, according to the number of inhabitants: the circumstances whereof, for number, place, and manner, are to be set down before the end of this present parliament.

The document also proposed that the current parliament should be dissolved on the last day of September 1648, and for new parliaments to be elected every two years, with the people being the sovereign authority over Parliament and not vice versa. Then there was a list of those aspects of political life that Parliament could not alter – in essence a bill of rights which included freedom of religion; the right to refuse conscription; indemnity against prosecution for acts committed during the civil war; a requirement that all laws be applied equally to all citizens; and that no law should be 'evidently destructive to the safety and well-being of the people'.

Henry Ireton now launched an attack on the first clause arguing that the call for parliamentary seats to be distributed 'according to the number of inhabitants' implied a universal male franchise. 'This doth make me think,' he declared, 'that the meaning is, that every man that is an inhabitant is to be equally considered, and to have an equal voice in the election of those representers . . . and that if that be the meaning, then I have something to say against it.' Ireton declared that this measure went against 'the civil constitution of this kingdom, which is original and fundamental', and that the existing electors, who were subject to a property qualification, should remain. This was the moment when the question of democracy was forced into an open debate.

Maximilian Petty's reply was brief and to the point: 'We judge that all inhabitants that have not lost their birthright should have an equal voice in elections.' Thomas Rainborough then gave reasons why all men should be allowed to take part:

> For really I think that the poorest he that is in England hath a life to live as the greatest he; and therefore truly, sir, I think it's clear, that

every man that is to live under a government ought first by his own
consent to put himself under that government; and I do think that the
poorest man in England is not at all bound in a strict sense to that
government that he hath not had a voice to put himself under.

Rainborough had followed the belief in an individual Christian
conscience to its natural conclusion and did not find anything in the
Bible to contradict it: 'I do not find anything in the law of God that
a lord shall choose twenty burgesses, and a gentleman but two, and
a poor man shall choose none. I find no such thing in the law of
nature or the law of nations.'

In response Ireton argued that only men of property had a real
stake in the kingdom, since their own fortunes were tied up in it –
they had 'a permanent fixed interest' – and while there was a natural
right to live in England, there was no natural right to vote. Moreover,
if those without property were to be in power, then they would simply
vote to take away all wealth from those who possessed it:

> We all agree that you should have a representative to govern, but this
> representative to be as equal as you can; but the question is, whether
> this distribution can be made to all persons equally, or whether amongst
> those equals that have the interest of England in them?

Edward Sexby accused Ireton of suggesting that men would go against
God's commandments and steal land that was not theirs, while on
the question of the franchise Rainborough asked: 'I would fain know
what the soldier hath fought for all this while? He hath fought to
enslave himself, to give power to men of riches.'

John Wildman believed that fear of anarchy was a distraction from
the real issue: 'Instead of following the first proposition to inquire
what is just, I conceive we look to prophecies, and look to what may
be the event, and judge of the justness of the thing by its consequence.
I desire we may recall whether it be right or no.' A proposal should
be judged on its rightness, not on an estimate of its possible results.
Yet it was consequences that mattered most to Cromwell and Ireton.

Although the words of Rainborough, Petty, Sexby, Wildman and
the other agitators seemed outlandish for their day, they reflected and
inspired the beliefs and hopes that were widespread in England. With

regard to the many public discussions held (and pamphlets and posters produced) during the revolutionary decades of the seventeenth century, the historian Christopher Hill commented that 'The eloquence, the power, of the simple artisans who took part in these discussions is staggering.'[11] He quoted John Milton with approval, who wrote of the 'noble and puissant nation, rousing herself like a strong man after sleep and shaking her invincible locks . . . a nation not slow and dull, but of a quick, ingenious and piercing spirit, acute to invent, subtle and sinewy to discourse, not beneath the reach of any point the highest human capacity can soar to.'

The Putney Debates lasted until 11 November, though they were only recorded for three days in total. As there seemed little chance of consensus in the open forum, Cromwell set up a committee to draft an agreement arising from the discussions. This document reflected a surprising number of the proposals in the original 'Agreement of the People', including that the current parliament should be dissolved before September 1648, and elections held every two years thereafter, with Parliament sitting for six months. Proposing that the government be carried out with a council of state, the document assumed that the monarchy and House of Lords would continue but with power residing in the Commons.

In addition, two crucial questions were addressed. First, it was decided that religious freedoms, conscription and indemnity for war acts should remain outside the purview of the new parliament, giving a clear indication that these matters must be settled before September 1648. This was a remarkable victory for the troops and the Levellers. Second, the document proposed that Parliament itself was to decide on the qualifications for voting, but that all who had made some contribution to the war, and all who had joined the army before the battle of Naseby were allowed to vote, while those who had fought against Parliament were to be disenfranchised until the third elected Parliament. Tithes were also to be replaced by a fairer system of tax which was yet to be determined.

The agitators and Levellers at Putney were the first group in history to argue for representative government in a nation state, for a written constitution to protect the citizen against the state, and to define certain universal rights: the right to silence (in resistance to widespread use of torture); the right to legal representation; freedom of conscience and debate; equality before the law; the right to vote; and the right to remove tyrants. None of these demands had been previously recognised by a national government.

However, relations between the agitators and the senior officers began to break down immediately after the debates. The Levellers within the council were becoming impatient with the officers' emollient attitude towards the king and the House of Lords. At the same time, Cromwell was manoeuvring to negate the power of the agitators. Two elements combined to defeat the Levellers' purpose. The first was the realisation by Cromwell and Fairfax that Leveller ideas, which they had considered a minority influence that could be managed without difficulty, had infiltrated widely into the ranks and officers of the army – that much was clear from the debates themselves. While allowing the drafting of a sympathetic agreement, they acted swiftly to curtail the growing power of the agitators and their Leveller colleagues. The agitators requested a meeting of all the army regiments in order to affirm the new agreement, but the senior officers could see the dangers this held for army unity.

At the next meeting of the General Council, Cromwell, with Fairfax now in the chair, declared universal male franchise a recipe for anarchy, and ordered the agitators to return to their regiments. In order to swing the waverers behind him, Fairfax revealed that he had requested from the Commons an increase in the army's monthly funds from £60,000 to £100,000, and the setting aside of bishops' and deans' lands to pay the arrears of soldiers' wages.

The other element that wrecked any hope of a democratic England was the revival of war sparked by the escape of the king. On 11 November 1647, Charles fled from Hampton Court with the intention of reaching France, but on the Isle of Wight he was detained by the governor and taken to Carisbrooke Castle. Parliament sent him another set of proposals (the Four Bills) with instructions to sign them. These required him to surrender authority over the army and navy for twenty years, to seek the approval of Parliament for any military action, to grant the right to Parliament to sit wherever it wished, and to annul all honours granted by him since the beginning of the conflict. But he also received delegations from the Scots who were concerned about a radical group taking power in England. Charles signed an agreement of Engagement with the Scots on 26 December and relied, for a final time, on their invading England. In the meantime there were rebellions in the south and west and in Kent and Essex, mainly against Parliament rather than in favour of the king, though these differences were becoming blurred.

Within the New Model Army itself the Levellers were stoking the fires of rebellion. At an army rendezvous at Ware in Hertfordshire on 15 November, just four days after the king's escape, Colonel Rainborough (no longer an army officer, and therefore not authorised to be present) presented Fairfax with a petition seeking the full implementation of the 'Agreement of the People'. Fairfax ordered him from the field, but a more serious challenge came with the arrival of the regiment of Colonel Thomas Harrison, without officers and led by their agitator Joseph Aleyn. They too had no right to be at the rendezvous, and were wearing copies of the agreement pinned to their hats. A dressing down from Fairfax, and the obvious refusal of the other regiments to join the rebellion, restored order. The troops had shown their feelings but they were part of an army, and swore obedience. Fairfax told each regiment in turn that the agents and agitators had combined with outside elements to divide the army against itself. He then had his own declaration of the army's requirements for itself and for the country read out. These included settlements of pay and indemnity, and fixed-term parliaments chosen through free elections.

Fairfax was gaining control over the situation when the regiment of Robert Lilburne entered the field, having been in open rebellion against its officers for the past eighteen days. They too wore copies of the agreement pinned to their hats and were not so easily cowed; only when Cromwell and other officers rode into the ranks with swords drawn did the men come to some kind of order. Fairfax carried out a court martial of several ringleaders and condemned them to death. He then reprieved them and selected just three to draw lots; the loser was shot in front of the regiment by the other two. This was the symbolic and brutal end of the nascent rebellion, and the end of any chance of Leveller domination of English politics.

Further rendezvous at Watford and Kingston proved harmonious and, in the early months of 1648, the New Model Army was cut by half with radicals purged and troublesome regiments reduced. Armed insurrections in parts of England and Wales and the intervention of the Scottish army provoked what has become known as the Second

English Civil War. Parliament was much harsher with those involved in this war; after the battle of Preston (August 1648), where Cromwell defeated the Scots, and the sieges at Pembroke (July) and Colchester (August), leading royalists were hanged. In September, with all rebellion crushed, a delegation was sent once again to negotiate with the king. Exasperated by Charles' intransigence, Henry Ireton persuaded Fairfax to abandon the talks and impose the army's own proposals; the king was transferred to Hurst Castle and, on 6 December, Ireton excluded all Members of Parliament still in favour of negotiation with the king.

Those who were left – the Rump Parliament – passed an ordinance on 1 January 1649 to set up a High Court of Justice to try the king. Charles refused to answer the charges against him, as he argued that there was no higher authority than the king and the court had no right to try him. For the prosecution Chief Judge John Bradshaw asserted that the ultimate authority in the country lay with the people: 'Sir, as the law is your superior, so truly sir, there is something that is superior to the law and that is indeed the parent or author of the law – and that is the people of England.'[12]

The Rump Parliament believed that as long as Charles lived he would be a danger to the stability of the country, and that he must be executed. Nevertheless, the parliamentary court needed to show where their authority was founded. Thus the crisis of the 1640s saw the beginnings of modern political philosophy, leading to the publication in 1651 of Thomas Hobbes' *Leviathan*. The book proposed the idea of society functioning through a social contract between rulers and ruled, which became the philosophers' answer to the question of legitimacy and how society should be governed. The social contract would be taken up in different forms by John Locke and Jean-Jacques Rousseau, from where it had a direct influence on political activists during the French Revolution.

On 26 January 1649 Charles was convicted of being 'a tyrant, traitor and murderer' by a court that called on the authority of 'the people of England'. Four days later he was executed in front of the Mansion House. There were further Leveller rebellions in April and May, put down by an increasingly disenchanted Fairfax. It was now Cromwell and Ireton who were controlling events. Cromwell led a military expedition to Ireland to suppress a Catholic rebellion in 1649 and, as head of the army, invaded Scotland in 1650 and 1651. By the time he returned to London, the Rump Parliament was in disagreement about a series of crucial measures on dissolution and elections. Cromwell became exasperated by this indecisiveness and, on 20 April 1653, dismissed Parliament by force and took effective control of the country; his Protectorate lasted until 1658. In 1657 he was offered the Crown by Parliament but, after agonising, refused: 'I would not seek to set up that which Providence hath destroyed and laid in the dust, and I would not build Jericho again'. After his death in 1658 his son Richard succeeded him but, with little support, was forced to resign in May 1659.

When the monarchy was restored in 1660, Parliament was able to exercise the control it had sought over the earlier Stuart kings. It was Parliament that invited Charles II to assume the throne and, when his successor James II refused to bow to its control, Parliament showed that it did possess the ultimate power in the kingdom by deposing the king and inviting William of Orange to occupy the throne. The conditions placed on the monarch by Parliament, laid out in the English Bill of Rights of 1689, the triennial Act of 1694, and the Act of Succession of 1701–2, saw the foundation of a constitutional monarchy and of the famously 'balanced' constitution, where commons, lords and monarch all played their part. Britain's political stability and success on the international stage in the eighteenth and nineteenth centuries was ascribed to this 'ideal state', but it would be difficult to argue that this was a step towards democracy. Democracy, torn from the soldiers on the field at Ware, now became a dirty word – all subsequent reforms in Britain were introduced on the basis that they would hold democracy at bay. It was only in the 1880s that the word was again used in a virtuous context.

The Glorious Revolution of 1688–9 became the founding myth of English constitutionalism, and in this ideology it is Parliament rather than the people that is sovereign. In fact sovereignty lies with 'the Crown in Parliament', a suitably grand and deliberately obscure form of words that allows the monarch to retain certain powers while surrendering the government of the country to Parliament. The Crown's powers have gradually become more ceremonial, but there remains to this day the possibility that the monarch could step in at a time of political or constitutional crisis to restore stability.

After 1700 many Europeans began to realise that parliaments had great potential as instruments of government, and this was largely due to the example of Britain. The country's imperial expansion, facilitated by an extraordinarily well-organised and successful navy (the modern equivalent of the Roman army), followed by the Industrial Revolution, gave the country huge economic success at home and abroad. Its constitution and the political stability it brought was a shining example to those like Voltaire who argued that national status did not depend on autocratic monarchs, and to those seeking liberty for the individual. Whether the British constitution and the nation's power were causally linked is difficult to determine; what is clear is that Britain became a more open society than most of its European neighbours.

However, closer inspection of electoral politics in eighteenth-century Britain shows an alarming degree of nepotism, corruption and self-serving, with few formal checks and balances. A seat in Parliament was won through family connections or through buying off the small number of electors in a constituency. Once they had been elected most MPs took little part in Parliament and the country was effectively ruled by a small coterie of grandees, mostly from the House of Lords and therefore not even answerable to the supposed representatives of the people. Of the twenty-four prime ministers who served between 1721 and the Reform Act of 1832, sixteen sat in the House of Lords.

The borough of Scarborough, assiduously described by historian Jack Binns, provides a typical story: 'Between 1715 and 1831 there were thirty-six elections and by-elections held in the borough of Scarborough, yet only seven of them were contested . . . central government exercised control over at least one and often both of the constituency seats.' But even when there were contested elections, politics were of little importance and 'personal and family rivalries were more relevant . . . a truly independent candidate was most exceptional.' In the 1760s Lord Granby, commander-in-chief of the army, arrived in the constituency with massive government support. In 1768 he put up his illegitimate son George Manners who won the election by twenty-nine votes to twenty-four and the seat was kept in the family for the next sixty years.[13] While national issues like war and religion had an effect, many elections were fought on local issues, with candidates promising financial rewards to gain support.

Despite all this, elections did involve more than just unworthy candidates and corrupt electors. The campaigns mobilised large sections of the population and candidates put themselves in front of the people; in many places this turned into a carnival complete with banners, rosettes and brigades of supporters. Those without a vote joined in the fun and had a chance to berate or cheer the candidates. Those standing would make a grand entrance on election day, and when the result was declared there were parties with bonfires, dancing and drinking; this was politics as entertainment.

In eighteenth-century Europe politicians were from a narrow social range – a situation that endured until the mid twentieth century. The House of Commons was typical: sons of peers and members of the gentry dominated, and promoting their family's interests was as important as party politics. These were gentlemen with an interest in the nation's affairs but a bigger interest in their own. The voters came from the gentry too: in Britain in 1800 there were 350,000 electors in a total population of ten million. Lewis Namier's ground-breaking studies of Parliament in the eighteenth century revealed how British politics was shaped by a small elite, all related to each other.

Yet that century also saw economic growth which brought affluence, education and political consciousness. In some parts of Europe, such as Scotland, the Dutch Republic, Sweden, Belgium and northern France, close to 100 cent of males were literate by 1800. This, together with changes in tax laws, brought a boom in sales of newspapers, periodicals and books. Britain was again at the forefront with 2.5 million papers sold in 1713 and 12.6 million by 1775. By 1789, the German states of the Holy Roman Empire had 200 newspapers read by three million people. Dutch papers were read in France, where papers were suppressed; after the outbreak of the French Revolution in 1789 a hundred newspapers sprang up immediately. Readership of papers was much bigger than their print runs suggest as reading rooms, coffee houses, lodges, literary societies, academies and pubs all bought copies. Politics extended its reach to an ever larger part of the population.

The democratic impulses of the Levellers, working through the New Model Army, failed to win the day. The inheritance of the conflict that swept through the British Isles in the 1640s was a denial of democracy in favour of a Parliament attended by the wealthy and well-connected and controlled by a small elite. The British Parliament's assumption that it spoke for the people was no more valid than that of the old medieval parliaments, and its electoral practices were certainly questionable. Nonetheless, for the next century the custom of elections became firmly established in Britain and other parts of Europe where politics became part of public discourse. And when more and more of the British population gained economic power through the organisation of industrial workers in the late nineteenth century, they finally gained access to political power through elections to Parliament – the same Parliament that had turned down the democratic proposals of their ancestors. No one knew about the transcripts of the Putney Debates until they were discovered in an Oxford archive in 1890. The generation that rediscovered the Levellers was to be the first to see full democracy come to Britain.

DEMOCRACY IN AMERICA

The Citizen-Elector

Democracy came to flickering life in the late medieval cities of Europe, in the valleys of the high Alps and in the ranks of the New Model Army. Important though these developments were in the history of democracy, they are dwarfed by the subsequent extraordinary political history of the United States of America. At the same time as European citizens were losing out to ever more powerful states, the United States established a democracy on a scale that had never previously existed.

The new system was not only sustained for longer than in every other democratic state but, in its first seventy or so years, the United States invented and put into effect a series of democratic practices and principles that gave the world a model. By the 1840s every white male adult citizen had the right to vote in state and federal elections; almost every important public official was elected; a series of national institutions was established to protect the citizen from the power of the state and the potential 'tyranny of the majority'; bodies at national, regional and local level harnessed and curbed the authority of the federal state; political parties emerged that not only raised funds for electioneering but encouraged participation and a political culture of mass engagement; and the difficult concept of a loyal opposition was established.

The story of how all this came about has often been neglected in favour of the grand rhetoric of Jefferson and Adams. But practice came long before theory. In this chapter we will first look at the roots of democracy in the American colonies: the Puritan churches and the old English boroughs. Neither made American democracy inevitable, but without them it would not have come into being.

The *Mayflower* set sail from Plymouth in September 1620 aiming for the area of the Hudson river, but the ship drifted north and made land at Cape Cod in Massachusetts. Despite meeting the onset of a northern winter, the Puritan passengers believed they had come to create a community in which God's will could be practised – to build, in the later words of John Winthrop, 'a city upon a hill'. The Puritans had escaped religious persecution in England and were seeking a place nearer to God. Yet despite the *Mayflower*'s mythic status, the eastern seaboard had already been settled by Europeans. The English colony at Jamestown in Virginia, founded in 1607, was a commercial enterprise with a population of traders, artisans and indentured servants working their way to freedom.[1] Two important strands of American life were therefore established right from the start – the buccaneering individualists of Virginia and the puritanical communities of Massachusetts.

While Dutch, Spanish, Swedish, Danish, Finnish, German and French settlers came to North America, the sheer number of immigrants from Britain was to be decisive and overwhelming. After an uncertain and brutally hard beginning – almost half of the *Mayflower*'s passengers did not survive the first winter – 18,000 Puritans had made the Atlantic voyage by 1642, and by 1700 there were 100,000 living in New England. Further immigration saw other sects such as the Quakers settle in large numbers in Pennsylvania, spreading west from the seaboard towards the Appalachians.

Although different religious groups were present, the early colonies were dominated by Nonconformist Protestants. In almost all cases they had a strong belief in both the community of the church and the individual value of each member. The ways in which these churches were governed is vital because, as one historian of the period has written, in the early decades of the New England colonies 'church and town governments were virtually indistinguishable'.[2]

It is important to understand how different Puritan congregations were from the Catholic and Anglican churches from which they had ceded. For the American Puritans there was no separate institution called 'the church', governed and officiated by some remote power. The church was its members not its clergy or its buildings; it was, in

the words of William Ames, founder of Congregationalism, 'a fellow-
ship of faithful believers'.[3] The term Meeting House, used by Quakers,
shows that its purpose was functional rather than sacred – in contrast
to the holy status of a Catholic church.

While Nonconformist churches were essentially founded in the
faith of their members, they were not open to all comers. Individuals
joining the church agreed to behave in certain ways and rules of
behaviour were extremely strict: the Puritans believed that power
brings responsibility and that the community cannot be ruled by those
who lead irresponsible lives. Moreover, the central tenet of Calvinist
theology was that the elect show themselves worthy of God's grace
by leading lives of simple piety. Each member of a Puritan church
signed a covenant, a solemn rite of passage dividing them from the
rest of the community. Moreover, each local church was a distinct
unit, and while they met together in a local synod where matters of
faith could be discussed and disputes resolved, the synod had no
powers of its own. Indeed, the Puritans were keen to limit the authority
of the institution to which they belonged.

In Massachusetts towns like Salem, Lynn, Weymouth, Cambridge,
Medfield and Marlborough, every local church held an annual General
Court comprising all the members. The freemen, meaning the male
members, would elect a number of assistants who would administer
the government of the church community (effectively the town) and
they in turn would elect a governor. A group of church elders emerged
who were regularly elected as assistants and governors, often holding
office for substantial periods. In these deeply religious communities
it was assumed that they spoke for God.

The Puritan system of church membership served as a model for
American democracy before the War of Independence and for several
decades afterwards. Nonconformist churches were the bedrock of
many of the settler towns of the East Coast, organising secular as
well as religious society. The government of the early colonies was
driven by the practical need to have an effective administration –
someone had to build roads, dam rivers, punish miscreants and so on.
Its structure was dictated by the lack of any overarching authority
and by the deeply held beliefs of the Nonconformist churches in the
equality of the faithful.

However, to become a fully fledged democracy the United States had to overcome one central element of Puritanism. Sixty years after independence, the French politician Alexis de Tocqueville commented that Puritanism 'corresponded with the most absolute democratic and republican theories'.[4] Yet Puritans did not believe in fundamental rights for all; they believed instead that government allowed the opportunity for communal and individual redemption. They saw that this would be of benefit to everyone and serve as a model for those outside the church; but government itself was too serious a business to allow everyone to partake in it. In an echo of Aristotle, they took the view that government must be left to the good – that is to the members of the church.

Two other aspects of early colonial life, both inherited from English practice, are relevant to our story here. First, ballots and town government followed English patterns; as one historian has argued, 'it remains a fact of great importance in American history that the English people . . . were very familiar with elections of one kind or another'.[5] As early as 1632 the Massachusetts settlers decided that each township should elect two representatives (as in England) to confer with the assistants and the governor, and that a quarterly general court should hear the views of all the freemen. Secondly, restrictions on voting were not only based on the Puritan belief in the worthiness of the faithful: American colonies followed English practice in restricting voting rights to those in possession of freehold property.

In the course of the eighteenth century, the American population grew prodigiously. From a total of around 50,000 in 1650 and 250,000 in 1700, it was 5.3 million in 1800. Boston grew from around 3,000 inhabitants in 1660 to 7,000 in 1700, and then to 24,000 in 1800.[6] The new immigrants were no longer solely Nonconformist Protestants escaping persecution; many were economic migrants in search of a better life. As the population grew, the religious dimension of community life decreased and the town meeting took over from the church as the centre of community affairs. There was also a dilution of the Puritan ideal as the wealthy and powerful began to dominate these meetings, using them to advance their own interests. Membership of a town meeting was limited not by church covenant but by variations on property ownership, including the forty-shilling law dating back to 1430. Nevertheless the meetings, as the historian Hugh Brogan has written, 'provided essential training in self-government' and each town was in essence 'a city-state, a direct democracy of the purest classical kind'.[7]

In the eighteenth century a freehold qualification existed in many colonies. New Hampshire required £50 value; Rhode Island £40 value or forty shillings annual rent; Virginia a hundred acres unsettled or twenty-five acres improved; North Carolina and Georgia, fifty acres straight. While in England the number of freeholders decreased between 1750 and 1860 as a result of the Enclosures Acts, in the colonies the cultivation of ever more land meant a continuing increase in freeholders. One Robert Park had come to Pennsylvania from Ireland as a tenant farmer, but was eventually able to buy 500 acres of good land for £350. In 1725 he wrote to his family that it was 'the best country for working folk and tradespeople of any in the world'.

At the same time as the cities were growing, settlers were occupying the fertile plain between the coast and the Appalachians. These were independent Pennsylvanian farmers, setting up remote homesteads far from the reach of town governments. The village, as known since time immemorial in Europe, was absent here; instead family farms were the basis of rural society. The descendants of these early farmers, hardy individuals wary of authority, were to play a big role in America's self-image and in its politics.

European settlement of North America was not a benign process; the destruction of the indigenous population and the forced transportation of millions of Africans to work as slaves, showed a brutality that contrasted with the religious morality of the settlers. The settlement of the continent was continually bedevilled by the violent rivalry between European nations. Wars between Britain and France erupted with regularity from 1689, culminating in the conflict known in Europe as the Seven Years War (1756–63) and in the United States as the French and Indian War. This conflict fundamentally changed the relationship between Britain and her thirteen American colonies. Up until then the mother country had been content to let them manage their own affairs, albeit with certain restrictions – insisting on the use of British vessels for all international trade, for example – but during the war, thousands of regular British troops were sent to the colonies, pushing aside any concerns of the Americans in pursuit of the strategic necessity of defeating the French.

The war and the British victory had a raft of unintended consequences. The British thought their colonists incapable of defending
themselves, so more troops were stationed in the colonies. The
Americans, on the other hand, had seen the British troops fighting
first hand and realised that they were far from invincible, while their
own irregular forces had performed with credit. Moreover, the withdrawal of France to the west of the Mississippi left open a vast area
to be exploited by settlers, and though the British government tried
to preserve this area for the indigenous population they were widely
ignored. The most important consequence of the war, however, was
that the British government, with its exchequer deep in debt, was
forced to recover the expense of stationing troops in North America
by imposing taxes on the colonies.

First came the Sugar Tax of 1764, then the Stamp Act of 1765, and
in 1767 the Townshend Acts introduced taxes on tea, paper, paint, lead
and glass. The American colonists became angry at the British authorities and began to organise resistance. Riots against the Stamp Act in
1765 and 1767 were followed in 1770 by the deaths of five colonists at
the hands of British troops. Benjamin Franklin was typical of colonists
outraged by this new aggression. Formerly a staunch royalist, Franklin
wrote of holding 'a Looking-Glass in which some Ministers may see
their Ugly Faces, and the Nation its Injustice'.[8] Committees of
Correspondence and clubs such as the Sons of Liberty exchanged
information, grievances and strategy and showed the development
of a distinctively American identity. Liberty was in the air and the
colonists were feeling their way towards social rebellion – New York
farmers rose against British landowners, and North Carolina planters
took on their legal overlords. In 1773 a group of Boston militants
destroyed a cargo of tea owned by the East India Company – the
famous Boston Tea Party – leading to a clampdown by the British.
In September 1774 a Continental Congress of colonial representatives
met in Philadelphia, where they decided on a boycott of British goods.
Open revolt now looked inevitable, but the British were ill-prepared
to deal with it: in the early 1770s the Townshend taxes were only
raising around £300 a year, a minute proportion of the £170,000 it
cost to maintain British troops in the colonies, while the number of
troops was, in any case, wholly inadequate to subdue the
population.

On 18 and 19 April 1775, General Gage made his famous march from Boston to Lexington and Concord to seize a colonists' weapons cache. The local militia were forewarned by Paul Revere and William Dawes, and their leader John Parker told his men, 'Don't fire unless fired upon, but if they mean to have a war, let it begin here.' So the War of Independence began. In June the colonists were defeated at the Battle of Bunker Hill, but by then the Continental Congress was the de facto government of an emerging nation in rebellion.

In fact many colonists were initially loyal to the British; the task of the rebel forces was to keep the conflict going for long enough to persuade their fellow colonists and outside forces – in particular France and Spain – that independence was a serious possibility. The early months of 1776 saw the American army under George Washington take Boston from General Howe, but Washington was forced to withdraw from Long Island, New York City and Quebec. When the Continental Congress met in Philadelphia that summer, the military outlook was at best difficult, at worst bleak. Nevertheless, the Congress decided it must push ahead with independence. Thomas Paine's pamphlet 'Common Sense', which argued for the rights of the colonists to govern themselves, had made a huge impact earlier in the year, eventually selling over 500,000 copies. The Declaration of Independence, drawn up in the midst of war principally by Thomas Jefferson, was agreed by the Congress on 4 July 1776. It declared both the possession of natural rights by all people, and their right to remove any government that aimed to destroy those rights:

> We hold these truths to be self-evident, that all men are created equal, that they are endowed by their Creator with certain unalienable Rights, that among these are Life, Liberty and the pursuit of Happiness. That to secure these rights, Governments are instituted among Men, deriving their just powers from the consent of the governed, That whenever any Form of Government becomes destructive of these ends, it is the Right of the People to alter or to abolish it, and to institute new Government, laying its foundation on such principles and organizing its powers in such form, as to them shall seem most likely to effect their Safety and Happiness.

Despite the confidence of the declaration the war was going badly for the Americans. In late December 1776 Washington pulled off a major tactical coup, crossing the Delaware river to take Trenton and Princeton in New Jersey, but 1777 saw further reverses with General Howe taking Philadelphia and General Burgoyne bringing 8,000 British troops south from Canada. However, a major turning point occurred in October 1777, when Burgoyne found himself cut off in upper New York State and was forced to surrender. Washington withdrew the Continental army to Valley Forge in Pennsylvania to wait out the winter of 1777–8 and emerged in a much stronger position. The French were encouraged to enter the war in early 1778, providing a fleet that successfully challenged British monopoly of the coastal seaway. They were followed into the war by Spain and the Dutch Republic. Once Washington secured the central section of the colonies, the situation in the south, after a disastrous defeat at Camden, started to go better for the Americans. Their troops were able to pin down General Cornwallis in the city of Yorktown, while French ships prevented British naval support reaching the isolated army. In October 1781 Cornwallis surrendered with 8,000 men and the war was effectively over.

The end of the conflict brought a vast number of problems for the new country. In an uncanny echo of England in 1647, the American leaders found themselves in command of an army that they could not pay. With no monetary or legal resources to support it the paper currency introduced to finance the war was worthless. A crisis was avoided only by a direct appeal from General Washington to the unpaid troops. Meanwhile, with no central authority the individual states had to press on with the process of government, including building relations with foreign powers. The national government had been formed under the Articles of Confederation agreed in 1777 and ratified in 1781, but these confirmed the primacy of the states working together in a loose confederation. Soon the interests of different states began to clash; some began to mint their own currency, and issues such as seaboard states over-taxing imports en route to the interior threatened to tear the confederation apart. In this atmosphere political leaders understood the need for a legal and political framework that would spell out the relations between the states. In May 1787 representatives of all the states except Rhode Island met at a constitutional convention in Philadelphia to hammer out some form of agreement.

While the Declaration of Independence was a piece of grand rhetoric crafted largely from the educated pen of Thomas Jefferson, the Constitution was a working document pieced together during four months of wrangling, trade-offs and compromise. By September, the Convention had agreed a constitution that was a victory for those who intended to build a new government, rather than tinker with the existing one. The so-called Federalists argued successfully for a strong central government with some authority over the individual states, while the Anti-Federalists saw the national government as a servant of the states, co-ordinating their requirements and activities. The proposed federal Constitution was then sent out to the states for discussion and ratification, where the same arguments were replayed. The 'Federalist Papers', written by James Madison, Alexander Hamilton and John Jay and published in the *Independent Journal* and the *New York Packet* in 1787 and 1788, were an attempt to persuade the congress of New York State to ratify the constitution.[9] The articles eloquently argued the case for an 'extended republic' headed by a single chief executive or president, but it is doubtful whether they affected the outcome of the vote – the stature of Federalists such as Washington, Jefferson and Madison was probably the decisive factor.

Once the Constitution was circulated, it was clear that a major element was missing: there was no reference to the rights of citizens. This was corrected in 1789 when the ten amendments known as the Bill of Rights were added. It is here that we see connections across centuries and across the Atlantic, since the rights laid out are enlargements of proposals first put in writing by the English Levellers and later put into law by the English Parliament of 1689. The states now ratified the federal Constitution one by one, with Rhode Island and Vermont (which had ceded from New York State) holding out until 1790 and 1791 respectively. Benjamin Franklin wrote: 'Our constitution is in actual operation and everything appears to promise that it will last. But in this world, nothing can be certain but death and taxes.'[10]

The United States now had a constitution that spelled out the relative powers of its federal and state governments and their structures, including the separation of legislature, executive and judiciary; it gave details of how Congress and the president should be elected, and what their powers should be; it also proposed a Supreme Court as a guardian of this Constitution. This was an impressive political structure that gave the nation legitimacy as a federal republic, with guarantees for the civil and political rights of its citizens. But how democratic was this new country?

Large-scale political participation was in the bloodstream of the American colonies and their citizens. Would this survive the transition from colonial semi-autonomy to full nationhood, and if so, what form would it take? We know the answer to the first question – democracy did survive. The answer to the second shows us just how much these matters are decided not in fine minds and meeting rooms, but in the jostling confusion of everyday life and in the assumptions and deter-mination of the population. Having agreed the Constitution and Bill of Rights, the great task of the Founding Fathers was to provide a federal government that built on, and stayed true, to the spirit of the local foundations of democracy.

The Declaration of Independence had stated 'that all men are created equal, that they are endowed by their Creator with certain unalienable Rights, that among these are Life, Liberty and the pursuit of Happiness'. This ringing sentence, forged in the midst of war against a king, gave reason why men should not be ruled by a tyrant; but just because men are created equal does not mean they remain that way. The matter of who had the right to vote was still based on property and the new federal government left matters of eligibility to the individual states (as had previously been the case with the colonies). In six states voting rights were relaxed, while others kept their existing arrangements; all states required at least some property to qualify.

This doesn't sound like the birth of a democracy but the next five decades saw a steady move from a freeholder to a male citizens' fran-chise. In New York in 1787 the vote was opened to all freeholders, no matter what value, and ballots were brought in for state elections. At the same time, however, Congress ordained that new states admitted to the union should have a fifty-acre freehold as their voting qualifica-tion – a more stringent test than was current in all the existing states, showing that many of the federal grandees were lagging behind local customs and impulses.

In fact the idea of a limited democracy along British lines, with Congress elected by a small number and drawn from an elite section of society, had been considered at the Constitutional Convention. When the matter of allowing states to set their own voting quali- fications had been discussed, the Virginia delegate Edmund Randolph declared 'our chief danger arises from the democratic parts of [the states'] constitutions'. This was a clear warning against spreading the franchise too widely, but there was also an understanding that the legitimacy of any government – and a war had just been fought to throw off one unpopular regime – could only come through the sovereignty of the people, and this meant a democracy based on widespread participation of its citizens. In reply to Randolph, Benjamin Franklin declared that 'The love of country flourishes where the common people have the vote, and withered, as in England, where they were denied it.'[11] On the other hand, James Madison had argued the case for a 'large republic', while warning of the dangers of a federal democracy: 'By enlarging too much the number of electors, you render the representatives too little acquainted with all their local circumstances and lesser interests; as by reducing it too much, you render him unduly attached to these, and too little fit to comprehend and pursue great and national objects.'[12] Despite Madison's arguments and Randolph's fears, the attempt to bring in a freehold qualification for all states was defeated and the Federal Convention effectively approved the piecemeal enlargement of the franchise that was going on anyway.

The Americans were aware of how the British tripartite constitution (Crown, Lords and Commons) had brought stability and prosperity, and many wanted the same kind of 'balanced' government in America. The federal president, Senate and House of Representatives reflected the tripartite bias. Originally the idea of a senate came from the still common belief in a natural elite, but this was not sustained for long in the United States and the Senate became one element in the struc- ture of government rather than a body representing a different group or estate in society. The two houses of Congress solved another problem for the Federalists: how to ensure that all states felt equally valued, while also reflecting the distribution of the population. The Senate had two representatives from each state, while constituencies for the House were based on population. This too was an echo of British practice, which drew a distinction between county and borough constituencies.

However, while the structures might have been similar, practice and cultural assumptions were totally different. In Britain it was assumed that the Whig landowners spoke for everyone and voting was almost incidental to the process of politics, since society had its 'natural' leaders; in America voting became central since this was the process through which authority arose. Americans began to recognise this by calling their new country a democracy, by which they meant a country where leaders were chosen and could be removed by the people. As early as 1809, in an atmosphere clouded by the threat of renewed war with Britain, the renowned journalist and preacher Elias Smith wrote: 'The government adopted here is a DEMOCRACY. It is well for us to understand this word, so much ridiculed by the international enemies of our country . . . My Friends, never let us be ashamed of democracy.' [13]

Important differences remained among the American people. A good number of the Founding Fathers, including George Washington, Thomas Jefferson and James Madison, were Virginia landowners who viewed the United States as a country of gentlemen farmers caring for a nation expanding slowly across the continent. They believed in small-town America and were dismayed at the growth of cities; they disdained rich industrialists and merchants, fearing that the accrual of political power by a wealthy class would undo the principles on which the new nation was founded. Jefferson expressed his concerns thus: 'I hope we shall crush in its birth the aristocracy of our monied corporations which dare already to challenge our government to a trial by strength, and bid defiance to the laws of our country.'[14]

The main figure who fought against the patrician disdain for commerce was Alexander Hamilton. An incomer from the Caribbean who was not loyal to any particular state, he saw his adopted land as a country with a strong and stable centre not a collection of states come together for individual convenience. He believed that a powerful federal centre could join the political, agricultural and commercial interests of the country in a bond that would benefit them all. Hamilton's key proposal, put forward in 1790, was for a national bank which would work with the federal government to manage the nation's financial affairs. The debate over the bank split the nation because it went to the heart of what the country should be. Here was a divide that offered different versions of America – a country of homesteads and townships with small government, versus a capitalist powerhouse harnessing the talents of the merchant class to the strength of federal government.

During the debate a crucial question emerged: are citizens expected to put aside their personal interests and act (and vote) in the interests of the people and nation as a whole, or does democracy rely on the notion that if everybody acts in their own interest, then the interests of the whole will also be served? In the Pennsylvania assembly William Findley, an ex-weaver, spoke on behalf of debtors and holders of existing paper currency against the re-chartering of the bank. Robert Morris, the wealthiest merchant in Philadelphia and an old-school patrician, argued that Findley had interests in the case and his views should therefore be discounted. Findley replied that his opponent's neutrality was a sham since he had an interest in re-chartering the bank; he also argued that it was legitimate for those with interests to argue on their behalf, so long as they declared their interest and didn't stop others with opposing views doing the same. To our ears this sounds like a fairly rational argument, but at the time it was utterly revolutionary. It challenged the customary assumption that politicians must be disinterested and should pursue some disembodied 'public good'; instead they should acknowledge that they, and politics generally, were part of the messy trade-offs and competing interests of society.

This debate reflects a wider development, in which the dominance of the landowning gentry was giving way to a more commercial society in which citizens took pride in working for a living. In fact, the small leisured class of wealthy landowners were increasingly despised as their claim to act in the interests of the nation became more difficult to sustain. Benjamin Franklin wrote in 1782 that an American would be prouder if 'a genealogist could prove to him that his Ancestors and Relations for ten generations had been Ploughmen, Smiths, Turners, Weavers . . . and consequently . . . useful members of society, than if he could only prove that they were Gentlemen, doing nothing of Value, but living idly on the Labour of others.'[15] This belief in work being more noble than inherited or unearned wealth helped to sustain America's democracy.

Thomas Jefferson believed the federal state should remain as small as possible, while Alexander Hamilton felt that a well-organised union of states with a powerful energetic centre could lead to national prosperity. This divide introduced partisan politics to the United States. Jefferson competed with John Adams (from the same Federalist Party as Hamilton) for the presidency in 1796 – the first contested presidential election. Jefferson lost and was appointed vice president, but he differed diametrically from Adams on relations with the French, as well as on the powers of central government, and decided to withdraw from Washington rather than serve in a coalition. Jefferson was able to take the presidency in 1800, defeating Adams in a rerun.

The invaluable gift that this first divide, with men of established national stature on either side, gave to the politics of the nation was the concept of a loyal opposition. It was vital for stability that debates about important matters such as war, federal power and citizens' rights could take place without the participants being accused of disloyalty. Democratic politics in the United States, just as in ancient Athens, had to learn to take ownership of the conflicts in society and contain them within legitimate forums. Democracy demands that the executive be held to account and that robust debate be carried out without fear of persecution; that opposition to the government be valued as a loyal part of the nation's political process.

When Jefferson stood against Adams in 1800, no one could accuse either of disloyalty to the nation. Since the previous election, politicians at different levels had been aligning themselves with either Jefferson's Democratic-Republicans or Adams' and Hamilton's Federalists, so that parties were winning elections at different levels and in different arenas. It was possible for a party to lose presidential elections but retain power in the Senate, allowing the possibility of winning the presidency or power in Congress next time round. Political rivalry could be fierce, however: in one of the most shocking incidents in American politics, Alexander Hamilton was killed in a duel by his political opponent Vice President Aaron Burr in July 1804.

By 1800 a system of rival political parties was becoming entrenched. In a nation where most of the population were descendants of recent immigrants, or immigrants themselves, we might expect factional politics to have emerged with political parties representing Scots or Irish, Puritans or Quakers, farmers or shippers; but it seems that the sheer multiplicity of society worked against this – no group was numerous enough to win power on its own, so political parties cut across ethnic, religious and social boundaries. The result was that, by the early 1800s, American voters had fallen for party politics in a big way. The carnival atmosphere – speeches, banquets, the sporting element of winner-takes-all – began to be a national obsession, a defining characteristic of the new country. Journalists relished the opportunities for skulduggery, rumour and personal attacks; local politicians worked hard and ingeniously, and a fair few figured it was a good way to make some money. More seriously the public and journalists responded to the abilities of politicians to address important issues in rhetorical terms, persuading, cajoling and entertaining large numbers of people in public gatherings. New immigrants – the population rose to eight million by 1814 – were gripped by the novelty of, and enthusiasm for, elections and party rivalries.

This first phase of party politics began the process of getting people used to loyal opposition; it saw the vast range of interests in society begin to coalesce and become organised by the presence of parties with a realistic chance of gaining power; and the parties began to organise themselves, giving energy to the political process. This was, however, a brief phase. By the time the United States went to war with Britain (1812–15) both Federalists and Republicans had become internally divided; the Federalists faded away as more people joined the Republicans who, in turn, became less like a party and more like a governing coalition.

Despite the growing appetite for the spectacle of politics, the Virginian gentry still felt their role was to serve the public good, and this held them back from self-promotion or criticism of their peers. Jefferson wrote 'If I could not go to heaven but with a [political] party, I would not go at all.' He and his fellow patricians did not like the discipline and compromise necessary for party politics. Yet for all its brevity, the first party system had begun to discover *by practice* how to build institutions and arrangements that would turn the utopian dream of the Declaration of Independence into a workable political system that would, above all, survive.

A new phase of American politics opened with the presidential election of 1824. For the previous twelve years party politics had stagnated as the Republican Party dominated at all levels. However, in 1824 the party could not agree on a presidential candidate, which led to four men standing as Republicans. John Quincy Adams from New York, the son of the second president John Adams, was the only one to have the full backing of his state party; as the Secretary of State to the outgoing President James Monroe, he also had strong connec tions to the Virginia establishment. Adams' main opponent was an entirely new kind of politician. Andrew Jackson came from Tennessee, well outside the heartland of US politics, and had become a national figure through his command of the victorious forces at the Battle of New Orleans in 1815. Jackson brought a transforming energy to American democracy but, although he gained the most electoral college votes, no candidate won an overall majority. Under the existing rules the House of Representatives had the power to decide the winner and they chose Adams. The result infuriated Jackson's supporters, and the next four years saw mudslinging of every kind between the two camps. Jackson's supporters portrayed Adams as corrupt and accused him of gorging at the public trough, and of turning the White House into a gambling den (Adams had brought in a billiard table). In response Jackson was accused of being a murderer, bigamist and slave trader. While it may not have been dignified, it certainly brought to an end the cosy Virginian ownership of national politics. The two men split the Republicans and two new parties were born: the Democrats, headed by Jackson and his running mate Martin van Buren, and the Whigs.

The 1828 presidential election saw further advances in American democracy, as members of the electoral colleges were now mandated by the popular vote (previously they had acted independently) and party members gained a bigger say in policy.[16] This was arguably the first democratic presidential election, with an impressive turnout of 58 per cent, which was largely the result of Andrew Jackson's populist style, his wooing of a wide range of voters and the arrival of a host of news-papers with an interest in national politics.[17] The election was won by Jackson and by the time of his inauguration in 1829, only Virginia and North Carolina still carried a freehold qualification for voters – and Virginia's was abandoned in 1830. Elections were drawing a bigger percentage of a larger electorate from a growing population; by the 1840 presidential election, turnout was 78 per cent.

The new political parties were quite different from their pre-decessors – more tribal, populist, organised and dedicated to winning.

Party candidates had previously been chosen at meetings within Congress, but from 1828 party conventions brought a mass of party members into the process as well as providing forums for the open discussion of policy. The so-called Albany Regency, the Democrat political organisation that originated in New York in the 1820s, was a prototype for the political parties of the future. It was a well-organised machine with electoral victory as its main objective. While parties were essentially groupings of like-minded people, the Albany Regency brought in a sense of order and discipline so that voters knew what the party, as well as its individual candidates, stood for. One of its leading lights, William E. Marcy, wrote: 'When they [New York politicians] are contending for victory, they avow their intention of enjoying the fruits of it. If they are defeated, they expect to retire from office. If they are successful they claim, as a matter of right, the advantages of success. They see nothing wrong in the rule that to the Victor belong the spoils of the Enemy.'[18] New York politician Martin van Buren reinforced the hold of parties by handing the gift of patronage to the state legislature: whoever won got to appoint around 4,000 officials, who would then work to keep their jobs by having the ruling party re-elected. Van Buren took this practice to national politics when he became president in 1837.

This second phase of political parties in the United States (formally called by historians the Second Party System) saw Democrats vying with Whigs in a much more organised and aggressive way than in the days of Jefferson and Adams. The system lasted until, in the face of its impotence to keep the nation together, Abraham Lincoln broke it apart on the eve of the Civil War. Political parties had existed elsewhere, notably in Britain, for at least a century before the founding of the United States, while in other countries, such as France, political factions had represented different groups within society; but it was America that gave birth to the modern political party, complete with comprehensive ideology, the ability to turn interest or prejudice into policy, and tribal loyalties. The chutzpah, razzmatazz and enthusiasm that American parties engendered gave democratic politics an extraordinary energy.

The United States had no role models for how to build a nation. Citizens slowly learned *from experience* to accept that organised political activity, in support of government or in opposition to it, was legitimate. Eventually parties became essential to the survival of a politicised society by articulating public needs and resolving contentions. In a nation where every voter had an opinion, parties worked to build coherent policies based on consistent ideologies. It wasn't the Constitution or the Founding Fathers who articulated the great issues of the nation, it was the political parties, their members and their meetings. The party system brought so-called 'ordinary' people into government, transforming people's understanding of their society in ways that were beyond contemplation in Europe. It soon became clear to many that, with elected and appointed posts carrying salaries, party work and loyalty could lead to a decent living. As has often been said, if an honest man could make a good living, a dishonest man might do even better. Yet once the parties were well established, the flip side of their powers became apparent too. As we have seen in New York, so many public offices were in the gift of elected officials that party bosses wielded immense power making them effectively invulnerable to voter opinion or choice.

As well as developing political parties, the United States was undergoing a quiet revolution in the franchise. One state after another changed the voting qualification from adult males who owned property to those who paid taxes. By the 1840s this move was complete, and in almost every state the vote was given to all adult white males. This wasn't always with the purest of motives: in the South, giving the vote to every white male was a way of signifying their superiority to slaves, and taxpaying qualifications were revived in the South after the Civil War in order to exclude black people from voting. Nevertheless, male citizenship became broadly identical with the right to vote.

While presidential and national elections were the great events of the political calendar, American democracy was well served by the layers of institutions that stood between the individual and the state. Alexis de Tocqueville gave an account of his 1831 travels through the United States in his book *Democracy in America*. He remarked on the power and effectiveness of local government, the various church bodies and local societies that looked after their members' interests in a different way to the potentially all-powerful state: 'The Americans make associations to give books . . . in this manner they found hospitals, prisons, and schools . . . Wherever at the head of some new undertaking you see the government in France, or a man of rank in England, in the United States you will be sure to find an association.'[19] The leading British political philosopher and Member of Parliament John Stuart Mill had originally regarded local boards and boroughs, with their narrow parochial concerns, as impediments to good government; but after reading de Tocqueville he understood that their presence was essential, and their occasional contrariness and inconvenient rules were necessary safeguards for the individual against the power of the state.

The history of the United States shows how political arrangements reflect the culture of society, but also how they are limited by the forces operating within that same culture. There remained profound problems that the combination of Constitution, votes for all adult white males, and vibrant parties did not address. The prime issue was slavery. Though many were against slavery, no party was prepared to stand on a platform of national abolition. In 1854 Abraham Lincoln, in response to the Kansas–Nebraska Act, which repealed an agreed limit on slavery, was forced to form a new Republican Party with the explicit intention of holding the Union together in the face of secession by the Southern states.

It was the legal enslavement of black people that made Abraham Lincoln, in the midst of war, reassess the meaning of American democracy. On 19 November 1863 he attended the dedication of the cemetery for the dead killed at the battle of Gettysburg in Pennsylvania. The Gettysburg Address is notable for its brevity – Lincoln spoke for just three minutes – and for its eloquent power. It is highly significant that in his speech Lincoln evoked the Declaration of Independence rather than the Constitution, reminding his audience that America had failed to put into practice the principles on which it was founded: 'Fourscore years and seven ago our fathers brought forth on this continent a new nation, conceived in liberty and dedicated to the proposition that all men are created equal.' For Lincoln, the war dead had given their lives so that a nation founded on the principle of equality at birth should survive. Though he does not use the word, his final flourish is a call to arms in defence of democracy, which he understood to be in the gift of the people, not their leaders: 'we here highly resolve that these dead shall not have died in vain, that this nation under God shall have a new birth of freedom, and that government of the people, by the people, for the people shall not perish from the earth'.

America's ability to remain a democracy was doubted by some in Europe as late as the 1830s – and if it did survive that hardly proved that democracy was a stable form of government. In 1832, one British commentator wrote:

> Against the single example of the United States we quote the whole history of democracy, the turbulence and destruction of the Greek states; the overthrow of the liberties of the Roman republic; the confusion of the Long Parliament, followed by the iron sway of Cromwell; the horrors of the French Revolution; the feebleness of the South American Republics; we read one convincing tale, the despotism of the many occasioning the misery of all, and terminated by the absolute power of the few. It is repeated from Athens to Bogota.[20]

Yet Americans had few fears that democracy would bring their country to its knees – on the contrary, they were proud of the system they had created. And people all over the world, in Europe and South America in particular, took inspiration from the United States – an independent nation that survived and prospered by becoming ever more democratic.

FRANCE, 1789–95

The Citizen-Activist

The events of the French Revolution have been endlessly described and endlessly argued over. A new political world seemed to dawn in 1789 only to collapse among the addictive bloodletting of the Terror just five years later. A dazzling combination of inspiration and warning, the French Revolution was an earth-shaking political event. In the biggest and most powerful nation in Europe – a continent on the verge of dominating the world – the long-established powers were overthrown and eventually replaced by the prototype of a modern nation state.

Where and how does the Revolution and its aftermath fit into a history of democracy? The application of a particular form of reason to revolutionary politics meant that there was only one possible true way to govern the country – any other path was seen as treason, a betrayal of the Revolution and the people of France. In the end the physical destruction of opponents became the way in which people showed their power; this is the dark legacy of the Revolution. The belief in a single path, the use of terror against political opponents, the illegitimacy of any form of opposition, the assumption of acting 'for the people': all these ideas were to be taken up by self-styled revolutionary regimes across the world in the following two centuries. The creation of the modern centralised state controlled by a small group or a single dictator also left its mark on subsequent history. In the story of democracy this surely is the villain, the dragon that must be slain before democracy can function.

On the other hand, France gave its people political rights and freedoms that went beyond even those enjoyed by the citizens of the newly born United States. In the 1790s, twenty rounds of elections were accompanied by pamphlets, posters, meetings and speeches that galvanised the nation. French governments brought in a series of land reforms, progressive taxation, pension schemes, famine relief and state funding of schools. They standardised weights and measures, and introduced a fair justice system and effective structures to administer their vast country. They inspired people to seek democracy and promoted the belief that every individual has certain fundamental rights that must be preserved. History allows these contradictions to coexist – and for people with the best of intentions to do great harm.

In the 1780s France was the ragged giant of Europe. For over a hundred years its strategic position, enormous natural resources and huge population, combined with the diplomatic and political skills of a series of able ministers, had made France the great military, economic and cultural power of the continent. From the 1750s that position had been challenged by Britain's growing power at sea and by Prussia's aggressive militarism on land. Nevertheless, France remained the dominant political and cultural force in Europe: its language was spoken in every court, its fashions were followed everywhere, its writers and artists avidly read and admired.

But in the course of the eighteenth century French society had become divided. The king at Versailles was surrounded by courtiers who prospered and perished through their closeness to the autocratic regime. The government survived so long as France, a land with huge agricultural capacity, could feed its people, raise sufficient tax revenue and defend itself against its enemies. However, the spread of printing and literacy and the enlargement of government had led to the emergence of a new type of citizen. Lawyers, government officials, doctors and merchants – as well as the likes of Voltaire and Diderot – became avid readers, connected through their clubs, societies and meeting houses to information and ideas from outside their localities. These educated men knew about political liberties in Britain, the Netherlands, the United States and the German states, and were aware of the contrast with their own situation.[1] While French writers such as the political philosopher Montesquieu took the lead in analysing different methods of government, none of this could be put into practice in their own country. And then there were the millions of poor, both in the squalid cities and in the countryside where 80 per cent of French people lived. The desperate poverty of the peasants and urban poor, treated more as beasts of burden than humans, helps us to understand the explosion of violence that was about to come. When the Bastille was stormed on 14 July 1789 the governor, de Launay, was captured, his head cut off and carried at the end of a pike. Eight days later the royal governor of Paris, de Sauvigny, along with his father-in-law Foulon – who had stated that, if hungry, the poor should eat hay – were caught and beheaded. Foulon's head was similarly paraded, this time with his mouth stuffed with hay.

All this was yet to come when in the spring of 1789 Louis XVI, under pressures from his advisers, summoned the Estates General to Versailles. By the late 1780s the French government was bankrupt; the country had fared badly in wars in Europe and the Americas, and a series of bad harvests saw many on the brink of starvation. The previous century had seen a succession of long-lived Bourbon kings rule from on high, chosen by God to reign over the people, but the France of the *ancien régime* was not the centralised autocracy that is sometimes portrayed. The understandable focus on Paris ignores the extraordinary multiplicity of the kingdom – a huge territory held together by just two elements: allegiance to the king and the Catholic religion practised by 97 per cent of the French people. Over the centuries French kings had successfully ruled by making deals to absorb different provinces, principalities, dukedoms and bishoprics, yet each of these regions retained a different set of powers and jurisdictions in which towns had the right to levy tolls and taxes, different languages were spoken and different weights and measures used. Life for most French people centred on their local market town, while nationwide commerce was made almost impossible by regulation and appalling infrastructure – it was easier for the eastern provinces of France to trade with distant Prussia than with Paris. A recent history gives the example of the Corbières region of Languedoc, whose 129 parishes, all home to Occitan speakers, were administered separately from Carcassonne, Narbonne, Limoux and Perpignan, while the internal boundaries for judicial matters were different again from those for tax or church matters. In this one region there were fifty different units used to measure land, with the same terms varying widely in different areas – a *sétérée*, for example, ranged from 0.16 to 0.51 hectares. Tax on salt, the major indirect tax in France, varied from 60 livres to 1.10 livres depending on where you lived.[2]

Despite its grandeur, the Versailles regime had little reach into these distant provinces. Just six small ministries looked after a country of twenty-eight million people; understandably it relied on local agents and administration. A series of fifteen *parlements*, created by monarchs from 1300 onwards, had some jurisdiction over legal matters and, in some cases, taxation; but their powers and reach varied enormously – the Paris *parlement* controlled almost half the territory of France, while others were based around a small district.

Local culture and identity were at the centre of life in pre-revolutionary France. Between 600,000 and 700,000 people lived in Paris, and Lyons, Marseilles and Bordeaux all had well over 100,000 people – for comparison Bristol, England's second biggest city, had around 60,000 inhabitants – with Nantes, Lille, Rouen and Toulouse not far behind. In tightly packed medieval towns artisans worked in skilled crafts and small manufactories – thousands of weavers, glass-makers, printers, smiths, woodcarvers and masons lived alongside butchers, bakers and shopkeepers. Though referred to as common people, the masters and journeymen of each trade took great pride in their knowledge and expertise. There were also bigger factories – a wallpaper factory in Paris employed 350 workers – but most craftwork was small-scale with workers getting together in illegal unions known as *compagnonnages*. The unskilled worked in building or domestic service, interspersed with seasonal work in the countryside. For the urban worker life was unremittingly hard – sixteen-hour days with entire families living and working in two rooms.

The French middle classes tended to follow careers in public admin-istration and the law. Putting money into land to gain seigneurial rights was also regarded as a wise investment and a way of getting on to the lower rungs of the nobility. This wasn't just social snobbery – being a member of the nobility opened up opportunities that were closed to others: French army officers had to show four generations of nobility, for example. (The adopted soubriquets of the revolutionaries Maximilien de Robespierre and Georges d'Anton, for example, betray their families' noble aspirations.) The middle classes were distinguished by their education and, though the regime banned any books seen as seditious, radical material was circulated freely and discussed in clubs where the urban bourgeoisie gathered. Along with serious political works came satire of various degrees of crudity – the king was frequently portrayed as impotent, despite his queen having given birth to three children.

For most rural French subjects unremitting toil on the land was the focus of existence, with continual food shortages making life precarious at best; life expectancy in the country was lower than fifty years. A series of good harvests from the 1750s had seen the population rise by around three million; the vast population and the complex edifice of society had all to be sustained, in the end, from the labourers in the fields. Smallholding farmers and peasants worked around 40 per cent of the land, though this was often enfeoffed so that feudal payments had to be made to seigneurs. As harvests failed in the 1780s, food riots erupted in the cities, while in the countryside resentment at tithes and feudal taxes simmered beneath the surface.

Artisans, peasants and bourgeoisie comprised the 99 per cent of the population that made up the so-called Third Estate. The nobility, or Second Estate, numbered around 125,000 or 0.4 per cent of the population. Their prime source of income was land, of which they owned around a third, with seigneurial rights over most of the remainder. Though the ennobled seigneur on his country estate had little in common with one of the king's fabulously wealthy inner circle, nobility gave access to privileges as well as income. Nobles often owned village mills and olive presses, and had the authority to forbid any competition; they collected levies on land sales and marriages and had the right to unpaid labour on their own land at harvest time. Important occupations were also reserved for the nobility – the Genevan Jacques Necker was the only non-noble in the king's ministry, for instance – and, whatever differences lay between them, they had a collective interest in maintaining the status quo.

The church was the First Estate of the realm, with around 170,000 clergy – 0.6 per cent of the total population – serving the faithful. While parish priests were meagrely paid, bishoprics were reserved for noble families and lavishly rewarded. Church income came from the tithe paid on harvested produce and from its own enormous land holdings – around 10 per cent of France – and urban estate. In Angers, for example, the Church owned 75 per cent of the town property. It employed priests, estate managers, servants, clerks, masons, lawyers and bailiffs. In many rural parishes the priest was virtually the only literate inhabitant; while most Parisians could read, marriage records from Luc-Vendée suggest that only 0.5 per cent of bridegrooms could sign the register legibly.

The *ancien régime* began to fail in the 1780s when taxation no longer provided the government with the revenue it needed, and French agriculture was not producing enough to feed its population. At the same time, members of reading clubs, masons' lodges and salons began to shake off the strictures of censorship and talked openly of concepts such as the citizen and the state, morality in public life, and the benefits of meritocracy. A trade agreement with Britain in 1786 badly affected the textile industry, while poor harvests in 1785 and 1788 brought peasants near to starvation and decreased the feudal income of the nobility. The latter reacted aggressively, imposing and increasing taxes; the feudal concept of *noblesse oblige*, where privilege goes hand in hand with the responsibility to protect, was exposed as a sham as the nobility looked after their own interests. But the aristocracy too was under pressure from above – from a king needing to keep the country solvent.

In 1788 Louis XVI sought financial assistance first from his assembly of Notables, then from the Paris *parlement*. The members of the *parlement*, however, aware of the currents of dissatisfaction and dissent running through the country, advised him instead to call a meeting of the Estates General, an ancient body that had last convened in 1614. Elections to choose the representatives of the three estates were called for March 1789. The clergy and nobility (though together representing just 1 per cent of the population) were to have 300 representatives each, the Third Estate 600. All the districts that had been in existence in 1614 (known as *baillages* and *sénéchausées*) were used as constituencies for the election of 1789, with others added to accommodate changes in the population.

The election was a two-stage process: in each district an open meeting was held to choose delegates; those chosen would then attend a formal constituency assembly that would itself select the deputies to be sent to Versailles. Eligible voters in the Third Estate elections comprised all men over twenty-five who paid direct taxes – which meant that in practice most men qualified. In Paris only, the qualification was higher, requiring six livres in taxes, which disqualified half the adult male population. The Third Estate elections were complicated by different rules in rural parishes and in towns where members of trade and merchant guilds formed electoral colleges, each choosing one delegate for every hundred members.

These electoral procedures are something of a surprise since France was an autocratic country with no supposed democratic tradition, and the Estates General had not been summoned for over 160 years. At these elections there were no political parties nor even organised tendencies, and the government did not try to influence the choice of candidates. Instead, each constituency is thought to have chosen the men most prominent in their communities. The candidates were united in their belief that the people of France should have a say in their government; the political identity of most deputies would emerge only after the election.

It is easy to understand why the 1789 elections energised the country: they were the perfect forum for an outpouring of grievances and a source of hope for a better future. Englishman Arthur Young was in the Atlantic port of Nantes in the weeks after the calling of the Estates was announced. 'Nantes is as enflamed in the cause of liberty as any town in France can be', he reported; 'the conversations I witnessed here prove how great a change is effected in the minds of the French, nor do I believe it will be possible for the present government to last half a century longer.'[3] The elections had an electrifying effect on the population: the meetings were widely publicised, the virtues of candidates debated, and the prospect of the people being involved in the destiny of France was celebrated. Politics suddenly became the centre of free and open discussion in a society where subversive ideas had been suppressed. It was this energy and enthusiasm that gave the deputies of the Third Estate the confidence to act as they later did. In this election such giants of revolutionary history as Mirabeau, Robespierre and the Abbé Sieyès began their political careers.

For the duration of the campaign the government lifted the strict censorship on political publications and over 4,000 pamphlets were published in the twelve months from May 1788. In addition the constituency assemblies kept lists of grievances – *cahiers de doléances* – to be used as aides-memoires by the representatives of all three estates at Versailles. These invaluable historical documents show agreement between the estates on the need to create a fairer tax system and apply laws consistently across France. But while the peasants spoke of removing feudal service and the urban bourgeoisie advocated a new society where opportunity was open to all, liberty was a right and privilege must end, the nobility wanted a reinforcement of privilege and hierarchy, a diminished role for the king and enhanced power for themselves.

In May 1789 the deputies of the Estates General were summoned to Versailles. Here the two worlds collided: on one side the extraordinary opulence of the royal court, its palace as big as a small town, its monarch a semi-god; on the other the lawyers, merchants and doctors of Amiens, Besançon and Marseilles. If the king thought the commoners of the Third Estate would be dazzled and intimidated by Versailles, he badly miscalculated. The 600 deputies knew they carried the expectations and hopes of the population and that the king, in contrast, was isolated. When the Third Estate deputies were ordered to wear black suits and cloaks marking them out as the most inferior in this deeply hierarchical place, this simply gave them an abiding sense of solidarity. During strained negotiations, the deputies refused to approve taxes without political reform and, on 10 June 1789, they announced that the Third Estate was the sole representative body of the people. After inviting members of the other estates to join them, on 17 June the deputies of the Third Estate declared themselves to be the National Assembly of France. On 20 June, Louis barred the deputies from entering their meeting hall; in response they assembled in a nearby hall where they took the famous Oath of the Tennis Court, in which they pledged to stay in session until they had devised and agreed a new constitution for France. In view of Louis' attempts to deny them a meeting place, they declared that they were the National Assembly wherever the deputies chose to convene. They were now, through their own assertions, both legislature and constitutional convention.

The deputies drew their power from the people who had elected them, and were prepared to put this power up against the customary authority of the king and the nobility. Although Louis still controlled the army – in fact 20,000 foreign mercenaries had been stationed in Paris – events at Versailles were being carefully watched from the capital where riots had already forced the partial withdrawal of the troops. Most common Parisians had been denied the right to vote in the elections to the Estates General, but it was they who were to save the new National Assembly. On 12 July Thomas Jefferson, America's 'Minister to France', witnessed a confrontation between German and Swiss troops, in the service of the king, and a crowd of Parisians: 'The horses charged, but the advantageous position of the people, and the showers of stones obliged them to retire . . . This was the signal for universal insurrection, and this body of cavalry, to avoid being massacred, retired towards Versailles.' Two days later, a crowd of around 8,000 stormed the Bastille prison in Paris, freed the prisoners and beheaded the governor. Crowds had already raided customs posts, which they believed were preventing grain from reaching the city, and had plundered fifty-two wagons of wheat grain from the Saint-Lazare Catholic seminary. The king was made impotent by the inability of the army to act against the citizens of Paris; Jefferson was astonished to see crowds taking arms from the Hôtel des Invalides while 'a body of 5,000 foreign troops, encamped within 400 yards, never stirred'.[4] The control of the city by the new order was made permanent by the formation of a National Guard, loyal to the Assembly and commanded by General Lafayette.

In the power vacuum it had helped to create, the National Assembly was given the opportunity to shape the future of the nation. The legitimacy given to its deputies by the elections had caused royal authority to crumble in a way that no one could have predicted. The king's ministers urged him to give way to the Assembly and, on the morning of 15 July, Louis went to the deputies and asked for their help in restoring order. It was an abject surrender of power.

The following day, in an extraordinary ceremony, Louis XVI was brought from his glittering palace in Versailles to the menacing streets of the capital. Around 60,000 Parisians lined the streets armed with muskets stolen from the Bastille and the Hôtel des Invalides, as well as pikes, swords, scythes and other makeshift weapons. The king's carriage was flanked by the members of the assembly on foot, as it made its way through the crowd. Some shouted '*Vive la nation*'; none shouted '*Vive le roi*'. At the Hôtel de Ville the president of the Third Estate and new mayor of Paris, Jean-Sylvain Bailly, asked the king to accept the gift of a tricolour cockade. After this public humiliation, Louis was escorted back to Versailles by a troop of the National Guard.

The sudden collapse of the authority of the royal regime was greeted in towns across France by immediate action as nobles were forced from office and alternative councils and local militias set up in place of the apparatus of the Bourbon state. Crucially, throughout France, rank-and-file soldiers took the side of the people as they refused to pay dues, taxes and tithes. In the countryside, desperation and hope combined as villagers turned on their seigneurs, making bonfires of the feudal records that had kept them in servitude. In early August the National Assembly formally abolished the feudal system: hunting privileges, serfdom and unpaid labour were all outlawed in the so-called August decrees.

If the elections of the Third Estate deputies had begun to politicise the nation, the takeover of power by the National Assembly released another torrent of political energy. The avalanche of pamphlets continued as politics became the source of people's hope and the focus of their anger. For many historians, this is the real legacy of the French Revolution. We take for granted that politics is where the nation's destiny is decided, and that politicians are there to represent our interests and solve our problems; but it was this revolution and the accompanying elections that for the first time in modern Europe made politics the focus of people's lives and their concerns about their country.

The next milestone in the rapidly changing situation came on 26 August, when the Assembly issued the Declaration of the Rights of Man and of the Citizen. This contained seventeen principles, beginning with the ringing declaration that: 'Men are born and remain free and equal in rights.' The document goes on to say that 'The principle of all sovereignty resides essentially in the nation. No body nor individual may exercise any authority which does not proceed directly from the nation.' For centuries, France had been ruled by an autocratic dynasty; sovereignty was bestowed on kings by God and their realm belonged to them. The Declaration threw all this out. The sacred tone of the document was a deliberate echo of royal pronouncements, designed to give gravitas to a universal statement; it was intended not only as the announcement of a new Golden Age for France, but also for the world.

The Declaration owes an obvious debt to the philosophers and writers of the time, who had studied vast numbers of contemporary and ancient texts and drawn considered rational conclusions about how societies should be governed. Yet the distance between the resulting theory and the actual practice of government led them to envisage an ideal society where humanity somehow perfected itself. Jean-Jacques Rousseau is the exemplar of this tendency and his influence is evident in Clause 6 of the Declaration: 'Law is the expression of the general will. Every citizen has a right to participate personally, or through his representative, in its foundation. It must be the same for all, whether it protects or punishes.'

The General Will was Rousseau's central concept of a good society. His 1762 work *The Social Contract* opens with the famous phrase 'Man is born free, but everywhere he is in chains.' By this Rousseau meant that it is the structures of society, particularly modern European society, that imprison humanity, and that if these were shed, men could indeed live in liberty. But how was such an unencumbered society to be run? Rousseau believed that there must be a common purpose in society, the General Will, which is derived from the individual needs and desires of the people, yet transcends individuality. This abstract entity welds the people together into a coherent society: 'Each of us puts his person and all his power in common under the supreme direction of the general will; and in a body we receive each member as an indivisible part of the whole.'[5]

This is reminiscent of Plato's vision of a society that takes priority over the lives of its people, but Rousseau was nevertheless arguing that it is ourselves, not our possession of property or title, that makes us worthy of voting and running the nation's political affairs.[6] Yet, as the historian Jonathan Israel has pointed out, the history of the Revolution is often seen through the prism of Rousseau's ideas while the myriad radical voices that influenced the initial impulse to liberty and equality are ignored. The latter stages of the Revolution showed the triumph of Rousseau's idealism but the early phases were inspired by the pragmatic voices of the so-called 'radical

Enlightenment', including Pierre Bayle, Montesquieu, Voltaire, Denis Diderot and Baron d'Holbach, as well as foreign writers such as John Locke, Thomas Paine and Mary Wollstonecraft. While these thinkers differed in their views, they stimulated debates that questioned the principles of monarchy, social hierarchy, religious discrimination and church authority. Moreover, as de Tocqueville wrote about the Revolution: 'it is true that it took the world by surprise, and yet it was the result of a much longer work, the sudden and violent termination of an undertaking on which ten generations of men had worked'.[7]

The king refused to accept both the Declaration of the Rights of Man and the August decrees, and there were signs that officers in the royal army were preparing to move against the National Assembly. Once again the people of Paris intervened. On 5 October a group of around 7,000 women marched from Paris to Versailles accompanied by a detachment of the National Guard. They invaded the Assembly and sent a deputation to the king, effectively forcing him to accept the Assembly's decrees. Not content with that victory, the women insisted that the royal family and the National Assembly return to Paris with them, which they duly did on 6 October. This was an immensely important event which secured the Revolution. The Assembly had been saved by the intervention of the common people of Paris – people who had been denied the right to vote for their deputies. For Parisians, this was their revolution.

Once established in Paris the deputies of the Assembly set about the reconstruction of the country with enormous energy. While the *ancien régime* had relied on distinctions between groups, after 1789 France was a nation of free citizens bound by a common purpose – *liberté, egalité, fraternité*. Protestants and Jews were given equal citizen rights to Catholics. Government at all levels, as well as the judiciary, the army, the police and the church, was opened up through the banning of special privilege and the introduction of accountability and elections. The Assembly created thirty-one committees that went about their work with vigour. Eighty-three departments replaced the old hotch-potch of provincial administrations, each designed so that the regional capital was within easy reach of every commune. The special status of ancient towns or cities was deliberately downplayed

by naming the departments after geographical features – the department that contained Bordeaux, for example, was named Gironde
after its main river. Laws and decrees were translated into local
languages and the judicial system unified under one set of laws;
capital offences were drastically reduced in number, while brutal
forms of execution were replaced by the guillotine. Justices of the
Peace were elected and access to the courts made easy and affordable.
Mayors and senior councillors were subject to election (though with
a property qualification for candidates), while village councils were
freed from the grip of seigneurs and given responsibility for overseeing
public administration and works. In desperate need of funds, the
Assembly nationalised all church land and began to auction it off.
While there were objections to some of these measures, in general
they were immensely popular.

However, the National Assembly also put forward the proposal that
would divide France more than any other. The Civil Constitution of
the Clergy gave the government authority over the Catholic Church.
Parish priests were to be elected and, in a measure passed in November
1790, were required to swear loyalty to the government. Only around
half took the oath and wide regional variations showed a divided
France, with the west and south-west in particular proving resistant.
Here the church was the centre of community life, the parish priest
usually a local man, and informal meetings after Mass were used to
settle the community's affairs. For the government there was an
important issue at stake: it would not allow privileged positions to
exist in an egalitarian society; it could not permit, for example, a
church synod to make decisions that affected public policy. In the
same spirit, the government abolished trade guilds – believing that
membership would confer advantages not open to others – and in
June 1791 all associations of employers and employees were outlawed.
At the same time, political clubs sprouted throughout France – Jacobin
societies, the Cordelier Club in Paris, Friends of the Constitution and
fraternal societies – all in vigorous correspondence with each other
about the burning issues of the day.

After two years the Revolution had transformed society in line with
the vision of the Assembly and the wishes of the people of France,
but the mood of the country darkened in June 1791 when the king
and queen, fearful of ever more radical measures and deeply disturbed

by the takeover of the church, tried to flee the country in disguise. They were recognised and detained at Varennes before being returned to Paris in humiliation. Though the king's status was ostensibly intact, this was a turning point: Louis was de facto a prisoner in his own country, with foreign royalist powers likely to come to his rescue.

In September 1791 a new constitution was agreed by both the Assembly and the king. It was, in the light of what was to come, a remarkably conservative document. Though the Assembly was to remain the legislative body, the executive would be made up of the king and his ministers, with the king having a veto over legislation; the judiciary was made independent of both executive and legislature; and the franchise was restricted to active citizens.

While all agreed that in principle everyone – meaning every man: women were excluded from almost all of the rights granted to citizens – should have the right to vote, the Assembly restricted the franchise to those who it believed would vote responsibly. 'Active citizens' were men over twenty-five who paid three days' wages worth of taxes per year, were not a bankrupt or servant, had lived in the same constituency for a year and were enrolled in the National Guard. They were to choose delegates who would in turn elect the deputies to the new Legislative Assembly that was to replace the National Assembly. The 1791 constitution required delegates to be the owners or tenants of land that yielded a sum equivalent to at least a hundred days' wages. The constitution was therefore much more restrictive in requirements for delegates than the rules for the election to the Third Estate in March 1789. Out of an estimated 7 million adult males, about 4.3 million were classed as active citizens, and just 50,000 as potential delegates; this from a total population (including minors) of around 28 million. The Parisian journalist and politician Camille Desmoulins protested about the use of the term 'active citizen' making the point that someone who risks his life to open the gates of the Bastille is more active than a man who owns a grand property and does nothing.

Widespread poverty meant that, depending on the district, only between 10 and 20 per cent of the male population qualified to vote. The 1791 constitution decreed that elections be held every two years; no deputy could serve more than two successive terms, though it was permitted for deputies to stand again after an absence. In a remarkable act the National Assembly passed a resolution proposed by Maximilien Robespierre, deputy for Arras, forbidding its deputies from standing for election to the first Legislative Assembly. This was a fateful decision, robbing the new Assembly of the hard-won experience of the National Assembly deputies, while turning the politically ambitious among them into an alternative locus of power.

Elections were held in September 1791. The 745 deputies who were returned were all wealthy men, mostly from property rather than trade, with many trained as lawyers. Since the summer of 1789 many nobles had fled France and in November 1791 the Legislative Assembly passed a law requiring the so-called émigrés to return – or be condemned to death. The king predictably vetoed the measure, widening the gap between the monarch and the Assembly. In February 1792 Austria, led by Louis' brother-in-law Emperor Leopold II, formed an alliance with Prussia with the intention of invading France and freeing the king. By April France was at war with Austria, and by late July the Prussian army was marching on Paris, its commander promising to massacre its inhabitants unless the king and queen were released unharmed. The result was to radicalise further the population of Paris.

By now some members of the disbanded National Assembly seemed to regret their decision to hand over power to their successors and sought other avenues to exercise influence. In this crucial phase of the Revolution the Paris Commune began to grow in authority. It had been established in 1789 as the city's council with Jean-Sylvain Bailly as its first elected mayor. Bailly had been president of the Third Estate and led the deputies in taking the Oath of the Tennis Court but when, in July 1791, he ordered the National Guard to use force to disperse crowds on the Champ de Mars, both mayor and Commune lost popular support. On 9 August 1792 a group of radicals belonging to the Jacobin club, including Robespierre, took effective control of the Hôtel de Ville, declaring themselves to be the Revolutionary Commune. The following day a crowd invaded the Tuileries Palace and killed the king's Swiss guards, forcing the royal family to seek the protection of the Legislative Assembly. The Commune, flushed with success and now in effective control of Paris, refused to recognise the authority of the Assembly in their city, sealed its gates and began publishing lists of 'opponents of the Revolution'. In recognition of the fact that the king had been effectively deposed, the Legislative Assembly agreed that a new body, the National Convention, should be elected to draw up a new constitution.

While events were moving swiftly in Paris, the rest of the country was, at least in most part, in full support of the Revolution. The English writer Richard Twiss described what he saw when he travelled through northern France in 1792:

> In every one of the towns between Calais and Paris a full-grown tree (generally a poplar) has been planted in the marketplace . . . on top of this tree or pole is a red woollen or cotton night-cap, which is called the Cap of Liberty, with streamers about the pole, or red blue and white ribbons . . . All the coats of arms which formerly decorated the gates of the Hôtels are taken away . . . No liveries are worn by servants, that badge of slavery is likewise abolished.[8]

The people of Paris had saved the Revolution in 1789; now they became the controlling factor in its politics. The Jacobins in the Commune gained power through allying themselves with the wishes of the Parisian people – an apparently democratic impulse but one with toxic effect. The Legislative Assembly with its inexperienced members was, by August 1792, on the verge of collapse. Priests who had refused the oath of loyalty had been suspended and were now arrested for treason. Between 2 and 6 September, with Paris in a panic over the approaching Prussian army, 240 priests and around 1,000 other prisoners were executed, while many members of the Legislative Assembly, believing themselves in danger, fled the city. The novelist Restif de la Bretonne witnessed one execution:

> I saw a woman appear, pale as her underclothing . . . They made her climb onto a heap of corpses. They told her to cry out 'Long live the nation'. She refused disdainfully. Then a killer seized her, tore off her dress and opened her belly. She fell and was finished off by the others. Never had such horror offered itself to my imagination. I tried to flee; my legs failed.[9]

Finally, on 19 September 1792 the Legislative Assembly dissolved itself in favour of the newly elected National Convention. It is arguable that, up to mid 1792, the Revolution had seen a relatively smooth transition from an autocratic regime to a constitutional government based on liberal principles. This view is supported by the measure passed by the Legislative Assembly in August 1792 which gave, for the first time, votes to all men over twenty-one excluding only servants. A democracy seemed to have been created in the remarkably short space of three years. But an alternative power base had come into being in the form of the Revolutionary Commune, while the revolutionaries themselves were increasingly divided into factions. The principal division was between the Girondins and the Jacobins. Initially this was a personal and tribal divide as much as one of political ideology, with each faction being loyal to certain leaders – Brissot and Robespierre in particular. In fact the Girondists began as members of the Jacobin club, but as the Revolution developed the Jacobins became distinguished by a more radical stance, wanting to destroy everything that went before in order to maintain the purity of the new order.

For the history of democracy, 1792 is a dividing point. Until that time, the revolution had been controlled by the bourgeois lawyers and traders who sat in the Assembly, albeit with enthusiastic support from the lower classes; afterwards, as the events of 1792 showed, the working people of Paris – who became known as the sans-culottes – grew impatient with representative government and with the time taken for measures to take effect. They now demanded a direct democracy where each person had their say in the forums of power, which clashed head-on with the representative democracy of the bourgeoisie. Rousseau had been critical of the British parliamentary model: 'If the English people think they are free, they deceive themselves; they are free during the election of Members of Parliament; as soon as these are elected, the people are slaves: they no longer count for anything.'[10] The sans-culottes may not have been students of Rousseau, but the Jacobin leaders who sought to channel the power of the Parisian people undoubtedly were.

The elections to the National Convention were the first national elections held under universal male suffrage since ancient Athens. Not surprisingly, given the threat to the Revolution and the re-election of many deputies from the first National Assembly, the Convention was a more radical body than its predecessor. The French people were encouraged to believe that their representatives were delegates, elected to do their bidding; letters from constituents to Convention members were often signed 'ton egal en droit' – 'your equal under the law'. Measures were brought in that allowed electors to recall any deputy who failed to follow the mandate he was given – a clear element of direct democracy introduced in an attempt to overcome the perceived drawbacks of representative democracy.

Among the political clubs of Paris the Jacobins won the support of the capital's crowds, and took effective control of the National Convention. On 21 September 1792 the Convention declared France to be a republic. There was barely any history of a republican movement in France; in 1789 almost all politicians had wanted a constitutional monarchy and until the republican declaration France had been a kingdom with a deposed monarch. Now the power of the monarch was assumed by the National Convention which became an absolute ruler with no other institutions able to challenge or check its authority or actions. The Convention, which remained in session throughout the cataclysmic years of the Revolution, continued to be both legislature and executive. The undoing of any separation of powers (a concept outlined by Montesquieu) was made complete in April 1793, when the Convention appointed the Committee of Public Safety and the Revolutionary Tribunal which became respectively the de facto cabinet and supreme court of the land. And within the Convention itself, opposition to the ruling clique was suppressed: partly through ideology – the belief that there was a single unquestionable way to run the revolution – and partly due to the continual power struggles, the concept of a loyal opposition never developed.

In September 1792 the invading Prussian army had been held at bay at the battle of Valmy, mostly by a force of untrained volunteers. In December, with the nation still under threat from external and internal enemies, the king was brought in front of the Convention to answer charges of high treason and crimes against the state. The leading Jacobin Saint-Just declared: 'As for me I see no middle ground: this man must reign or die! He oppressed a free nation; he declared himself its enemy; he abused the laws: he must die to assure the repose of the people, since it was in his mind to crush the people to assure his own.'[11]

The king was found guilty by all 693 deputies. A majority voted in favour of the death penalty and, on 21 January 1793, the most powerful nation in Europe executed its monarch. Yet within a few months the new republic had to contend with a civil war as well as the continuing threat of invasion. A mass rebellion in the Vendée region of western France was combined with uprisings in towns and cities, including Lyons, France's second city. Some of the rebellions were pro-monarchy, some were against the suppression of Christianity, others still were led by the Girondins who were opposed to the Jacobin takeover of power. The Jacobin response in Paris was to arrest Girondin deputies to the National Convention (twenty-one were to be executed in October) and to take over the Committee of Public Safety.

The Jacobins were in power as France faced its gravest crisis; despite the victory at Valmy, the threat of invasion remained strong. In the summer of 1793 the regime instituted the famous *levée en masse*, conscripting all qualifying citizens into the army. The result was to make France a militarised nation intent on total war. With the survival of the new nation at stake, the war against Prussia, Austria and the counter-revolutionaries was to be different from anything that had gone before. Previous European regimes had been wary of mass armies, seeing their subjects in arms as a potential threat to themselves. Armies were usually small, led by aristocrats and bolstered in number by mercenaries. France's revolutionary leaders took the opposite view and called on the citizens as trustees of the sovereign nation. The French people responded with enormous vigour and commitment to the cause and the results were startling and far-reaching. The French army had already been a highly professional and meritocratic organisation; the *levée* now put at its disposal the resources of a huge nation, together with a highly motivated population, and the number of men in arms increased rapidly from 200,000 to 900,000.

The people of France were not fighting to gain territory or for international political leverage. They fought first to save their country, and then to free the people of other nations from tyranny. Thus their war, at least to begin with, was an ideological battle. For the next nineteen years the French army was virtually invincible. Whereas previous armies had tended to be tactical in battle, preserving their troops and trying to outmanoeuvre the enemy, the French forces drove straight for the heart of their opponents using weight of numbers and devastating artillery fire to sweep them from the battlefield. Events showed that the dream of many Enlightenment thinkers, that nations governed with the consent of their people could live in peace and tranquillity, was a fond illusion; they too would fight wars, not only to survive but also to bring freedom to their neighbours.

On 24 June 1793 the members of the National Convention passed the constitution they had been elected to promulgate. All men, including resident foreigners, were given the vote so long as they had lived in the constituency for six months. Each constituency had a roughly equal number of inhabitants, and a single deputy was directly elected. The new legislative assembly would be elected every year. This constitution, though ratified by the Convention, was overtaken by events and never brought into effect (although its electoral rules served France for most of the period from 1852 to 1940).

Meanwhile, in Paris the politics of the Revolution were entering a new dark phase. A paranoid group of men in power with a deep sense of moral purpose, the absence of any avenues for legitimate opposition, the application of strict reason to the messy world of politics, and the revolutionaries' eagerness to see every perceived enemy destroyed – all contributed to the internecine conflict that saw an endless stream of people put before a makeshift tribunal, before being beheaded in the Place de la Révolution. The Terror, which lasted from September 1793 to July 1794, has overshadowed the achievements of the Revolution – the land reforms, progressive taxation, pension provision, famine relief, school funding and, of course, the universal male franchise. The Jacobins may have believed that a period of dictatorship was necessary in a national emergency but their actions clearly contravened the fundamental document of the revolution, the Declaration of the Rights of Man. Like many who were to follow in their footsteps over the next 200 years, they believed they knew the true path, and that the wrongs done to individual human beings were a rational price to pay for the good of humanity.

By the spring of 1794 the revolution was losing any sense of purpose beyond its own preservation. Notable revolutionary leaders like Georges Danton, Olympe de Gouge (a leading campaigner for women's rights) and Camille Desmoulins were guillotined;

intellectuals and artists, including Antoine Lavoisier and André Chenier, were executed in the summer. The Revolution was like a sow eating its own farrow. In June the revolutionary tribunal dispensed with the need for witnesses and each day prisoners would make a cursory appearance in front of a panel before being taken off to the Place de la Révolution. This was not a battle of left versus right (terms invented during the Revolution): as the people of Paris pushed for yet more radical measures the Jacobins moved against their erstwhile supporters, arresting both 'extremists' and 'indulgents'. Political clubs and societies closed down; the phase of popular democracy, with the sans-culottes dictating terms to their leaders, had come to an end.[12]

No one seemed to know any longer what the Revolution was for. Maximilien Robespierre, who emerged as its effective leader during 1793, had agonised over the question through the months of the Terror. In February 1794 he came to the Convention to declare his beliefs:

> What is the end towards which we are striving? The peaceful enjoyment of liberty and equality; the reign of that eternal justice whose laws are engraved, not on marble or stone, but in the hearts of all men . . . What sort of government can realise these prodigies? Only democratic or republican government: these two words are synonyms.

But that democracy should not involve the participation of people in government; for Robespierre instead it was a semi-mystical process:

> What then is the fundamental principle of democratic or popular government, that is to say, the essential underpinning which sustains it and makes it work? It is virtue . . . which is nothing other than the love of the land of your birth and its laws . . . this sublime sentiment supposes a preference for the public interest above all particular interests . . . In the system of the French Revolution, what is immoral is impolitic and what corrupts is counter-revolutionary.[13]

This fatal combination of politics with morality brought about the Terror; it became impossible to disagree with your political opponents without, in effect, accusing them of being traitors. Robespierre and his colleagues implicitly dismissed Macchiavelli's notorious but far wiser analysis (based on years of experience in government) that moral purpose and politics should be kept well apart. They preferred Rousseau to Macchiavelli, Plato to Democritus.

The Terror came to an end once the foreign coalition army was defeated in June 1794: the nation was no longer in mortal danger. A coup on 27 July saw Robespierre arrested; he attempted suicide but, along with sixteen Jacobin colleagues, he was executed the following day. For the remainder of 1794 Jacobins were persecuted and led to the scaffold. Historians have pointed out that the loss of life in the months of the Terror – estimates vary from 16,000 to 30,000 – was far smaller than in the brutal suppression of the counter-revolution in the Vendée where between 120,000 and 450,000 died. Nevertheless, the Terror remains a potent symbol of the Revolution because of its seemingly addictive violence and its terrible warning of how the best intentions – those wonderful abstract concepts of *liberté*, *egalité* and *fraternité* – can produce the worst consequences.

The National Convention now backed away from its democratic tendencies. A new constitution introduced in 1795 brought in two chambers: a 250-seat Council of the Ancients, and a Council of Five Hundred (an echo of Athens). The minimum age for delegates was forty and thirty respectively, with a residency qualification of fifteen and ten years, as well as property qualifications. Direct elections were ended and the electorate shrank from seven million to around 100,000. Even so, the elections brought deputies who were hostile to the ruling five-man Directory, which annulled the results in many of the constituencies in both 1798 and 1799. In November 1799 another coup brought this system to an end and Napoleon Bonaparte, France's most popular general, to power. Napoleon put forward new constitutions in 1799 and 1802; each had complex voting arrangements that effectively presented him with a list from which he could choose suitable members of a senate, tribunate and legislature. Like his role model Augustus Caesar, Bonaparte retained the structure of a representative constitution, and simply controlled all the significant positions. In November 1804, after great successes in foreign military campaigns, Napoleon declared himself emperor.

The movement towards full male franchise and democracy was therefore halted, but the revolutionary constitution of 1793 gave future

French regimes a path to follow. Despite the chaotic results, the Revolution had effected a transition from an absolute monarchy to a political system that could respond to the popular will. Public education was understood as both a basic right of citizens and an important element of a functioning democracy. The Revolution's new administrative structures formed a model that would be followed across the world. The modern nation state, based on ethnic unity, a coherent culture and the combination of a strong centre and local autonomy, was first laid out in France.

But how successful was the Revolution in one key element of democracy – getting people to vote? Records of voting in elections in the revolutionary period are incomplete, but those that survive are telling. In the 1791 election, Paris had roughly 80,000 qualified electors, of whom 17,000 voted. They elected 946 delegates to choose their deputies – despite these delegates having put themselves forward, just 200 of the 946 voted. In the 1792 elections to the National Convention, out of a total electorate of seven million, only 700,000 voted. Why was this? A historian of French elections has commented that 'corruption, fraud, intimidation and violence were practised by the candidates of all factions and their supporters; even when the law provided for secret voting electors were often made to vote publicly in the presence of a mob'.[14] In the Paris constituencies for the elections to the Convention in August 1792, for example, voters had to declare their choice aloud 'in the presence of the people'. Yet this only partially explains the extremely low rates of turnout in a country that was energised by the politics of the revolution. The discrepancy between the right to vote and the practice of voting remains one of the great paradoxes of revolutionary France.

France brought the scent of liberty to much of Europe, through its conquests and its example. The nation state, ruled with the consent and involvement of its people, defined by its citizens rather than its monarchy, was a heady vision to aim for. France went a long way towards that goal before becoming engulfed in violence. Nevertheless the impact and legacy of the revolution has been enormous. As well as showing that liberty could be won (and potentially lost) by the simple act of sweeping away the established order, it brought a new kind of nationalism to bear where the people, language and culture defined the nation. These two concepts of liberalism and nationalism, born out of the revolution, were to dominate the politics of Europe and, by extension, much of the world, for the next 150 years. Democracy was an important element in this struggle. The initial effect of the French Revolution and the Terror was to turn people away from democracy – it seemed that giving power to the lowest orders would result in chaos and bloodletting – but the principles that sovereignty resided in the people and that all people had equal rights endured, though it was to be another half century before they resurfaced as political forces in Europe.

REPUBLICS IN LATIN AMERICA

The Subdued Citizen

While democracy enjoyed rebirth and relapse in France, the continent of South America was, within a few decades, embracing the liberating message of the Revolution. As in France, an apparently rock-solid regime that had been in place for centuries was swept away in just a few years and replaced with a series of new nation states. And, in common with their fellow rebels in North America, the would-be leaders of these new nations needed to create a legitimate authority that would give them the right to rule. While Brazil turned to monarchy, other nations sought legitimacy in republican democracy – the sovereignty of the Spanish crown was replaced by the sovereignty of the people. Democracy came to Latin America in the 1820s, well before most of western Europe, but from the beginning this democracy was restrained, hampered and undermined by the region's historical legacy.

It was Pascual de Andagoya who first heard rumours of a land where everything was made of gold – El Dorado, a place of fabulous riches somewhere to the south in a place the locals called Birú or Pirú. This was around 1520 and Andagoya was a young Spanish explorer who travelled from Panama to Colombia. He tried unsuccessfully to go further south, and on his return to Panama word spread through the community of Spanish adventurers. The recent conquest of the Aztec Empire in Mexico by Hernan Cortez had shown that such rumours sometimes had substance. Francisco Pizarro mounted expeditions from Panama in 1524, 1526 and 1530, each time drawn further south by talk of a great king ruling a vast empire. By 1534 he had discovered the Inca capital, destroyed the heart of the Inca Empire and executed the emperor. The conquistadores claimed the territory for the Spanish crown and established a provisional capital at Jauja. Then, in a significant move, Pizarro founded a new city on the coast at Lima – the centre of the Spanish American Empire was to be a port for shipping goods, not an inland administrative centre.

The Spanish came to South and Central America not as a nation intent on conquest, but as adventurers in search of gold. Like many other European colonies, Spanish America began as a series of trading posts, extracting riches from the surrounding territory using forced indigenous labour, and shipping them back to Spain. Lima had a monopoly of this trade. When the Spanish ventured further south from Peru, they crossed the Andes into present-day Argentina, establishing a settlement at Santiago del Estero in 1553. Earlier, Spanish explorers had also sailed down the east coast settling at Buenos Aires in 1536.[1] Similar cities sprang up at Asunción and Montevideo. Portuguese merchants began to farm sugar cane on the Brazilian coast, bringing slaves from Cape Verde and later mainland Africa, and Rio de Janeiro and a string of coastal towns were built to handle this traffic. São Paulo, Belém, Paramaribo and other trading posts were established by Dutch, Portuguese and Spanish merchants.

Once the conquistadores had claimed territory and suppressed the indigenous population, the Spanish crown took formal control of its colonies through a series of viceroys. In contrast to North America, the land was carved up between powerful courtiers and adventurers – those who first took possession, and those to whom the viceroy and the king owed favours. This structure of ownership gave shape to an economy based on the exploitation of land, first for minerals, then for pasture and crops. This was a rural economy with the main urban centres being conduits for trade, but not for the kind of pre-industrial manufacture that characterised European towns. The skills of indigenous people in textiles, pottery and metalwork were disregarded and all high-quality goods imported from the mother country. The colonial economy had no impulsion or incentive to innovate, diversify or develop.

In Spanish America, the rigid class structure of early modern Europe was retained with new wealth injected as a social agent. As in Spain itself a hierarchical Catholic society held on to its traditions with each colony run by a small elite of nobles administering a class of what we might call merchant-adventurers. Along with these came professional administrators, lawyers and civil servants acting for the government. These European subjects of the Spanish crown, known collectively as *criollos*, lived among a mixed population of indigenous peoples and imported slaves whose status was determined by race – mixed-race Indians or mestizos having the highest non-European status, black slaves the lowest. The longevity of the colonies meant that this strict hierarchy, held in place by brutal repression, became deeply embedded.

Ninety per cent of the exports from Latin America to Spain were silver and gold. As the British traveller Basil Hall described in the 1830s:

> The sole purpose for which the Americas existed was held to be that of collecting together the precious metals for the Spaniards; and if the wild horses and cattle which overrun the country could have been trained to perform this office the inhabitants might have been altogether dispensed with, and the colonial system would then have been perfect.[2]

The continent was divided into five viceroyalties: New Spain (roughly Mexico, Guatemala and Cuba); New Granada (Ecuador, Colombia and Venezuela); Brazil (loyal to the Portuguese Crown, which was united with Spain from 1580 to 1640); La Plata (Argentina, Paraguay, Bolivia and Uruguay); and Peru (including Chile). Peru controlled all trade with Spain: only Peruvian ports were allowed to receive Spanish goods, which then had to be carried over the Andes to the rest of the continent involving, for example, a 3,000-kilometre trek to Buenos Aires.[3] On the other side of the Atlantic only Cadiz and Seville were permitted to trade with the Americas. Twice a year a huge convoy of ships, heavily protected, would set out from Spain for Lima, laden with manufactured goods (textiles, china, furniture, weapons, machinery), returning with gold and silver bullion. The result of these restrictions was a booming trade in smuggled goods with British, French and Dutch ships around Buenos Aires, Santiago, Veracruz and Caracas feeding the needs of eager customers.

The infrastructure of the viceroyalties revealed their purpose – port cities dominated, built to manage the exploitation of the interior, and administrative centres were developed only where needed to guard the trade in commodities and pacify native populations. Vast tracts of land came into the possession of a small number of families. The owners' original intention was to seek gold and silver but later these huge estates, or haciendas, became agricultural land and their owners, the *estancieros*, the most powerful men in South America. Some historians have argued that the hacienda's patriarchal structure and rigid customs became a model, with *estancieros* creating South American societies in their image. While the *estancieros* monopolised land, merchants had a parallel hold on trade. In North America a rural and small-town middle class had formed a buoyant market for manufactured goods, providing the basis for innovation and the development of resources and skills; by the late seventeenth century these colonists were producing ships, textiles, glass, paper and building materials. The tiny manufacturing base in Latin America, in contrast, was manned by forced indigenous labour; it took until the mid nineteenth century for a small rural middle class to take root.

Simón Bolívar, the man who was to lead many of the Spanish colonies to independence, revealed how this system fed the resentments of rebels against the Spanish crown in the 1820s:

> The Americans, in the Spanish system now in place, have no other place in society than that of simple consumers; even in this they are burdened with shocking restrictions, such as the cultivation of European fruit . . . a prohibition on factories . . . and customs bans between American provinces so that they cannot trade, understand or even negotiate with each other. In the end, do you know what our destiny is? Fields in which to cultivate maize, grain, coffee, cane, cocoa and cotton . . . [and] the depths of the earth to excavate gold which never satisfies this greedy nation.[4]

But on its own terms the Spanish Empire was a success. For three centuries it kept the population pacified, while exploiting the continent's natural resources to great effect – something no other modern empire has been able to achieve over such a long period. Given this, it is remarkable how quickly the empire collapsed.

The rebellions against the Spanish crown in the early decades of the nineteenth century were born out of the resentments articulated by Bolívar and encouraged by events in North America and Europe. Spain's alliance with France and subsequent humiliation at the hand of Napoleon left many *criollos* frustrated and disgusted by the rulers of their mother country. A group of inspirational leaders including Francisco de Miranda, Simón Bolívar, José de San Martin and Bernardo O'Higgins emerged to turn rebellious sentiments into practical campaigns.

The low point of Spanish fortunes came in 1803 when Napoleon forced King Ferdinand VII to resign and placed on the throne his brother Joseph Bonaparte, who introduced a new liberal constitution. The Spanish rebelled against the French occupation and a ruling committee, or junta, established itself in Seville to rule in Ferdinand's name. In 1809 it declared the empire in South America to be part of Spain and invited colonists to elect representatives to attend the Junta Central in Seville. More than a hundred cities across Spanish America took part in the elections with large sections of the population, even those without a vote, becoming involved in the process. In practice only a small number of delegates represented the colonists in the legislative assembly, the Cortes, but a system of consultation was nevertheless established throughout Spanish America that would persist through all the political turbulence that followed. Ferdinand VII was restored to the Spanish throne in 1813 after the defeat of Napoleon in the Peninsular War, but by then most of Spain's American colonies were in a state of civil war between republicans, seeking autonomy, and royalists loyal to the mother country. The republicans were victorious.

By 1822 Simón Bolívar was president of Gran Colombia, a new state roughly comprising the old viceroyalty of New Granada. In the south, the Argentinian José de San Martin in alliance with Bernardo O'Higgins of Chile had become a dominant force. San Martin wanted to bring about a new monarchy in South America with a prince of Spanish blood, while Bolívar envisaged a new republic. In July 1822 the armies of San Martin and Bolívar independently drew closer to the great prize of the viceroyalty of Peru. In order to avoid a conflict between the colonists, the leaders agreed to meet at the key port city of Guayaquil. Bolívar gave a banquet for San Martin on 26 July at which he declared a toast to 'The two greatest men in South America,

General San Martin and myself'. San Martin, a professional soldier, knew that Peru could not be taken from the Spanish unless the two armies worked together, and Bolívar apparently made clear that he was both to command the forces and to govern the resulting republic. San Martin saw no option but to grant Bolívar the command of both armies. He gave up any claim to Peru and returned to Argentina and then to France; with San Martin the vision of a monarchy for Spanish America vanished.

The Portuguese colony of Brazil had also been profoundly affected by Napoleon's invasion of Iberia in 1807, with the Portuguese royal family decamping to Rio de Janeiro. In 1820 the new government in Lisbon asked their king to return but the Crown Prince Pedro remained in Brazil and refused to dismantle the machinery of independent government built up there during the exile years. In 1822 he declared independence, which was confirmed in 1823 by a victory over forces sent by the Cortes in Lisbon. Pedro was crowned 'Constitutional Emperor and Defender of Brazil'.

Once free from the control of the mother country, how should the ex-colonies be governed? What gave legitimacy to those leaders such as Simón Bolívar who had won power through military struggle? The question of territory added further complications: should the continent be divided into nations, and if so, how? Bolívar dreamed of uniting South America in one great republic, but it soon became clear that such an ambition could never be realised. Apart from the geographical obstacles, forces of liberalism and conservatism were fighting for supremacy in each of the colonies. Unlike the United States, there was no general acceptance of a particular political philosophy or system of government. A central problem was that Bolívar, the dominant figure in the north of the continent, while a staunch republican, was not a democrat. To him elections were 'the greatest scourge of republics and bring only anarchy'.[5] In 1815 he had written that events in South America 'have proved that wholly representative institutions are not suited to our character, custom and present knowledge', and in 1819 he declared: 'Complete liberty and absolute democracy are the reefs on which all republican hopes have foundered.'

Although this makes Bolívar sound like a trenchant anti-democrat, but he was a sophisticated political thinker with a comprehensive knowledge of political history. In 1819 he also wrote that Venezuela should be a republic and 'its principles should be the sovereignty of the people, division of powers, civil liberty, proscription of slavery and the abolition of monarchy and privilege'. But this did not mean democracy: 'Athens affords us the most brilliant example of an absolute democracy, but at the same time Athens herself is the most melancholy example of the extreme weakness of this type of government.' Bolívar saw the 'absolute democracy' of ancient Athens as a reason for the city's decline – a commonly held view in the nineteenth century. He therefore argued in 1826 that 'a life-term president with the power to choose his successor is the most sublime inspiration among republican regimes'.[6] It is hard to square this with 'sovereignty of the people' and 'the abolition of privilege' but Bolívar believed these could best be realised through a president who understood the needs of his people.

This was more akin to the Roman Empire than the Roman Republic, but nevertheless it was enshrined in the constitution that Bolívar drew up for Bolivia, the country named after him. Though he commanded great personal loyalty, this hardly stood as a way of securing the legitimacy to rule over a nation. The need for legitimacy had helped make the United States a democracy; the fact that the same requirement was not met in South America led to continual and bloody disputes for the next 170 years over who should rule. The Pan-Andean state imagined by Bolívar never came into being, and Gran Colombia disintegrated under its internal pressures, leading Bolívar to his most famous observation: 'America is ungovernable. Those who have served the revolution have ploughed the sea.'[7]

In each of the new nations the political revolutions of 1810–25 had happened without a change in the structure of society or its economic foundations. Instead of suffering a social revolution that would cast off hierarchies, the elites held on to power and adapted to the new political realities. The restrictions that Bolívar had complained of remained in place – the only difference was that they were no longer imposed by Spain. In fact the old divisions and rivalries within the viceroyalties between liberals and conservatives, and between centralists and those in favour of local autonomy, now became more acute.

The independence movements had been inspired by the doctrine of liberalism that drove the American and French revolutions, but how would this be implemented in societies that were seigneurial, hierarchical and racially divided? This became the enduring problem of Latin American culture: political leaders keen to implement liberal structures and policies were confronted by groups who benefited from the entrenched privileges of the Spanish era. If these groups had simply resisted all attempts at political or social change, the story of South America would have been simpler, but the *estancieros* often allowed change to happen on the surface, while working to undermine its effects on society.

Political instability persisted because no group – liberals, conservatives, *estancieros*, the church – recognised the legitimate right of others to rule; each wanted to maximise their own power, even if that came at the expense of the nation. This lack of national cohesion and loyalty was not altogether surprising in the early nineteenth century: no one in the 1810s thought of themselves as Argentinian, Venezuelan or Colombian. Yet they understood that they were different from the north: 'They [North Americans] were a new people,' wrote the Mexican liberal Servando Teresa de Mier in 1823, 'homogeneous, industrious, hard-working, enlightened, with all the social virtues, and educated by a free nation. We are an old people, heterogeneous, without industry, enemies of work, wanting to live from public employment like the Spaniards, as ignorant in the mass as our fathers, and impaired by the vices of three centuries of slavery.'[8] We have in recent times fought shy of ascribing characteristics of people in quite this way – in the story of democracy, more important than any cultural habits were the prevailing structures that allowed the rich and powerful to continue to control the levers of power.

The early internal struggles of nations like Argentina echoed those of the United States, with one faction pushing for a loose federation of provinces and another for a nation with a strong centre. In contrast to the north, however, these disputes were fought out in armed combat. In the decades after independence politics was bedevilled by the inherited culture of clans, factions, patronage, clientship and great families. Political ideology was less important than connections, kinships and access to powerful people.

Nevertheless, a form of democracy did begin to emerge. Like the French revolutionaries, the leaders of Spanish America wanted to abolish the corporate divisions of society, and recognised the essential

equality of men (women were universally absent from this consider-
ation). The young nations declared the arrival of this new political
world constitutionally; in 1811 Venezuela gave votes to all male citizens
and free coloured men over the age of twenty-one; in Chile all free
inhabitants were given equal political rights and the 1812 constitution
itself was ratified by the people through their representatives.
Elsewhere, the wording of constitutions left room for the manoeuvrings that were to characterise the continent's political future. In
Peru the constitution of 1823 declared that 'sovereignty resides in the
nation and it is exercised by the officials to whom the nation has
delegated its powers' – yet it left the method of selecting delegates
and officials open to interpretation. In this case the citizens were men
over twenty-five who owned property or were in a profession and had
no record of 'un-citizenlike' behaviour. In Argentina different provinces
made their own laws: in 1819 Santa Fe gave citizenship and the right
to vote to all adult men, excluding only public debtors; in 1821 Buenos
Aires gave the vote to every free man born in the country over the
age of twenty – including servants and labourers (the latter were
elsewhere considered not to be included in the term 'adult men');
the provinces of Salta and Mendoza followed suit in 1823 and 1827.

Despite these declarations of democratic intent, the subsequent history
of Latin America shows how the existing elites used the structures of
representative government to reinforce their own hold over power.
Alongside liberals and conservatives, federalists and unionists, reformers
and traditionalists, the Catholic Church also played a major social and
political role. Hugely wealthy through land, tithes, donations and property,
the church was seen by liberals as an obstacle to political freedom and
to a free-market economy in which every citizen was equal before the
law, regardless of creed or status. Conservatives, on the other hand,
believed the Catholic faith was the unifying force in new nations of
separate races, providing social cohesion. This view was expressed by
a supporter of General Santa Anna, urging him to become the dictator
of Mexico in 1853:

First and foremost is the need to preserve the Catholic religion, because
we believe in it and because even if we did not hold it to be divine, we
consider it to be the only common bond that links all Mexicans when
all the others have been broken; it is the only thing capable of sustaining

the Spanish-American race and of delivering it from the great dangers
to which it is exposed.[9]

These sentiments reveal the ongoing divide in Latin America. Liberals
believed in the nation state, in free enterprise and in free trade between
countries; conservatives still held to the idea of Latin America as a
continental entity, with Catholicism as the glue. Most significantly,
conservatives opposed any constitutional order that excluded the
church and the conflict over the role of the church significantly contributed to the continual political instability. During the nineteenth
century liberal republicans struggled to diminish the church's legal
privileges, influence over education and disproportionate wealth. Yet
the vast majority of the people remained deeply loyal to the church;
in particular, Catholicism retained deep roots in the countryside among
peasants and Indians.

As well as these internal conflicts, the new nations soon experienced
pressures from external powers that were to have a decisive effect
on their political destiny. The first great external influence was the
superpower that controlled almost every aspect of world trade and
international finance – the British Empire.[10] The old dreams of El
Dorado found an echo in the shares of South American mining
companies suddenly appearing on the stock exchanges of the world
in the 1830s, and governments in Colombia, Mexico, Peru, Chile and
Buenos Aires raised huge loans that they struggled to repay. Britain
saw the newly liberated South American countries as an opportunity
to expand its trade and influence, and while the navy offered protection against Spanish or French incursions, British capital and goods,
produced far more efficiently than in local economies, flooded the
continent. The national banks in Buenos Aires, Chile and Mexico
all failed, to be succeeded by banks controlled from Britain, such as
the London, Buenos Ayres and River Plate Bank Ltd and the London
Bank of Mexico and South America. Exploiting fully its economic
and financial advantage, Britain was able to extract trade agreements
that further tightened its commercial stranglehold on South America.

The United States, meanwhile, had recognised the new nations.
The Monroe Doctrine of 1823 declared that, although the United States
would not interfere in European affairs, it would resist efforts to extend

European monarchies to 'this Hemisphere' and would oppose any attempts by European powers to regain lost territories. However, Britain was far more important to Latin America than the United States and it was British recognition that Spanish America craved. The Foreign Secretary George Canning was aware of the delicacies of a constitutional monarchy recognising a group of republics, but finally went ahead in 1825. A British traveller wrote of that year: 'All the people in Bogotá are half-mad with joy as the Vice-President has just received the welcome intelligence . . . that the British Government has acknowledged the independence of Mexico, Colombia and Buenos Ayres . . . the Colombians galloping about like madmen, exclaiming, "We are now an independent nation!"'[11]

British banks and companies controlled key portions of the Latin American economy including railways, telegraphs and docks. They had little interest in developing the economy of the continent other than as a supplier of cheap commodities – beef and grain, nitrates and metal ores – for their own rapidly expanding home market. If Britain's dominance hampered development in the nineteenth century, an equally severe obstacle to economic prosperity and political stability was the long series of wars – such as those between Argentina and Brazil, and Mexico against France and the United States – that lasted up to 1867. Given the huge disruption caused by these conflicts, the slow pace of economic development is understandable.

How did these economic difficulties and inherited social structures affect the development of democracy? Most of the emerging nation states struggled to agree a constitution that would bind the people, the provinces and the centre together; powerful interest groups were not prepared to make sacrifices for the good of a nation that seemed to exist in name only. Into the vacuum that developed stepped the figure of the caudillo, a power broker who used networks of clients and patrons as well as his military skill (often commanding his own band of militia) to gain influence. He treated politics as a power game with the winner taking the spoils including whatever wealth was available. Caudillos existed at all levels of society, and the great patrician families had to learn how to deal with ambitious men from lower social orders, usually trading protection and stability for political power and its economic rewards. Once the royal bureaucracy was disempowered after 1820, the caudillos flourished and some became national leaders.

Simón Bolívar was the perhaps the first example, but others soon followed at regional and national levels. José Gaspar Rodriguez de Francia (1766–1840) forged the nation of Paraguay, while José Cecilio del Valle (1776–1834) tried to create a United Provinces of Central America. Argentina, however, was the prime location of caudillismo. The first caudillo to gain national power was Juan Manuel de Rosas (1793–1877). Born into a wealthy family, he lived the life of a rancher and gaucho while making his own fortune in the meat-packing business. Like other *estancieros* he ran his ranch like a miniature state, using his own armed men to deter rustlers. Rosas was first elected governor of Buenos Aires province in 1829. During a break from office from 1832 to 1835 he waged a savage war against the indigenous peoples of the pampas; this won him support from the ranchers – to whom he gave land – and a reputation for brutality. On his return to power he used control of the capital to dominate the country, though he did not manage to cement Argentina into a nation. Rosas became the epitome of the swashbuckling caudillo, using a combination of force and charisma while manipulating the electoral system to give him legitimate political power. But in 1852 the other *estancieros*, previously his tacit supporters, opted for stability over Rosas' chaotic personal rule and defeated him in battle. Argentina became used to internal armed conflict and to military forces regarding themselves as the creators of the nation. Only in 1880 did a truly unified country emerge – seven turbulent decades after independence.

This pattern was repeated across the continent as a series of charismatic leaders took control by allying themselves with powerful groups, using the electoral systems where necessary, and ignoring them when not. One result of this was a plethora of constitutions as governments sought to hang on to power by changing the electoral rules, or as military leaders staged coups and then handed control back to civilians. Peru, for example, declared itself independent in 1821; its constitution of 1823 abolished the monarchy, and three more constitutions followed in 1828, 1834 and 1839; the presidency changed hands no fewer than twelve times between 1826 and 1845. The constitutions were successively more liberal, establishing direct popular elections for president and assembly, but they did not provide stability in a country where different interest groups did not recognise the right of others to rule. In 1845 Marshal Ramon Castilla came to power and ruled as an effective dictator until 1862. A more liberal constitution in 1856 was swiftly followed by retrenchment to yet another constitution giving the president overwhelming powers; with brief interregnums, it remained in force until 1920.

Peru's neighbour Bolivia followed a similar pattern when Andrés de Santa Cruz assumed the presidency in 1829 and for the next decade ruled as a dictator. After 1840 Bolivia suffered from a series of coups and short-lived constitutions that offered democratic rights but could not, in practice, deliver them. Bolívar's birthplace of Venezuela was, if anything, even more unstable. The constitution of 1830 declared a democracy but in practice the country was ruled throughout the nineteenth century by a series of competing oligarchies. From 1830 to 1900 Caracas experienced at least thirty armed insurrections led by local caudillos aimed at deposing the sitting president.

In Mexico political liberalisation was enshrined in the constitution but the legal abolition of class divisions had little effect on the ground; one historian describes Mexico's situation in words that could be applied to any of the nations of South and Central America: 'its citizens were rigidly divided by barriers of class, geography and ethnicity, many of which stayed firm until the twentieth century . . . Elections were meaningless, and the great majority of the population remained marginal to national politics.'[12] The federal constitution of 1824 gave autonomy to twenty states and four territories; Mexico then encompassed a large swathe of present-day Texas, New Mexico and California, and this liberal constitution with regional autonomy attracted 'Anglo' settlers from the east of the United States. In 1835, however, a new constitution removed the autonomy of the states and centralised power in Mexico City. Thereafter the country was divided between conservatives backed by military leaders like Santa Anna, and liberals dominated by the figure of Benito Juarez. Power shifted, often violently, with elections playing little part in deciding who held power (Juarez was in fact re-elected four times to the presidency). The constitution of 1857 promised freedom of speech, assembly and the press, and reaffirmed the abolition of slavery, but implementation depended on who was in office. The archetypal Mexican caudillo, Porfirio Diaz, seized power in 1876 and ruled for thirty-five years; the constitution remained but elections were rigged and power maintained in the hands of a few.

Political attempts to forge the nations as liberal entities continued

in the face of the stark realities of power. In Argentina, the 1853 constitution provided for equality before the law by confirming the abolition
of slavery and of noble titles, and by providing all inhabitants, not just
citizens, with the same rights. These included freedom of the press,
rights to travel, property and association. All adult males had the right
to vote for deputies to the lower chamber and to the senate. The document is, for Argentines, central to their political history, which
nevertheless remained dominated by undemocratic powers.

From around 1870 South America began to enjoy greater stability and
prosperity; fewer conflicts between them and growing demand for
commodities meant that countries like Argentina, Chile, Uruguay and
Venezuela could make their way in the world. A more international
outlook saw an increase in liberal measures, which led to sustained
modernisation and the establishment of national banks, armed
services, schools and judiciary. In addition the development of railways
and telegraphs helped to unify these countries geographically. In
Argentina this allowed ever more expansion into the pampas where
most of the remaining Indians were driven off and the grasslands used
for cattle ranching. From 1880 to 1914, Argentina grew at an annual
rate of 5 per cent and became one of the richest countries in the
world. Expanding opportunities led to huge immigration, mainly from
Spain and Italy: the population increased from 2 million in 1870 to 5.5
million in 1920.

British banks and companies, in particular, reaped the benefits,
expanding their involvement and cementing their place as the dominant
economic force in the continent. British companies owned railways,
banks, merchant houses and processing plants, and Britain was the
main market for meat and wheat, sending manufactured goods to
Argentina in return. An Anglo-Argentine elite emerged, which joined
the *estancieros* to create a ruling class that controlled the country's
economy and politics. In a commodity and cash-crop market, small
farmers and producers were squeezed out. Land not already held by
big landowners was acquired by large-scale investors who employed
low-wage workers. The lack of a rural middle class – an innovative
group of producers and a possible market for manufactured goods –
continued, thereby deterring the development of a home-based industrial system.

The turn of the twentieth century was a boom time for much of Latin America but, although we are viewing its structural weaknesses with the benefit of hindsight, the precarious situation was widely understood at the time. The Argentine politician and historian Vicente Fidel López, writing in the 1870s, commented: 'We are the farmyard of foreigners, a piece of foreign territory because we have no independence.'[13] Even the mass influx of immigrants in the late nineteenth century did not alter the fundamental truths of Argentine society. With no internal market for goods, access to foreign markets remained the lynchpin of the economy. The internal conflicts in Argentina and other Latin American countries had allowed a dual society to develop. On the one hand liberal constitutions and periodic elections gave the appearance of liberal democracy. But because economic power was concentrated in a few hands (including British companies), this made the public face of politics a sham. In reality all meaningful power was held and negotiated behind closed doors.

Latin America remained a set of independent nations, unequal, social structures entrenched, with pockets of prosperity amid widespread poverty. Democracy had been inscribed in its constitutions but hardly practised in the corridors of power. Though it had a notable head start, Latin American democracy was, by the end of the nineteenth century, not wholly dissimilar from that in Europe, where political leaders paid lip service to liberalism and democratic principles, but power remained in the hands of a narrow section of society.

EUROPE IN THE NINETEENTH CENTURY

The Denied Citizen

'The battle is mine; and if the Prussians arrive soon, there will be an end of the war.'

This declaration by the Duke of Wellington came at just after four o'clock on 18 June 1815. The battle of Waterloo brought an end to the Napoleonic Wars and heralded the beginning of a new phase in European politics. The revolutionary and Napoleonic era in France had profoundly altered the geopolitics, but also the political language and assumptions, of the whole continent. The next fifty years saw European leaders and their citizens struggle to find a way to accommodate the new politics against the background of the vast technological, economic and social changes brought by industrialisation.

The French Revolution began the practice of national democracy in Europe and the French army's conquests of parts of Germany, the Low Countries, Italy and Spain – with most other countries forced into an alliance with France – spread the ideals of liberal politics. In November 1814, with Napoleon in exile on Elba, the major powers came together in Vienna under the guiding hand of Klemens von Metternich, foreign minister of Austria, to agree the boundaries of the states of Europe which had been mightily disrupted by two decades of French conquest.

In central Europe in particular, the changes had been profound. A host of independent kingdoms, principalities, cities and bishoprics making up the loose association of the Holy Roman Empire had previously been dominated by the kingdom of Prussia to the north and the Austrian Empire to the south. This 'soft centre' of Europe was organised into manageable units by Napoleon, and then amalgamated into the Confederation of the Rhine. After his defeat these lands returned to independence and, though the Holy Roman Empire was not resurrected, Prussia and Austria resumed their struggle for influence over the German-speaking centre of Europe. Once the French were forced out of Italy, Austria reimposed its rule over most of the north, including the most prosperous provinces.

In the wake of the defeat of France, the object at Vienna was to create a series of strong states with governments that recognised each other's borders as a path to peace and security. In this aim the Congress succeeded; for the next century wars between the major European powers were restricted to the Crimean War of 1854–5, the wars for Italian independence (1859 and 1866), the Prussian–Danish war of 1864, the Austro–Prussian war of 1866 (the Seven Weeks War) and the Franco–Prussian war of 1870–1 – a remarkable record in such a militaristic age.

The other aim of the Vienna Congress was that these states should be able to resist the revolutionary pressures that had brought down the *ancien régime* in France. Not only had the French armies conquered most of continental Europe, they had created states that reflected the philosophy of the Revolution, establishing constitutional government (even though in practice dominated by French appointees), equality before the law, and a practical code of government and legal jurisdiction. Governments all over Europe, while feeling forced to enact laws ensuring equality before the law and religious tolerance, brought in measures that held liberalism in check. Within the German states, Metternich persuaded a reluctant Diet to pass a series of laws aimed at restricting press freedom. Governments wanted to have more control of their populations: a register of the inhabitants of Berlin had begun in 1799 and a regular national census was introduced in France in 1836, in Denmark in 1840 and in Britain in 1841. More dramatically, in 1819 around 60,000 people demonstrated in favour of political reform at St Peter's Field in Manchester; fifteen were killed in an attack by the same cavalry troops that had fought at Waterloo, and the word Peterloo became a symbol of British radicalism suppressed by authority. The British Reform Act of 1832 was explicitly undertaken to quell the possibility of revolution, while the 1834 Poor Law replaced a set of local obligations for parishes to provide for the needy with a national system that ensured that anyone in receipt of help (through workhouses) should be worse off than anyone in work.

For more than thirty years the spirit of Vienna ruled over Europe, with regimes restricting access to power and the right to vote against the background of a struggle between liberal sentiment and conservative powers. In Britain, for example, the Combination Laws which outlawed trade unions were repealed in 1824 but ten years later the Tolpuddle Martyrs were convicted under an obscure law concerning the swearing of oaths – the liberal impulse behind the earlier measure being quashed by a conservative judiciary. In 1830 the French Assembly engineered the removal of the ageing Charles X from the throne, in favour of the supposedly liberal Louis Philippe; but once in power the so-called Citizen King showed himself to be as conservative as his predecessor. King Frederick William III of Prussia abandoned promises made in 1813 for a liberal constitution and, after the defeat of Napoleon, ruled as a dictatorial monarch. In all these cases the ruling powers paid lip service to liberal principles before retrenching.

While most citizens did not want a full-blown revolution on the scale of 1789, their needs were not met by the status quo. The *Restauration*, as the decades after the Vienna Congress became known, perpetuated the historic mistake of the *ancien régime* by failing to recognise, and deal with, the fundamental changes in society. Firstly, Europe was in transition from a principally agricultural, craft-based economy to a predominantly industrial, urban society. In 1855 Britain became the first European country to have more town than country dwellers; for Europe as a whole that point was reached in the late nineteenth century but the process was well underway by the 1840s, along with an overall growth of the population. Secondly, the urban middle classes – government officials, solicitors, tradespeople, shopkeepers, doctors, accountants – were increasingly exposed to political debate and ideas through newspapers, magazines and pamphlets. Communications were utterly transformed through the spread of railways, the telegraph and other new technology – in 1814 *The Times* of London bought a printing press that could turn out over a thousand pages a minute. In 1855 stamp duty on British newspapers was finally removed, the *Telegraph* emerged as the first penny national and the *Liverpool Post* and *Manchester Guardian* both became daily papers. In most European cities newspapers covered political debates and were shared in coffee houses and reading societies. By the middle of the century, the growing middle classes were becoming an informed and influential voice in European society.

This is the third point: these people knew very well that they were increasingly responsible for creating and managing the new society. They gained a definite self-identity and a confidence in their own virtue and worth and developed settled, hostile views about both the landed aristocracy that claimed the right to govern them, and the workers who served them. While the French Revolution left an overwhelming fear of rebellion from below, the middle classes also began to lose patience with their social superiors (but moral inferiors) who ruled the nations of Europe in their own interests. They did not simply want a greater voice in society, they wanted a different kind of society.

The model that revolutionary France had provided for those with liberal sympathies was a nation based on the sovereignty of its people. The boundaries of the French nation were no longer to be drawn according to the preferences and negotiations of monarchs and courtiers, but according to the wishes of the people: the French people were the French nation. Measures had been taken to give the people a common identity and a sense of unity and purpose, in return for which they were granted equal rights. The people had come together in this new nation and fought – first for its survival, then to punish its enemies and finally to build an empire. The French armies, filled with vast numbers of eager *citoyens*, had been extraordinarily successful: in just two decades, from 1792 to 1812, France had conquered almost the whole of continental Europe. This was the other great lesson of the revolutionary years – a nation based on a common culture, language and identity could achieve internal harmony and external greatness. It was these two tendencies – liberalism and nationalism – that were to dominate the politics of nineteenth-century Europe, with democracy hanging on to the coattails of these powerful forces.

The attempt to preserve the status quo in Europe finally and dramatically failed during 1848, the year of revolutions. Even though in employment terms Europe was still largely agricultural, in the early to mid nineteenth century industry was driving social change. Tensions between the incoming factory systems and the huge numbers of artisans and *Handwerker* in centres like Lille, Lyons, Aachen and Leipzig led to strikes and riots. Not only were factories pricing artisans out of their traditional markets, but the lives of factory workers were unenviable. Brought in from the countryside, illiterate, underpaid and mistreated, the life expectancy of a Lille factory worker in the 1840s, for example, was around thirty years, and real wages of French workers declined every year from 1817 to 1848. German workers saw their wages fall by a quarter during the 1840s and their working conditions too were appalling.

If those conditions gave cause for discontent among workers, this was matched in other sectors of society. Both the big merchant and banking families, whose power was growing, and the burgeoning middle classes became disillusioned with the inability of their rulers to manage the transition to industrialisation. The disastrous handling of government investment in railways and the catastrophic government-inspired overproduction of steel in the 1840s exasperated captains of industry and the bourgeoisie. In Germany, industrialists were also frustrated by the fragmentation of the domestic market, pressing for more political integration that would bring greater commercial possibilities. Taxation brought further discontent, particularly in regions where political power was held elsewhere – the taxes paid by the Italian provinces of Venetia and Lombardy, for example, kept the Austrian Empire afloat.

Interestingly the pressures on government from above and below were considerably lessened in Europe's two most developed industrialised countries – Britain and Belgium. Britain faced political challenges in 1848, but no revolution, because successive governments had already taken measures to reassure both industrialists and the middle classes. The political, commercial and banking systems, including the use of shares and public subscription schemes for infrastructure, were well suited to the needs of industrialists; the 1834 Poor Law act gave a green light to the exploitation of cheap labour, while the 1835 Municipal Corporations Act allowed the middle classes to run towns and cities. In Belgium, the constitution of 1831 was seen as a model of liberalism by the rest of the continent. The property qualification for those voting for the lower chamber of parliament was extremely low, a Senate of elder statesmen was a stabilising influence, and the monarch was required to swear an oath of allegiance to the constitution when assuming the throne. Here the government had effectively brought both merchants and middle classes inside the political sphere.

Yet constitutions and laws of political representation never tell the whole story. In other parts of Europe constitutions gave political rights without allowing the means for those rights to be exercised. In France around 240,000 men were qualified to vote and stand for election to the Chamber of Deputies, but more than two-thirds of the deputies in 1840 were drawn from the wealthiest 18,000 who paid over 1,000 francs in tax. Even if powerful industrialists could break into this world, the professional classes and the petite bourgeoisie were excluded. Political roadblocks were only part of the story. In Austria, France and Prussia arcane systems meant that students qualifying as lawyers, civil servants or doctors would often have to serve long apprenticeships and wait many years before positions became vacant. There were too many highly qualified people for the few positions available and governments were unable to provide solutions. All this created an atmosphere of impotence and frustration among the middle classes, who felt marginalised as political influence and social advancement was put beyond their reach.

While the effects of industrialisation were felt most keenly in the growing urban centres, the situation in the countryside was becoming dire. From 1800 to 1840 Europe's population grew from 190 million to 270 million, including a huge increase in some rural populations – 75 per cent in East Prussia, for example. Although there were significant improvements in productivity and more land came under cultivation, the strain on the food supply was immense. Migration from the country to towns and cities also caused social stresses. Where capitalist agriculture rubbed up against customary rights, as in central and southern France, there was violent resistance. The spectre of 1789 continued to haunt the quasi-feudal landlords of Europe, disturbing the tranquillity of their castles and manor houses.

In the 1840s many rural people were crushingly poor, spending 70 per cent of income on food, and terribly vulnerable to price rises in staples like potatoes and grain. The harvests of the early 1840s were bad across Europe and the destruction of the potato crop in 1845–7 caused widespread famine, especially in Ireland. There and elsewhere poor transport infrastructure, population growth and an unstable social system contributed to the catastrophe. In Ireland the situation was exacerbated by the woeful indecision and inactivity of the British authorities – another sign of the inability of governments to cope with the realities of the new economics. Living conditions for the rural and urban poor throughout Europe worsened dramatically as prices of staples soared: wheat and rye prices in Germany rose by 60 per cent in just two years from 1845; elsewhere rises of 200 per cent were recorded. One commentator wrote: 'The inhabitants of the province which is called the pearl in the crown of Prussia, Silesia, live in worse conditions than convicts.'

Natural disasters added to poor harvests. Devastating floods of the Vistula caused crop failures throughout the Austrian Empire, bringing thousands of starving destitute peasants into Vienna – yet the Austrian authorities were still exporting wheat. In many places people took matters into their own hands, occupying grain stores and mills, halting wheat convoys on canals and rivers. These disruptions in the countryside and the breakdown in authority brought itinerant workers to the cities – mostly young men with little to lose.

The social problems in the countryside exacerbated the existing problems in towns. Commerce became depressed as share prices fell and national finances were put in jeopardy while credit for businesses dried up; in Vienna, with the imperial government in debt beyond its means, major banks went under. None of these conditions are precursors to certain revolution – many of them occur at other times – but the uprisings of 1848 were not isolated events; rather they were indicators of change. The year 1848 is a staging post, a marker in the century in which democracy went from being a threat to civilised society to becoming one of its principal components. We need to look briefly at the events in the three major European countries affected – Austria, Prussia and first, France.

Following the defeat of Napoleon, the Bourbon line in France was restored through the figure of Louis XVIII (Louis XVII had died in 1795 without ever assuming the throne). To safeguard against another revolution, the Congress of Vienna insisted that the king adopt a new constitution, resulting in the Charter of 1814. This restricted the power of the monarch and made provision for a Chamber of Peers and a Chamber of Deputies, the latter elected under a restricted property franchise giving 90,000 citizens the right to vote. The king still had command of the army and the right to declare war; he also made laws with his ministers and sent these for approval to the chambers. His subjects enjoyed equality before the law, and freedom of religious worship, expression and the press were guaranteed. This constitution placed France broadly on the same footing as the other nations of Europe: a constitutional state with liberal safeguards, but with access to power extremely limited and arbitrary powers still held by the rulers.

On his death in 1824 Louis was succeeded by his younger brother Charles who was undone by the legacy of the 1789 Revolution. Charles proposed a law allowing nobles who had fled the country in the 1790s to claim financial compensation. The Chamber of Deputies refused to pass the law and the ensuing criticism of the king grew so loud that he proposed the reintroduction of censorship. This was again vetoed by the chamber which, in March 1830, passed a motion of no confidence in the king and his ministers. Charles dissolved both chambers but new elections returned an even more liberal house. The king reacted by issuing the infamous July Ordinances which suspended the press, dissolved the Chamber of Deputies and removed its right to amend legislation. The result was three days of revolution in which the people of Paris sought to take control of their city. The king abdicated and fled to Britain, to be replaced by the Duc d'Orleans, who took the name Louis Philippe.

Although a member of the royal family, the new Citizen King was known for his liberal sympathies – he had fought on the side of the revolution at Valmy and Jemappes. He introduced the Charter of 1830, which lowered the qualification for voting, allowing around 200,000 to take part in elections. Press freedom was restored and the power of the king to initiate laws was removed, while the revolutionary tricolour replaced the white-and-gold Bourbon banner as the flag of France. Yet despite this liberal beginning, Louis Philippe grew increasingly intransigent while his ministers, particularly Prime Minister Francois Guizot, failed to respond to the changes in French society.

In 1848 the forces that, as we have already seen, were destabilising Europe built to a head in France. Public demonstrations were banned, leaving no avenue for political dissent to be expressed. To circumvent the restrictions, opposition groups began a series of meetings called *campagne des banquets*, in which people met socially in order to discuss political concerns. These too were prohibited, removing the last avenue of protest. In response, on 22 February crowds surged through the streets of Paris into the Tuileries Palace and the Chamber of Deputies. 'A powerful mob, with sticks and iron bars, strove to burst open the gate and inflict summary vengeance on Guizot,' wrote an American visitor, Percy St John, 'The windows were broken with stones. Loud cries of *Vive la Reforme!* were followed by *a bas Guizot!*'[1]

In his novel *A Sentimental Education*, Gustave Flaubert described the same night:

> Impassioned speeches were being spouted on street corners; peals of bells rang out furiously . . . lead bullets were being cast and cartridges rolled; the trees on the boulevards, the public urinals, benches, railings and gas lamps had been torn down . . . by morning Paris was covered with barricades. Resistance was short-lived; the National Guard was joining in everywhere and by eight o'clock the people of Paris found themselves in control.

The demonstrations and riots of February 1848 succeeded in overthrowing the government because the National Guard joined the rebellion, but also because the king and the ruling elite had lost confidence in their own ability to govern. As Flaubert commented: 'Gently, of its own accord, the monarchy was melting away.'[2] On 23 February Guizot resigned and, in the wake of the deaths of fifty-two demonstrators, the king abdicated soon afterwards. A provisional government was rapidly formed and, on 26 February, the Second Republic was declared as the spirit of 1789 surged through the nation. Elections to a Constituent Assembly were held on Easter Sunday under universal male suffrage creating nine million new voters, though residency restrictions of three years excluded large numbers of itinerant workers.

Republican hopes of a new dawn were soon dashed, however, as the church in particular brought its full influence to bear on parishioners. France was divided between a conservative countryside and the radical cities; most people were still rural dwellers and more than half the deputies elected were from conservative parties. A riot in Rouen against the election results led to the shooting of fifty-nine people – the counter-revolution had begun within two months of the revolution itself.

The Executive Commission that formed the new government excluded the radical republican leader Louis Blanc, and a botched invasion of the Assembly by protestors on 15 May gave the government the pretext for arresting a number of other radicals. An uprising of workers in Paris, known as the June Days, was ruthlessly suppressed by troops who killed around 1,500 demonstrators with a further estimated 15,000 deported to Algeria. The Parisian middle classes, while wanting liberal reforms and access to power for themselves, were content to see a repression of militant working-class elements. This was a crucial divide that presaged the political development of Europe for the remainder of the nineteenth century.

In November 1848, a new French constitution was agreed with universal male suffrage. A single Assembly of 750 deputies elected every three years would in turn choose a Council of State to propose legislation; a directly elected president with executive powers would serve for four years. At this point France seemed well on the way to being a democracy, albeit with only men allowed to vote. Then Louis-Napoleon, nephew of the emperor and heir to the Bonaparte line, put himself forward for the presidential elections of December 1848; his name gave him a huge majority.

To start with Louis-Napoleon ruled in conjunction with the Assembly, but in December 1851, after being refused a constitutional amendment to allow him to run for a second term, he staged a *coup d'état*. An insurrection against the coup was led by, among others, the writer Victor Hugo who described the events on the streets of Paris on 4 December: 'Suddenly, at a given signal, a musket shot being fired, no matter where, no matter by whom, the shower of bullets poured upon the crowd . . . In the twinkling of an eye there was butchery on the boulevard a quarter of a league long.'[3] One year later, Louis-Napoleon dissolved the Second Republic and declared the Second French Empire, with himself as Emperor Napoleon III. Though elections continued to be held, democracy had lasted just three years.

In 1848 the Austrian empire covered much of present-day Hungary, the Czech Republic, Slovakia and the north Balkans, as well as northern Italy and parts of Poland and the Ukraine. The emperor of Austria, Ferdinand I, was also king of Hungary, Bohemia and Venetia-Lombardy. The constitution gave him authority to choose his ministers; the elected Diet was simply a consultative body and the Austrian foreign minister, Metternich, was the most powerful man in the empire. Having steered his country through the Napoleonic Wars by first negotiating an alliance with France and then joining the victorious allies, the presiding master of the Vienna Congress was still in office thirty-four years later. Yet the Habsburg Empire faced the same pressures as France. The growing professional and merchant classes regarded the imperial government as economically incompetent and demanded reform of the constitution and more involvement in government. At the same time, the countryside of central Europe was undergoing its own revolution. Feudal systems of ownership and service were breaking down under commercial pressures, which gave the peasantry more freedom and enabled landowners to produce food more efficiently; but free trade undermined the security of rural labour and food supply. In addition, Austria was plagued by nationalist uprisings among Poles, Magyars and Italians, soon to be joined by Slovaks, Czechs, Romanians, Croatians and Slovenes. In the nationalist world inspired by France, a polyglot empire seemed an anachronism as different groups saw their future in ethnic states, or at least in entities that would protect their group identities.

The financial and social pressures eventually led to a crisis in the Austrian government. The revolution in Paris had shown the vulnerability of any administration that did not act swiftly. In March 1848 the conservative Metternich was forced from office and the following month a more liberal constitution was introduced for the German areas at the heart of the empire, though government procrastination delayed its implementation. Reforms introduced in the Papal States had encouraged Italians in Austrian-ruled Venetia and Lombardy to push for the same, while the Hungarian Diet adopted its own liberal constitution, which amounted to a declaration of independence. The reaction among the Slav sections of the empire was immediate, with a pan-Slav congress convening in Prague in June with the intention of gaining greater political rights.

In the summer of 1848 radicals in Vienna, frustrated by government delays, pushed for further change under the banner of the 'party of progress'. In May the atmosphere in the capital became so hostile that the imperial court fled to Innsbruck, though the emperor was persuaded to return in August. The problem for radicals across the empire was that once reforms were introduced and elections held, voters largely returned conservative deputies, since these were the prominent men in their districts. This led to more frustration and, in October 1848, Viennese students started a riot which ended in the lynching of Count Latour, a member of the cabinet. Most of the city's bourgeoisie, an estimated 100,000 people, together with the emperor and his court now left Vienna, which was bombarded by the Austrian army killing between 3,000 and 5,000 people. In December the political crisis was brought to an end when the emperor was persuaded to step down in favour of his nephew, Franz Josef, who began an extraordinary sixty-eight-year reign by declaring martial law and immediately reversing most of the liberal reforms. Liberal politics in the Habsburg Empire were at an end and remained suppressed until the catastrophe of 1914.

The German states had been reduced by Napoleon's reforms and the Congress of Vienna to thirty-five monarchies and four free cities. They were grouped together in the German Confederation, though this was simply a diplomatic alliance – even George IV of Britain had a seat as king of Hanover. The aim of the Congress of Vienna had been to stabilise this potentially troublesome area through good relations between its two dominant forces – Prussia and Austria. As long as the conservative leaders of those countries stayed in place, the situation seemed to hold. King Frederick William III promised in 1813 that he would institute a constitution for Prussia, though when he died in 1840 it was still unwritten. His major achievement was to diminish Austrian influence by forming a customs union, or *Zollverein*, with the other German states, and deliberately excluding Austria. When Frederick William IV succeeded his father he eased restrictions on the press and again promised a constitution for Prussia, though he balked at an assembly elected by the people. The national assembly called in 1847 was a Diet of representatives from the provinces of the Prussian kingdom with limited tax-raising powers, and subject to the king's summons.

Prussia loomed large over the German Confederation, but the dominant feature of the era was the rise of liberalism, which carried with it the desire for a single German nation. Peasants, artisans, middle-class professionals, shopkeepers, merchants and industrialists all had reasons to be dissatisfied with the status quo. Germany was still a traditional agricultural society but it was moving towards industrialisation. As elsewhere in Europe both industrialists and the bourgeoisie believed that the government was incompetent at handling modernisation. A banking framework with flexible rules on credit, for example, had not been developed anywhere except in Britain and Belgium, while both infrastructure and the education system were unsuited to the growing industrial and commercial demands. The changing economy brought into being new phenomena such as the economic cycle in which demand periodically slackens and unemployment increases; the first signs of cyclical unemployment were felt in Cologne as in Vienna and Paris.[4] Peasants in southern Germany invaded the great castles of their landlords and Ludwig, king of Bavaria, already embroiled in a scandal, abdicated in March 1848, after the news of Louis Philippe's demise brought crowds on to the streets of Munich. The end of feudalism brought liberated peasants into the growing cities in search of work in industry; this pitted industrial and artisan workers against each other, while the middle classes demanded liberal reforms but also a crackdown on violent rebellions by peasants and workers.

What made the situation in the German lands unique was the desire for national unification. A united Germany appealed to liberals as a way of moving from a hodgepodge of autocratic kingdoms to a constitutional state with guarantees of political rights and freedoms. Merchants and industrialists also saw the advantage turning the *Zollverein* into a single German market for their goods. The stumbling block – remarkably, in view of future developments – was the Prussian ruling class, which saw a German nation as a threat to its power.

In 1847 Frederick William IV convened the Prussian Diet in order to raise revenue for railway building, and in time-honoured fashion the Diet demanded reforms in return for taxes. The king realised that liberal support would be useful to him in his struggle with the landowning gentry who dominated the Diet, so when riots erupted in Berlin in March 1848 on the news of Metternich's dismissal, the king seemed to embrace the cause of German nationalism and announced his intention to grant reforms.

By this time a German national state had become a central aim of all those pushing for political reform. A group of liberal politicians from across the German Confederation met at a 'pre-parliament' in

Frankfurt from 31 March to 4 April 1848 to prepare the ground for a Constituent Assembly which would draw up a German national constitution. This became the Frankfurt Assembly, which was voted in under restrictive conditions that excluded most working people – voting qualifications varied from one state to another – and sat from May 1848 to May 1849. While the assembly wanted to form a nation state it could not agree whether this should be monarchical, republican, federal, democratic, secular, Catholic or Lutheran; or whether it should include just the members of the Confederation, or all German lands including Austria. The Assembly's internal contradictions became clear as it sought to establish liberal measures, such as equality before the law, while also courting Frederick William as a monarch under whom it might serve.

In March 1848 a squabble erupted between Denmark and the German Confederation over the duchies of Schleswig and Holstein.[5] The conflict made German unity an issue for the whole of Europe; more importantly it opened a divide between nationalism and liberalism. Both German nationalists and Prussian liberals had encouraged Frederick William to invade Schleswig-Holstein but when Prussia was forced by international pressure to withdraw in 1852, the kingdom lost its credibility as the potential leader of a liberal Germany. The king, frustrated at this failure, dismissed his liberal ministers and the reactionary Junkerparlament dominated by the great landowners resumed its powerful position. From 1852 onwards, the hope of liberals that Prussia might become part of a German nation based on a liberal constitution evaporated. The constitution drawn up by the Frankfurt Assembly was a dead letter. A reversal began that was to have profound consequences. The belief in a united Germany as a vehicle to promote liberal politics was replaced by a vision of national unity as a way of making Germany a great power that could dominate the heart of Europe. The twin legacies of the French Revolution – liberalism and nationalism – were fatally separated.

While violent protest and repression flowed and ebbed across mainland Europe, in Britain events took a different turn. In 1846, after a fierce national debate, Prime Minister Robert Peel successfully pushed the Repeal of the Corn Laws through Parliament. Allowing imports of cheap corn was a blow against the landowning classes and favoured

FORUMS OF DEMOCRACY I

(*Above*) Greek amphitheatre, Epidaurus.

(*Right*) Piazza del Campo and Palazzo Publico, Siena.

Simon Bolivar el Libertador

THE STRUGGLE FOR
DEMOCRACY

(*Above*) The Tennis Court
Oath, 20 June 1789.

(*Above left*) Simón Bolívar,
the liberator of Latin
America.

(*Right*) Fighting at a
barricade in Berlin, 1848.

(*Left*) The great Chartist
meeting on Kennington
Common, 10 April 1848.

CASTING THE VOTE

(*Above*) First Presbyterian Church members
voting on decisions, California.

(*Above*) Woman voting during the first
post-liberation elections in Korea, 1948.

(*Right*) Women voting at the British
General Election, 1964.

(*Above*) South African voters, 2007.

(*Below*) Voters in Kashmir, 2011.

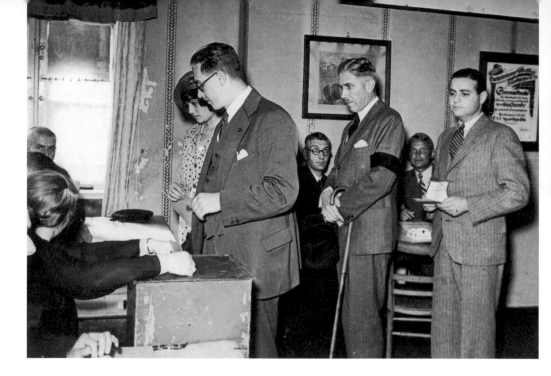

DEFEAT AND SURVIVAL

(*Above*) German Chancellor Franz von Papen (*centre*) at the ballot box, 1932.

(*Left*) US President Harry Truman in the voting booth, 1950.

(*Below*) John F. Kennedy and Richard Nixon at a TV studio for the first ever televised debate between US presidential candidates, 1960.

DEMOCRACY NEW AND OLD

(*Above*) Soviet President Mikhail Gorbachev and Russian President Boris Yeltsin in the Russian parliament after the failure of the coup, August 1991.

(*Below*) US President Barack Obama shakes hands with visitors at the Lincoln Memorial in Washington, 2011.

FORUMS OF DEMOCRACY II

(*Above*) Government and opposition face each other in the British House of Commons, eighteenth century.

(*Below*) Voting in the European Parliament, 2011.

both industrialists and their workers. A central argument was that, if people had to spend less of their income on bread, they could spend more on manufactured goods, which would allow industry to prosper. The beginning of a shift in power from agriculture to manufacture was palpable. In contrast to France, Austria and Prussia, in Britain a conservative government was prepared to go against its traditional allies in the face of changing commercial realities.

In terms of parliamentary modernisation, the Reform Act of 1832 had ironed out some of the absurdities in the existing system, giving a fairer distribution of votes – but the Act had been sold to Parliament and the king on the promise that it held back, rather than advanced, democracy. Earl Grey, sponsor of the bill, was clear on the issue: 'The principle of my reform is to prevent the necessity of revolution . . . [there is no one] more dedicated against annual parliaments, universal suffrage, and the ballot than I am.'[6] A classic nineteenth-century liberal measure, the Reform Act gave political rights to the middle classes, introducing a property qualification for voters to replace arcane rules, while excluding the workers. In response a loose organisation of like-minded reformers drew up the People's Charter in 1838, which called for universal male franchise, equal constituencies, annual elections, secret votes, the abolition of property qualifications, and payments for MPs. Chartism, as it become known, is generally reckoned to be the first mass working-class movement. The Chartists, who brought the possibility of democracy to the world's most powerful country, not only fought for political reform but also persuaded working people that the right to vote was important to their lives. This promotion of the benefits of democracy to working people went against the grain of the times and was led and sustained by newspapers in the industrial north of England.

In 1839 the Chartists sent a petition to Parliament, which the House of Commons refused to hear – a snub that convinced some radicals that force was the only route to real political change. Later that year twenty Chartist supporters were killed while trying to free colleagues from imprisonment in Newport, South Wales, but further uprisings failed to materialise. Instead, in May 1842 the Chartists presented another petition to Parliament, this time signed by three million people. Again Westminster rejected it. Some Chartists now stood for election – Feargus O'Connor, editor of the *Northern Star* and leading

Chartist, became the Member for Nottingham in 1847 – but others attended hustings and then withdrew in protest at the lack of democracy in the system. With the forces of Parliament and state ranged against them, Chartists had to rely on the mass of support for their aims. With rebellions threatening to overturn governments across Europe, the British state was acutely aware of the dangers.

On 10 April 1848 around 150,000 Chartist supporters gathered on Kennington Common in London. More than 100,000 special police were drafted in, and the army was told to ensure that the demonstrators did not cross the Thames. But Chartism was an overwhelmingly peaceful movement and the meeting, which had been called to show support for O'Connor's presentation of a new petition to Parliament, passed without violence. Nevertheless the government was sufficiently frightened to pass legislation banning public assemblies, and brought in a new Treason Felony Act. Chartism continued after 1848 but the government intervention effectively took away the movement's momentum.

What, then, was the fate of democracy in Europe after 1848? In retrospect, we can see a pattern that was roughly followed in most of central and western Europe. Conservative regimes that had stayed true to the repressive spirit of the Vienna Congress were either overthrown or forced to liberalise. The pressures for change came through an alliance of liberalism and nationalism inspired by the French Revolution and given impetus by social pressures. This change was, however, short-lived and conservative forces soon regained the ascendancy across the continent. Post-1848 conservatism was, though, quite different from what had gone before; it began to embrace the popular desire for national unity and identity.

For the French revolutionaries, liberalism and nationalism had been inseparable. But the disappointments of 1848, in particular the failure of the attempt to ally the growing sense of national identity with the desire for wider access to power, brought a sea change. The formerly progressive middle classes, while still wanting access to power for themselves, embraced nationalism at the expense of democracy. This was the birth of what has become known as classic liberalism. Freedom from the restraints of religion, monarchy, trade tariffs and government rules was thought sufficient to deliver sustained prosperity and a decent society – at least for the middle classes. In Germany in particular, but also in France and Austria, the forces of reaction became allied with nationalism – conservative opinion swung behind the notion of a state based on its people *and* its traditions. This was a crucial development in European history. Conservative forces built on the nationalism that had swept France in the revolutionary years and decoupled it from the liberalism that had first inspired the revolutionaries.

Nevertheless, the conservatives who ruled after 1848 understood that they needed to take account of the liberal forces in society. Liberals in all countries wanted to strengthen their parliaments against the whims of monarchs and aristocrats by broadening the franchise to bring in the middle classes. But for them constitutional and competent government was the prime concern, rather than the will of the people expressed through universal suffrage. Indeed the concept was derided even by campaigners like the Italian nationalist Count Cavour, who declared: 'No people should be electors unless their income and intelligence indicated that they . . . had a vested interest in the social order.'[7]

After 1848 conservative forces resumed their dominance but by the mid to late 1860s liberal and nationalist pressures, often at odds with each other, began to have an impact on all European states. The complex series of wars that led to Italian unification began in 1859 with a Piedmontese army, led by Cavour and supported by France, taking Lombardy from Austria. At this point Cavour was intent on control of the north rather than unifying the whole of Italy but the following year Giuseppe Garibaldi, leader of an irregular force, was persuaded by Cavour to lead an expedition to Sicily. Garibaldi took Sicily then Naples (both previously independent kingdoms) and declared his intention of announcing a kingdom of Italy from its historic capital of Rome. In June 1861, despite Rome and Venetia still being outside Italian control, Cavour said on his deathbed 'Italy is made.'

Garibaldi's role as a common soldier turned rebel leader conveyed the inspiring message that autocratic rulers could be overthrown in the name of nationalism and reform. But here again liberal measures had their limits. The Italian constitution of 1861 (which lasted until 1946) gave the king sole executive power, command of the armed forces, the right to declare war, to appoint all ministers, to make treaties and alliances and to appoint the members of the Senate.

Consequently the republican movement led by Garibaldi failed to secure power, and Garibaldi himself was arrested in 1862. While the lower chamber was elected, the bicameral parliament was only entitled to approve legislation, with a right of veto over taxation or changes to the boundaries of the kingdom. Unification was bought at the price of quashing dissent and diversity. In 1861 Cavour had written to king Victor Emmanuel of the difficulties with Naples: 'We must impose national unification on the weakest and most corrupt part of Italy. As for the means, there is little doubt: moral force, and, if that is insufficient, then physical force.'[8]

While in Italy nationalism took precedence over liberalism, in other parts of Europe pressure for liberal reforms was being felt and heeded in the 1860s. In Britain the Reform Act had begun to make the parliamentary system more consistent (though the franchise remained severely restricted). Despite the decline of the Chartist movement, organisations like the Reform League and the Reform Union brought middle-class liberals together with trade unions of skilled workers in pushing for universal male suffrage. Others, such as John Stuart Mill – author of *On Representative Government* – advocated reforms that would enfranchise the so-called respectable working class while keeping the masses at bay. This was a classic nineteenth-century liberal strategy, and in 1866 Liberal Prime Minister William Gladstone drafted a bill to extend the vote to skilled workers. However, elements of the Liberal Party rebelled, leaving the incoming Tory Benjamin Disraeli to pass an amended bill extending the franchise to all householders, as well as men paying £10 in rent. This halfway measure allowed conservatives to talk of defending the country against democracy, while satisfying growing liberal sentiment. Nevertheless, in the coming decades democracy began to be spoken of in some quarters as a desirable aim – the spirit of Putney was about to be revived.

In France Louis-Napoleon, who had declared himself emperor in 1852, kept the universal male suffrage brought in by the provisional government of 1848. The problem for liberals here was the impotence of parliament compared to the power of the executive, dominated by the emperor. Louis-Napoleon recognised the need for reform, if only to head off a republican movement, and in November 1860 modest measures allowed the Assembly to revise some bills and required ministers to sit in parliament. Restrictions on press freedom were lifted in 1868, giving a further boost to liberal politics, and the elections of 1869 gave the liberals enough power to demand an executive drawn exclusively from parliament. In 1870 Emile Ollivier was appointed first minister and asked to draft a new constitution, which, though full of contradictions – making the emperor head of state and president of the Council of Ministers, while calling the nation a 'parliamentary' empire – was passed overwhelmingly by a plebiscite in May 1870. Within a few weeks, however, the empire was brought to an end by invading Prussian armies. As one historian has written, 'The Second Empire almost solved the problem of reconciling monarchy and democracy – but not quite, and not in time.'[9]

The Prussian invasion also led directly to another political upheaval in the French capital. The Paris Commune was a result of the French surrender to Prussia and the formation of a new government under Adolphe Thiers. The people of Paris distrusted Thiers, believing he was working to restore the monarchy after the deposing of Louis-Napoleon in July 1870. They also deeply resented the Prussian insistence on a victory march through their city. Once the parade was over and the Prussians returned home Thiers ordered the regular army to disarm the Parisian National Guard and confiscate their 400 cannon. Two army units rebelled, executed their generals and joined the National Guard. Other troops followed and Thiers ordered an evacuation of police and all government officials; from March to May 1871 the people of Paris had control of their city. The commune declared itself in favour of a republican democracy and elections to a commune council were held on 28 March 1871, returning a mix of skilled workers and professionals. Its policies were secular (separating church and state) and progressive (abolishing night working, for example), and though they only met for sixty days, the council members planned free education and other social measures such as the abolition of prostitution. Women too were heavily involved in the framing of commune policies.

On 21 May French troops loyal to the Thiers government entered the city and over the next two weeks took control of Paris. The reprisals were brutal – estimates of the number of commune supporters killed in fighting or executed vary from 10,000 to 50,000, with around 7,000 more deported to New Caledonia. Another French revolution had come to a bloody end and full democracy was yet again postponed.

In Prussia, the political situation became entangled in the expansionary policies of Otto von Bismarck, who not only dominated European politics but also embodied the new alliance of conservatism and nationalism, while effectively manipulating a democratic constitution to restrict access to power. Bismarck began his career in 1851 as Prussia's envoy to the parliament of the German Confederation; his eight years in Frankfurt changed him from a sceptic to a full-blown advocate of German unity. After spells as ambassador to Russia, France and Britain, Bismarck returned to Berlin in 1862 to serve the new king, Wilhelm I, as minister-president and foreign minister. After provoking war against first Denmark (1864), Austria (1866) and then France (1870–1), Bismarck brought about his goal of a united German Empire and, in the aftermath of the Franco–Prussian war, saw Wilhelm crowned as Emperor of Germany in the palace of Versailles on 18 January 1871.

The North German Confederation, which had been formed in 1866, provided the constitution for the new empire with the emperor or kaiser – an office reserved for the king of Prussia – assisted by a chancellor who was appointed by and responsible to him. The Reichstag of the united Germany, first elected in 1871, was elected by a universal male franchise, while the upper house or Bundesrat contained representatives of all the German states. Bismarck needed the support of a majority in the Reichstag, and his management of its members, together with his closeness to the kaiser, was the key to his power. The chancellor was initially able to work with the liberal majority as they found common cause in oppressing the large Catholic population. As liberals lost their majority, Bismarck was nimble enough to bring in conservative measures that brought him popularity with the new mood of the Reichstag and its electors.

All adult males could vote in elections to the Reichstag – but how little this meant became clear when, in 1878, Bismarck outlawed the main socialist party, the SDAP (later SPD). But he was an astute politician, and coupled his banishment of the party with the introduction of a system of social welfare that provided health and accident insurance, as well as pensions. His message to the people of Germany was clear – you don't need socialism to have social benefits. Despite these popular measures, the chancellor's impregnable position made a mockery of German democracy – the voters had no power to remove him from office, while he continued to bring in laws that removed authority from elected bodies.

In the twin monarchies of Austria and Hungary democracy also continued to be severely restricted. Voters in Hungary had to possess property of such value that most were disqualified. In Austria the Reichsrat was indirectly elected from four groups – landowners, chambers of commerce and urban and rural taxpayers – in effect excluding most of the population. In Hungary the constituencies were manipulated to deny Slav voters the chance to elect their own representatives, with Magyars dominating the outcome.

Russia, meanwhile, was growing in strength as a result of the dissolution of the Ottoman Empire. The comparatively liberal reign of Alexander II had seen the emancipation of serfs in 1861 and measures to reform the judicial and penal systems, as well as the introduction of representative local government. Pressure for change in Russia had the same origins as elsewhere: an increasingly literate middle class combined with industrialists advocating a competent modernising regime. Yet Russia remained an autocracy and, frustrated at the lack of political change, revolutionary groups like the Narodnaya Volya (People's Will) turned to violence. Ironically the tsar was assassinated in March 1881, just days after his minister of the interior, General Loris-Melikov presented him with a proposed plan for a parliament or Duma. Even these faltering steps were scuppered by the assassination, and all political reforms were quashed.

The period from 1840 to 1880 gave birth to the doctrines of classic liberalism. For nineteenth-century liberals freedom from the powers of monarchy, aristocracy and the church had brought in an age of free trade and enterprise, progress and prosperity. It was only in the late nineteenth century that this position began seriously to falter. Free trade worked for dominant economies but not for others, and freedom from regulation worked for the powerful but not for the rest. All of this became clear just as the industrial working class was beginning to realise its own power – and one use to which this power was put was the demand for democracy.

EMBRACE AND RETREAT

The Idealised Citizen

In the 1860s workers in almost all countries were working and living at some level of poverty. Though some had won political rights there were many barriers to voting, and politics was of little concern compared to the problems of getting enough to eat and surviving sickness and disease. Thirty years later the industrialised world had utterly changed. Cities were transformed by electric lighting and new methods of transport, including trams and underground railways. The spread of express rail services, steamships and refrigeration changed the food supply systems of the world. Europe could now feed itself on grain imported from the North American prairies and Australia, on beef from North and South America, and on sheep from Australasia. The result was a massive reduction in basic food costs. While in 1874 American grain was selling in Liverpool at 20 cents a bushel, in 1881 it cost just 2 cents; bread in London cost 17.5 pence in 1873 and 4.5 pence in 1905.

Cheaper food, which allowed more money to be spent on other goods, benefited the overall economy. One temporary outcome, though, was a crisis in rural Europe as small farms and even large estates could not compete in markets that had become flooded with imports. A staggering thirty million people migrated to the United States from Europe between 1836 and 1914; Argentina alone received three million immigrants from southern Europe between 1895 and 1914.

While rapidly expanding cities created new problems, governments and city authorities at least understood the need to tackle them. Widening and paving streets, installing sewerage and lighting systems, taking abattoirs off public streets, collecting refuse and creating parks – all these measures began to change cities from dark, unhealthy and dangerous places to centres of entertainment and shopping. Bloomingdale's opened its New York store in 1886, Galeries Lafayette opened in Paris in 1896, Macy's in New York in 1901, KaDeWe in Berlin in 1905 and Selfridges in London in 1909, all putting goods on display and making shopping enjoyable. People moved to cities for the excitement they offered, as well as the opportunities for work. With more money to spend, millions of urban Europeans and Americans built a working-class culture born of mutual support, seeking escape from the drudgery of factory work through music, theatre, sport and entertainment. Newspapers, which had grown tenfold in circulation from the 1830s to 1880, had been mainly liberal in tone and content, aiming at the aspiring middle classes. Faster, cheaper printing and widespread elementary education brought a whole new market on stream by the 1880s and 90s. In Britain the *Daily Mail* was founded in 1896, followed by the *Mirror* in 1903, both firmly aimed at working-class people, and a host of magazines such as *Tit-Bits* (1881) were published for a female readership.[1]

As well as pressure for change from a newly confident and educated working class, politicians were faced with growing evidence that societies and industrial economies functioned better if everyone was valued. Contemporaries began to write about society as a single organism, requiring all of its parts to function well in order to prosper. Despite the social and physical separation of the classes, bourgeois philanthropists became concerned about the plight of the urban poor. But if this all boded well for a widening of political rights, resistance to the embrace of democracy was still well entrenched.

Politics and society remained heavily paternalistic and hierarchical. Most political leaders were elderly men – Gladstone, Bismarck, Franz Josef and Prime Minister Henri Brisson of France were typical – while society in general remained highly stratified with each class jealously guarding its position from those below. Armies of domestic servants waited on the wealthy and the middle classes, with no social contact between the two.[2] In Britain the divide exemplified by servants and masters was confirmed in education. Ever aware of social status, the

British bourgeoisie emulated the schooling of the aristocracy and sent their children away to boarding schools. Here they were isolated not only from society and from the opposite sex, but also from the commercial and industrial world; most prepared for a life in the professions and studied a curriculum based on the classics.

This rigid social setting, combined with increasing overall prosperity, technological change and mobility, led to the breakdown of classic liberalism, paving the way for the development of the role of the state as protector and provider. Nineteenth-century liberals believed in free trade unfettered by government interference, a free hand for the hard-working middle classes to prosper and to govern their country and their towns, and some help for the deserving poor. But this attitude could not hold. The infrastructure of society – the armed forces, education, highways, public sanitation, police forces and prisons – all had to be paid for. Tax on income, anathema to the liberal philosophy which saw it as a penalty for hard work, was introduced or made permanent across Europe and in the United States. The state now became not only the guardian of national security and the manager of the economy, but the guarantor of citizens' rights and the provider of education, health and pensions. In this situation, where the state provided so much in return for taxing almost everyone, the case for democracy with a full adult franchise grew stronger.

In this changed reality, the fault lines of European politics were redrawn. A new form of liberalism emerged which favoured the expansion of the state, and with it the extension of political rights. Progressive politicians now embraced the advance of the state as a way of delivering political and social benefits to the whole of society through the implementation of democracy. Opposing this tendency were conservatives who clung to the belief that freedom meant self-help, not state intervention or expansion. Conservatives in effect continued the traditions of the old classic liberalism.

In Britain the Liberal Party was out of power almost continuously from 1885 to 1905, but on its re-election it shed the anti-state stance of its forebears and brought in sweeping changes including the introduction of pensions, housing schemes for workers, health insurance, extending votes to all adult males and, eventually, to women aged over thirty. Public spending in Britain rose from £133 million in 1890 to £272 million in 1910. Social legislation brought in school meals, limits on working hours and minimum wages in key industries. These were crucial developments that were echoed in other parts of the industrialised world.

The forces behind these political shifts included organised labour which played a major role in bringing democracy to the industrialised world. After 1870 workers became more concentrated in large factories, shipyards and mines where economies of scale were necessary to bring profits and to deliver massive engineering projects. This not only gave workers the chance to become organised but also gave them immense economic power, which in Britain was highlighted by a series of strikes, including the famous 1888 Bryant & May match-workers strike, led largely by women, and the 1889 London Dock Strike.

This economic power enabled workers' organisations to make some gains, but trade unions began to see that they needed political power to win real improvements in the lives of working people. Many union members and officers embraced socialist ideas, which envisaged a fairer society with wealth distributed more equally among the population.[3] In their influential 1890 book The 'New' Trades Unionism, Tom Mann and Ben Tillett argued that unions were not just there to help their members but 'to make trades unionism become the all-powerful instrument for abolishing poverty'.[4] Unions were democratic bodies themselves, with workplace shop stewards and officers elected by the members, who could see how their own organisations offered a voice to working people that contrasted with the restricted access to Parliament. Some working-class candidates stood for the Liberal Party, but their selection was a rarity. The Bradford Manningham Mills strike of 1890 demonstrated the growing power of unionism with socialist intent, and in 1893 a group of trade unions formed the Independent Labour Party. The constitution of the party declared its aim 'to secure the collective and communal ownership of the means of production, distribution and exchange', but this avowedly socialist intention was less significant at the time than the boost the party gave to the development of democracy in Britain. By giving organised labour a political voice, the ILP brought working people into the political process and made democracy – in which every citizen had full political rights – an imperative for Parliament.

In order to gain seats and influence, the ILP needed the support of the whole trade union movement. The turning point came with a court ruling on a railway strike in South Wales. In 1900, members of the Amalgamated Society of Railway Servants took strike action against the Taff Vale Railway; in response the railway sued the union for losses caused by the strike. At the time it was widely assumed that such actions would fail, but the courts upheld the case and fined the union £3,000 damages plus £19,000 in costs. The Court of Appeal found for the union, however, granting immunity under trade union legislation. When in July 1901 the House of Lords reversed the decision, the verdict was a shock to both trade unions and liberals across the country. Union leaders now feared that they would be unable to protect their members, let alone pursue any wider political aims. It became apparent that the only course was to make changes in the law by an increase in the parliamentary presence of workers' representatives. After the Taff Vale rulings affiliated membership of the Labour Representation Committee increased from 375,000 to 861,000 in less than two years, and the next election returned twenty-one Labour Members of Parliament.

The channelling of working-class power into the political process happened in different ways in other industrialised countries. In Germany, for example, the avowedly Marxist SDAP (Sozialdemokratische Arbeiterpartei, Social Democratic Workers' Party) had been banned by Bismarck in 1878 for advocating revolution and the overthrow of the government. Legalised in 1890, the renamed SPD pledged loyalty to kaiser and country, though it retained a Marxist programme and campaigned for nationalisation of key industries. In the 1912 election, the SPD won the most seats of any party in the Reichstag. However, this victory brought home the ability of existing interests to hold on to the levers of power. The failure of the majority of the population or their representatives to gain real access to power remained an issue throughout Europe.

In other parts of the world, governments brought in laws to extend voting rights, to limit the arbitrary use of power by the state, and to provide universal secular education and welfare. The colonisation of much of Africa and Asia, where the indigenous people were given virtually no rights, made this a partial process at best, but in most sovereign states the structures of democracy were strengthened. In Argentina free education was guaranteed in 1884 and universal male suffrage conducted through ballots was introduced in 1912. In Brazil a coup in 1889 brought the empire of Pedro II to an end and established a republican government with a democratic constitution.

In France, the eventual establishment of a broadly agreed constitution for the Third Republic in 1877 was followed by laws on free secular education in 1881 and 1882, and the separation of church and state in 1905. In Denmark the results of the 1901 elections led to the de facto founding of a constitutional monarchy when the king was forced to accept the will of the people and invite the left-wing Venstre party to form a government. In 1905 Norway and Sweden peacefully dissolved their ninety-year union, with Sweden effectively granting its neighbour independence, paving the way for further constitutional monarchies with increasing powers for elected parliaments in both countries. A bill of rights was passed in Austria in 1867, and by 1907 all male citizens could vote in elections to the Reichsrat. Italy had been a constitutional monarchy with a democratically elected parliament since unification in 1861; here, universal male suffrage was formally introduced in 1913.

In Russia a series of mass strikes forced Tsar Nicholas II to agree in October 1905 to a state Duma with legislative powers, elected by universal male suffrage, together with basic civil rights for all his subjects. In the Ottoman Empire, a constitutional monarchy was introduced and parliament convened in July 1908. The so-called Meiji constitution, adopted in Japan in 1890, followed the abolition of feudalism and created an elected Diet, an independent judiciary and placed limits on the powers of the emperor. In China the declaration of a republic on 1 January 1912, with Sun Yat-sen as its leader, brought thousands of years of imperial rule to an abrupt end.

In the United States moves to strengthen democracy were more subtle but just as essential. Since the end of the Civil War in 1865 the political parties had colluded with industrialists in using economic muscle to ride roughshod over the rights of American citizens, showing that the fears expressed by Jefferson and others had been well-founded (see Chapter 6). Manufacturing, mining, steel and railroad companies bought up competitors, created monopolies and then raked in vast profits. Out of these they funded the campaigns of politicians who gave them the freedom to do what they liked. Some resistance to the so-called 'robber barons' began with the passing of anti-trust laws in the 1890s, but these were left unused until Theodore Roosevelt came to the White House in 1901. He helped to revive American democracy by taming powerful monopolies like the Rockefeller-owned Standard Oil Company and J. P. Morgan's US Steel. As well as corrupting politics, their activities had been hindering the economy by quashing competition, so the government stepped in to regulate commerce but also to provide a fair deal for consumers. This was another new role for the state – as citizens the people had political rights but Roosevelt understood that economic management of an industrial state meant protecting the interests of customers as well as workers.

The extension of democratic rights to adult men in countries across the world served to highlight the anomalous position of women. In the United States the campaigner Susan B. Anthony cast her vote in the 1872 presidential election and was arrested, tried and sentenced to a fine of $100 for voting illegally. The situation began to change in the 1890s with women being given the vote in New Zealand in 1894 and Australia in 1902. The cause of women's votes gripped the public imagination of Britain from 1905 when members of the Women's Social and Political Union first disrupted a public meeting; they were arrested, refused to pay their fines and were sent to prison. The criminalisation of respectable women shocked the country and gave the campaign dramatic impetus. A series of actions culminated in 1913 with Emily Davison fatally throwing herself in front of the king's horse in the Derby. The WSPU suspended its activities at the outbreak of war in 1914, but women in Britain were granted limited voting rights in 1918 and full rights in 1928. A similar campaign in the United States led to the passing in 1920 of the 19th Amendment to the Constitution, which forbids discrimination in voting based on gender. In Germany, Austria, Poland, the Netherlands and Belgium, women were granted voting rights in 1918 and 1919. The end of the First World War represented a high water mark for democracy with virtually every independent nation introducing reforms that promoted democratic institutions and practices. Why, then, did all this fall apart soon after?

There were plenty of reasons why people should be discontented with the progress towards democracy and with the practical effects of democratic reforms. Firstly, for all the progressive measures of the early twentieth century, poverty, poor health and inadequate housing

persisted in all industrial cities. In part this was due to the massive
influxes of people from the countryside and from non-industrialised
regions, but it also owed much to the unchanging inequality of most
societies. In 1905 the journalist and Liberal MP Leo Chiozza Money
pointed out that in Britain, 14 per cent of the population owned 50
per cent of the wealth; he estimated that 1.25 million were rich, around
4 million comfortable and the remaining 38 million poor.[5] Charles
Booth's *Life and Labour of the People of London* (1886–1913) showed that
30 per cent of the capital's population were unable to feed, clothe and
house themselves adequately. British cities were typical of those across
industrialised Europe and the Americas. Huge increases in national
wealth and in average income, together with political rights for more
working people, had not lessened the real hardship among a large
section of the population. There is no necessary link between democracy and lack of poverty, but one impulse for reform came from the
belief that democratic governments, elected by all, would give more
attention to the alleviation of poverty. This view was strengthened by
the belief in society as an inclusive entity.

The other major shortcoming of this period of democratic reforms
was the continuing domination of politics by a small section of society.
Members of parliament and cabinet ministers in almost all countries
were drawn from the upper echelons of the middle classes and the
aristocracy. Where parliaments did contain working-class or socialist
representatives these were prevented from exercising power; although
the SPD became the biggest party in the German Reichstag in 1912,
it had little influence over the imperial cabinet that ruled Germany.
Here and elsewhere governments were presenting themselves as
democracies, with democratic institutions and open elections, while
deliberately restricting access to power.

The question of access to power is a perennial issue in democracies.
It is often near-impossible to find documentary evidence of the explicit
exclusion of particular groups or social classes. Restriction of access
is achieved by much more subtle and, in some cases, unconscious
means – people in power tend to choose others like themselves, or
even people who they know, to serve with them. Selection procedures
for candidates can be fair and open and yet still overwhelmingly return
candidates from particular social groups. For the historian the evidence
lies in the result, not the intention. If electors are, in one election

after another, given the power simply to choose between two or three wealthy candidates from privileged backgrounds then a crucial element of representative democracy is removed.

While governments were introducing democratic reforms, the very idea that democracy was the best form of government, and that political and social progress meant development towards democracy, came under attack from two directions. First, Marxists believed that revolution, in which the working class took power away from the bourgeoisie, was the next stage of history. There would then follow a dictatorship of the proletariat, in which the need for politics would disappear as material goods were shared equally according to need. The other direction of attack, which emerged after 1918, was from ultra-nationalism, which viewed parliamentary democracy as an impediment to clear, forceful leadership: a compromise-ridden talking shop that failed to give each nation the greatness it deserved.

Socialist ideas and movements, often intertwined with anarchist or syndicalist groups, were widespread throughout the industrialised world in the late nineteenth century. The plethora of ideas born out of the desperate plight of workers were given form and substance by Karl Marx, but he was only one voice among many. Socialists believed that government policies should be aimed at bringing maximum benefit to as many citizens as possible and most wished to bring that about within democratic states; 'scientific socialists', as the followers of Marx called themselves, believed that a new kind of society in which workers would own the means of production and distribution was historically inevitable. In an industrial world where all the material necessities of life could be met by clattering machines in gigantic factories, it seemed to Marxists that control of the machinery would inevitably lead to satisfaction of all material needs. Syndicalists on the other hand took trade unions as the model, envisaging a society based on syndicates of unions in which co-operation rather than competition was the basis of economic organisation. Yet another group, the anarcho-syndicalists, believed in the abandonment of the state and the direct participation of workers in all political and economic aspects of their lives. Massive inequality and endemic poverty gave force to these groups. Moreover, political ideas and campaigns materials could spread quickly around the world with agitators and union organisers travelling by rail and steamship carrying their persuasive oratory to wherever workers were being oppressed.

How did the upsurge of revolutionary socialism show itself? In France there were several notable incidents: the 1893 bombing of the National Assembly by avowed anarchist Auguste Valliant; the 1894 assassination of President Sadi Carnot, again by an anarchist; and the notorious Trial of the Thirty the same year, which was held to justify the resulting clampdown on press freedom. In 1901 President McKinley of the United States was assassinated by Leon Czolgosz, a self-styled revolutionary. In North and South America, agitation by anarcho-syndicalists brought repressive measures from regimes terrified by the prospect of revolution. In Russia a revolutionary group assassinated Tsar Alexander II in 1881; the empress of Austria was assassinated in 1898 by an anarchist who declared 'I wanted to kill a royal. It did not matter which one.' In 1900 King Umberto of Italy was also murdered by an anarchist. Political violence was used in less spectacular acts in Scandinavia, Argentina and Mexico.

While none of these assassinations brought down governments, the first sustained blow struck by revolutionary socialism was the Russian Revolution of 1917. The regime that was overthrown was far from being a fully functioning democracy. Nevertheless, the earlier revolution of 1905 had restricted the powers of the tsar and brought in an elected Duma. The first elections in 1906 were by indirect universal male suffrage, but by the time of the fourth Duma elections in 1912, the rules had been changed to favour the nobility and those with property – which meant that the tsar and his ministers continued to run the country. In early 1917, with Russia embroiled in a disastrous war and the tsar away at the front, the liberal and socialist Duma deputies forced the tsar's abdication and formed a provisional government. This was intended to hold power only until the Constituent Assembly had been elected by universal male suffrage, which would then draw up a new constitution for Russia. But before the Constituent Assembly had a chance to meet, the Bolsheviks seized power from the liberal–socialist coalition in October 1917.

The Bolsheviks did not believe in elections. In 1907 Lenin had written: 'The most democratic bourgeois republic is no more than a machine for the suppression of the working class by the bourgeoisie, for the suppression of the working people by a handful of capitalists.' He characterised elections as exploitation, 'under which the oppressed classes enjoy the right to decide once in several years which representative of the propertied classes shall "represent and suppress" the people in parliament'. Though it seems to repudiate the freedoms that we associate with democracy today, in the context of the time Lenin's analysis was persuasive – the ruling classes were, in many countries, using democracy to legitimise their own hold on power. Lenin instead argued for a 'soviet, or proletarian democracy' in which the working class formed the government.[6]

Democratic structures are not immune from corruption and, in particular, from the abuse of powers of patronage and influence. From the 1880s parliaments were widely criticised as corrupt and indecisive. The harmonious world that the bourgeoisie were creating for themselves was viewed with disdain and anger by growing numbers of people who were either excluded from this comfortable existence, or viewed it as stifling. The appeal of adventure and even war as an active and decisive antidote to the tedium of white-collar life was strong among the middle classes, particularly intellectuals. In 1909 the Italian Futurists caused a sensation across Europe, arguing that war was hygienic and that innovation was all that mattered; others claimed that violence would invigorate a Europe of dull middle-class mediocrity. Writers such as Georges Sorel, Vilfredo Pareto and Roberto Michels argued against democratic compromise, and politicians like Karl Lueger in Austria and Francesco Crispi in Italy used the exposure offered by democratic elections to campaign for reactionary measures that weakened liberal democracy in their countries.

This desire for heroic action combined with an assertion of national pride was soon put to the test. In 1914 Germany precipitated a war in which it had most to lose. Between the founding of the German Empire in 1871 and the outbreak of war, Germany had become an industrial giant. Coal production had increased eightfold, and German steel production was greater than that of Britain, France and Russia combined. Its chemical and electrical industries dominated the world through capacity and innovation. Germany's population had increased from forty-one million to sixty-five million, of which more than 60 per cent lived in towns and cities (as opposed to 33 per cent in 1871) and 40 per cent were employed in industry. Despite this extraordinarily beneficial situation, the German and Austrian military managed to convince their governments that they were under imminent threat of attack from an alliance of France and Russia, and must strike first.

Politically the country was split between the Prussian-led establishment under the kaiser and chancellor, and the socialist SPD. Despite strong reservations, the widespread working-class support for war in 1914 persuaded the SPD deputies in the Reichstag to vote in favour of the war credits requested by the chancellor.

Germany and Austria were soon battled into a murderous stalemate with the Allies. America's entry into the war in 1917 was decisive – an acknowledgement of the rise of the United States as an industrial giant – and President Woodrow Wilson was to be the dominant figure in the subsequent peace talks. As Germany faced defeat in 1918, its military commanders Erich Ludendorff and Paul von Hindenburg made two decisions that would haunt German democracy for the next fifteen years. Firstly they decided that President Wilson's 'Fourteen Points' offered the best chance of a peace settlement (though these were pushed aside by France and Britain); secondly they handed power to the civilian government in the ostensible hope that this would produce a more favourable outcome. Both the immediate and long-lasting effect was to hand blame for the surrender and, moreover, the humiliating terms of the eventual settlement, to the civilian parliamentary government. This was a deliberate move by the German army command. Ludendorff blamed the politicians for the defeat, suggesting to the kaiser that he 'bring these groups into government whom we have in the main to thank for the fact that matters have reached this pass . . . Let them eat the broth they have prepared for us.' These words implied that the German army, 'undefeated in the field', had been stabbed in the back by the liberal and SPD deputies in the Reichstag, and that victory could have been theirs were it not for the defeatism shown on the home front.[7] This was hardly an auspicious beginning for a new era of republican parliamentary government.

At the end of hostilities in November 1918, events in Germany moved at a frantic pace. President Wilson insisted on the removal of all wartime leaders before peace negotiations could begin. The kaiser abdicated and left Germany for Holland on 9 November; Friedrich Ebert, leader of the socialist SPD, became chancellor the same day and immediately declared Germany to be a democratic republic. This was an opportunity for the giant of the European mainland to become a fully democratic state.

The new commander of the German army gave Ebert his support and the Armistice was signed on 11 November. Socialist groups opposed to the SPD because of its pro-war stance had set up workers' councils across the country which threatened the authority of the new government. But in the coming months Ebert was able to satisfy their needs by agreeing reforms with industrialists and trade unions, including working hours, wage bargaining, union recognition and works councils. Elections to the National Assembly in January 1919 allowed all men and women over the age of twenty to vote. The turnout was 83 per cent and the Assembly, dominated by the SPD, the liberals and the Centre Party, voted by 262 to 75 to accept the new constitution. Ebert had managed to avert the communist revolution that many people had feared and others hoped for.

The Weimar constitution, with its guarantees of rights and its sophisticated system of checks and balances, appeared a model blueprint for a liberal parliamentary democracy. Universal suffrage for men and women, elections to the Reichstag by proportional representation and four-year parliamentary terms gave the republic an impeccable set of democratic credentials. Perhaps only the extensive powers given to the president – elected for a seven-year term, with the authority to choose a chancellor and cabinet and dissolve the Reichstag, and with supreme command of the armed forces – looked out of balance. Nevertheless, one historian has since called it 'on paper, the most liberal and democratic document of its kind the twentieth century had ever seen'.[8] However, the reality on the ground put it at risk from the beginning.

As the spectre of communist revolution subsided, the German people were faced with harsh economic reality. In 1919 industrial production was 40 per cent of its pre-war level, while the nation's overall income had shrunk by a third. There were around 600,000 widows and over a million children orphaned by the war, as well as millions of wounded soldiers. All believed they were entitled to state care but the constitution's promise of welfare provision for the needy could only be met by taking more in taxes from an already impoverished population. In addition the war and its ending had brought a rift in German society between nationalists and communists that was played out in street violence, including the murders of Kurt Eisner, socialist leader of Bavaria, and Karl Liebknecht and Rosa Luxemburg, communist activists in Berlin, in early 1919.

Moreover, the terms of the Versailles treaty were punitive. Alsace and Lorraine, taken over in 1871, were returned to France; the provinces of Malmedy and Eupen were annexed by Belgium, and the Saarland and Rhineland were occupied under the supervision of the League of Nations for fifteen years, after which they were to be demilitarised zones. Worse still for Germany was the physical separation of East Prussia from the rest of Germany by a newly independent Poland. Severe limits were placed on the size of the German army and navy and, to add insult to injury, the infamous Clause 231, which became known as 'the war guilt clause', declared Germany to be the aggressor responsible for the war and imposed harsh reparation payments. This was deeply resented by the German people who still believed they had fought a noble war of self-defence. An immediate payment of 20 million gold marks was to be made and the reparation commission agreed a total figure of 269 billion marks, eventually reduced to 132 billion, to be paid over the following decades. When the Weimar deputies reluctantly agreed to the Versailles conditions in June 1919, the German people's views of their new parliament took a dramatic turn for the worse. The war guilt clause and the demand for the handover of war criminals, including the kaiser, were regarded as a national humiliation, a foreign imposition intended to deprive Germany of its noble traditions.

Although the Versailles terms haunted successive governments, they were far from fatal to Germany's future prosperity. While it lost productive regions like the Saar, the remaining territories were virtually free from war damage, making possible a revival of much of German industry and commerce. Strategically the collapse of the Austrian Empire and the civil war in Russia left Germany as the dominant force in central and eastern Europe. Both Britain and France were also severely weakened by the war and after the Versailles conference the United States withdrew from Europe to focus on its domestic concerns.

Nevertheless, the damage to Germany's national pride was immense, providing vital ammunition to nationalist right-wing groups. The continuing occupation of the Rhineland and the annual humiliation of reparation payments kept a poisonous feeling of national betrayal alive for the next twelve years. The June 1920 elections, the first held under the Weimar constitution, showed that the brief honeymoon was over. The SPD lost nearly half its votes, as did the Catholic Centre and Democrat parties – an overall decline of liberal and centrist parties from 76 per cent in 1919 to 43.6 per cent. The winners were parties positioned to the left and right in a kind of 'holier than thou' spectrum of extremism.

These parties opposed the Weimar constitution and the practice of liberal democracy – a vote for any of them was a vote against democracy itself. As the historian Ruth Henig has noted, after the 1920 election Germany was 'a democracy without a majority of committed democrats'.[9] The tragic irony of Weimar history is that the democratic constitution allowed these parties a voice in the parliament that they intended to destroy.

In the next thirteen years, there were seven elections and fourteen different governments. The system of proportional representation meant that centrist parties managed to keep some hold on power through forming coalitions, but that often bore little relation to the way that votes were cast. The Catholic Centre Party, for example, was part of every Weimar government while polling between 11 and 14 per cent of the vote. Each German political party represented narrow sectional interests based around class and religion: those of the working class, Catholics, conservative Prussian landowners, businessmen, bureaucrats and professionals. Various explanations for this sectionalism have been put forward: the relatively recent emergence of the country from a large number of states, the fragmented nature of German society, religious divisions, and the legacy of Bismarck's divisive policies. While some have blamed the democratic Weimar parties for not reaching out beyond their narrow constituencies, their position was made near-impossible by the continual onslaught on the legitimacy of the democratic system.

While the elected parliament and governing coalitions of the new republic struggled to win the full support of the people, there were groups eager to put forward their own vision of Germany's future. Most prominent of these were the Freikorps, consisting largely of soldiers who had served in the war. The Freikorps mixed the brotherhood of the trenches with virulent nationalism and anti-communism, which soon turned into hatred of the Weimar system. Important to these groups and to a large section of the German people was the so-called Reich myth, which tied together inspirational elements of

Germany's past – from Charlemagne to the Holy Roman Empire – to suggest that building an empire was a historic destiny that the Germany people should fulfil.[10] The Reich myth explicitly dismissed the notion of Germany as part of a western tradition based on liberalism and democracy.

From 1920 to 1923 ultra-nationalist organisations like the Freikorps grew in strength and boldness. Encouraged by a powerful right-wing press which held parliament in contempt, these groups carried out a low-level campaign of terror. They murdered more than 350 political opponents between 1918 and 1922, but the German judiciary turned a blind eye: only one perpetrator was punished. In March 1920 the cabinet was forced to flee to Dresden when members of the Freikorps invaded government buildings in Berlin and the army declined to defend the government; the attempted coup was defeated only by the intervention of Berlin workers.

A low point for the young republic came in late 1922 when the economy suffered from hyperinflation. The French government accused Germany of using inflation to avoid making reparation payments and in January 1923 French and Belgian troops occupied the Ruhr. This dealt a further blow to the faltering Weimar state. Groups of Freikorps readied themselves to take the law into their own hands and march against the French, while socialists planned a takeover of the government. By November 1923 inflation reached its peak, with a loaf of bread costing three billion marks and a glass of beer four billion. In this deepest of crises the Weimar government did, seemingly against the odds, manage to pull the country round. This was largely due to the emergence of a leader who was prepared to take unpopular decisions. Gustav Stresemann, leader of the People's Party and a centre-right politician with widespread support, secured the crucial backing of the army commander General Seeckt for a series of measures to end the Ruhr crisis and restore the economy. An end to all resistance to the French caused outrage on the right, which Seeckt moved swiftly to suppress (including the arrest of Adolf Hitler). An ingenious solution to hyperinflation involved placing all German real estate under mortgage and giving this measure priority over all other financial instruments. At the same time a stable new currency, the Rentenmark, was created. While in the short term wages went down and prices went up, Stresemann's achievement lay in convincing the German people that, in the long term, the situation would improve – which it did.

For the next four years the Weimar Republic prospered. Stresemann had become foreign minister in August 1923 and carried out a successful campaign to restore Germany's reputation in the world. Relations with France improved dramatically – in 1929 the allies agreed to withdraw troops from the Rhineland, five years ahead of the agreed date – and investments, in particular from the United States, flooded into the country. Between 1923 and 1928 Germany's industrial production more than doubled, becoming second only to the United States, with real wages increasing by more than 20 per cent.[11]

Yet this golden age of the Weimar Republic still contained unresolved problems that put its democracy in continual peril. A key difficulty was that all the centrist parties had to work together in order to gain a workable majority in parliament, forming a 'bourgeois centre bloc'; there was no discernible difference between them. When things went badly, therefore, it was the whole centre that took the blame, leaving as the only alternatives the extreme parties of left and right. The system of proportional representation that allowed small parties to get into parliament also meant that coalition policies were worked out between politicians, rather than in the public forum of election campaigns. After each election another coalition of centre parties formed the government, with the same group of politicians appearing in different ministerial roles. The electors thereby lost the power to remove their leaders – and if they wanted to retain the moderate democratic parliament they had no alternative. The extreme parties were therefore able to argue that, in order to achieve a real change of power, the system had to be destroyed.

Goebbels called Weimar 'an old man's republic', with young Germans disproportionately voting for parties of the far left and right. A clear indication of the hostility to the republic and its parliament came in 1925 with the election of Paul von Hindenburg, chief of the general staff in the First World War, as president; this seemed to show that the majority of the German people preferred a military to a civic leader. Despite Stresemann's achievements many Germans still felt bitter about the humiliation of Versailles, and the reparations paid to France in particular continually undermined the standing of the Weimar institutions – Germans remembered that it was the politicians not the army who had surrendered in 1918. Indeed, rather than calming German nationalism, Stresemann's diplomatic successes led to a continual clamour for him to 'do something' about the hated Polish corridor, which divided one part of Germany from another.

There were other forces in Germany that worked against democracy. While German industry and the big cities enjoyed a boom, rural Germany struggled with the legacies of the period of hyperinflation. Right-wing groups were quick to exploit this and to make common cause between farmers and the middle classes who felt crushed between the powerful trade unions on the one hand and big business on the other. Nationalist groups, supported by major newspapers, called for Germany to be reborn, to be freed from the shackles imposed on it by Versailles and by the petty manoeuvrings of the Reichstag governments. The programme of the German National People's Party began: 'All of our thoughts, our burning desires and our struggles are dedicated to the greatness and freedom of the fatherland. [Germans are] a people whose *Lebensraum* has been brutally cut down, whose freedom to live has been cast in chains through senseless treaties.'[12] Nevertheless the country may have been able to overcome all these anti-democratic forces in time; if prosperity had continued to increase and Stresemann had continued his patient diplomacy (he died in October 1929), then the Weimar parliament might have won over the German people.

But then, just three weeks after Stresemann's death, the Wall Street Crash precipitated, or at the very least accelerated, the end of democracy in Germany. Investment from the United States dropped by 80 per cent and export markets for German goods in Europe dried up. The government had severe difficulties in meeting social security payments to the increased numbers of unemployed. There was a rapidly growing feeling throughout the country that the state simply did not have the expertise, decisiveness or ideas to deal with the situation, or to offer a way forward. Many people were looking for a viable alternative.

The economic crisis brought about a hardening of views among powerful groups in German society. By mid 1930 captains of industry and finance as well as major newspaper proprietors regarded the SPD-led government as a disaster that was likely to lead to communist takeover. Their influence with Hindenburg and the centre-right parties in the Reichstag forced the resignation of SPD leader Hermann Müller as chancellor in March 1930. At this time the principal right-wing nationalist party was the German National People's Party (DVNP) which had won 19.5 per cent of the vote in the previous 1924 federal election; the Communist Party had won 12.6 per cent. The National Socialist Freedom Movement, which was a combination of the German Völkisch Freedom Party (DVFP) and the National Socialist German Workers' Party (NSDAP or Nazi Party) had won just 6.5 per cent of the 1924 votes. The new government, a so-called 'grand coalition' led by Heinrich Brüning of the Catholic Centre Party, staggered on. At the next election in September 1930 the Nazi vote leapt to 18.3 per cent, making them the second largest party in the Reichstag, with the Communist Party a close third. A fatal weakness of the Weimar system now became clear, as the constitution allowed Brüning to continue as chancellor through by-passing the Reichstag and ruling via presidential decrees from Hindenburg. The Reichstag met for ninety-four days in 1930, forty-one days in 1931 and just thirteen days in 1932. Weimar democracy was staggering to an end.

By September 1932 official unemployment reached 5.1 million, and in an atmosphere of hopelessness and frustration the Nazi message of national renewal gained ever more appeal, particularly among the young. Many looked to Italy where Mussolini had developed the new political philosophy of fascism, combining revolution and tradition and advocating a powerful state. Parliamentary democracy looked increasingly like an old-fashioned, restrictive and corrosive system.

The Nazis appealed strongly to nationalist sentiment, using violent imagery to depict Jews and other races as subhuman. The idealisation of the German race was a perverse extension of the ethnic nationalism that had dominated the nineteenth century. Jews had been a settled group in Germany for centuries, but the Nazi message began to resonate in the 1920s and 30s because, among other reasons, this was a time of great movements of people. Some of this was brought on by industrialisation and rural poverty; among the millions of migrants were Jewish people moving from poverty and repression in eastern Europe in search of a better life in Germany and elsewhere. People of all kinds left the countryside to work in steel mills, chemical plants, railway yards, shops and offices, swelling the populations of Europe and America's great cities. Lower-middle-class office workers, bureaucrats and shopkeepers, whose rising numbers made them a significant political force, felt adrift in this changing society.

Hitler had attempted an armed coup during the crisis of 1923; this time he decided that the Nazi Party should take power through the existing democratic channels. In the March 1932 presidential election he stood against Hindenburg, forcing a second round of voting which the incumbent won, but in which 37 per cent voted for Hitler. After this humiliation Hindenburg refused to continue supporting the government through presidential decrees and a Reichstag election was called.

In the July 1932 election support for the Nazi Party more than doubled to 37.4 per cent, giving them 230 seats out of a total of 608. The communists were the other main party to make gains with 89 seats; the country was becoming polarised into mutually hostile camps. A minority government led by Franz von Papen of the Centre Party continued in power until a no-confidence vote precipitated yet another election in November 1932 in which the Nazi vote decreased but the communist vote increased significantly.

A weak centre and powerful parties on the extreme right and left, both hostile to the parliamentary democracy in which they served, created an unsustainable situation. It was the growing power of the Communist Party that led the German establishment to press Hindenburg to act. Industrialists and others saw a looming threat of civil war between right and left; an influential group wrote to the president calling for decisive action. On 30 January 1933, with extreme reluctance, Hindenburg appointed the Nazi leader Adolf Hitler as the new chancellor of Germany. Some of those instrumental in the appointment believed that they could control the excesses of the Nazi Party and that this would not be the end of democracy but a chance for its renewal; others were happy to see the demise of the Weimar Republic. Franz von Papen showed how divorced from reality he was when he said of Hitler's appointment as chancellor: 'No danger at all, we've hired him for our act.'[13]

At this stage Hitler was by no means in complete control of Germany; the events of the next weeks were to show how German democracy was finally suffocated by mainstream politicians working in consort with the Nazis. Hitler intended to bring the Weimar constitution and the Reichstag itself to an end; but to do this required a two-thirds majority, which in turn required a further election. This election was fought specifically on a platform of ending democracy. Hitler asked Hindenburg to dissolve parliament and new elections were set for 3 March. Hitler told his cabinet that 'The forthcoming election of the Reichstag is to be the last election. Any return to the full parliamentary system is to be absolutely avoided.'[14]

On 27 February 1933 the Reichstag building caught fire; the Nazis blamed a communist arsonist, which gave the government a pretext to arrest and intimidate thousands of communist politicians and supporters. 'This is a God-given signal', Hitler declared. 'If this fire, as I believe, turns out to be the handiwork of communists, then there is nothing that will stop us now crushing this murder pest with a fist of iron.'[15] In the subsequent wave of oppression the internal powers of the individual states within Germany were swept aside by the Nazi-led government with Hindenburg's agreement in what was, in effect, a *coup d'état*.

In the March election the Nazis won 288 seats, the SPD 120 seats and the communists 81 seats. Other far-right parties had 70 seats between them, giving the Nazis and their allies a comfortable combined majority in the 674-seat Reichstag, but still short of the two-thirds needed to change the constitution. On 23 March the Enabling Act was voted on in the Reichstag. The votes of the 81 communist deputies, most of whom were in detention, were discounted, and just 94 of the 120 SPD deputies were present. In the crucial vote the Centre Party, which had been part of every Weimar government, chose to put its 74 votes in favour of the Act. Hitler was thereby given the authority to rule without recourse to parliament for four years. The democratically elected parliament had voted itself out of existence.

While Hitler's ascent to power was not inevitable, it was a product of both circumstance and history. Germany's response to the depression and the rise of extreme parties on left and right was different from other countries going through similar crises. The Reich myth, which spoke of a Greater Germany, inspired both National Socialists and the conservatives in Germany, and has been cited by historians as a major factor in the destruction of German democracy. But the catastrophe of 1933–45 also had origins in the nineteenth century. The ethnic nationalism that advocated a united Germany had originally

been a liberal vision, yet from the 1860s it was claimed by conservatives and became part of the imperial culture. Germans were not
unique in their racist doctrines: the conquest of other races in Africa
and Asia and the superiority of white Christians was an assumption
shared by many Europeans before 1939; the supremacist views of the
Nazis, based on a heady mix of paranoia and self-glorification, fell on
fertile ground in the centre of Europe.

Though they differed dramatically, both fascism and communism
had no time for the negotiations, compromises and complexities, or
the containment of conflict by discussion and resolution that characterise democratic politics. Both turned away from the humdrum reality
of managing a free democratic society and called instead on an ideal
view of the world. It is no coincidence that Plato's *Republic* was
Mussolini's inspiration.

We have spent most of this chapter looking at the decline of democracy in Weimar Germany, partly because it is the most disastrous case
of a democracy falling apart from within, and partly because of its
impact on the rest of the world. Let us look at what was happening
in other countries at this time: how was the apparently irresistible
advance of democracy halted in some countries while it survived in
others?

From Finland and Romania in the east to the shores of the Atlantic,
Europe in 1918 was a continent of liberal constitutional democracies.
Yet, as Eric Hobsbawm has pointed out, 'the twenty years between
Mussolini's march on Rome [in 1922] and the peak of the Axis success
in the Second World War saw an accelerating, increasingly catastrophic, retreat of liberal political institutions'.[16] In Europe during
this period democracy survived only in Ireland, Britain, Finland (intermittently), Sweden and Switzerland, while in the Americas only the
United States, Canada, Costa Rica, Colombia and Uruguay continued
as functioning democracies.

All the other nations whose democratic credentials were stated
earlier in this chapter were taken over by right-wing authoritarian
regimes dedicated to the destruction of democracy. The reasons for
this varied. France, the Low Countries, Denmark and Norway were
invaded by Nazi Germany which imposed regimes on their populations, but out of twenty-seven European countries, seventeen had

representative assemblies either dissolved or sidelined before the outbreak of war in 1939. Italy became the first fascist state, predating Hitler's ascent to power by more than a decade. Created by Benito Mussolini, who took power in 1922, the Fascist Party appealed to the frustrated sense of Italy's past greatness and played on the threat of communism, with a seductive mixture of tradition and revolution. Other takeovers were made by, as Hobsbawm calls them, 'old-fashioned authoritarians or reactionaries'. In Hungary, Finland, Poland, Yugoslavia, Romania and Spain, right-wing traditionalists took power, emboldened by Hitler's success in Germany. In Lithuania an authoritarian regime seized power in 1926; in Latvia and Estonia in 1934 right-wing coups resulted in the abolition of parliament. In 1934 a new constitution made Austria a one-party fascist state which, in 1938, was absorbed into Germany.

Across the world similar nationalist or militarist movements were coming to power. In Japan the military came to dominate the government under a constitution that allowed the emperor an unusual degree of power, culminating in the 1931 invasion of Manchuria, and Japan's withdrawal from the League of Nations. The fledging constitutional Republic of China became embroiled in a long civil war between the governing Chinese Nationalist Party (Kuomintang) and the Communist Party, a dire situation exacerbated by the Japanese occupation of much of China, which lasted from 1931 to 1945.

In September 1930 Argentina experienced its first military coup of the twentieth century. The army leaders wanted 'orderly progress' towards the national greatness that they believed the country deserved. Intent on excluding workers from power, they kept an ostensible form of democracy and manipulated elections. There was a similar story in Brazil where, in the same year, a disputed election was followed by a military coup which brought Getúlio Vargas to power as a dictator. In the 1930s, all over the world, authoritarianism, militarism and fascism seemed to be the future.

Even in those countries that continued as democracies, anti-democratic and anti-liberal forces grew stronger. In Britain the British Union of Fascists, led by Oswald Mosley, reached a peak in 1934 with a claimed membership of 50,000. In October 1936 an attempt by the so-called blackshirts to march through a Jewish area in London's East End led to the famous Battle of Cable Street, where local people confronted Mosley's supporters, showing that they could not claim support among the working classes. In France the 1920s were a stable period dominated by a centre-right electoral pact known as the National Bloc. The delayed reaction to the financial crash of 1929 brought in a brief government headed by socialists and the Radical Party (in reality a centre party) in 1932. After a right-wing attempt to invade and take over the Chamber of Deputies in 1934, the 1936 elections resulted in a resounding victory for the combined left under the banner of the Popular Front, headed by Léon Blum, the first Jew to lead France; he was succeeded by another leftist politician in Eduard Daladier. But right-wing groups such as Action Française also had support – in 1934 the AF had 60,000 members – and much intellectual opinion was sympathetic to Hitler's aims of eradicating communism. As in Britain, but unlike Germany, the French political system enabled voters to choose from different parties which, while in competition for power, were each committed to democracy. The ability of voters to make a meaningful choice between popular democratic parties averted any serious reversion to extremism.

In June 1940 France was invaded by German forces; an armistice was signed on 22 June and came into effect three days later. On 10 July the National Assembly voted by 569 to 80 votes to hand extraordinary powers to Marshal Philippe Pétain, the country's military commander in the First World War, and France was divided into a German-occupied zone in the north, an Italian zone in the south-east, with the remainder being a 'free zone' run from the spa town of Vichy. The Vichy government and its supporters believed that France had followed the wrong path in the 1930s, continuing with democratic government when it needed the strong hand of a dictator.

The United States also saw a rise in right-wing groups, partly as a reaction against the threat of communism, but also as a harking-back to a mythic America. Racist right-wing groups who glorified the South from the time before the Civil War, grew stronger in the 1920s. The Ku Klux Klan was refounded in 1915 and by the 1920s had grown to a formidable organisation wielding political influence in a number of states. Public authorities went along with the change of mood and racial segregation was even introduced into offices of the federal government. By 1930 access to public spaces, including areas of Washington DC itself, was forbidden to black American citizens. The so-called Jim Crow laws, which legalised racial segregation in the United States, were cited by Hitler as evidence that Germany was only following the example of other nations in introducing the Nuremberg Laws of 1935.

A more subtle but pervasive change came over American society at the same time, signalled by the hugely influential columnist Walter Lippmann in books such as *Liberty and the News* (1920) and *The Phantom Public* (1925). Lippmann argued that while journalists must always endeavour to tell the unvarnished truth, the average citizen could not be expected to spend his or her life immersed in the minutiae of political debate and policy. In the past democracy had moved from the age of direct participation at the town meeting to the era of active, public-spirited citizens sending their representatives to Washington. Now it was entering a new phase in which citizens were no longer engaged in politics, leaving the nation in need of leaders who could articulate policy and carry it through with the help of experts.

This vision of a 'passive democracy' was the flip side of the 1920s rise in American consumerism. The ability of industrial and commercial organisations to satisfy entirely the basic human needs of food and shelter had come to pass by the turn of the twentieth century. But this represented a real problem for capitalism, which was built on the idea of continual expansion of goods and services: American industrialists worried about a future where everyone would have enough to eat and a decent home to live in – surely they would then stop buying.

The answer to the problem came through a new way of viewing human needs. Companies should not regard their customers as being in need of goods per se – crockery, shoes, radios or sofas – but as being in search of happiness. Rather than simply announcing the availability and price of goods, advertising now began to depict the ideal worlds that such goods would allow you to enter. A set of plates would enable you to eat your tea, but a dinner service was part of a new vision of American life. Americans were changing from the rugged energetic individualists whose ploughs tamed the wild prairies into seekers after social status.

The effect on politics was immediate. Presidents Warren Harding (1921–3), Calvin Coolidge (1923–9) and Herbert Hoover (1929–33) all saw the value of giving the public an endless supply of consumer goods and services. The function of the government became the satisfaction of these needs by providing economic prosperity to voters. This made governments popular and fuelled economic growth. It also had a more subtle effect: as Lippmann had predicted, so long as people were driven by the need for ever greater satisfaction through consumption, they would not be engaged in political activism, and the governing elite would be left to get on with running the country. While the Great Depression of the 1930s temporarily halted this development, passive democracy would become a significant element in the future of America and much of the West.

With the stock market collapse of 1929 affecting the United States more than any other country, why did the American people continue to support the democratic system? The answer lies in part in the possibility of change and renewal that American politics continued to offer. In his acceptance of the Democratic Party nomination in 1932 Franklin Roosevelt declared: 'This is more than a political campaign, it is a call to arms.' When he took presidential office in 1933 America's industrial output had been halved and unemployment stood at 25 per cent. Roosevelt put a raft of federal programmes into action, following the model developed by the British economist John Maynard Keynes of using government spending to boost the economy. The president was supported by voters who understood that radical action was required, and by offering an optimistic vision of the future Roosevelt prevented an economic crisis from becoming a political one; his radical action meant a renewal of democracy, not its abandonment.

While we have seen the specific reasons for the collapse of democracy in Germany, why did so many other countries follow suit? Democracy is a rarity in human history, existing in only a tiny minority of times and places. The dynamics of human society always give some the opportunity to gain power and, when they do so, they tend to work hard to retain that authority. Thus the central pillar of democracy – giving the powerless the right to remove their rulers – works in direct opposition to the wishes of the powerful. Democracy can only survive when powerful groups in society see it as being in *their* interests. The ways this comes about are as diverse as the societies of humankind, but it is clear that it takes time for the interests of democracy to become identical with the interests of industrialists, bankers, the press, the army and the civil administration. In many countries in Europe, Asia and South America in the 1920s and 1930s these groups – or some of them at least – had not fused their interests with the relatively recent democratic institutions, and so were unwilling to work for the continuation of democracy. They were, in turn, able to persuade their populations that democracy was not in *their* interests either, and so democracy fell.

It would be the military triumph of the United States and its allies in 1945 that utterly changed the history of democracy and reverted the previous collapse. The United States was able to impose democratic structures on the vanquished, often in a deliberate attempt to prevent the spread of communism. Just as important, however, the great powers of Europe were forced to accept a diminished role in the world and began the slow process of decolonisation. The emergence of democracy in the ex-colonies began with the largest of them all: India.

INDIA

The Independent Citizen

If you were looking for a country in which to establish the world's newest democracy, then India in 1947 would not be high on your list: a British colony that had never been a nation, its society based on a hierarchy of castes, divided by religion and speaking a host of languages, with most of its population in poverty and in continual threat of starvation. Above all India, unlike every other modern democracy, was not European. (Democracies in North and South America had been established and run by European immigrants and their descendants.) And yet a democratic political system did take root in India, and has persisted to the present day. The 2009 elections to the lower house or Lok Sabha of the fifteenth parliament had an electorate of 714 million, of whom over 420 million voted – more than the combined electorates of the United States and all the countries in the European Union. Politics has become the lifeblood of India where millions of voices can make themselves heard, and thousands of competing claims are aired, negotiated and resolved in public.

Explanations for this remarkable story are as diverse as India itself and focus on the question of whether the key elements that allowed democracy to flourish after independence were deeply embedded in Indian culture, or whether democracy was a novel concept to which the new nation managed somehow to adapt. It is now widely acknowledged that independence was a staging post rather than a rupture in the story of democracy in India – democracy was embedded in the subcontinent well before the British formally left. There is also a view that British rule should be seen within the continuum of Indian history; from this perspective colonial rule left an influential legacy but much of Indian culture had remained untouched within the colonial period. Independence simply allowed the prevailing culture to continue as before, but now with Indian people in control of the political centre. However, we need to balance that reading of history with an acknowledgement that contemporary India is a modern creation that combines innovation and adaptability with a remarkable continuity. To understand these abstract arguments we need to look at the history of India before and after the arrival of the British.

Ever since the fourth and third centuries BC, when the territory of India was ruled by the Maurya Empire, the subcontinent has accommodated a simultaneously diverse and unified set of cultures – people in different areas shared cultural practices while varying in their customs. Both Hinduism and Buddhism spread across the region, uniting South Asian people not just in religious belief but in cultural and social attitudes. Hinduism developed into a social structure during the so-called Classical Age, lasting from the ninth to the seventeenth century AD. During that time parts of the north-west of India were invaded and settled by Muslims from Persia, the Mughals, while the Hindu Vijayanagara Empire became a dominant force in the south from the fourteenth to the seventeenth century. The Mughal Empire became fully established under Akbar the Great (1542–1605), eventually reaching from Kabul in the north to Calicut in the south and to the Ganges Delta in the east. The Mughals did not interfere with the Hindu faith of their subjects and Akbar used a combination of Muslim and indigenous leaders, known as jagirdar, to run the empire. These local governors collected taxes and organised the defence of their regions through a team of administrators (zamindars). The empire made use of established authorities in some areas, while in others it brought in administrators and officials to create an effective imperial bureaucracy. The Mughal court was peripatetic and the 2,000 jagirdar were expected to attend regularly at whatever location was chosen by the emperor.

The key feature of the empire was the autonomy granted to the regions: so long as local leaders brought in taxes and did not challenge the authority of the centre they were largely left in peace. But this same autonomy contributed to the break-up of the empire; by the eighteenth century the Mughals became the victims of their own success. By that time the different regions had grown in prosperity and self-confidence. Provincial leaders became more lax at sending taxes to the centre, which in turn became progressively weaker. Rebellions within the regions, for example the Deccan wars beginning in 1670, successfully challenged the central authority. After the death of Aurangzeb, the last great Mughal emperor, in 1707 many of the jagirdar cut their links with the imperial court, setting up quasi-independent states in Hyderabad, Bengal and Oudh. The end came when Delhi was sacked by a Persian army in 1739, and the Mughal Peacock throne taken as a spoil of war. The empire did not vanish but the Great Mughal became just one of many regional leaders, each with their own power base.

The subsequent takeover of the Indian subcontinent by the British was such a gradual affair that it can be seen as a continuation of the Mughal system of government under another name. The involvement of the East India Company began in 1615, when Sir Thomas Roe led a mission to the Mughal emperor Nuruddin Salim Jahangir. For the next hundred years employees of the company traded with parts of the empire, some of them establishing trading posts on the subcontinent. During all this time the company was independent of the British government, though it was granted special privileges, first by Elizabeth in 1600 and subsequently by Oliver Cromwell, King Charles II and then by the British Parliament in 1708. In return for its privileges the company paid considerable sums of money to the British government. Its main trade was in cotton, silk and other textile products such as indigo dye, but there were lucrative sidelines in opium and tobacco. As its operations expanded the company set factories and built small fortresses to protect its property. In 1717 it was allowed by the Mughal emperor to trade in Bengal without paying customs duties. Extensive trade there and in other parts of India and East Asia allowed the company to prosper, but without any plans for conquest: there seemed no reason to want political rule so long as trade was lucrative and stable.

The Seven Years War of 1756–63 changed the situation. In 1757 Robert Clive led forces of the East India Company, supported by the Great Mughal, against the Nawab of Bengal and the French at the battle of Plassey. Clive's victory made the company the de facto rulers of Bengal, the jewel in the crown of India, but there was still no indication that the protection of British interests would lead to a whole-scale takeover of the subcontinent; the British simply became part of the existing power structure.

Nevertheless by 1780 the company's trading function had become virtually political: in the absence of any other authority, East India Company officials were administering a large and prosperous part of east India, including the collection of tax revenues. Partly because of the gradual assumption of authority, company officials found themselves working in an Indian system with interactions between Indians and British at all levels. This was not a unified imperial design but a set of practical arrangements.

In its commercial role the East India Company was content to co-exist with Indian people and Indian culture. Yet many individuals and groups in Britain were eager to bring the fruits of civilisation to a people who, according to Charles Grant, board member of the company, and an evangelical Christian, were 'long sunk in darkness, vice and misery' and in need of 'the light and benign influence of the truth [and] the blessings of a well-regulated society'.[1] While Christianity failed to make a strong impact on Indian soil, the education of a significant number of the Indian elite was to be an important legacy of British rule. Eventually the British came to regret creating a group of highly knowledgeable and able Indians who could challenge their authority at every level (a practice that was not repeated in Britain's African colonies). Educated Indians began to think about an Indian nation that transcended region, creed and caste.

In the first half of the nineteenth century the East India Company changed decisively to become a dominant and conquering military power. Victories over the Maratha Empire in the south and coercion of local leaders in the north-west gave the company control of the whole of India by 1850. This undeclared takeover was made formal by the Indian Mutiny of 1857, which utterly changed the relationship between the British and India. By that time the East India Company employed around 200,000 Indian troops, known as sepoys, along with 40,000 British soldiers, to enforce its powers. Different factors inspired the mutiny, including measures to enforce sepoys to serve outside India and the erosion of privileges enjoyed by high-caste sepoys. The trigger was the introduction of a new Enfield rifle; the technique for loading was to bite open the paper cartridges, and rumours spread that the cases were stiffened by soaking in either pork fat – which was anathema to Muslim soldiers – or beef dripping – which was unacceptable to Hindus. While the main conflict was confined to the Ganges plain, the company's authority collapsed in many parts of India. The British government assumed direct control of British forces; the crushing of the rebellion was brutal and left Britain with no serious rivals for power.

After the mutiny Britain consolidated its position through the appointment of a viceroy; the East India Company was abolished and India became a British colony. The subcontinent was now divided into districts, each under the authority of a District Officer who was typically drawn from the British upper-middle classes. The development of railways, roads, the telegraph and later the telephone made possible the government of the subcontinent as one entity. At the same time upper-middle-class Victorian life with its social hierarchies and rigid conformity was exported to India. This allowed little contact between British and Indians. In the same way that they regarded their own working classes, the British colonial masters treated the Indians with condescension, charity and occasional brutality; those who cared about Indian people argued that the British were running the country for the inhabitants' own benefit.

The British government of India lasted from 1857 to 1947. During this time Indians were well aware of political developments in Britain, of the changes in electoral law and the democratic pressures applied to both Liberal and Tory parties. In 1885 the Indian National Congress was formed, not as a political party but as a kind of club or society for educated Indians to discuss and to bring influence to bear on the political future of their country. The election of a reforming Liberal British government in 1906 brought notable changes to the subcontinent; that year also saw the foundation of the All India Muslim League. The India Councils Act of 1909 (known as the Morley Minto Act) gave Indians some elected seats on legislative assemblies which had previously been entirely appointed by the British, and also reserved a number of seats for the Muslim minority. While British appointees remained in the majority, it marked the beginning of a parliamentary structure for India at district, provincial and imperial level.

After 1918, when all British men over eighteen and some women over thirty were given the vote, Indian demands for real political rights grew stronger. In 1919 the British government granted Indians greater participation in the machinery of government, which provided a catalyst for more focussed discussions by the Indian nationalists in Congress and the Muslim League. Indians had not previously thought of themselves as a nation, now they had to work out what that concept would mean in practice. What was India, and what should it be? Some Hindus wanted a nation based on their religious culture – but where would that leave the large Muslim minority? Some wanted political unity, others a loose federation. These ideas were hotly debated.

Into this open and voluble debate came the extraordinary figure of Mohandas Gandhi. The son of a provincial politician, Gandhi had trained in London as a barrister before working in South Africa from 1893 to 1914. There he experienced direct racism and, in a campaign to give the Indian community political rights, developed the idea of satyagraha (literally 'truth force'), a combination of adherence to the truth and non-violent protest. In satyagraha people would disobey unjust laws en masse and accept punishment as a form of radical protest. Gandhi returned to India in 1915 and became leader of the Indian National Congress in 1921 with the avowed aim of winning Indian independence from Britain. His adoption of a simple style of dress, wearing the traditional dhoti made from homespun cloth, was the physical representation of his belief that the soul of India lay in its villages and their people.

The satyagraha movement organised campaigns of non-cooperation throughout the 1920s, while Gandhi's skills in reaching out to ordinary Indian people turned Congress from a small club of educated Indians into a national organisation involving all classes and regions. In early 1930 Gandhi instituted a campaign against the tax on salt, culminating in the famous 400-kilometre march from Ahmedabad to the Dandi salt works; more than 80,000 Indians were imprisoned during that campaign. At the heart of Gandhi's work was the realisation that India could not be created simply by getting rid of the British: the nation had to be built from the bottom up.

The template for the new nation of India was introduced by the 1935 Government of India Act, which set up a federation of semi-autonomous provinces in which Indians were given more voting powers. In practice, however, the federal system didn't work: provincial ministers were controlled by the central command of the Congress Party, which was now the dominant force in Indian politics. Jawaharlal Nehru, the scion of a wealthy Kashmiri family and educated in Britain, was now the leading organiser of the independence movement; it was the combination of Gandhi's charisma and popularity and Nehru's political skills that were to provide the basis of the movement. In the meantime the majority of the allocated Muslim seats were taken by members of the Muslim League, whose leader Muhammad Ali Jinnah was eventually to advocate a separate state for Muslims. The system introduced by the 1935 Act gave politicians in the provinces a chance to get involved in government, and officials in district and provincial councils learned political skills – how to manoeuvre, compromise and organise. In addition, by 1940 the Indian Civil Service, the great machine of government administration, had become ever more 'Indianised'; there were by then more Indians than British officials in its top ranks.

After 1945, independence was inevitable. British troops had been taken elsewhere during the war and the costs of reoccupying India were prohibitive; Britain and India were in any case finding that they had little use for one another. Economically they were going their separate ways as India began to behave more like a developed country – increasing the literacy of its population, producing its own manufactured goods and importing commodities from elsewhere. Moreover the United States, which was bankrolling the reconstruction of Europe, was hostile to British imperialism, and the British public wanted reconstruction at home, not overseas.

As independence loomed tensions rose between the Hindu and Muslim communities, each feeling threatened by the potential dominance of the other in different parts of the country. Inter-communal violence was particularly bloody in the Punjab, which was home to Sikhs, Muslims, Hindus, Christians, Jains and Buddhists. Nehru wrote of the violence: 'I must confess that recent happenings in the Punjab and in Delhi have shaken . . . my faith in my own people. I could not conceive of the gross brutality and sadistic cruelty that people have indulged in.'[2] In 1947 the British prime minister Clement Attlee appointed Lord Mountbatten as viceroy with a mandate to clear the path for Indian independence. Mountbatten was a genial figure, bringing Indian leaders into his social circle and striking up a close friendship with Nehru in particular. Nehru for his part fought in Congress for a secular vision of India opposing Hindu nationalism and offering protection to India's millions of Muslims. Both Nehru and Mountbatten were frustrated by the intransigence of Jinnah, whose concerns for political rights for the Muslim minority turned into a demand for a separate state; but Nehru understood that the reality of communal violence in which tens of thousands were killed meant that the dream of a united independent India could never be fulfilled. In the end Nehru, Jinnah and Mountbatten agreed on the partition of the country into the states of India and Pakistan and independence was formally declared at midnight on 14–15 August 1947.

Though partition was traumatic, the new Indian and Pakistani governments dealt with the administration of its aftermath with extraordinary speed and success. Refugees were settled and government offices, revenues, armed forces and other bodies efficiently divided. In India the Constituent Assembly was given the task of drawing up a constitution for the new country. How this should be drafted was still far from clear. Gandhi believed Congress should disband now that the work of independence was done; however, the party continued but remained a collection of different opinions and approaches. Some within Congress believed that partition had given the green light to an avowedly Hindu state, and there was a possibility that the powerful Indian bureaucracy could be used to serve an oligarchy of the educated elite. Democracy, though, remained the favoured option within Congress, and it was Nehru's principal achievement to push for a universal franchise and to make the extension of political rights an engine of economic and social development.

The constitution was signed into law in January 1950: India had become a democratic republic. The preamble to the constitution followed its western predecessors in making the people sovereign and enshrining certain rights, including equality and free expression:

We, the people of India, having solemnly resolved to constitute India into a sovereign democratic republic and to secure to all its citizens: Justice, social, economic and political; Liberty of thought, expression, belief, faith and worship; Equality of status and of opportunity; and to promote among them all Fraternity assuring the dignity of the individual and the unity and integrity of the Nation.[3]

The constitution gave the national government more power than some people liked, but this was considered necessary by others to create a modern state. The right of the president to dissolve governments of individual states (the so-called President's Rule) was problematic, but it reflected fears of a break-up of India into separate states.

The new state set out to create a free, equal and prosperous society; but the Indian government's task of maintaining stability while giving the people freedom of choice posed the eternal question of how to balance liberty and order. Indians had been constrained under the British and now they were free, yet society had to function in an orderly way. Stability was helped by three factors: the political neutrality of the army, a highly professional Civil Service that acted as a buffer against political disorder, and, in the first decades of independence, the dominance of Congress; so pervasive was Congress that India was for a while that apparent paradox – a one-party democracy.

Jawaharlal Nehru served as prime minister and foreign minister from 1947 until his death in 1964. The son of a wealthy Indian lawyer, Nehru witnessed British democracy with all its merits and faults at first hand when he studied at Harrow school and Cambridge. The long campaign for independence, together with the influence of Gandhi, undoubtedly shaped his political outlook and by 1947 he was aware of the difficulties and possibilities that India faced. Nehru saw clearly that the new nation could easily be ruled by an oligarchy of the highest castes and wealthiest families for their own good. Such a ruling class would follow the paternalistic approach of the British rather than engaging the population in politics, social issues and embarking on reform of education and health care. From the start Nehru was concerned about the behaviour of public officials: 'They tend to revert to the days of British rule, when they looked down upon the public as some kind of enemy or opponent which had to be put down. This is a dangerous development, because it undermines the prestige of Government with the people.'[4] Nehru provided a popular patrician figurehead but also ensured that democracy engaged ordinary people.

Like America's Founding Fathers, Nehru became disillusioned and exhausted by the scale of the task and by the pettiness and opportunism of politics, but he had the support of a collection of able and experienced administrators and politicians. In particular his relationship with the deputy prime minister, Vallabhbhai Patel, allowed dissent within Congress to be expressed through the political process rather than behind closed doors. Nevertheless after Patel's death in 1950 Nehru took more control of Congress, his secularism winning out over the Hindu nationalism of his deputy's supporters.

Nehru's greatest gift to Indian democracy may have been his love of elections and campaigning. He relished the opportunity to get out among the voters and preach the creed of democracy; subsequently elections became a vastly important public rite inculcated into the identity of the nation. Indians discovered a passion for politics that they have never lost; unlike in Europe, in India it is common practice to argue politics with complete strangers. Nehru understood that this continual nurturing of democracy was crucial to its survival. He also treated Lok Sabha with respect and seriousness, attending parliament regularly, making it the forum for important announcements, and taking notice of the opinions of members even when they threatened to hold up legislation. In contrast to post-colonial leaders around the world, Nehru argued against repressive government measures, such as restricting press freedom, and used them only reluctantly. As one Indian historian has written: 'Nehru's commitment to democracy and civil liberties was total. To him they represented absolute values and not a means to an end.' When asked what his legacy would be, Nehru replied: 'Hopefully 400 million Indians capable of governing themselves.'[5] Nehru pursued a socialist domestic agenda with a foreign policy of non-alignment. While some have criticised the slow pace of economic development in the first decades of independence, the emphasis on building up education and maintaining stability and national unity have underpinned the recent surge in economic growth.

Before Nehru's death in 1964 other political parties struggled to make headway. The socialist and communist parties had both started life as sections of the Congress party before breaking away, but the willingness of Congress to encompass some of their beliefs made life difficult for them. The Bharatiya Jana Sangh (BJS) was founded in 1951 as a Hindu nationalist party, but communalism was unpopular in India after Gandhi's assassination by a Hindu. It was also illegal to appeal to religious beliefs in elections and the BJS struggled for support. The Swatantra Party became India's first secular conservative party, set up in 1959 to represent laissez-faire economics and free trade in opposition to Nehru's socialism, but it too failed to lure its ideological soulmates from under the comfortable umbrella of Congress. The dominance of Congress was self-perpetuating – anyone wanting to get on in politics naturally looked to Congress as a vehicle.

Congress elected Lal Bahadur Shastri as Nehru's successor. Shastri had been chosen by a group of senior party members who became known as the Syndicate and when Shastri died of a heart attack in January 1966, the Syndicate turned to Nehru's daughter Indira Gandhi, expecting a popular young woman without her own power base to be malleable. The new prime minister took office at a difficult time with India suffering food shortages and spiralling prices. The 1967 elections saw huge losses for Congress; though it narrowly retained a majority in the Lok Sabha, it surrendered outright control of most states. Significantly, many of the Syndicate members lost their seats leaving Indira Gandhi in a more powerful position. In November 1969, the old guard, resentful of her growing status, expelled the prime minister from her own party. Mrs Gandhi immediately set up her own political organisation, called Congress (R) (for Requisitionists), which later became Congress (I) (for Indira). Some 220 MPs joined her, while 68 stayed with the rival Congress (O) (for Organisation). The consequent elections in February 1971 were a personal triumph for Mrs Gandhi: Congress (R) won 352 of the 518 seats, giving a powerful mandate to the new party formed around her. Her astute handling of the Bangladesh conflict of 1971 further increased her authority and stature at home and throughout the world.[6]

Yet it was under Indira Gandhi that India came closest to losing its democracy. In June 1975 the Allahabad High Court convicted Mrs Gandhi of electoral fraud in her constituency during the 1971 elections, and ordered her to be removed from her parliamentary seat and banned from parliament for six years. This effectively disqualified her from the office of prime minister. In an extremely tense atmosphere, with crowds of supporters and detractors gathering in Delhi, Mrs Gandhi refused to comply and instead asked the country's president to declare a state of emergency. Fakhruddin Ali Ahmed, a member of the Congress Party who had been picked for the role by Mrs Gandhi, obliged and the emergency began on 26 June 1975. At the same time the President's Rule was invoked to bring the only two states ruled by opposition parties – Gujarat and Tamil Nadu – under central government control. Thousands of opposition activists were arrested as civil rights were suspended and censorship introduced. A botched slum clearance programme, combined with a campaign of forced birth control run by Gandhi's son Sanjay, only added to the growing discontent. Some have argued that Indira Gandhi was defending the country from an effective coup in 1975, but the length of the emergency works against this claim; Mrs Gandhi extended the emergency twice before calling elections in 1977. In the event Congress was humiliated at the polls, losing power for the first time in India's history to the Janata Party – an alliance of opposition groups. The emergency had shown the extent to which Congress had been altered by the Gandhi family, with independent figures being replaced with personal favourites. The result was a narrow clique that had little connection to party members. On 23 March eighty-one-year-old Morarji Desai became India's first non-Congress prime minister.

When the loose alliance of Janata fell apart Indira Gandhi returned to power in 1980, but by the time of her death in 1984 Congress had become just one of a variety of parties competing for the main ground of Indian politics, along with others representing sectional interests. Rajiv Gandhi, Mrs Gandhi's son and successor, lost the 1989 election with a coalition of the National Front and BJP (the reincarnation of the old BJS) coming to power under V. P. Singh. The dominance of Congress may have created stability in the early decades of independence, but the development of alternatives was crucial to stable democracy. Ensuring that voters had the chance to remove their leaders from power was essential – which made the 1977 ousting of Indira Gandhi such a momentous event.

Other voices have come to the fore in Indian politics in the last two decades, most notably those challenging the right of the educated elite to represent the country as a whole. People like Mayawati, a dalit woman who was elected chief minister of Uttar Pradesh in 1995, explicitly speak for a certain section of the population. While this risks the factionalism that India had previously avoided, this new development has transformed the Indian people's long-held beliefs about authority, and who has the right to govern.

It was Mahatma Gandhi who said that no political system can be created that does not, in the end, depend on people acting well. Democracies need to build institutions that guard against abuse, as well as providing access to power and the ability to bring down leaders. Indian democracy is far from perfect: the system has been manipulated, abused, undermined and patronised. Yet maintaining the unity of the nation while at the same time giving voice to its people has been India's biggest challenge and its greatest achievement.

Like the United States, India has a boundless appetite for the carnival of politics, and a social structure that, in practice, favours parties over factions. Elections are a massive logistical feat, combined with a festival atmosphere and the dramatic tension of a passionate contest. No national party can rely on a single-caste appeal, so they select candidates to suit constituencies with different caste, communal and economic identities; indeed there is evidence that the democratic system is breaking down caste boundaries. Indian democracy depends on strong parties, which are well governed, open to dissent, inclusive and secular. When this is not the case – when parties follow sectional interests – democracy suffers.

Indian parties have been able to give coherence and direction to the vast number of local interests operating in a national forum. In its first decades in power Congress had been quite unlike other parties, allowing open debate on the formulation of policy. While the removal of rulers from power proved difficult, the democratic institutions allowed people to register assent and dissent on government at all levels. The upper house or Rajya Sabha comprises representatives elected by state bodies and gives a powerful voice to the states in the national government. The federal system, where each state has a reasonable degree of autonomy, also allows dissent about regional issues to be handled without threatening the centre. Potentially divisive issues, such as language, have been treated with sensitivity – the creation of new states in Gujarat and Maharastra in 1960 and Haryana in 1966 were a response to language groups' demands for more autonomy. In the early decades a free press forced the state to focus on its main priority: feeding a vast population. In the gradual improvement of many people's living standards, Indians have been able to see the practical benefit of a government answerable to its population.

Having politics as the centre of the nation's life has encouraged able and ambitious people to see politics as a viable, meaningful and prestigious career to pursue, while the military has refrained from interfering in politics. The Civil Service has also remained impartial though public administration is plagued by corruption and stifling bureaucracy; the police, in the words of one analyst, are 'more of a liability to democracy than a support to it'.

India remains a contradiction, particularly in the context of the economic liberalisation of the last twenty years. The country has taken on the trappings of a modern commercial society; with this and with democracy come a host of assumptions that have become embedded in western culture – individual autonomy and rights, freedom of choice, free will – that are not seen as necessary truths within Indian culture. The ways that these values have been adopted are perhaps the greatest achievement of the Indian National Congress. The party embodied these contradictions – its members were Indian people fully aware of their cultural history, yet also familiar with the tenets of western liberalism. In the fifty years from the founding of Congress in the 1880s they debated how liberalism might be applied in their own country; from the 1930s they took the chance to apply these ideas, and it was through the leadership of Gandhi that they then shared their vision with the people of India. But while Gandhi wanted to return to a traditional India, building outwards from the virtues of village life, Nehru saw that an independent India must operate in a world of nation states, each fighting for its share of influence and prosperity, and so must have a strong centre.

India's democracy has continued while many others in Asia have foundered. We have seen some reasons for its endurance in this chapter, but we must acknowledge the limitations of any explanation. The story of democracy in India is thrilling and inspiring; it has shown that democracy can succeed in difficult circumstances, and that it can give millions of people respect and dignity, born from the knowledge that their voice is valued. The reasons for the triumph of Indian democracy did not make its continued existence inevitable, but India has shown the world what is possible.

THE POSTWAR WEST

The Consumer-Citizen

Europe in May 1945 was a devastated continent. Nearly six years of mechanised warfare, including vast artillery bombardment and carpet-bombing of major cities, had reduced the industrial heartland to a wreckage of twisted metal and rubble. Cities like Warsaw, Hamburg, Coventry, Dresden, Plymouth, Leningrad, Caen, Berlin and London had suffered huge amounts of physical damage and horrendous human casualties. Somewhere between eleven million and twenty million people were displaced, with many having no home to return to. Only when the last months of the war revealed the horrors of the Nazi extermination camps did the full scale of Europe's tragedy begin to be understood.

The magnitude of the devastation made decisive action a priority while the division between the victorious powers immediately became apparent. At peace conferences held at Yalta (February 1945) and Potsdam (July 1945) the Soviet Union, the United States and Britain effectively divided Europe into two spheres of influence, with the liberal democracies faced by a communist bloc.

Western Europe was in a state of political uncertainty. The experience of the Weimar years and the 1930s loomed large in the collective memory; there was every possibility that the west of the continent could again become a battleground for extremists. The decisive influence was the attitude of the US government. While the Versailles conference of 1919 had agreed large-scale reparations from the defeated nations, in 1947 the United States agreed a major programme of economic support for the whole of Europe, which became known as the Marshall Plan. The Soviet Union refused the offer of help for itself and on behalf of those countries within its sphere of influence marking a de facto division of political power. The $25 billion of aid granted to Europe between 1945 and 1951 represented around 10 per cent of US annual GDP, a colossal figure.

The United States also sought to stabilise the defeated nations of Germany, Austria and Italy by bringing them into a new military alliance. On 4 April 1949 the North Atlantic Treaty, promising mutual support and military co-operation, was signed and NATO was born. The United States, Canada, Belgium, the Netherlands, Luxembourg, France, Great Britain, Italy, Portugal, Norway, Denmark and Iceland were the founding members, with Greece and Turkey joining in 1952 and West Germany in 1955. In the same year as West Germany's decisive entry, the Warsaw Pact between the Soviet Union, Hungary, Czechoslovakia, Poland, Bulgaria, Romania, Albania and East Germany was signed, signalling not only the formal division of Europe, but the demise of democracy in those countries that had fallen under Soviet influence.

In the meantime western Europe began the task of rebuilding democracy, and this involved limiting the influence of communism. Western European communist parties generally claimed to be in favour of democracy, but despite this the advance of communism was seen by the US and Britain as a major threat. Italy had the strongest communist party and its potential destabilising influence was heightened by the fragility of Italy's existence as a nation: in the early 1950s the Italian language was spoken exclusively by only 20 per cent of the population – most spoke their local dialect – and the great majority did not have a secondary education. Southern Italy was notoriously backward in economic terms with Calabrians, for example, earning just half the national average wage. The war had heightened internal divisions and the north of Italy showed signs of wanting to form a separate state. Massive aid from the United States created the economic conditions necessary for unity around a stable government with a special fund established to aid the south; elections held in June 1946 abolished the monarchy and the constitution of the Italian Republic was agreed the following year.

Of the three main Italian parties – Socialists, Communists and

Christian Democrats – it was the Christian Democrats who dominated the post-war years at national level, while the Socialist and Communist parties controlled the industrial cities in the north; areas of public and civil life were simply carved up between these different political interests. This was not an ideal democratic outcome as voters were often denied a realistic choice between competing parties – the route to power was through internal party struggles rather than open elections; but the central element of the system was that the Christian Democrats kept the communists from achieving national power, and therefore earned the trust of the United States and other Western governments. Nevertheless the Communist Party continued to have popular support – around 34 per cent as late as the 1972 – and was an effective force in local and regional government as well as, many people believe, providing Italy with a vibrant alternative political culture.

How did the other defeated nations fare? The fate of Austria and Germany shows us something that is difficult to explain and would have been impossible to predict: each country seemed to embrace democracy with the determination with which, fifteen years earlier, it had chosen extreme nationalism. In the case of West Germany some intellectuals regretted that consumerism and the search for prosperity blocked any deep political or cultural transformation, but to Germany's neighbours the achievement of building a peaceful country with a high regard for democratic values was admirable. The 1949 election was a close contest between the right of centre Christian Democrat party (CDU) and the SPD. While both parties did not formally accept the division of Germany, the CDU was eager to position Germany within the emerging western block, while the SPD wanted to make the country a neutral buffer between east and west. As West Germans began to feel the material advantages of the western alliance, support for the SPD ebbed dramatically until its revival under a new young leadership in the 1960s. This left CDU leader Konrad Adenauer as the architect of post-war German politics. In many ways he was its embodiment too.

Born in 1876, Adenauer had been a prominent figure in German regional politics between the wars. His ousting as mayor of Cologne in 1933 and his arrest and imprisonment by the Nazis in 1945 gave him enough credibility to win the approval of the Western powers. In keeping with the history of Catholic parties since German unification the CDU, while culturally conservative, was socially progressive, building a welfare system and pursuing an interventionist industrial policy. Co-operation between the state, industry and unions created a form of democratic capitalism that differed dramatically from the American free-market approach. This so-called Rhenish model was a significant development in which the democratic state supported key industries while insisting on the involvement of workers' representatives in the management process. The nation's federal structure meant that power continued to be decentralised with the individual states or *Länder* able to promote their own commercial and industrial revival, much in contrast to the centralised tradition in Britain and France. In order to prevent the instability of the Weimar years, the position of chancellor was made more secure, and the president's role downgraded.

Austria followed a similar path to democracy, though here the post-war period was more painful than in West Germany. Both main political parties in Austria had reason to want to forget the past. The Austrian People's Party had opposed the 1938 *Anschluss*, but under its previous name had staged the 1934 coup that ended Austrian democracy. The Social Democrats, in contrast, had supported the *Anschluss* which was now a source of considerable shame. Austria never did go through a period of public repentance for its crimes as a nation; instead, deeply aware of three communist neighbours on the country's doorstep, the two parties formed a series of coalition governments that brought stability and prosperity.

Almost all the nations of the West had been deprived of democracy through Nazi occupation. The Benelux countries, Norway and Denmark re-established democracy after 1945 while Sweden, which had stayed neutral during the war, and Finland continued as democratic states. Scandinavia entered a long period of centre-left social democracy and stable affluence. The emergence of these countries as the most democratic, on all objective assessments, in the world is noteworthy.[1] In the present day we look on Scandinavia as a model of successful liberalism, but these countries were relatively poor in the nineteenth century, with huge numbers of rural Swedes, for example, leaving for a better life in America. Industrialisation came relatively late, and it is only in the post-war period that prosperity has been continuous. Scandinavia had seen democratic practices and institutions widened and strengthened, along with most of Europe, in the 1920s; after the privations of the immediate post-war period the region entered a virtuous circle whereby increased democracy brought, or at least coincided with, greater wealth. Whether this is the full explanation for the flourishing of democracy is doubtful; we can cite the long tradition of communitarian living, the networks of mutual support (as seen in Amsterdam in Chapter 4) and the customs of citizen involvement as elements in Scandinavian and Dutch culture that reinforce democracy.[2] All these exist elsewhere to some degree, but it is perhaps the coincidence of these cultural factors with prosperity that has cemented democracy so firmly.

Britain experienced a major political change after 1945. The war had exposed millions of voters to the unfairness of the hierarchical society that had survived into the 1940s, while also showing that shared sacrifice had its rewards. The Labour Party offered an alternative based on public ownership of key services and industries, and embarked on the introduction of a National Health Service and extensive welfare provision. The landslide defeat of Winston Churchill in the 1945 election was one of the most significant moments in the country's democratic history: a man possessed of extraordinary charisma who had led the nation to victory was thrown out of office by the electorate.[3] The real triumph here was the persistence of democracy through the operation of parliament. It was a parliamentary debate in May 1940 that had made clear the need for a national leader of Churchill's stature, while the national coalition government under Churchill dissolved itself back into separate parliamentary parties in May 1945, in preparation for the July election. Throughout the war and after, Britain's democracy was able to adapt to the needs of a crisis that could hardly have been more grave.

While Britain's parliamentary system had remained intact throughout the conflict, in France the Fourth Republic was founded out of the wreckage of the war, with a new constitution coming into operation on 13 October 1946. The leaders of the Third Republic were widely held responsible for not only the catastrophic defeat by Germany in 1940 and the widespread collaboration with the Nazis, but the failure to deal with the depression of the 1930s. However, the demise of the Third Republic did not result in the rejection of liberal democracy. The Fourth Republic re-established a parliamentary democracy with a largely ceremonial president. In the elections of November 1946 the Communist Party of France (PCF) won the most seats and entered a coalition government with the Socialist Party (PS) and the Workers' Party (SFIO). The socialist leader Léon Blum led the coalition but in late 1947 the government fell apart and was replaced by a new grouping in which a number of centre-right parties replaced the communists. The participation of the PCF in parliamentary elections and the first coalition allayed many of the fears about French democracy. From 1947 the centre struggled to hold on to a majority in the National Assembly: over the next eleven years there would be twenty-one prime ministers from six different parties. Charles de Gaulle, hero of the liberation of France in 1944, was adamantly opposed to the constitution of the Fourth Republic, advocating a presidential system rather than parliamentary government. Nevertheless the Fourth Republic did set France on a democratic course by offering a credible alternative to the discredited establishment, rebuilding the industrial and economic infrastructure, and taking the first steps to the formation of a European trading alliance, which was to become the EEC and later the EU.

The one area of consistent failure was the country's relations with its colonies. First in Indochina then in Algeria, France tried to retain power in the face of highly motivated and organised nationalist forces. In Algeria, French settlers fought a virtual civil war with Algerian nationalists and, by doing so, exposed the weakness of the French government and of the parliamentary multi-party system. In Algiers in May 1958 a group of French ex-generals, supported by ethnic French settlers, attempted a coup against the colonial power; France itself was at risk of being torn apart. At this time of national crisis an authoritative, unambiguous voice was needed. In June 1958, Charles de Gaulle was persuaded to become head of government and immediately sought powers to bring in a new constitution that would give full executive powers to the president. The constitution of the Fifth Republic became law in October and de Gaulle was elected president by an electoral college in December 1958, for a term of seven years.[4] French democracy had shown itself ready to change in the light of new circumstances, in order to survive.

In March 1946 Winston Churchill had given his famous speech in Fulton, Missouri:

From Stettin in the Baltic to Trieste in the Adriatic an iron curtain has
descended across the continent. Behind that line lie all the capitals of
the ancient states of central and eastern Europe. Warsaw, Berlin, Prague,
Vienna, Budapest, Belgrade, Bucharest and Sofia, all these famous cities
and the populations around them lie in what I must call the Soviet sphere.

The countries of eastern Europe rapidly became authoritarian states
ruled by communist parties supported by the full weight of Soviet
power. Democracy was quashed and any deviation from the correct
path was severely punished, as the world discovered in 1956 with the
crushing of the Hungarian uprising. It was clear what the Hungarian
protestors wanted, as a *Daily Express* reporter witnessed: 'I can hear
the roar of delirious crowds made up of student girls and boys, of
Hungarian soldiers . . . and overalled factory workers marching
through Budapest and shouting defiance against Russia. "Send the
Red Army home," they roar. "We want free and secret elections."'[5]
This was not to happen anywhere in eastern Europe for another
thirty-three years.

In the West, democracy went hand in hand with increasing prosperity and a consensus based on centrist politics, bringing a degree
of complacency to those in high office. This was shaken first by the
social and cultural changes of the 1960s and then by the economic
upheavals of the 1970s. The 1960s showed that open democratic governments, committed to individual rights, could still fail to reflect the
needs of a rapidly changing society. While social changes coursed
through society, governments struggled to keep pace. Laws to legalise
homosexuality and abortion, to make divorce easier and to outlaw
racial and gender discrimination were passed, but often in the teeth
of opposition from an increasingly outmoded ruling elite. This old
guard was gradually pushed aside and the democratic process was
given new energy in the 1960s by a generation of younger leaders
including Willy Brandt, Harold Wilson and Olaf Palme who followed
John F. Kennedy's lead in bringing a more charismatic conversational
style to politics, engaging with citizens through the fast-growing
medium of television. Authority figures could no longer rely on the
respect and deference of their subjects, or of journalists. Instead they
had to be ready to argue their case, and those who could do so with

wit and flair reaped the rewards of communicating directly with millions of voters who wanted leaders like themselves, not stuffy patricians who claimed always to know what was best.

The 1960 US presidential election was the first to carry televised debates between the candidates, and the contrast between a calm, authoritative Kennedy and an uncomfortable Richard Nixon has gone down in political folklore as the deciding factor in the election. That may be an exaggeration, but looking good and sounding right on television has become essential to any modern democratic leader.

Just as important has been the continuing development of a varied and often partisan newspaper market. Press barons have political views and are not afraid to use their newspapers to put pressure on elected governments. But other papers argue for the political views of their readers, at least as they see them, to be heard. A free press is recognised as an essential element in a functioning democracy but allowing the press to do its job without abusing its power is, as with most elements of democracy, a matter of fine judgement based on experience and understanding.

One exception to the style of media-friendly politicians came in France, where the venerable General de Gaulle remained as president from the first day of the new republic. The apparent implacability and social conservatism of the Gaullists – television and radio were state-controlled and discrimination against women was endemic – led to a build-up of pressure for change. In May 1968 radical students found common cause with Renault car-workers and other trade unionists and turned the streets of Paris into a running battleground. At one point de Gaulle travelled to Germany to confer with the army commander in the French zone of occupation about a possible military takeover of France; but Prime Minister Georges Pompidou persuaded de Gaulle, now seventy-eight years old, to dissolve parliament and hold elections in which voters overwhelmingly backed the Gaullists, preferring reform to revolution. However, when de Gaulle put his personal popularity on the line in a referendum the following April, France rejected him.

Events in France in 1968 showed that maintaining a democratic society needed more than the ability to win elections. Being able to call on a majority to vote for you is the route to gaining power, but the exercise of power involves an understanding of those who are opposed to you. The street demonstrations and burning barricades were a sure sign that politics was failing to encompass the conflicts in French society and to give them an open forum. We should recognise some cultural differences here: in France street protests have been part of political life since before 1789, and often represent a serious barrier to government policy (they brought down governments in 1789 and 1848 and came close in 1968). In Germany and Britain, on the other hand, demonstrations have a different history, showing strength of support for an issue but without threatening the government. Extra-parliamentary activity is an essential part of the functioning of a democracy, and any government that restricts the right to protest loses its democratic legitimacy. De Gaulle believed that the demonstrators had gone beyond their right to protest and that he could therefore ignore their demands. It is curious that this most French of leaders so misunderstood French political tradition.

Germany and Italy also experienced political rebellion, though of a different kind. As the 1968 protests in West Germany faded away, student leader Rudi Dutschke called for a 'long march through the institutions' – in other words, the radicals should now turn their attention to entering and changing the political parties and the political process in Germany. Many chose to do this but a few, led by Andreas Baader, Gudrun Ensslin and Ulrike Meinhof were impatient for revolution and chose violence. Initial support for the so-called Baader-Meinhof Gang evaporated when they moved from robbing banks to kidnap and murder. Most of the leaders were captured in 1972 and Baader, Ensslin and Jan-Carl Raspe committed suicide in prison in 1977.

While democracy in West Germany was never seriously threatened by internal terrorism, the picture was different in Italy where left-wing and right-wing groups both turned to violence for political ends. The Brigate Rosse, or Red Brigades, was founded in 1970s by a group of students headed by Renato Curcio. Initially involved in factory sabotage, the group turned to political kidnapping and, in 1974, murdered two members of a neo-fascist party in Padua. A 1975 manifesto declared that the group would 'strike against the heart of the State, because the State is an imperialist collection of multinational corporations'. While using clichéd language, this did show that the age-old struggle for control of the state was continuing, and that political leaders

needed to do more than promote prosperity while manoeuvring themselves into perpetual power. In 1978 the Red Brigades committed their
most spectacular act in kidnapping and then murdering ex-prime
minister and prominent politician Aldo Moro. A year later they
murdered a leading trade unionist thereby alienating their support in
almost every sector of society. In 1980 a neo-fascist group planted a
bomb in the railway station of Bologna – a city known for its left-wing
politics – killing eighty-five people. The war between violent extremists threatened to destabilise the country, with the police regularly
accused of being neo-fascist supporters. In the end popular disgust at
the violence brought the country back from the brink and Italy's
imperfect democracy survived.

Spain and Portugal were the exceptions to the post-war restoration
of democracy in western Europe. In Portugal Antonio Salazar had
come to power in 1932 as part of the right-wing storm sweeping
through the continent; he assumed oppressive powers and developed
a network of secret police that crushed all dissent, as well as keeping
a tight hold of Portugal's imperial possessions. Salazar remained in
office until a brain haemorrhage forced him to step down in 1968. His
successor Marcelo Caetano promised democratic reforms but did not
deliver; he was forced from office in the so-called Carnation Revolution
of 1974 and democracy was instituted. In Spain, General Francisco
Franco held on to to the leadership he had won in the civil war against
the elected republican government in 1939. He died in office in 1975.
The dramatic finale of Spanish authoritarianism came in February
1981, when a group of soldiers attempted a military coup, wishing to
restore a full-blown monarchy to replace the liberal democracy that
had followed Franco's death. On the evening of 23 February, Lt. Col
Antonio Tejero led 200 armed soldiers of the Guardia Civil into parliament and ordered everyone to 'await the arrival of a competent
military authority'. While most members of the Cortes lay on the
floor for their own protection, the minister of defence and the acting
prime minister both stood and ordered the rebels to surrender. At
midnight General Alfonso Armado arrived with orders from King Juan
Carlos: Tejero must surrender. The soldiers ignored Armado, but when
the king broadcast to the nation at 1.15 a.m. he disowned the rebels
and spoke up for the democratic constitution. The coup attempt had
failed and Spain's transition to democracy could continue. Nevertheless

the long persistence of these authoritarian regimes in Portugal and Spain is a notable fact in twentieth-century European history. Their survival was undoubtedly helped by the tolerance of the United States, which was more interested in combating communism than promoting democracy – both countries became members of NATO. Salazar and Franco also showed that the modern state, heavily centralised and with total control over the armed forces and police, could resist any trends towards democracy among its neighbours and in the wider world.

The other south European country with a troubled post-war political path was Greece, which presented the most immediate problem for the West after the end of the war. The communist partisans who had fought throughout the German occupation were not ready to accept the return of the government-in-exile: a fierce civil war began and continued until 1949, when a pro-Western government gained power. The internal divisions remained, with both Western powers and the Greek military paranoid about a communist takeover. In 1965 King Constantine dismissed the government and in the run-up to elections in 1967 there were fears that the United Democratic Left (an alleged cover for the illegal communist party) would become part of the new government. This was the pretext for a military coup which began the so-called Rule of the Colonels – an oppressive regime which suspended political parties, freedom of the press and all civil liberties. Torture of political activists and opponents became widespread. Democracy was finally restored in 1975.

While the nations of Western Europe and their political leaders were rebuilding their societies, moves were also being made to create a supra-national body. The rivalry and hatred between France and Germany had infected Europe and European politics for centuries through a chain of conflicts from the Napoleonic and Franco-Prussian wars of the nineteenth century, to the two world wars of the twentieth. The French politician Robert Schuman had experienced this first-hand: his parents were French citizens living in Lorraine which was annexed by the German Empire in 1871. Schuman was born a German citizen and studied at schools and universities in Luxembourg, Munich, Berlin and Strasbourg. When Alsace-Lorraine was returned to France in 1918 he became a French citizen and in the Second World War fought in the Resistance, was arrested by the

Gestapo and narrowly avoided being sent to Dachau. When Schuman became French prime minister in 1947 he immediately sought ways of ending the spiral of violence and hatred, and was the driving force behind the Council of Europe, set up in 1949 to monitor the provision of fundamental freedoms within the boundaries of Europe. But Schuman had a vision of further co-operation, particularly in economic and industrial matters. In 1950 a group of countries signed the Schuman Declaration, agreeing to co-operate in the production of steel and coal; from this evolved the EEC, with six original members – France, Germany, Belgium, the Netherlands, Luxembourg and Italy – formally joined together in 1957 by the Treaty of Rome.

The economic community expanded over the decades: Denmark, Ireland and Britain joined in 1973, Greece, Spain and Portugal in the 1980s, Austria, Finland and Sweden in 1995, and countries from eastern Europe in the following decade. In 1993 this economic union took a significant step when, in the Maastricht Treaty, the members agreed to work towards 'an ever closer union among the peoples of Europe', and to implement a common currency (with some countries opting out of this provision). While the EU is a body comprised of fully democratic states, the democratic credentials of the body itself have always been the subject of fierce debate. The power of the elected European Parliament to oversee the workings of the appointed Commission have been strengthened in response to public concerns, but there will always be tensions. Citizens of Europe want the EU to be more accountable but worry that an elected president, for example, would be too powerful. Yet the existence of the EU has seen the prosperity of its member states increase to the point where today's Europeans are the wealthiest generation in human history.

While Western Europe benefited massively from the protection and financial support of the United States after the war, America itself experienced an extraordinary economic boom. The US economy trebled in size between 1940 and 1950 and, thanks to GI bonds, returning servicemen had dollars to spend on retraining and consumer goods, while a sense of optimism gave companies the confidence to invest in increased capacity. The United States became extremely wealthy: GDP per capita remained more than double that of major European countries throughout the late 1940s and the 1950s. In 1959 there were more cars in the United States than in the whole of the rest of the world. The war also ended with US forces in control of many areas across the globe, from western Europe to South-East Asia, the Pacific islands and Japan. The United States president was the undisputed leader of the free world. But there were two worms in the wholesome apple of this free and prosperous country, and each of them weighed against its credentials as a freedom-loving democracy. The first was virulent anti-communism; the second, the legalised segregation and denigration of black citizens.

President Harry Truman's place in democratic history rests on two conflicting episodes. He carried through the Marshall Plan, and promoted and sustained democracy in the defeated countries of the Axis powers. At the same time, Truman fell victim to the red-baiting whose legacy still haunts and hobbles the American democratic system. After assuming power in 1944 on the death of Franklin Roosevelt, Truman led the Democratic Party to heavy defeat in the 1946 mid-term elections. The Republicans took both houses of Congress and the president was widely assumed to be a lame duck. He then threw a lot of energy into persuading America and a hostile Congress to accept the Marshall Plan; but in order to do that, Truman, together with Secretary of State George Marshall and Assistant Secretary Dean Acheson, had to sell the plan as the best way to save Europe from communism, rather than as a way of boosting economic recovery. This encouraged those members of Congress who had begun to see anti-communism as a good way to win votes to become more strident.

Though anti-communist hysteria reached its peak in the early 1950s, the notorious House of Representatives Committee on Un-American Activities began its work well before then. In March 1947 the committee announced its intention of holding 'a secret investigation of Communism in motion pictures'. Why they started with Hollywood remains something of a mystery but, after hearing from a series of 'friendly witnesses', the committee subpoenaed nineteen who were suspected of links with the Communist Party; eleven of these took the stand. One was the German dramatist Bertolt Brecht, who returned to Europe the following day; the other ten included the director Edward Dmytryk, the producer Adrian Scott and the writers Ring Lardner Jr and Dalton Trumbo. These so-called Hollywod Ten were imprisoned for contempt after they refused to answer whether they were members of the Screen Writers' Guild or the Communist Party. At the hearing Trumbo asked the committee's permission to read a statement. This was refused but the statement is a powerful defence of democracy and artistic independence, ending with the warning: 'You have produced a capital city on the eve of its Reichstag fire. For those who remember German history in the autumn of 1932, there is the smell of smoke in this very room.'[6]

Truman's shock victory in the 1948 presidential election – the Democrats also regained Congress – might have reversed this situation but in fact the hysteria got worse. In 1949 the Soviets exploded an atomic bomb and the communists led by Mao Zedong took power in China. Then in January 1950 a state department official, Alger Hiss, was found to be in the pay of the Soviet Union. These events and the behaviour of those who capitalised on them led to years of paranoia and persecution which had a profound and lasting effect on America. Though the American people eventually recovered their senses – and their sense of justice – the American government never quite did. This was mainly due to the work of Joseph McCarthy who, not content with persecuting individuals, took on the government itself.

An undistinguished senator from Wisconsin, McCarthy became famous overnight when, in February 1950, he claimed in a speech that he had a list of communists working as a spy ring in the State Department who were 'known to the Secretary of State'. The claim was never substantiated but was followed by similar allegations about Voice of America, the United States army and the Truman administration. Money flowed in to McCarthy's campaign and he won re-election to the Senate. Through the House Un-American Activities Committee the democratically elected government, along with thousands of citizens, found itself badgered and demoralised at every turn. The result was a paralysis of American political and cultural life.

At the same time, the United States was expanding from an industrial giant to a world superpower. The need to combat Soviet influence was a major element in America's global reach as it sought to limit the spread of communism around the world. The 'loss' of China in 1949 was held against Truman by his political enemies, and the US government had to avoid a similar situation developing elsewhere. The defence industries and the military now became the beneficiaries of extraordinary largesse from the federal government. This, together with the rapid development of civil aviation, also changed the economic geography of the country. The West Coast, Washington state, the south-west and, in particular, California gained massively from federal investment in research and development, infrastructure, equipment, training, real estate and manpower. The sunbelt became the power house of hi-tech defence, while the rust belt of the industrial north-east would soon begin to wither away.

The effect on politics in Washington was profound. In 1961 President Eisenhower, who knew the military better than most, warned in his farewell speech of the dangers of the military-industrial complex. By then it was too late. The federal government was under continual pressure from defence and other industrial lobbyists, their clients giving vast sums of money to political campaigns. Even upright Congress members were under pressure to bring jobs and investment to their constituents. In all of this the insidious taint of McCarthyism remained, even when he had been exposed as a hypocrite: it was somehow unpatriotic to reduce military spending or to seek peaceful resolutions to conflicts. Populist politicians bundled this up with providing welfare, or taxing the rich, as a sign of weakness and therefore being un-American.

As a global superpower the United States became a major factor in the political destinies of smaller nations, and therefore in the history of democracy. In the first major conflict after 1945, America led a United Nations force in support of south Korea against Chinese-backed communist troops from the north. Once the Korean War (1950–3) had been fought to a standstill and the spread of communism in East Asia halted, at least temporarily, the US acted elsewhere in the world to protect its national interests, often through subterfuge. The strategy was based on the firm belief that the Soviet Union had total control over the communist world, including China, and that Stalin, like his US counterparts, viewed the world as a chessboard in which individual states could be won or lost to the cause. The installation of communist regimes in Czechoslovakia in 1948 and China in 1949 seemed clear evidence of this. Signs of incipient communism, real or reported, in any nation were enough to send the State Department and the CIA into destructive action.

The first tangible effect of the CIA's new role was the organising of a coup in Iran in 1953, at the request of their ally Great Britain. Iran had a history of constitutional governments struggling against the power of the autocratic shahs. In 1951 parliament chose Mohammad Mossadegh, a popular national figure, as prime minister. The shah, although concerned about Mossadegh's growing power, had no choice but to confirm his appointment. The new government nationalised much of the British-owned oil industry and through emergency powers Mossadegh brought in democratic reforms, restricting the power of the shah and reforming land ownership. All of this brought enemies at home, but particularly overseas in the form of Britain and its secret service. The British were too weak to act alone and sought help from the United States who, through the CIA, funded and supported Mossadegh's internal enemies leading to his arrest for treason. The shah's autocratic position was restored. By the time of the coup there was little doubt that Mossadegh had, through a series of emergency measures, extended his power beyond his democratic mandate – but how far this was made necessary by Britain's destructive influence is open to argument. While his actions were hostile to Britain's commercial interests, Mossadegh was not a communist, as Churchill argued; he was in fact both a supporter of the shah and an admirer of the United States. The coup became a leitmotif for American intervention in the Middle East, where democracy with all its inconvenient outcomes was crushed in favour of compliance.

The same pattern was followed, with similar results, in Latin America. In 1954 the CIA organised a military coup in Guatemala that removed the elected government of Jacobo Arbenz Guzmán. Until 1944 the country had been ruled by a military regime that encouraged foreign investment; as a result the United Fruit Company, based in the United States, ploughed money into Guatemala, buying controlling shares in its transport and utilities. Subsequently civilian governments began to take more control of the country, bringing in labour protection and expanding state ownership of the infrastructure. Guzmán, who was elected in 1950, extended this process, including the acquisition of vast holdings of uncultivated land owned by the United Fruit Company. Alan Dulles, director of the CIA, had formerly been on the board of the UFC, while his brother John Foster Dulles, Secretary of State, was a shareholder. Lobbying by the UFC soon convinced the US government that there was a danger of communism gaining a foothold in the Americas.

In June 1954 Castillo Armas led a coup against Guzmán supported by American ships and planes. Guatemalan democracy had been strangled in its early years. Armas' incompetent and corrupt government was the beginning of a long period in which a succession of military regimes fought against insurgents demanding political rights. The toll of decades of political conflict is estimated at between 140,000 and 250,000 Guatemalans dead or disappeared, in a country of thirteen million people. Only in 1993 was democracy restored.

Guatemala set the pattern for interventions by the United States in the affairs of Latin America. The freedoms that were so valued and trumpeted by the government and citizens of the world's major democratic power were routinely and deliberately destroyed in what became known as 'Uncle Sam's backyard'. Why did the leading nation of the free world become such a destructive force in the history of democracy?

One answer of course lies in the strategic battle with communism, the great chess game played out across the globe in which countries were pawns to be grabbed and held no matter what. From the 1960s to the 1980s a series of nations were caught up in the struggle between the Soviet Union and the United States, each seeking to extend their sphere of influence. The resulting internal polarisation in these countries proved fatal to the development of democracy. Chile had had a long period of restricted democracy in which a small group held on to the strings of power, interrupted by temporary military takeovers. The election of a reforming president, Eduardo Frei Montalva, in 1964 brought in a period of social change, with the state providing education, housing and rights for agricultural workers, but the underlying divisions in the country were exposed following the election of the socialist Salvador Allende in 1970. Allende was no puppet of the Soviet Union. He had criticised the Soviets over the invasions of Hungary and Czechoslovakia, and trade with Russia did not increase during his time in office; in fact when he went to Moscow in 1972 in search of more financial support he was turned down. Nevertheless his political programme was avowedly socialist, including nationalisation of the copper industry, Chile's most lucrative exporter. Support from the United States was subsequently cut off and in 1973, with the economy in crisis, the CIA backed a military coup led by Augusto Pinochet. The coup remains the most incendiary of the US interventions in Latin America because of the state terror inflicted by Pinochet on socialists, trade unionists and anyone suspected of political opposition. Thousands of Chileans fled into exile bringing with them first-hand reports of mass torture and murder. Whatever Allende's failings, the horrors of the Pinochet years stood as a lasting rebuke to US intervention.

In some countries the United States intervened overtly, in others covertly by giving tacit support to regimes that promoted themselves as anti-communist, and were prepared to allow US corporations free rein. Latin America now became a byword for military dictatorships. In several countries, armed guerrilla movements – some right wing, some Marxist – fought wars of subversion against the authorities. In El Salvador in the 1980s the conflict descended into civil war with each side backed by foreign powers; in Bolivia and Colombia the inability of the state to control its own territory led to the rise of criminal cartels with extraordinary power.

While the United States was using military, financial and covert powers to protect its interests, the Soviet Union was doing the same. Those who look back to the Cold War as a time of stability need to remember that democracy was the victim of the stand-off between East and West. This depressing pattern continued into the 1990s, when the collapse of communism ushered in a new era of geopolitics.

Apart from the struggle against communism there was another reason why the United States and its Western allies often worked against democracy in the rest of the world. Industrialists and corporations in America, Britain, France, Germany and Italy who produced goods and commodities at low costs in poor countries, and then sold them in the wealthy First World, were making fortunes. Corporations had little interest in developing the economies or political systems of these countries. Indeed, democracies that elected leaders with a popular mandate to take greater control of the country's affairs, to develop local industries and increase prosperity, were perceived as a real threat to the interests of these companies. It was far easier to deal with an autocratic regime that could be corruptly enriched while suppressing the demands of the general population. And so long as Western governments, predominantly the United States, saw the interests of its corporations as identical with the interests of the nation, democracy was unlikely to be allowed to flourish in the developing world. Nor did this strategy benefit Americans themselves. Corporations relocated manufacturing to places where there was cheap labour with little concern for the fate of their former workers. The hollowing out of the great American cities followed as blue-collar jobs disappeared and inner cities became industrial wastelands. While the GDP of the United States grew, the wages of blue-collar workers in real terms fell steadily.

Inside the United States another political story was unfolding. Montgomery, Alabama, in common with other towns and cities in the American South, had legalised racial segregation. Legend has it that, at the end of the working day on 1 December 1955 Rosa Parks was too tired to move out of her seat to make way for a white man. In fact, as she later said, she was tired of the mistreatment handed out to her and other black people. Rosa Parks was not the first black person to make this kind of protest but she was in the right place at the right time.[7] Segregation was America's dirty secret.

The continuation of segregation after the Civil War was a malign outcome of Washington two-party politics. The uncertain outcome of the 1876 presidential election, in which twenty crucial electoral college votes were disputed, led to a deal wherein the Democrats allowed the Republican Rutherford Hayes to take the presidency in return for the withdrawal of federal troops from the South and an effective free hand for Southern states in their treatment of black citizens. From that time on every administration in Washington relied for its survival on the support of Southern Democrats.

What made Rosa Parks' protest so significant was the support she rapidly gained from other black activists in Montgomery. When her case came to trial, a local preacher named Martin Luther King helped to organise a black boycott of the Montgomery public transit system. A year later the Supreme Court ruled that the segregation of buses in Alabama was illegal. African Americans made up around 20 per cent of the population of the United States. By the 1960s in every country in the free world, discrimination on grounds of skin colour was not only illegal but generally considered immoral and backward (South Africa and Rhodesia were the pariah exceptions); yet in the South of the United States blacks were not only barred from public places and facilities, they were, through a series of arcane rules, effectively prevented from voting. Before 1965 only 383 out of 15,000 African Americans of voting age were registered to vote in Dallas County, Alabama. In Wilcox County none of the eligible 6,085 African Americans were registered – while 2,959 whites out of a total white population of only 2,647 were registered to vote! In the protests against segregation in the 1960s, political rights were not eventually handed down from on high by far-sighted people of power and influence who had been convinced by rational argument; they were won by sheer persistence, hard work, organisation, passionate belief and overwhelming courage in the face of murderous intimidation.

America's dirty secret was exposed as photographers and TV crews showed a watching world the brutality of the police and the quiet courage of protestors. The federal government understood that it had to act. African Americans were escorted by federal troops through hostile crowds into previously segregated colleges, laws were passed to outlaw discrimination and rules that disenfranchised blacks were swept away with the 24th Amendment to the Constitution and the Voting Rights Act of 1965. Nevertheless for African Americans in the South, voting would never be easy. Black politicians emerged as mayors and congressmen but African Americans had to be persuaded, after decades of discrimination, that they were voting for something that was meaningful to their lives. The scenes in Florida in the 2000 presidential election, when thousands of black people were prevented from voting through bureaucratic 'error', only served to confirm this feeling. It has, perhaps, taken the election of an African American president to make African Americans feel fully enfranchised.

The black civil rights movement in the United States coincided with the winning of political rights by tens of millions across Africa and Asia. As European nations divested themselves of their colonies, a host of new nations were born. Most of them, as we shall now see, began their lives as democracies.

DEMOCRACY AND DECOLONISATION

The Exploited Citizen

On 6 March 1957, British Prime Minister Harold Macmillan, together with the Duchess of Kent and Dr Kwame Nkrumah, gathered in Accra to oversee the birth of a new country. In an elaborate series of ceremonies the old Gold Coast Legislative Assembly was closed at midnight, and the new parliament of Ghana opened for business next day. Ghana became an independent democracy and, even though it initially retained the British queen as head of state, in 1960 it declared itself a republic. In the 1950s the democratic world greeted the prospect of new independent democracies springing up across the African continent – the whole non-communist world was, it seemed, ready to embrace democracy.

Ghana was the first of Britain's colonies in sub-Saharan Africa to gain independence, and 1957 is often taken to mark the beginning of decolonisation. The picture is more complicated, however, and we need to take into account in particular what happened the previous year in Egypt. But before looking in detail at certain individual countries we should acknowledge that each nation in Africa had a different experience of both colonisation and decolonisation, with widely varying patterns of exploitation, liberation and independence. Most have subsequently gone through at least one period of democracy, but for some, democracy has been tried and failed many times over.

After several decades of political and financial control by Britain, including a period as a protectorate, Egypt was granted nominal independence in 1922. The country was a monarchy, but the British high commissioner remained the power behind the throne. Britain had formal power over the one million foreign residents, over foreign affairs and security, and over the Suez Canal. Most importantly, Britain retained control over Egyptian cotton production, ensuring that raw cotton was supplied direct to the mills of Lancashire. By 1952 elements of the Egyptian army had become impatient with the autocratic rule of King Farouk and the continuing British dominance of Egypt. A group known as the Free Officers seized power on 22 July in a bloodless coup, with the intention of setting up a parliamentary democracy; as elsewhere in Africa, it was a group of nationalists outside the structures of government rather than the established Egyptian political elite who took power. The democracy never came to pass. After Gamal Nasser emerged victorious from a deadly power struggle among the officers, the new constitution, agreed in January 1956, allowed for a single party to select a candidate for president, who was then approved by a popular vote.[1]

In common with many ex-colonies, Egypt saw the urgent need to develop an industrial and manufacturing economy: cotton should be made into finished products in Egypt, not Lancashire. The industrial plan involved building a huge dam across the Nile to supply power and to regulate the river. However, raising capital for the project proved almost impossible, and the new government turned to its only assured source of revenue, the Suez Canal. The nationalisation of the canal was carried out with financial probity but was unacceptable to the British. Prime Minister Anthony Eden plotted in secret with the French prime minister, Guy Mollet, to concoct a pretext for an invasion of Egypt, to retake the canal and install a more friendly government.

On 29 October 1956 Israel invaded the Sinai desert; the ensuing hostilities allowed Britain and France to intervene as peacemakers and protectors of the canal. While the invasions were successful in military terms, they were a political catastrophe. At almost the same time the Soviet Union had invaded Hungary to crush political dissent; to the wider world, and to President Eisenhower in particular, the Anglo-French action was indefensible. He threatened to sell US holdings of Britain's currency – which would have spelt disaster – while other allies even proposed expelling Britain and France from NATO. A ceasefire and withdrawal were agreed and within months Eden was replaced by Harold Macmillan, who was to oversee the decolonisation of British Africa.

The lesson for Britain and France, and for their African colonies was, or should have been, threefold. First, power had shifted to the United States with the Soviet Union as the only other global power. The United States was avowedly against the continuation of imperialism, and Britain and France needed to find ways of giving true independence to their colonies. The second lesson was that when power is won through military struggle it is difficult for genuinely democratic government to emerge. Control of the army gives control of the state, and control of the state gives control of everything – including the constitution. Thirdly, the transition from supplying agricultural produce to making industrial goods was a massive and, for most African countries, an impossible task. The industrialised nations were intent on protecting their own interests and excluding competition. For all the fine words about development, African countries have found entry into the modern industrial world continuously blocked.

Nationalists across Africa were inspired by Nasser's boldness and vision and by the real possibility of freedom from their colonial masters. In the 1950s a wave of young African activists emerged, including Kwame Nkrumah and Nelson Mandela, to stand alongside Nehru and Martin Luther King as champions of non-European peoples. In the decade after Suez almost every remaining colony in Africa gained independence.

In the 1950s the Gold Coast was, in many ways, an ideal British colony. Its cocoa and bauxite production brought in export earnings, while a settled level of prosperity had allowed the development of schools providing a basic education in English and the founding of a university. With only a small number of European settlers, Ghanaians occupied senior-level posts in the administration with some winning seats on local and colonial councils. The cocoa business was owned and run by Ghanaians and a middle class of professionals and business leaders took seriously the potential that the future offered.

The Gold Coast had, along with other parts of West Africa, been developed as a coastal colony, with the port of Accra used to ship hardwoods, cocoa, bauxite and other minerals out to Britain. The British set up a constitutional convention in the late 1940s, which recommended a democracy with a franchise limited by earnings and property. In calculated opposition to this proposal the activist Kwame Nkrumah organised a self-styled People's Assembly, which proposed a universal franchise and a second chamber consisting of traditional chiefs. When in 1951 Britain was forced by international pressure to agree to elections under universal franchise, Nkrumah won a landslide and was asked by the British Governor General to form a government. It was widely recognised that self-government was a step towards independence, and in 1957 Nkrumah declared full independence within the British Commonwealth. In 1960 he brought in a republican constitution which, by replacing the British queen as head of state, broke formal connections to the former colonial masters.

By this time adherence to democracy had been replaced by the more abstract goals of national achievement and pan-Africanism. Nkrumah's own background and personality was instrumental in this. In his time as a student in London in 1945 Nkrumah had, in contrast to Nehru's patrician experience of Harrow and Cambridge, lived in cheap lodgings and had argued politics with African students, none of whom had any real expectation of gaining power in their own countries. Nevertheless, in the 1950s two of the poorest countries in the world – Russia and China – had transformed themselves through Marxist politics into nations that were respected and feared. Some began to ask: why should the same not happen for Africa?

When Nkrumah returned to the Gold Coast in 1947 he brought with him a Marxist ideology and personal ambition, along with a strong African sense of group loyalty. As in the Soviet Union and China, a small group of people who had worked together in the early years were to be rewarded with high office. In Ghana and elsewhere a self-styled vanguard of pioneers saw themselves as the makers of a great future against all the odds. This was a different type of party politics, in which the party became a self-serving clique whose own goals took precedence over everything else. Nkrumah's governing party, the CPP, began as a Western-style party but it came to resemble a clan structure in which loyalty to the head and to the party became more important than the task of governing the country. Parties became the obstacles to the reforms they were supposed to introduce.

For similar reasons, Ghana and other ex-colonies changed from a parliamentary to a presidential system of government. British parliamentary politics had a long tradition of robust debate, often based on mocking your opponent. This did not work in cultures where respect for those who are placed in authority is what holds the social system in place. In African culture, figures in authority are restrained through social forces which amount to a sophisticated means of allowing and checking power. This is hard to replicate in a Western system which grants massive formal powers to elected leaders.

The Ghanaian republican constitution gave immense powers to the president, including the appointment and dismissal of judges, civil servants and military leaders, as well as making him commander-in-chief of the armed forces. The opposition MP, Victor Owusu, argued that the new constitution could have been written in one sentence: that 'the President shall be responsible for the running of the government, for the dispensation of justice, and for the making of laws in Ghana.'[2] Of the twelve opposition members who voted against the new constitution, eleven were later imprisoned.

Like Egypt, Ghana saw industrialisation as the key to prosperity and it too needed a dam to provide hydroelectric power for industrialisation. But although the Akosombo dam was built, the foreign contractors who extracted bauxite refused to process it on site; instead it continued to be shipped to North America and Europe for manufacture, giving Ghana a minute margin on its own natural resource. Like so many other African countries Ghana seemed doomed to be an exporter of commodities rather than a manufacturer. Worse still, the loans to finance the dam were repaid by raising taxes on cocoa producers, putting the country's prime resource at risk.

Even before becoming a virtual dictator Nkrumah had introduced measures allowing the government to imprison without trial anyone accused of treason; strikes were also outlawed as he urged trade unions to motivate workers rather than campaign for their rights. It was an offence for anyone 'to show disrespect to the person and dignity of the head of state.' The result was predictable: nobody was prepared to question or criticise the government. Nkrumah shared Nasser's socialist principles, which made Ghana unattractive to American investors, and he was forced to move closer to the Soviet Union. Investment from the West dwindled and the economy suffered. In 1964 Nkrumah put forward further amendments to the constitution which made him president for life and the CPP the only legally permitted political party. Democracy had been officially laid to rest.

These developments beg the question of how the rest of the country, and in particular its parliament, allowed democracy to be sidelined so easily. Members of parliament were mostly from the middle classes – teachers, building contractors, shopkeepers, clerks and farmers. Industrial and commercial concerns were not well represented, neither were workers, while the MPs owed their good fortune and large salaries to the patronage of the CPP. Nevertheless, the Assembly did debate controversial matters openly and its committees, including a vigorous public accounts committee, did question ministers about their behaviour, but without questioning government policy itself. Discussions within the Assembly were tolerated by Nkrumah because they kept his ministers in line, without affecting his own power.

One further aspect of the withering of democracy in Ghana, and which has wider relevance, has been explored by the historian Trevor Jones. As in other former British colonies, English was the language of government and of the law, and also of political debate; but people going about their daily lives spoke Dangme, Nzema and Ewe, or any other of the nine major languages in Ghana. Indigenous languages were and are the tools of normal living, while English became the language of abstraction, a product and a tool of political separation, an anti-democratic device used by government ministers to obscure and conceal the real state of the country. This tendency is endemic in established democracies but is most obvious where the language of authority is different from the language of life.

In 1966, while on a state visit to China and North Vietnam, Nkrumah was removed from power in a military coup said to have been backed by the CIA. He never returned to Ghana and lived in exile in Guinea until his death in 1972. His rise and fall mirrors that of other charismatic African leaders, and he remains a heroic figure to many because of his belief in African unity. He was inspired by the belief that Africa could come together as a single entity, but his enthusiastic vision was not matched by the desire to nurture a pluralist democracy in his own country. Democracy was devised to give Ghana the legitimacy it required for independence and to give Nkrumah the authority to rule; once that authority had been established, democracy withered away.

There were mitigating factors of course. Nkrumah's vision of an industrialised economy had been hopelessly optimistic but was in tune with the times. The world expected the ex-colonies to 'develop' while at the same time the economic policies of wealthy industrial countries effectively ensured that countries like Ghana remained in relative poverty while producing cheap commodities.

A more complex reason for the failure of democracy in Ghana and elsewhere is the legacy of colonial exploitation. We saw in Chapter 11 how India was governed in the years before independence and on the surface Ghana seems to have had the same advantages, with Ghanaians holding administrative posts in the colonial regime. But there were important differences. The British rule in Ghana was purely exploitative, plundering the country for its natural resources and, while in India the British had fitted into an existing governing system, in Africa they imported their own alien political and administrative culture. In addition, some argue that Britain deliberately slowed the development of a well-educated class of African citizens, learned from the lessons of India and discouraged the spread of political ideas. In fact Britain set up so-called Government Colleges in several ex-colonies, including Nigeria, to teach the art and science of administration – although critics maintain that these colleges simply trained Africans to think like Europeans rather than develop new ways of governance more appropriate to Africa.

Many post-colonial African leaders simply followed the colonial powers by exploiting the wealth of their own countries after their industrial ambitions were frustrated, but does this explain their indifference to democracy? Here we need to understand how much was at stake for these leaders. Having led their countries into independence they had little option but to cling on to power – the alternative was to lose everything. In Ghana and other countries the notion of a loyal opposition – that is, a political system in which parties win and lose power but always live to fight another day – was unknown. In addition the concept of political parties, so beneficial in the United States and later in Europe, was the bane of African politics. There each party became associated with an ethnic group while the tradition of party discipline and loyalty to the leader turned parties into vehicles for corruption and megalomania. African respect for kinship and patronage makes a Western-style system difficult to operate. In addition, the colonial powers bequeathed a toxic institution that ill-fitted the indigenous culture: the modern centralised state, with its monopoly of power, its control of the military and its vulnerability to takeover by small groups, made every African country a candidate for instability.

After Nkrumah's exit there followed fifteen years of military dictatorships and two more constitutions before Jerry Rawlings, a flight sergeant in the Ghanaian air force, came to power in 1981. After suspending the defunct constitution, Rawlings ruled as a virtual dictator until 1992 when he introduced a new constitution and called elections. He was elected president in 1992 and 1996, before giving way to a new president in 2000.

The situation of some other African countries was complicated by large numbers of European settlers who resisted the handover of power to the indigenous people. The interior of Kenya had been 'discovered' in the nineteenth century by British pioneers wanting to control the headwaters of the Nile. Settlers began to farm the fertile highlands, assisted by a colonial government that helped them drive Africans off their lands and force them to work on the colonial estates. Asian traders who had worked on the coast for centuries were moved to the interior to provide services in the growing city of Nairobi. Kenya became a highly prized colony, offering British settlers a lavish lifestyle in a beautiful setting, while producing crops for the home market. Some Kenyans sought to take advantage of the opportunities opened up by the imperial markets, and it was the frustrations of this aspirational group that sparked the Mau Mau rebellion of the 1950s. In the end the British found in Jomo Kenyatta, a man they had previously imprisoned, a figure who could unite the different interests and give assurance to British farmers. After lengthy negotiations, elections in May 1963 saw Kenyatta become the first prime minister of an independent Kenya. His party, KANU, effectively represented the majority Kikuyu people, guaranteeing him a permanent majority. Though Kenyatta was seen as a political moderate he too amended the constitution to give himself increasing powers. In 1964 Kenya was made a republic with Kenyatta as its president and head of government with control over the armed forces. The main opposition party was merged with KANU, and in the 1969 elections all other parties were banned and their leaders arrested. Kenyatta won uncontested presidential elections in 1970 and 1974 and died in office in 1978.

In southern Africa Britain tried to ease the path to independence by creating a federal structure comprising Northern Rhodesia (Zambia), Southern Rhodesia (Rhodesia, later Zimbabwe) and Nyasaland (Malawi). The idea was to combine the labour resources of Malawi with the minerals of Zambia and the farming wealth of Rhodesia in an interdependent triangle that would be controlled by the quarter of a million white farmers of Rhodesia. But the federation fell apart as its imbalance was exposed. Malawi broke away in 1959 and Britain was forced to grant the small country independence. Zambia was also granted independence but its copper mines continued to be controlled from South Africa; the royalties paid to the Zambian government were paltry. In Rhodesia, moves towards independence with equality for all were resisted by the large white population. In 1965 the white Rhodesia Front made a Unilateral Declaration of Independence and set up an exclusively white government. A long war of liberation ended in 1980 when Robert Mugabe was elected prime minister. The new constitution reserved some seats for whites, but politics were dominated by Mugabe's ZANU PF party. Here too political parties were formed along ethnic lines with the Ndebele minority kept out of power at every level. A similar divide plagued the Portuguese ex-colonies of Mozambique and Angola, as well as Zaire, where civil wars supported by outside interests devastated these potentially prosperous countries for decades. New African countries became pawns in the global chess game of the Cold War, with the Soviet Union and the West supporting those who served their interests. In some states, like Kenya or Tanzania, that support enabled one person or group to remain permanently in power; in others, such as Angola or Zaire, it meant that different factions could fight long wars using prodigious amounts of Soviet or American equipment. Either way, democracy was the victim.

The continent's wealthiest country was to have the most protracted transition to a democratic system of government. The formation of the Union of South Africa in 1909 paved the way for its status as a British dominion; in 1910 the South Africa Act enfranchised whites and gave them political power over all other races. Black Africans could not own or rent land outside designated areas. In 1948 the National Party took office and brought in a policy of separation between the races, known to the world from its Afrikaans name of apartheid. In 1960 Harold Macmillan told the South African parliament of a 'wind of change blowing through the continent of Africa' and advised them to begin making overtures to black Africans. A few months later the Pan-Africanist Congress organised a march at Sharpeville where police fired on the demonstrators, killing sixty-nine people. The white security forces were given almost unlimited powers and black activists, including members of the African National Congress (ANC) like Walter Sisulu, Nelson Mandela and Steve Biko were arrested, tortured, murdered or imprisoned.

In the 1970s a stalled economy left many young black people without work. Schoolchildren in Soweto rioted when they were threatened with education only in Afrikaans – as well as this being the language of their oppressors, they argued that they needed English to get jobs. Pressure from the outside world during the 1970s came to nothing, and in the 1980s highly conservative governments in both Britain and the United States had little interest in imposing sanctions on the white supremacists in Pretoria. But as the South African economy began to crumble, global industrialists started to use their muscle in favour of change. In September 1985 Gavin Relly, chairman of the mining company Anglo-American Corporation, led a group of South African industrialists to Lusaka to meet Oliver Tambo and other ANC leaders.

With the end of the Cold War in 1989, any reason for supporting the South African regime as a bulwark against communism came to an end; for the United States in particular, South Africa became an embarrassment, its avowedly racist system an affront to democratic countries and their leaders. In August 1989 President F. W. de Klerk replaced P. W. Botha and, realising that the country was on the verge of collapse, began making overtures to black organisations – first to the Inkatha Freedom Party representing Zulus and then, inevitably, the ANC and its leader Nelson Mandela. By now the struggle against apartheid attracted global attention and the world watched on television as Nelson Mandela walked free from jail after twenty-seven years' imprisonment. Mandela's management of the transfer of power from the apartheid regime to the democratic majority was masterful and in May 1994 he was elected president under the new democratic constitution. Though other parties have emerged since, the ANC remains in control of the political process; the most dramatic transfer of power has been within the ANC itself, when President Tabo Mbeki was ousted as leader in December 2007, to be replaced by Jacob Zuma, who became the country's leader at the next election in 2009. South Africa was the last country in Africa to be returned to its indigenous people.

Since decolonisation the African continent has seen a continual struggle against economic adversity, civil conflict, outside interference and, above all, poverty. The birth of the new nations coincided with European post-war economic growth, which had to be fuelled by more and more imports of commodities. As David Birmingham has written: 'The large bank reserves of colonial Ghana were not used to pipe water to African villages but for metropolitan construction, and the groundnut plantations of Tanzania were not aimed at enriching the farming poor in Africa but at providing margarine rations in the British welfare state.'[3]

In that sense, once the colonial powers no longer had any obligation to look after their subjects, they could exploit them more freely. Partly as a consequence, the economic position of most African countries went through an alarming decline in real and relative terms. In 1960 Ghana was ranked 64th in the world by GDP; by 2000 it had fallen to 112th. In the period from 1960 to 2006 GDP per capita had increased in Ghana from $170 to $573, and in Nigeria from $99 to $792, increases of around 3.5 and 8 times respectively. Over the same period, GDP per capita in Greece rose from $487 to $21,000, and in Italy from $804 to $31,500, increases of around 43 and 38 times. When we remember the massive retreat in democracy in the West in the 1930s, caused in large part by the depression, then we should not be surprised by the fragility of African democracy.

In addition, the structure of the centralised state meant that most African presidents were able and eager to build powerful military forces to protect their power; but in many countries generals became irritated by the grandiosity or incompetence of their civilian governments and simply took power for themselves – usually with a promise to bring back a truly democratic government at the earliest opportunity. The military took power in Sudan in 1958, Algeria in 1965, Ghana and Nigeria in 1966, Sierra Leone in 1967, Uganda in 1971, Madagascar in 1972 and Ethiopia in 1974. In many African countries the armed forces are held in high regard by the population; lack of educational opportunities has pushed many able young men into the army where they can cultivate contacts beyond their villages, and with force at their disposal they have the ability to intervene in their nations' politics.

The seventeen sub-Saharan colonies of France followed a somewhat different path to the British colonies. France was a more reluctant decoloniser, and French culture had filtered into the lives of its colonial subjects – in a sense the French in Africa were more like the British in India. Independence was granted rather than actively fought for, so that France controlled every aspect of decolonisation. The notable exception was the Algerian War of independence of 1954 to 1962, in which French settlers refused to recognise the claims of the indigenous Algerian people. The conflict brought down the Fourth Republic as Charles de Gaulle was given extraordinary powers to quash the rebels. De Gaulle gradually changed his stance, however, and in 1962 finally granted independence.

Elsewhere in Africa, the French instituted a system for granting independence while retaining some degree of control. In 1960 Africans who had served in senior positions in France were made the new leaders of their countries in what de Gaulle called 'a French system where everyone plays his part'. De Gaulle appointed his political ally Jacques Foccart to manage the process, declaring that: 'the decolonisation . . . must succeed as a friendship, with us accompanying the people of these countries'.[4] The desire of France to maintain ties with her colonies in what became known as Françafrique, was expressed by French prime minister Edgar Faure as 'independence as interdependence' and given the motto *partir pour mieux rester* – 'to part in order to stay together'. France openly claimed 'limited sovereignty' and its troops were deployed in support of regimes of differing types, though none were democracies. France invested in its African ex-colonies and got a healthy return, through export markets and secure mineral and energy supplies. In the end, promotion of democracy was of little importance compared to nurturing a compliant Francophone elite.

Asian ex-colonies fared little better than African countries as democratic states, at least in their first decades. The British and Dutch had carved up a portion of South-East Asia in 1824, with Britain assuming control of Malaya and the Straits settlements (including Singapore) while the Dutch took the so-called East Indies. This agreement was reflected in the eventual boundaries of the nations of Malaysia and Indonesia. In 1945 Indonesian nationalists, having declared independence two days after the Japanese surrender, began a bitter liberation war against the Dutch. After independence was granted in 1950 the nationalist leader Sukarno put forward a constitution that ensured full democracy and human rights for all citizens; but by the following year Sukarno had begun to criticise the multi-party parliament for its internal disputes, arguing that this was contrary to the traditions of Indonesian society which were founded on discussion and consensus under the guidance of wise elders. The country now entered a period of so-called Guided Democracy in which Sukarno became increasingly powerful and dictatorial. By that time Indonesia had also become caught up in the Cold War, with Sukarno allying his country with China and the Soviet Union. The subsequent withdrawal of American aid left the country in a parlous state and, in 1968, brought the military leader and fervent anti-communist General Suharto to power. Democracy did not return to Indonesia until Suharto was forced from office in 1999.

Malaysia shows a more complex picture, where an apparently open democratic structure masks a one-party state, with almost all the seats in parliament won by the ruling UMNO party. Criticism of the government is heavily curtailed in a country where harmony between the Malay, Chinese and Indian communities is the principal priority for the state, which aims to bring this about through economic means rather than by encouraging an open society.

Malaysia's neighbour Burma won independence from Britain in 1948, shortly after the assassination of Aung San, the leader who had unified the different nationalist elements. Here a form of constitutional government lasted until 1962 when a military coup brought Ne Win to power for the second time. His vision of a country whose economy and daily life were totally controlled by the state has endured. In 1988 a new military leadership brought in some reforms and arranged for elections in 1990, which were won by the National League for Democracy led by Aung San's daughter, Aung San Suu Kyi. Yet the resulting assembly was not allowed to meet, and although a National Convention was called in 1993 to draw up a new constitution, it soon became clear that the military leaders would not allow a meaningful result. Widespread street protests in 2007, provoked by the regime's incompetence in the wake of devastating floods, were quashed by the army. In Burma the militarised state seems determined to resist all pressure for reform.

The United States was able to extricate itself from direct colonial rule by granting independence to the Philippines immediately after the Second World War. A democratic system brought Ferdinand Marcos to the presidency in 1965, but after winning a second term Marcos brought in martial law in 1971 and stayed in office until forced from power by massive popular demonstrations in 1986. The Marcos regime, supported initially by the United States as an anticommunist ally, became a byword for authoritarian corruption and self-enrichment.

Further north the situation was tragically complicated by the reluctance of France to give up its prize colony of Indochina, comprising Vietnam, Cambodia and Laos. Vietnamese nationalists, who had fought alongside the Allies against the Japanese, forced a humiliating French withdrawal from the north after the debacle of Dien Bien Phu in 1954. The Geneva Accord of that year saw the country split in two with the north being governed by the victorious Vietminh, and with free elections scheduled for the south. When these elections seemed likely to give the Vietminh and their leader Ho Chi Minh a mandate to govern, Ngo Dinh Diem, leader of the temporary government of the south, declared himself president of the new Republic of Vietnam. By this time the United States, fearful of China's expansionism, had become a key player in the region, supporting any regime that attempted to contain communism.

Involvement in Vietnam proved catastrophic, with the United States fatally confusing an independence war with its own global campaign against communism. The eventual outcome, after huge of loss of life on both sides, was the formation in 1975 of a single independent country run by the Communist Party.

The principal legacy that imperial powers bestowed on their ex-colonies was not democracy but the state. As we saw in Ghana and Kenya, the strong central state that emerged in Europe in the late Middle Ages and shaped the political development of modern Europe, became the West's gift to the world. The imperial powers believed that ensuring that each colony possessed a centralised bureaucracy and executive, as well as a strong military to provide stability, set the most judicious path for post-independence. Most importantly, the state had to possess a monopoly over the use of violence within its territory; it could not survive if individuals or groups could use their own military forces, powers of imprisonment, or any other forms of quasi-judicial punishment against its citizens. In Europe this power had been balanced by individual rights that the state could not override, and by the development of open government and political debates through which conflicts in society could be accommodated and mediated. A state that was not constrained in this way had a monopoly of power as well as force, as was to become apparent in the ex-colonies.

But the West's legacy went beyond the simple transplanting of a particular political structure. Nineteenth-century Europe had seen the rise of the nation state, an apolitical entity based on a unified culture, ethnicity and language – France, Italy and Germany being the prime examples – but rather than taking care to construct countries based on similar unifying characteristics, Europeans simply invented them after their own convenience.

Iraq provides a good example. Iraq was the original name of the capital province of the Abassid caliphate, based in Baghdad from 1253. Under the Ottoman Empire, whose centre was Istanbul, the area was controlled by the regional governor of Baghdad. After the fall of the Ottomans during the First World War, the British created the mandate of Mesopotamia and the Hashemite kingdom of Iraq by drawing together Kurdish areas to the north and Shia regions to the south of the capital. Iraq was therefore cobbled together with little thought for its long-term viability – there are accounts of national boundaries being drawn by British officials who flew over the desert with a map and pencil on their laps. A similar story can be told almost anywhere across the old Ottoman Empire; boundaries between Lebanon and Syria, for example, were designated by France under a League of Nations mandate in the 1920s, giving Lebanon a historically new demographic mix of Christians and Muslims, while the Kurdish homeland was divided between Turkey, Iraq, Iran and Syria.

In West Africa colonial boundaries were drawn inwards from the coast, each colonial power claiming whatever lay inland from its trading ports. Nigeria was created out of the territories of three major ethnically distinct peoples – the Yoruba, Ibo and Hausa – and a host of smaller groups. In eastern and southern Africa, Europeans settled in great numbers in the interior, and boundaries followed the agreements made at the Congress of Berlin of 1878, which stipulated that settlement granted the right to rule.

The process of decolonisation itself was chaotic, confusing and contradictory. Decisions were made for pragmatic reasons – to serve the former imperial powers' national interests, to provide stability, to create countries that would continue to have political and economic ties to their former imperial masters, or to solve problems of nationalist rebellions. It should have been clear from the start that each of the ex-colonies would face mountainous difficulties in trying to run and sustain a system of government supported by open democratic politics. In each case small groups were effectively handed the keys to a state modelled on the imperial power's own government, and leaders were expected to fight off rivals for power at the same time as allowing the practice of loyal opposition and regular transfers of power to take hold. Political parties were meant to emerge as engines of democracy as they had in America, rather than as vehicles of despotism. In addition the system was supposed to overcome ethnic and cultural divisions within the new states. Local cultures based on kinships networks were disregarded as primitive and corrupt and would, it was believed, disappear under the shining light of the new dispensation. But politics, as we have seen elsewhere, is a *part* of culture, not separate from it; and so almost every newly independent nation began a painful struggle for survival burdened with the political culture of another time and place.

THE COLLAPSE OF COMMUNISM
IN EUROPE

The Citizen Triumphant

On the morning of 10 November 1989 the West German President Richard von Weizsäcker stepped through a gap in the Berlin Wall near to the Brandenburg Gate, and into no-man's-land. From the other side an armed lieutenant of the East German border guard walked towards him. The president and his party froze as the officer drew near. The lieutenant hesitated but then gave a salute: 'Welcome, Mr President, everything is going to plan; no reports of any disturbances.'[1]

This astonishing encounter took place on the morning after the fall of the Berlin Wall. It was, in miniature, the acknowledgment that the authority of the West now ran into the East, that the communist system of government had died a remarkably peaceful death.

From 1945 to 1989 Europe had been divided into a democratic West (with the exceptions noted in Chapter 12) and a communist East, the frontier falling roughly along the line where the Soviet and Anglo-American forces met in the spring of 1945. Any notion of a happy workers' state was strangled at birth by brutal oppression throughout eastern Europe. To live in East Germany, Poland, Czechoslovakia, Hungary, Romania or Bulgaria was to live in fear and accept a life of rigid conformity. Citizens were encouraged to spy on each other and to become part of the huge and sophisticated system of secret surveillance. Memoirs, novels and plays by dissenting writers showed societies gripped and wearied by sustained paranoia – a picture confirmed by the later discovery of millions of secret-service files. It also became increasingly clear that communism was failing to deliver the material prosperity that was sweeping the West: eastern Europe was drab, its architecture and public spaces soulless and inhuman. If anyone had doubts about the value of democracy, then here was the answer – this was what society without democracy looked like.

Although communist regimes followed the Soviet model of ruthless totalitarianism, cracks occasionally appeared. The crushing of the 1956 Hungarian uprising by Soviet forces revealed that communism was being held in place by force and not the will of the people. The measures needed to keep the system in place also became starkly clear in August 1961 when Berliners woke to the sound of hundreds of trucks entering the city. Construction workers from the eastern sector then began the task of building a fifteen-kilometre wire fence with an average height of 3.6 metres, which was soon replaced by a solid wall. The Berlin Wall was an admission of failure dressed up as victory. Prior to its construction around 1,500 people per day had been fleeing from the Soviet controlled sector of the city into West Berlin. The wall was built to keep the people in; even the 60,000 or so East Berliners who commuted daily to work in the western sector were now prohibited from crossing the border. West Berlin, an enclave within the communist German Democratic Republic, was now the frontier between two ideological blocs. When President Kennedy visited the city in June 1963 he famously declared: 'Two thousand years ago the proudest boast was *civis Romanus sum*. Today, in the world of freedom, the proudest boast is *"Ich bin ein Berliner"* . . . All free men, wherever they may live, are citizens of Berlin, and, therefore, as a free man, I take pride in the words *"Ich bin ein Berliner."'* During the twenty-seven years of the wall's existence an estimated 5,000 East Germans successfully crossed to the West; a hundred are thought to have been shot by border guards in the attempt.

The suppression of the Hungarian uprising and the construction of the Berlin Wall kept the lid on dissent within the Eastern bloc – but only temporarily. In the so-called Prague Spring of 1968, Czech citizens began to demand political freedoms. The new leader of the communist government, Alexander Dubček, began to introduce reforms including greater freedom of speech, a mixed public and private economy and the promise of some democratisation. Employing the phrase 'socialism with a human face', Dubček and his allies argued that the previous policies had simply outlived their purpose and that it was time for change. In response, on the night of 20 August 1968 200,000 Warsaw Pact troops invaded Czechoslovakia; totalitarianism was restored by force.

Hungary in 1956 and Czechoslovakia in 1968 were indications of both the desire of the people for change, and the power of communist governments to resist. Dissent was forced underground throughout the Eastern bloc but by the 1980s the communist monolith began to crumble. The first signs of change came in Poland, where significant strikes had taken place in the early 1970s when the government brought in economic reforms which included steep price rises. A general strike led to Moscow replacing the ailing president Władysław Gomułka with the more dynamic Edward Gierek in December 1970. In common with other eastern European leaders, Gierek expanded the economy by inviting loans from the West, which chimed with the 'Neue Ostpolitik' of the West German chancellor, Willy Brandt. While this boosted the economy in the short term, in the long term it was disastrous, building up debt while protecting Polish industry against the modernisation that it desperately needed; by 1980 80 per cent of Polish export earnings were used to pay interest on its foreign debt. One result of Gierek's looser grip was a flourishing underground publishing industry as well as greater contact with the West. By the late 1970s a loose opposition movement had been founded around the Committee for the Defence of Workers (KOR). A crucial development came in October 1978 when Karol Wojtyla, Archbishop of Kraków, was elected Pope, taking the name John Paul II. The Catholic Church had been vigorously oppressed but despite this Poland remained an overwhelmingly Catholic country. Ignoring advice to tread carefully, John Paul II made an historic visit to Poland in June 1979 during which he preached a message of human and national rights to congregations totalling six million. Polish people felt that the world was at last on their side.

In the summer of 1980, with the economy in crisis, workers in the shipyards of Gdansk and the coal mines of Silesia organised a series of strikes and factory occupations. In September the workers formed a single national trade union named Solidarity under the astute leadership of an electrician named Lech Wałęsa. With its huge membership – growing to ten million by 1981 – Solidarity became a beacon for all those working for democratic political reforms.

The declaration of martial law in 1981 and the arrest of Solidarity's leaders did nothing to solve Poland's problems. A stalemate continued through the 1980s as the country, along with the remainder of the Eastern bloc, stagnated economically while the West, having survived the economic turbulence of the 1970s, enjoyed a consumer-led boom. In 1988 GDP per capita in Poland stood at $1800; in France it was $18,000.

By 1988 Solidarity was pushing for complete political reform. A series of strikes in the summer brought the government to the nego-tiating table, as the new Soviet president, Mikhail Gorbachev, was now signalling the end of the 'Brezhnev doctrine' which had justified Soviet military intervention in eastern Europe. But by now Poland was just one factor in the unfolding drama gripping the Soviet bloc. The June 1989 elections were a disaster for the Communist Party and were the first tangible sign of the emergence of a new order in eastern Europe. On 3 July the Soviet envoy to Poland announced that the country should be in control of its own destiny.

In common with its satellite countries, the Soviet Union experienced a long period of economic stagnation during the 1970s and 80s. The historic expansion in heavy industry in the 1920s and again during the Second World War had symbolised the momentum of the revolution, showing a dynamic country pushing ever forward into a communist future; but by the 1970s the difficulties of organising a sophisticated economy to satisfy the needs of 290 million people through a central-ised state apparatus were woefully apparent. Essential goods would simply disappear from the marketplace while others were obtainable only on the black market with hard currency. The Soviet Union, the once great producer, became a nation of empty shops.

The Soviet economy had seen a gradual decline in growth rate from around 5 per cent in 1960 to around 2.7 per cent in 1978, after which it ground to a complete halt. The disastrous and expensive war in Afghanistan, which began in 1979, and a drop in the oil price – a major Soviet export – from its peak in the late 1970s, contributed to the slump and to a growing sense of lassitude.

It was in this atmosphere that the young and dynamic Mikhail Gorbachev quite suddenly found himself elected to the post of general secretary of the Communist Party, and effective head of government.

Gorbachev's rise through the ranks of the party had been steady, but he had benefited from the deaths, in rapid succession, of Leonid Brezhnev (November 1982), Yuri Andropov (February 1984) and Konstantin Chernenko (March 1985). Gorbachev had already made his mark in the West when, as head of Soviet delegations to Canada in 1983 and Britain in 1984, he struck a markedly different tone to his dour predecessors; Margaret Thatcher famously declared Gorbachev to be 'someone we could do business with'.

Once Gorbachev assumed power in March 1985 he proposed reforms to get the stagnant economy moving. He decided that economic impetus would only come from social and political reforms. His programme of perestroika, or restructuring, was intended to allow and encourage citizens to be more creative and take initiatives to improve economic activity; but this could only come about if the system itself, which was widely acknowledged to be ossified and corrupt, could be opened up – hence the other famous concept of glasnost.

However, glasnost suddenly exposed the Soviet Union as being on the verge of bankruptcy, with its people living at subsistence level. The image of the country as a military superpower was shown to be a piece of sustained bravado supported only by diverting a massive proportion of the nation's wealth into defence. The invulnerability of the Red Army had been disproved during the Afghan War (which Gorbachev ended) and the idea that the Red Army was poised to sweep across Europe at the first sign of NATO weakness, for so long the central plank of western military thinking, was exposed as an illusion. In addition the explosion at the Chernobyl nuclear power plant in April 1986 made the world doubt Soviet claims to be a high-tech power.

Gorbachev showed himself to be a courageous reformer, releasing political prisoners and rehabilitating victims of Stalin's purges. In January 1987 political reforms put forward to the Party Plenum included multi-candidate elections and the appointment of non-communists to positions of authority. He also proposed injecting private enterprise into the state system by allowing co-operatives to run businesses for the first time since Lenin's short-lived reforms of the 1920s. The opening of co-operative cafés and shops in Moscow in the summer of 1988 marked an extraordinary change for a country where everything had been owned and run by the state for seventy years.

Democracy was finally introduced to the Soviet Union in March and April 1989 as elections were held to a new 2,250-seat Congress of People's Deputies. One-third of the deputies represented ordinary constituencies, one-third large national territorial constituencies and one-third public bodies – a hundred of these seats were reserved for the Communist Party. The Central Committee could nominate individuals; they did not have to take part in competitive elections, but they had to win 50 per cent support from voters. Over 80 per cent of the electorate went to the ballot box in the spring 1989 elections. Future Russian president Boris Yelstin won his seat through a competitive election for the Moscow national territorial seat, with record-breaking five million votes. Yeltsin was a former first secretary of the Moscow City Communist Party and had lost his high position in the party after criticising the Moscow Politburo.

While 90 per cent of deputies were Communist Party members there was a split between reformers and conservatives; new parties were only beginning to form, but a new bloc of 400 influential deputies came together to push for more reform. The Congress met in May; its first task was to elect representatives to the governing body, the Supreme Soviet. Mikhail Gorbachev became chairman of the Supreme Soviet and, on 15 March 1990, was elected unopposed as the first ever president of the Soviet Union.

In July 1989 Gorbachev made a historic speech to the Council of Europe in Strasbourg. He spoke of a 'common European home', and added: 'The social and political order in some countries changed in the past, and it can change in the future too, but this is entirely a matter for each people to decide. Any interference in the internal affairs, or any attempt to limit the sovereignty of another state, friend, ally, or another, would be inadmissible.'[2] It was this call for a 'return to Europe' that had the greatest emotional pull and inspirational weight for the people of the communist bloc.

Gorbachev still believed that communism had much to offer – his vision of Europe involved socialist states living contentedly alongside capitalist countries. His belief that communism should and could exist within a democratic system was behind the reforms in the Soviet Union, where he planned to build a society that was essentially socialist, with the Communist Party still in control, but with freedom of speech, political pluralism and a mixed economy. The contradictions in this system rapidly became apparent and reformers, led by Boris Yeltsin, were keen to exploit the weaknesses in Gorbachev's arguments. Once Gorbachev had conceded the case for political pluralism, free speech and free elections, it was impossible for the Communist Party to maintain its special position.

The sessions of the Congress were televised, giving Soviet viewers their first taste of open political discussion in which their political masters underwent savage criticism. Television channels, most of them supporting reform, began airing programmes that included fierce debate: programmes like *Vzglyad* and *600 Seconds* became well known for unearthing scandals within the ruling elite. On one programme Margaret Thatcher explained that Britain kept its nuclear arsenal out of fear of aggression by the Red Army; most of the Soviet audience were themselves fearful of the West and had never encountered the opposite view. *Komsomol Pravda*, the official newspaper of the communist youth organisation, became a voice for reform, alongside the newly founded *Nezavisimaya gazeta* (Independent News) and the long-established investigative magazine *Ogonyok*. The journal *Argumenty i Fakty* (Arguments and Facts) claimed a world-record circulation of thirty-five million in 1990, showing a vast appetite among the public for political news; in contrast the print run of *Pravda*, the official Communist Party paper, declined from a peak of twelve million in the mid 1980s to just one million in 1991.[3] The problem for Gorbachev was that debate became centred on the incompetence and corruption of the existing powers.

Boris Yeltsin took full advantage of the opportunities for plain speaking, winning himself a national reputation by attacking Gorbachev at every opportunity. In the summer of 1990 Yeltsin was elected the president of the Supreme Soviet of the Russian Republic. The relations between the Soviet centre and its constituent republics were now at crisis point. In March 1990 Lithuania declared itself independent, followed by Latvia in May – though neither declaration was accepted by Moscow.[4] In July 1990 Yeltsin left the Communist Party and the Russian Congress of People's Deputies voted to leave the Soviet Union. In March 1991, 98.9 per cent of citizens of Georgia voted for independence. In June Yeltsin stood as a candidate in the first democratic elections for the president of Russia and won 57 per cent of the vote. He immediately banned political parties from factories and other workplaces – the traditional power bases of the Communist Party. A new treaty was drawn up, making the Soviet Union a federation of the remaining republics – each of them promising democratic constitutions – with joint foreign and security arrangements. The treaty was due to be signed by the individual republics and by the increasingly marginalised Mikhail Gorbachev on 20 August 1991.

The old guard, unwilling to let the Soviet Union crumble into history, now made a dramatic last move. While Mikhail Gorbachev was on holiday in the Crimea, Vladimir Kryuchkov, head of the KGB, put an established plan into action. A group of senior Communist Party figures flew to the Crimea on 18 August 1991 and ordered Gorbachev to reverse his policies by declaring a state of emergency, or step down. He refused to do either. On the conspirators' return to Moscow a state of emergency was declared, television, radio and newspapers were shut down, and tanks and troops were brought into the heart of the city.

When Boris Yeltsin heard the news he immediately made his way to the White House, his official residence as president of Russia, arriving at 9 a.m. on 19 August. With the broadcast media under the control of the coup leaders, Yeltsin's supporters distributed leaflets around the city, calling for citizens and the army not to support the 'reactionary' coup, and instead to take part in a general strike. Yeltsin also called for Gorbachev to be allowed to address the nation. The world watched, transfixed, as the fate of a world superpower was played out in the streets of Moscow.

The White House became the focus for resistance with Yeltsin supporters putting up barricades, while the commander of a tank division sent to 'guard' the White House declared his loyalty to Russia and its president. The decisive moment in the unfolding drama came when Yeltsin made a rallying speech from the top of a Red Army tank. He denounced the coup as a reaction against democracy, and told the crowd why it would not succeed: 'Despite all the difficulties and severe trials being experienced by the people, the democratic process in the country is acquiring an increasingly broad sweep and an irreversible character.'[5] The following day a half-hearted attempt to take the White House was abandoned, and the coup leaders were forced to fly back to the Crimea to negotiate a resolution with Gorbachev. When he again refused to co-operate, the conspirators returned to Moscow where they were arrested.

The Communist Party was now seen as a danger to the new democracy and Yeltsin immediately nationalised all the property owned by the party in Russia and took control of its archives. Gorbachev resigned as general secretary and within three months the party was outlawed in Russia. Then, in December, Gorbachev signed the treaty that formed the Commonwealth of Independent States and formally dissolved the USSR. After six tumultuous years as leader of his country, he resigned as Soviet president on 25 December and the hammer and sickle flags were lowered from the flagpoles of the Kremlin. Almost miraculously the Soviet Union had managed a virtually bloodless transition from communist totalitarianism to pluralist democracy. Gorbachev's liberalisation of the Soviet Union had succeeded, but his vision of a society that combined state-sponsored communism with liberal democracy was shown to be a mirage. Democracy is unpredictable and ungrateful, and, as Churchill could have told him, is apt to make fools of leaders.

In response to the changes in the Soviet Union, communist countries in eastern Europe began making moves towards democracy. In May 1988 the hardline leader of Hungary, János Kádár, was forced from office and a reforming, though still communist, regime under Károly Grósz took power. The new government loosened restrictions on foreign travel and, following Gorbachev's lead, announced plans for multi-party elections in February 1989. A crowd of more than 300,000 people turned out in June to see Imre Nagy, the hero of the 1956 uprising, reburied in Heroes' Square in the centre of Budapest. By then Hungary had begun to dismantle the wire fence along its border with Austria – the Iron Curtain was being torn down.

In September 1989 the foreign minister Gyula Horn announced that any East Germans seeking refuge in Hungary would not be returned, but would be free to travel to the West. Under West German law, East Germans arriving in the country were automatically granted full citizenship. In September 1989 an estimated 13,000 East German citizens travelled to Hungary and then simply walked over the border into Austria. The great symbolic dividing line between liberal democracy and communism, the Berlin Wall, had become an irrelevance.

East Germany had always been the poster boy for Soviet-style communism, its economy flourishing in comparison to the other communist countries, but by the late 1980s it had fallen severely behind its extraordinarily successful and prosperous neighbour to the west. By the autumn of 1989 there were demonstrations all over East Germany, during which the mood began to change. At the first mass rallies people saw escape as their aim and chanted 'We want to leave'; by late September getting to the West was no longer the goal; instead East Germans wanted to change their own country, and chanted 'We are staying'.

On 18 October Erich Honecker, long-time leader of East Germany, stood down and on 4 November half a million people gathered at a demonstration in Alexanderplatz in East Berlin. The new government headed by Egon Krenz first allowed their citizens to travel to the West through Czechoslovakia before deciding, on 9 November, to open their own borders. The specified date of 17 November got lost in the confusion of the announcement and word spread like wildfire across Berlin that the border to the West was now open.

'To my right is a mass of revellers,' reported the BBC's Tim Weber from the Brandenburg Gate on the night of 9 November, 'dancing, singing, drinking champagne and having the time of their lives. To my left – a thin line of armed men, nervously holding their Kalashnikov assault rifles, shifting uneasily from foot to foot. Separating them is the wall.' Soon people from east and west began to climb on to the wall and began attacking it with hammers and pickaxes. The following day East Berliners flooded through the open border crossings. When Tim Weber went the other way he found 'A ghost town, with a few lonely policemen shuffling along empty sidewalks.'

Little more than a week later a series of demonstrations in Czechoslovakia built to a peak when half a million people gathered in Prague's Wenceslas Square to demand political change. A two-hour general strike on 27 November brought the country to a standstill, and the following day the communist government announced that it would step down and arrange free elections. On 10 December a non-communist government was appointed and the last communist leader Gustáv Husák resigned. On 28 December Alexander Dubček, leader of the Prague Spring of 1968, was elected speaker of the federal parliament; the next day dissident playwright and national hero Václav

Havel was made president. Full elections held in June 1990 gave democratic support to the Havel government.

In Bulgaria too the long-time leader Todor Zhivkov and his deputy were ousted in November 1989, to be replaced by the reformist Andrey Lukanov. The Communist Party abandoned its monopoly, allowing multi-party elections to take place in June 1990, though the country remained plagued by the corruption that had been endemic under the old regime.

The final act of the democratic revolutions of eastern Europe was played out in Romania. As well as being a totalitarian state, Romania had suffered for twenty years as the personal fiefdom of President Nicolae Ceauşescu and his immediate family. The absurdity of Ceauşescu's self-aggrandisement and his final humiliation should not distract us from the terrifying nature of his regime, in which torture and murder were common political weapons and which kept the population on subsistence-level poverty. While being Stalinist in his rule, Ceauşescu had remained more independent of Moscow than his neighbours, and felt no need to follow Gorbachev's lead. Thus, unlike other communist leaders, Ceausescu refused to step down after the fall of the Berlin Wall. The Romanian rebellion began in the city of Timişoara on 16 December as a protest against the eviction of a Hungarian priest. During the next four days protestors ransacked the local Communist Party headquarters, and when the government bussed in workers armed with clubs to beat the demonstrators, most of them ended up joining the protest. On 20 December Ceauşescu returned from a visit to Iran and gave a televised address to the nation. A mass rally was arranged for the next day, in which the leader would address his people and condemn foreign interference that he claimed was responsible for the turmoil in the country.

The drama played out on the balcony of the Romanian Communist Party headquarters on 21 December 1989 is, along with the tearing down of the Berlin Wall, one of the emblematic images of the collapse of communism in Europe. Shortly after Ceauşescu had begun his lacklustre speech to over 100,000 by reciting the achievements of communism, parts of the crowd began to whistle, jeer, boo and laugh, while there were sounds of gunfire from outside the square. Ceauşescu misunderstood completely what was happening and began to promise wage rises for workers, before stumbling to a halt. Chants of 'Death to the murderer' and 'Down with the dictator' were heard. While his wife urged him to keep talking, they were both ushered inside for their own safety. It was an ignoble end to an ignoble rule. Street battles continued overnight and the next morning thousands more protestors gathered in defiance of an order limiting groupings to five people. The newly appointed defence minister ordered troops back to the barracks and as demonstrators invaded the Central Committee building Ceauşescu and his wife managed to flee in a helicopter. The pilot and crew soon understood the changing situation, and the Ceauşescu were abandoned on a roadside near Pitesti with their secret police bodyguards. Police took them back to Bucharest where on 25 December they were given a two-hour trial, found guilty and sentenced to death. They were immediately taken outside and shot.

Ceauşescu was not quite the last East European dictator to be forced from office. That distinction falls to Slobodan Milosevic, who took advantage of the break-up of Yugoslavia to attempt a Serbian takeover of the neighbouring ethnically mixed territory of Bosnia–Herzegovina. The resulting war lasted from 1992 to 1995 and was the bloodiest conflict on the European mainland since the Second World War. Milosevic's power waned after the end of the war and ended with his arrest in 2001 on charges of corruption and abuse of power.[6] Yugoslavia had by then broken into its constituent states, each making steps towards liberal democracy.

How, then, did these countries fare as democracies? The citizens of eastern Europe wanted political freedoms for their own sake but also because they believed that democracy would deliver a more prosperous life. Given the great difficulties experienced by all the Eastern bloc countries in the years immediately after 1989, it is worthy of note that they have all stuck, albeit with variations, to a broadly democratic course. The transition from a central-command economy to a mix of public and private enterprise – the quid pro quo of democracy was the requirement for citizens to embrace a market economy – was particularly traumatic because in the West influential neoliberal leaders, institutions and economists were in favour of withdrawing the state from virtually all economic activity. The privatisation and selling of state-owned assets and companies – from airlines and tele-communications to gas and water suppliers – had become a central plank in the Anglo-Saxon economic model. The loans and grants that the former communist countries received from bodies like the International Monetary Fund and the World Bank were conditional on states agreeing to sell off industries and utilities. The results varied from the traumatic to the catastrophic.

Gorbachev had tried gradually to adapt the Soviet command economy through a series of measures; but once Boris Yeltsin was president of Russia this stage-by-stage process of transforming the economy was abandoned. Economists and political advisers believed that the different state sectors were so intertwined that only a complete abandonment of state ownership would work. In early 1992 Yeltsin announced his plans for a market economy in Russia, including free pricing, privatisation of industry and property, banks, private retail stores and free trade with the rest of the world. At the same time an austerity package saw interest rates pushed up to choke off inflation and a severe cutback in government spending on welfare and other services. The GDP of Russia dropped for the four years from 1990 by 13, 19, 12 and 15 per cent successively. State assets were bought up in dubious deals by power brokers who became hugely wealthy on the proceeds. The economic reforms were, on the surface, in line with the precepts of democracy: giving power and freedom to the individual and removing the restrictions imposed by the state. But the democratic reforms in Russia had taken a centralised state from a small clique of communist leaders and handed it to a small clique headed by an elected president. To function effectively democracy requires institutions like the judiciary, parliament, a free press and a strong civil society to moderate the power of government. Despite the euphoria of the late 1980s, all these factors were still extremely weak compared to the power of the Russian state. Instead of a democracy, the Yeltsin government became an oligarchy in which powerful men enriched themselves and became more powerful in the process.

By the late 1990s Yeltsin's economic policies were proving disastrous. Russia had failed to develop a manufacturing economy, relying on commodities like oil, gas and metals for 80 per cent of its exports. When the Asian financial crisis developed in 1998 and the oil price dropped, confidence in the Russian economy drained away; debts piled up, workers went unpaid and inflation soared to 84 per cent. The value of the rouble plunged against the dollar, and the Russian economy was widely regarded as a 'basket case', while its citizens saw their savings disappear and their wages drop dramatically in value. Inhabitants of Moscow and other cities began to go hungry. The Russian people responded to adversity with their usual mix of stoicism and ingenuity. Used to relying on their own efforts, Muscovites became prodigious growers and producers of food to get themselves and the country through the winter of 1998. The crisis eased once the price of oil climbed again on the international markets.

Once Vladimir Putin gained office (he was made prime minister in 1999 and elected president in 2000) the state began to take back control of essential industries and the so-called oligarchs were brought to book. However, democracy was severely curbed with free speech curtailed, journalists being harassed and even assassinated, while the space for open debate about policies was eliminated. The reimposition of a strong state, which has been popular among Russians who feel that their country is regaining its prestige after the humiliation of 1998, has also meant that the economy has developed very slowly. Russia remains a supplier of commodities to manufacturing economies rather than a manufacturer of goods – a notable contrast with China.

The reasons for Russia's dire situation were numerous and complex, but in essence the development of both a mixed economy and a pluralist democracy depend on certain relations of trust. A sophisticated modern economy cannot function without people – investors, managers, workers, consumers – having trust in a robust financial system, in their suppliers, in their customers and in the fairness of the legal system. It is entirely understandable but nevertheless hampering, that the Russian people, after their experiences of a corrupt communist system followed by a disastrous period of laissez-faire private enterprise in which their savings were wiped out, should have little trust in any of these bodies. The enduring problem has been that economic and political concepts and structures have been applied to Russia – by the IMF, the World Bank, the Russian government – as if it were a laboratory rather than a country with a deep and abiding culture and history. Indeed Russian culture was seen as an obstacle to freedom rather than the most precious and meaningful portion of people's lives. Putin's recognition of this has won him popularity among Russians, even at the expense of a more open society. The primary goal of his leadership has been to restore the reputation of the Russian state, without which little can be achieved; but this simply takes us back to the enduring problem of who controls the state, and how.

Other countries suffered some of the same shocks as Russia – notably Poland in 2002 when its shipyards were first privatised, then shut down by their new owners, before being renationalised. Some have been cushioned from the worst effects of sudden change by joining the European Union. While no guarantor of either pluralist politics or prosperity, the EU provides mechanisms for investment together with easy access to the richest market in the world. The conditions for membership encourage the implementation of democratic institutions and practices; partly as a result every country in Europe has become a democracy.

All the ex-communist countries entered the democratic world in the new era of globalisation. This meant that as well as following certain political and economic policies, they became part of the global trading network in which every country, weak and strong, has found it necessary to make common cause and to co-operate in order to get what it wants or needs. The EU has provided a convenient and powerful alliance for some, but those outside its gilded walls have struggled.

The former republics of the Soviet Union have chosen different paths, with Russia ensuring that it retains control of those that border its territory, so that countries like Ukraine and Georgia find themselves squeezed between courtship by the West and a jealously watchful Russia. At the same time the rapid expansion of the EU has brought other nations, notably Turkey, within its circle of aspiring members. Turkey has been in informal talks with the EU over membership for decades, and has improved its democratic credentials.

Mikhail Gorbachev's reforms also had an impact in China, the most populous country in the world. While still a communist and non-democratic state, China deserves mention here because its situation as a growing economic superpower raises fundamental questions about the relationship between political and economic freedoms. First we need to backtrack to see how Chinese communism developed in quite a different way to the Stalinist Soviet Union. Historians have pointed out that Chinese communism, as advocated by Mao Zedong and others, always ran counter to the central tenets of Stalinist communism which focussed on centralisation, collectivisation and heavy industry. While Stalin believed that a truly socialist society, in the Marxist sense, had eliminated all contradictions, Mao always argued that there would be differences between the people and their rulers, and that these should not be suppressed because to do so would be to 'abolish politics'. Mao believed in progress not stasis, and progress came out of continual contradictions as described by Marx in his theory of dialectics. This may sound high-flown but it was born out of essential differences between Russian and Chinese culture, and its practical effects were profound.

In the wake of the Soviet success in the Second World War, the Stalinist view of agriculture and industry was taken by most communists as a paradigm for development. The peasants must be made to produce as much as possible as cheaply as possible to feed the industrial workers who would build the capacity for the country to become a great power. When the Chinese communists came to power in 1949 Mao saw things differently, believing that impoverishing the peasants would, in the long run, destabilise the country. Instead, villages were given a degree of autonomy and allowed to use their surplus labour to produce surplus goods. Increasing the purchasing power of peasants would benefit everyone in the long term, providing customers for industrial goods. Mao even believed in a decentralised army which would allow China to defend itself through guerrilla warfare. 'Centralise only what must be centralised and leave the rest alone', he wrote.[7] Unlike Stalin, Mao believed that institutions should be continually renewed and replaced as circumstances demanded. This essential difference between gradual development and continual change is what separated the Soviet from the Chinese experience.

But if Mao was such an advocate of giving power back to the people, why did his policies have such a disastrous effect on the Chinese population? In the Great Leap Forward of the 1950s, Communist Party leaders paid lip service to the freedom of peasants while continually demanding that they hand over more of their produce. The result was a famine in the countryside in which millions died. In another move driven by Mao's personal ideology, peasants were forced to leave agriculture to work on small-scale steel production of no real value; meanwhile, infrastructure projects of potential benefit failed because of a lack of expertise, as trained engineers, along with skilled workers of any kind, had been eliminated. And in the Cultural Revolution of the 1960s, the fury of the discontented young turned the idea of continual renewal into a brutal and chaotic disaster.

Mao himself must bear the blame for the results of his actions and for the punishments meted out to tens of thousands of 'rightists'. If he had simply encouraged decentralisation, initiatives by the people and criticism of the leadership then the Chinese people would not have suffered to the degree they did; but Mao was a theorist, not a practical administrator. His ideology led him to believe that if everyone was as good as each other, then even people trained in such crucial areas as engineering, agronomy, manufacturing or construction were continually replaceable. Indeed anyone who claimed to possess useful knowledge about a certain field was suspect, so that teachers, scientists and technicians were sent into internal exile as a form of punishment, leaving the country bereft of skilled and educated workers.

As China entered the 1980s, it therefore had a quite different background to the Soviet society that Gorbachev and Yeltsin sought to reform. China had begun making tentative steps to reform from Mao's death in 1976. Though these were initially at a low level, the Chinese government began encouraging small-scale enterprise and giving local officials rewards for encouraging industry in their areas. This staged approach developed through the 1980s and 1990s and was a deliberate rejection of the growing Western belief that all the state enterprises must be either kept in state control, or privatised together. While there was no meltdown of the kind seen in Russia in the early 1990s, the piecemeal approach did cause some problems. The agricultural sector, for example, where individual producers were still trading with local state bodies, became more impoverished as industry and commerce surged ahead dragging up prices that farmers had to pay for machinery, while the state kept food prices low. Indeed the pricing of goods became a major difficulty for a system which, in Mao's time, had valued work in a totally different way. Allowing enterprises to make a profit, and thus to create inequality in a communist system, has proved contradictory in theory but achievable in practice – at least so far. What then has that meant for democracy?

Mao's death in 1976 had been followed by the emergence of Deng Xiaoping as the most powerful figure in China. Almost immediately Deng and Hua Guofeng, Mao's anointed successor, made speeches calling for a pragmatic rather than an idealistic approach to China's future. Newspapers began debating the need to be able to elect and remove government officials. In October 1978 a group of students began pasting newspaper articles, posters and then personal messages on to a blank wall in one of Beijing's main thoroughfares. The so-called Democracy Wall was encouraged by Deng, partly because many posters condemned his rivals, the notorious Gang Of Four, and strengthened his hand in pushing reforms through the party machinery.

However, Deng himself became the target of attacks as posters and articles contained demands like: 'When people ask for democracy they are only asking for what is theirs by right . . . Are they not justified in seizing power from the overlords?' Nor were these anonymous contributions. In this case the writer was Wei Jingsheng, editor of the journal *Explorations*. Chen Erjin, a peasant-turned-schoolteacher, published a journal called *Crossroads Socialism* which argued that oppression came not from the traditions of China (which Mao had always sought to overthrow) but from the communist system itself. Chen used Mao's own teachings to advocate a second revolution that would bring full democracy – not the half-baked democracy of the West, but one that would embrace all areas of life including factories and communes as well as government – while also ensuring civil rights and the separation of powers. While *Crossroads Socialism* was the most prominent and influential, similar kinds of journals sprang up in cities across China during 1978 along with demonstrations demanding 'freedom and democracy'. By March 1979 the authorities had lost control of the situation; Deng now changed his view of the Democracy Wall, which was cleaned of all material while the writers and editors of the new political journals were arrested and imprisoned. This encouragement of openness followed by oppression became the signature of Deng's leadership.

Ten years after the Democracy Wall, the democracy movement re-emerged in an even more dramatic way. The death of Hu Yaobang, a prominent former general secretary of the Communist Party, in April 1989 proved to be a catalyst for gatherings in Tiananmen Square in Beijing. Two years earlier Hu's forced resignation had been a setback for reform-minded Chinese; they now intended to use his funeral to show their continued support for democratic reform. Around 100,000 people gathered in the square on the eve of the funeral on 21 April.

Some made speeches in front of the Great Hall of the People, while others sang songs calling for change and renewal. It was not a uniform movement – while students wanted more reforms, workers protested against the inflation and corruption that economic reforms had produced. Nevertheless, there was a general sense of grievance at a leadership that was immune from criticism and from the hardship suffered by ordinary people.

The protests escalated in the run-up to a planned visit to Beijing by Mikhail Gorbachev. To the Chinese leadership, the economic difficulties in Russia were a warning of what might happen in China if liberalisation moved too fast. On 13 May, two days before Gorbachev's visit, a group of students camped in the square went on hunger strike over the refusal of the leadership to negotiate. They were joined by hundreds of others as the protest became the focus of worldwide interest. Students from the Academy of Fine Arts made a ten-metre high statue of the 'Goddess of Democracy', which faced the portrait of Chairman Mao across the square.

The protest caused deep disagreements within the Communist Party leadership.[8] While Premier Li Peng wanted to crush the rebellion, General Secretary Zhao Ziyang wanted to persuade the students to end their protest, and was prepared to accede to some of their demands. Deng Xiaoping, who remained the most powerful figure, was for the first weeks unsure of how to proceed. He saw reform as the future path for China but, at the same time, wanted to control the pace and breadth from the top. A generous view would understand that Deng's generation had lived through the chaos of the Cultural Revolution and feared a similar upheaval if the students were allowed to have their way; but at the same time Deng was content to restrict access to power and to maintain control of China.

Deng finally came down on the side of Li Peng. Zhao Ziyang was placed under house arrest and, on 4 June 1989, troops were ordered to clear Tiananmen Square. There is some evidence that the leadership did not intend a brutal crackdown but that troops panicked when surrounded by angry protestors. Nevertheless any leader sending troops to confront unarmed citizens must be held responsible for the consequences. The conflict was particularly badly felt in a country where the notion of a People's Army was not mere rhetoric but a deeply felt part of the nation's psyche. It is estimated that 3,000 people were killed in the massacre. The official line that the protest was the work of 'a tiny, tiny handful' of people was contradicted by the authorities' claim that the troops had been overwhelmed; and while stressing the seriousness of the situation as justification for their actions, they also admitted that the protest had been supported by the people and intellectuals of Beijing.[9] Whatever China's leaders may have told themselves, the crushing of the protest was watched with interest in Pyongyang, Yangon, Tehran and elsewhere – the message received was that brutal force against civil rebellion worked.

The story of China since 1989 has been its economic growth; after a brief period of reaction, in which price controls were re-extended and small enterprises shut down, reform resurfaced. A stock exchange was created and state enterprises became joint stock companies with some autonomy, and price controls on essential goods such as grain and oil lifted. In all this the individual citizen faces both opportunities and hazards. How this affects the global political situation, with China set to be the biggest economy in the world, will be crucial for the future history of democracy.

Western observers who criticise the absence of democracy tend to forget that China, unlike the Soviet Union, went through huge upheavals in the 1950s and 60s in which millions died; for many Chinese, stability is paramount and the majority are wary of those calling for dramatic and rapid change. The regime has exploited this feeling by promoting nationalism and prosperity at the expense of freedom of expression and democracy. Both Jiang Zemin (effective leader of China from 1997 to 2003) and his protégé and successor Hu Jintao (president from 2003) have shown hostility to democracy, while also following some precepts of an open society. In 1998 Jiang gave signals that political pluralism would be welcomed, and then imprisoned three citizens who set up the China Democratic Party. The Falun Gong religious sect was allowed to hold meetings before being suppressed and persecuted. An artist like Ai Weiwei has been given sufficient freedom to attain global stature, but was then arrested and secretly detained under an arcane law. While laws have been brought in that give rights to citizens, the Communist Party reserves the privilege to overrule these laws – which is exactly what happened in the prosecution of the China Democratic Party. In fact the Communist Party acts as a state within a state, its members concerned primarily with their positions, influence and rewards within the party system. The party controls the state; access to political power comes only through the party, and its procedures, while open to endless analysis, are not open to scrutiny. Nevertheless, the National People's Congress, previously a rubber-stamping organisation that always voted unanimously, now occasionally votes against measures sent from the State Council.

Rather than trying to predict where all this might lead, historians and political commentators are now inclined to ask what preconditions for democracy exist in China. Several of these are favourable, and have echoes in historical situations where democracy has arisen and been sustained. So, for example, China has a fairly homogeneous population and while there are religious and ethnic differences none of these – apart, perhaps, from Tibet – threaten the unity of the country. Significant class divisions and deference politics are also not a big factor in Chinese society. Chinese culture favours solutions to conflict in which each party retains its dignity, a precondition of the formation of a loyal opposition. And while the Chinese government has its share of corruption, it has handled the economic transition competently at almost all levels. The government also has effective control over its territory, though government at local levels is often inadequate due to a lack of democratic transparency and accountability.

At the same time Chinese intellectuals have, according to Western analysts, generally failed to forge links with democratic reformers among the general population. Nevertheless, economic change has brought about a further liberalisation of society; the economy is effectively pluralist, with millions of individuals and institutions making decisions where once everything was controlled from the centre. Economic development has meant the rapid evolution of a legal system where contracts can be freely entered into and enforced through an acknowledged authority. And, while the growth of an affluent middle class has not itself brought calls for democracy, China has developed a thriving civil society that runs in parallel to officialdom. In the meantime China still locks up dissenters and executes more people than all the other countries of the world put together.

15

DEMOCRACY SINCE 1989

The Informed Citizen

In March 1991, President George Bush declared the emergence of 'a new world order'. His speech was made in the aftermath of the expulsion of Iraqi forces from Kuwait, where the victory of the 'international community' over a rogue state had followed the fall of communism in the Soviet Union and eastern Europe. These events had changed the political map of the world, giving capitalist liberal democracies untrammelled dominance of the globe with the United States as the sole superpower. Life under communism, as millions of east Europeans could testify, had been oppressive, restricted, bitter and joyless; democracy was clearly the model for all governments. Bush's defeat in the US election of 1992 brought an administration under Bill Clinton eager to embrace this new world, and with little interest in propping up military dictatorships just because they were anti-communist. At the same time the world became ever more interconnected through trade, finance and technology-based information networks. In this chapter we will look at what these changes have meant for democracy in different parts of the world and at the emergence of new democratic mechanisms, before looking at the experience of living in a democracy, and asking what the history of democracy can teach us.

Since the 1980s we have lived in the age of globalisation. Relaxing trade barriers and allowing the free and instantaneous flow of capital has made everyone part of the same trading network. Those who trade in money and commodities have been vastly enriched but many hoped that in the process international investors would put money wherever they got the best return and that these injections of cash would bring development, jobs and resources to the poor parts of the globe, making the whole world an economic level playing field.

In this Washington model of free trade the rich world would invest to make profits but, in order to do that, would engage with poorer countries as active trading and investment partners. The theory was that this partnership, in contrast to the old exploitation, would be best brought about through democratic open governments freeing the entrepreneurial spirit of their peoples while subjecting themselves to the rule of international law. While not always actively promoting democracy – American foreign policy has generally favoured the pragmatic over the ideological – in the 1990s the United States was inclined to favour democratic change.

However, following the election of George W. Bush in 2000, United States policy shifted in a more ideological direction. Under the influence of the so-called neoconservatives, the administration took a proactive view of promoting democracy in other countries, even to the point of armed intervention against tyrannical regimes. This policy was pursued with vigour after the terrorist attacks on New York and Washington in September 2001, but had actually been articulated before then by the British prime minister, Tony Blair. In a remarkable speech in Chicago in April 1999 Blair spelled out a doctrine of intervention. First stressing that 'globalisation is not just economic. It is also a political and security phenomenon', he then declared that 'The most pressing foreign policy problem we face is to identify the circumstances in which we should get actively involved in other people's conflicts.'[1] The message was that the world is now so interconnected that powers like the United States and Britain must have the right to intervene in other countries' internal affairs in order to protect their own interests. Though Blair did not mention bringing democracy to those countries, his words chimed perfectly with the ideas of the incoming Bush administration.

This vision lasted only until reality defeated the bland notions of exporting 'freedom and democracy' around the globe. Immediately after September 2001 Afghanistan was invaded by UN-approved NATO forces, its Taliban government ejected, and arrangements put in place for a democratic system to emerge. Ten years on and NATO, under the name ISAF (International Security Assistance Force), is still engaged in the country. Local leaders control their own territories, consisting of impassable terrain, with a fierce sense of ownership. They will co-operate with the central government when it suits them; whoever controls Kabul dominates only one small part of a vast territory. The United States and its allies have been forced to curtail their ambitions for a democratic polity in Afghanistan; a state with control over its territory is now their goal, though whether even this is achievable is doubtful.

Following September 2001, the United States administration also advocated 'regime change' in Iraq. A combination of professed motives included punishing those responsible for the 9/11 attacks, preventing the use of 'weapons of mass destruction', and the new American vision of exporting democracy and freedom to other countries. Other motives that were less openly discussed included access to Iraqi oil and the country's strategic location, bordering the key states of Iran, Syria, Jordan and Saudi Arabia. Having a compliant ally in such a location would be a significant geopolitical gain for the United States. This time, however, the international community did not agree with the legality of an invasion and the United States had to go it alone, with Britain as its junior partner.

Once Saddam Hussein was deposed the transition regime run by the US oversaw elections in January 2005 to a 275-member Transitional National Assembly charged with drawing up a new democratic constitution. This election was boycotted by the Sunni minority, with just 2 per cent turnout in some Sunni provinces. The Assembly appointed Kurdish leader Jalal Talabani as president and the Shi'ite Ibrahim al-Jaafari as prime minister. The new administration, acting under American supervision, agreed a constitution in October 2005 and elections to a permanent Council of Representatives were held in December 2005. Turnout in this second election was nearly 80 per cent with relatively little disruption to the voting process. A new Prime Minister, Nouri al-Maliki, led a coalition government. Iraq had become a democracy.

Two questions then arose which echo earlier episodes in the history of democracy and bring into sharp focus the need to understand the practicalities of democracy. First, was the democratic government the real power in the land, and was it acknowledged as such by the population? And second, would democracy win the approval of the people by delivering a decent life? The answer to the first question remains in the balance though it is unarguable that, despite the reduction in troop numbers, the United States is a powerful force in the country, along with Iran and internal groups – some using violence – who remain outside the democratic system. In 2006, in an interview on CNN, al-Maliki tried to counter the impression that the United States remained the real power in the land: 'I consider myself a friend of the US, but I'm not America's man in Iraq.'

On the second question, life in Iraq has remained a desperate struggle. After eight years, comparisons with the Saddam regime are no longer tenable; instead people want to know why, in a country rich in oil, the capital city has power for only six hours a day, and why, despite the billions of dollars pumped into Iraq, no one seems to be able to do anything to improve the country's infrastructure. The large-scale violence of the post-invasion years has abated, but security remains a concern for all Iraqis. Another round of elections was held in March 2010 but it took eight more months for a fragile coalition government to form, with the president and prime minister retaining their positions. Being able to count numbers of parliamentary seats gives Iraq a comfortable familiarity for Western observers but this means little in the wider context of impotence and insecurity.

Iraq and Afghanistan are the most notable recent examples of attempts to implant democracy. Throughout Africa and Asia the architecture of democracy – parliaments, elections, civil rights – disguise the realities of power. As one commentator has concluded: 'State-building isn't working, and it isn't for lack of trying.' And, more worryingly for democracy in African countries, he states that: 'peacekeeping missions and elections, heralded as the way to lift these countries out of prolonged crisis, now effectively deepen their entrapment.'[2] Trying to make things better from outside often makes them worse.

If American global power had a brief and probably futile phase of exporting democracy, how has globalisation – the other geopolitical force of the age – affected the spread of democracy? The overwhelming trend of global trading has been to weaken the economic dominance of North America and Europe. These were the historic heartlands of democracy but they had a questionable role in encouraging global democratic development during the Cold War. Over the last two decades countries in Africa, Asia and Latin America have become more democratic, or returned to democracy for the first time in decades. However, for most elected leaders, the main problem has been how far to enter the international global network of finance, with its access to loans and foreign investment, but with dangers of the state losing control of its own economy by putting its fate in the hands of international speculators. Globalisation works both ways: in the 1990s traders and funding bodies like the IMF and World Bank wanted countries to show democratic credentials, but the price of joining the global market is that elected governments lose power to global forces that often seem beyond anyone's control.

Different regions of the world have taken alternative pathways through this forest of competing forces. In Latin America democracy has seen its strongest resurgence. In Brazil, Argentina, Chile, Bolivia, Venezuela and Mexico governments have taken different approaches to their own internal affairs and how to place themselves within the globalised system. The most successful, in particular Brazil, have focussed on building up a strong internal economy with a potent middle class, something that Latin American leaders have previously failed to do, while building trading alliances with other so-called emerging economies. In Venezuela and Bolivia, presidents Hugo Chavez and Evo Morales have taken another road – socialist and nationalist, defying the power of the United States. In all this, Latin America has shown signs of a genuine alteration in its view of itself. While previously Latin Americans believed that their history and culture put them at a disadvantage to Europeans and North Americans, it has recently shown signs of embracing the distinctiveness of its unique combination of cultures. A survey of world film in 2009, for example, said that 'without question the first decade of the new century belonged to Latin America'.[3] This respect for their own cultural history rather than someone else's is a fascinating element in the development of democracy – the belief that every person has the right to a say in who governs is rooted in respect for your fellow citizens. Democracy has long existed only in name in Latin America; it is beginning to be more deeply observed and widely practised.

In South Asia similar moves happened through the 1980s and 90s. In the Philippines, Ferdinand Marcos had ruled an ostensible democracy, though in reality a dictatorship, since 1965. The president had been supported by successive US governments as a bulwark against communism, but as a result of remarkable mass protests he was thrown out of power and a functioning democracy installed in 1986; a new constitution was agreed the following year. Indonesia finally shook off the dictatorial rule of Suharto and became a democracy in 1999. Malaysia remains an ostensible democracy, ruled by a succession of long-standing premiers. Prosperity has improved in the country but with little sign of democratic developments such as respect for political opposition or a free press. Burma, though, remains an intractable and brutal military dictatorship, defying the ability of the rest of the world to interfere in its internal repression – and showing how a determined clique can maintain power by keeping a tight grip on a centralised, militarised state. The same intransigence has persisted in North Korea.

At the time of writing, popular demonstrations and rebellions calling for democracy have brought changes of government in Tunisia, Egypt and Libya, while protests in Syria, Bahrain and the Yemen have highlighted the decades-long repression of political dissent in these countries and elsewhere in the Middle East. The success of these uprisings will be judged, in Western countries at least, by how democratic they become. But how far are we prepared to go in helping them? If a Middle East government were elected on a platform of nationalising its oil production, or developing its own petro-chemical industry, would the West allow that to happen?

In Africa too, the fall of communism has brought about the emergence of democracy as the only 'respectable' form of government. Where previously most leaders came to power through violent coups, since 1989 elections have been the route to government and the crucial acceptance by the international community that triggers financial and trade support. But this new generation of democratically elected African leaders has shown a marked reluctance to surrender power. Kenya was thrown into crisis in December 2007 when the incumbent president, Mwai Kibaki, was declared winner of a highly disputed election. After widespread violence that approached the level of civil war, a settlement was reached that brought in a power-sharing coalition government – a temporary solution that deprives the country of a viable opposition. In Nigeria, Olusegun Obasanjo was elected president in 1999 after sixteen years of military rule. After two terms he was replaced by another politician from his People's Democratic Party, Umaru Yar'Adua, who won power in 2007 amid widespread claims of electoral fraud. After his death in office, he was succeeded by his deputy Goodluck Jonathan, who won the next election in 2011, leaving the same party in power. In South Africa, there is little sign of a credible opposition that could defeat the ANC in national elections – the route to power is within the party rather than in public political forums. In January 2011 Laurent Gbagbo, incumbent president of Ivory Coast, was declared the loser in presidential elections. He refused to leave office and was only ousted by army units loyal to the victor Alassane Ouattara, with the help of French troops. As one analyst of African politics has written: 'if you lose an election there's a second way: you get mediators in and cut a deal.'[4] While power sharing like that seen in Kenya seems to defeat the principle of competitive elections, it may be the African solution to an African problem.

Across the world democracy has become a desirable end – both for citizens who want the benefits that it brings, and for leaders who need its legitimacy in order to enter the international system. It is the latter that often takes priority. As we have seen, voters are often denied the opportunity to remove their rulers from power, while the rights of citizens are routinely overridden by the state.

With so many countries becoming democracies while, at the same time, their governments ignore many of its essential elements, the old divide between democracies and other forms of government has given way to degrees of democracy. In this situation analysts have come up with ways of measuring and scoring democracies. The Economist Intelligence Unit published its first Democracy Index in 2006; the second edition, published in 2008, concluded that 'following a decades-long global trend in democratisation, the spread of democracy has come to a halt'. The 2010 edition was even more gloomy; its summary is entitled 'Democracy in retreat' and declares: 'there has been a decline in democracy across the world since 2008'.[5] In common with other bodies, the EIU does not decide whether a country is a democracy or not, but examines its performance through expert assessments of sixty questions providing information in five areas: electoral process and pluralism, civil liberties, functioning of government, political participation and political culture. Countries are listed according to their scores, and also categorised, in declining order of score, as Full Democracies (of which there were twenty-six in 2010), Flawed Democracies (fifty-three), Hybrid Regimes (thirty-three) and Authoritarian Regimes (fifty-five). Other international indexes include elements such as economic freedom, and focus less on public participation. As these indexes are not published in academic journals they are not subject to independent review. Nevertheless, the EIU Index does at least tell us that measuring democracy is a subtle and complex business, which involves factors beyond regular elections, universal adult franchise and secret voting. It is entirely possible, for example, to live in a society where free and fair elections are regularly held, *and* where citizens are imprisoned by state authorities without charge and without knowing the evidence against them.

The EIU ascribes the decline in democracy to a number of factors. The attempts to impose democracy in Afghanistan and Iraq have had a negative impact on its idealisation – when democracy becomes part of a package proposed by an invading force, then people become cynical. A similar effect has been seen in other parts of the world – eastern Europe, Russia, Latin America – where the initial enthusiasm for democracy has been tempered by harsh economic realities. When democracy doesn't deliver the anticipated prosperity, people can easily look for other solutions. More cynically, dictators throughout the world have learned better ways to protect themselves against being overthrown by popular rebellions, and high oil prices have enabled many to strengthen their grip on power.

In established Western democracies, the analysis picks out two trends: increasing curbs on civil liberties and 'a precipitous decline in political participation'. Taking this latter point first, some analysts see a historically significant shift away from representative democracy and towards so-called 'monitory democracy', in which groups that are outside the formal political system play a big role.[6]

This is a trend rooted in the history of democracy. We saw in Chapter 6 how Alexis de Tocqueville and John Stuart Mill argued for the essential importance to a functioning democracy of a dense array of institutions such as parish, borough and county councils, trade associations, school boards, local associations of political parties, public demonstrations and so on. Though often an inconvenience and irritation, these bodies and activities have always acted as a crucial check on the untrammelled power of the state. Yet in many nations the state has worked hard in recent decades to eliminate any institutions that present themselves as rivals for power in any sphere. Democratically elected leaders deplore this tendency when in opposition but find it suits them well once they are in power.

With little to stand between the individual and the state, the only power left to the democratic citizen is to vote at elections. But citizens want more than this. So traditional institutions, such as an independent judiciary and a free press, have been joined by congressional and parliamentary committees, judicial inquiries, and public hearings. All these are within the formal system but independent of the executive arm of government. In Britain for example, the government went ahead with the invasion of Iraq in 2003 in the face of strong public opposition, supported by a Parliament in possession of an inaccurate set of facts. While unable to prevent the government from undertaking the invasion, the democratic system has pressed a reluctant executive into setting up three separate inquiries into different aspects of the war. The latest inquiry, chaired by John Chilcot, forced both the ex- and the serving prime ministers to appear – the first time this has happened in British history. Government-appointed inspectors of prisons and schools, children's commissioners, and others produce reports that are often critical of government performance.

Outside the formal political systems a host of bodies publish reports, investigations and research findings into almost every aspect of government policy and behaviour. It is essential that, for their own sake, these bodies retain the trust of the public so that their reports are taken to be open, if not always unbiased. In fact independent bodies are so widely trusted that a report into overseas aid by Oxfam or Save The Children, for example, will often be taken more seriously than a government report. This is not surprising when, according to an EU-commissioned poll in 2004, only 10 per cent of British, 11 per cent of German, and 13 per cent of Italian respondents trusted political parties. Governments are similarly viewed with distrust. Political commentators often decry the fact that young people are more likely to join a single-issue pressure group than a political party – in the 1960s more than 10 per cent of registered voters in European countries were members of a political party compared to less than 4 per cent today – but as political leaders have increasingly deprived party members of any say in policy, people are simply seeking a more effective way to express their political views.[7]

There are recent signs that young people are becoming more active through public demonstrations, particularly when issues affect them directly, while the Internet has provided a new channel of expression. This first caught fire in Howard Dean's campaign for the Democratic nomination for US president in 2004. Young people were attracted by Dean's policies and most of his campaign funds were raised through Internet donations, where the average given was $80 in contrast to the massive corporate donations generally received by candidates. Dean's campaign also used the Internet to recruit and encourage activists. Barack Obama too resorted to the Internet in 2008, with activists organising web-based campaigns in target areas to good effect. Other politicians have courted the Obama team to learn the magic formula, only to find that there isn't one – the Internet is just one more way of promoting your candidate.

Measuring and monitoring may or may not dominate the next phase of democracy, replacing the original direct democracy of Athens and Graubünden and the representative Western democracies of the last two centuries. If it does it will be prey to the same difficulties, false friends, enthusiasts and champions as its predecessors. And who, we might wonder, will monitor the monitors? Will society be dominated by tensions between the elected representatives of the people and the self-appointed who claim to know what is best for the rest of us?

Even though the EIU Democracy Index throws its net widely, we should remember that it is measuring democracy rather than how well a society works, or the quality of life of its citizens, or their happiness (whatever that is taken to mean). The countries that score highest in the index are north European, ethnically homogeneous, wealthy countries with a history of communal working and living. We have seen in Chapter 12 that these countries have a cultural history of a strong commitment to society from their citizens in return for high social benefits. This can mean that outsiders find it difficult to find their way.

There is also a danger that ranking countries implies a kind of linear progression, with Europe and its old white colonies at the top and African and Asian countries at the bottom. Let us remember that democracy is a means to several ends. It was reborn in the modern world to give citizens control over the modern Western state. In cultures where democracy is struggling to establish itself it could be the structure of the state that is the problem rather than the commitment to democracy.

In Western countries democracy infuses every aspect of life. This doesn't mean that we are always thinking or talking about politics but we each live with the continual assumption that our views matter as much as anyone else's, that we should be free to express them, that politicians are there to solve the country's problems and, if they don't, then we have the right to kick them out.

These assumptions provide a framework for our lives, while also bringing their own problems. Politicians regularly promise more than they can ever deliver, and often mess things up because they are trying to be popular instead of effective. This tendency for deception, or more generously over-optimism, is actually one of the hallmarks of democracies – democratic politicians must lie and we must complain about their lying.

One of the curiosities of successful democracies is how different they are from each other and from what we might call a standard model (which gives us a clue as to why democracy is hard to export). Of the top ten democracies in the EIU Index, for example, seven are constitutional monarchies which give special, albeit limited, powers to one family. Some elect by various forms of proportional representation, others by winner-takes-all; some have powerful regional governments; some hold elections for everything from heads of state to police chiefs to school boards, while others would see this as an unwelcome intrusion of politics into civil society.

Most of the people I talked to about the subject of this book – all of whom were born and lived in a democracy – were surprisingly cynical. Democracy, they thought, was not what it used to be; politicians had taken power away from ordinary people and were, in any case, fairly hopeless at running their country's affairs. There is some truth in this – over the last thirty years power has been handed to a global financial system over which no one has real control and, in compensation for this loss of authority, national governments have centralised power within their own countries. Voters feel they have had little say in this process, which has had the greatest effect on their lives.

Living in a democracy does not guarantee a happy and fulfilled existence, nor a sense of contentment with governments or politicians. Even the most popular democratic leaders last around a decade at most. Indeed, discontent is an essential element of every democracy. We gripe and moan and rage, and occasionally write a letter or join a protest march – complaining about the government and politicians is, after all, our democratic right. That's all very well, but what if the biggest complaint is that there is no choice? Those who look back on the 1960s and 70s as a time when real choice was on offer need to bear in mind that this was a time of social upheaval, and that it followed decades of what was called the post-war consensus – it is perhaps in our nature to want consensus after conflict, and then to yearn for a vision that provides an alternative.

Our greatest failure would be to abandon democracy in favour of a more seductive political vision, and it is to our eternal credit that we have resisted this temptation – mostly. History shows that this can easily happen, even in the west European heartland of democracy. The catastrophic retreat of democracy in the 1930s in the face of economic depression must lead us to ask whether democracy is a luxury that only wealthy countries, or those with growing economies and prospects, can afford. The most powerful rebuttal to this is India, a country where the majority of its people have lived at subsistence level for most of its democratic history. For all its faults, Indian democracy should be our inspiration.

Nevertheless it would be easy to get too dewy-eyed about the establishment of democracy outside Europe and those countries settled by Europeans. For the last sixty years liberal democracies have dominated the world economy; in 1990 the US and the European Union produced over 60 per cent of the world's GDP; predictions for 2013 put the figure at between 40 and 45 per cent. Countries like China, Brazil, India and Indonesia will have as much, if not more, economic muscle as the old democratic West. Out of a total of 167 countries, their rankings on the EIU Democracy Index are 136, 47, 40 and 60 respectively; China is placed under 'Authoritarian Regimes' while the other three are categorised as 'Flawed Democracies'. Will prosperity induce greater openness, leading to democratic structures and practices, or will prosperity in China, for example, be limited without democratic developments? Can a nation that is politically restricted deliver widespread prosperity for its citizens? The truth is we don't know – because the situation we face is unprecedented. Indeed the search for historical precedents shows us that the history of democracy, for all its recent triumphs, has occured in just a few places and over short periods of time. Those of us who have spent our whole lives in democracies, and in a world dominated by them, are a fortunate minority.

Democracy can be an uncomfortable system to live in because democratic politics, when it works well, takes on the conflicts in society; and when it works badly it fails to control the power of the state. Other political systems offer a mirage, a vision of a society where all conflicts are resolved and harmony reigns, even if this is at the expense of individual liberty; only democracy reflects the reality of human existence – that we are complex creatures and often impotent in the face of our own nature. Democratic states can act out of concern, generosity and forethought, but also show arrogance, revenge, pettiness and short-sightedness – just like us. Democracy understands our complexity and deals with it, rather than pretending it does not exist.

However, one element of democracy is, if anything, a little too simple. Elections give politicians an opportunity to persuade us to vote for them. They need to use simple powerful messages, easily transmitted through headlines, soundbites and hearsay, which promise a better future for their electors. But government or, to use a more loaded term, statecraft is often a matter of not giving people what they immediately want; it is about devising and carrying through measures that are beyond everyday experience in the teeth of entrenched opposition.

Democratic governments have not found that an easy task. We began this book in the agora at Athens, the marketplace where traders plied their wares. Athenian democracy demanded that the citizens leave the agora, driven out by the vermilion rope, and make the climb up the hill to the assembly of the people. Arguably the greatest failure of democratic governments in our time has been the surrender of power to the international financial system in return for short-term prosperity for their electors. The traders of the agora once shrank before the power of the assembly; now our leaders must bend to the will of markets, the pnyx bends the knee to the agora. This will change, but only by making the world more democratic, not less.

The history of democracy tells us much, but can only teach us what we are willing to learn. We said at the beginning that every democracy is different and that there is no blueprint, no set of rules that will guarantee its success. The world is changing; existing democracies face new challenges, including economic gridlock and the possibility of catastrophic climate change, while people of different cultures are seeking ways to build democracies in their own lands. The history of democracy can offer some guidance but no easy answers beyond two simple truths. Firstly, democracies must continually create new ways of working if they are to survive, and new democracies must invent their own structures and practices without undue interference if they are to endure. The second truth, learned through a century of unimaginable cruelty, is that, when we give up democracy – through the seductions of demagogues or at the point of a gun – our lives are inconsolably diminished.

A democratic society is the expression of a multitude of lives; it is never 'achieved', it is always a work in progress. It is a continual act of communal creativity – and the energy required to keep creating is immense, as are the forces ranged against it. Nepotism, patronage, self-interest, cynicism, apathy and the seductions of a quiet life are powerful lures that we can only intermittently overcome, yet overcome them we must if we are to flourish.

NOTES

Prologue

1. Bernard Crick (2002) *Democracy: A Very Short Introduction*, OUP, Oxford, p 1.

1 *Athens and the Ancient World*

1. For a map of ancient Athens see Meier, p. 382. • 2. Ostracism was named after the *ostraka*, pieces of pottery on which members of the people's assembly scratched the name of the person they wanted to see expelled. The ostracism vote was held every year; if there were more than 6,000 votes cast in total then the person with most votes would be banished from the polis for ten years, and given only ten days to leave. The measure was brought in to prevent a tyrant emerging to take power in the city. It was first used in 487 BC, and a further fifteen times until 415–407 BC: it remained on the statute book but was never used after this date. • 3. See, for example, Popper. • 4. Solon wrote poems that were a defence of his measures, but these are suspected of being altered and added to by later writers. For a full historiography of Athenian democracy see Hansen, Ch. 1. • 5. Herodotus, Book 1, 29. • 6. See, for example, Hornblower • 7. Aristophanes, *The Knights*, ll 48–9. • 8. Aristophanes, *The Archanians*, ll 19–39. • 9. Thucydides, Book 2, ll 35–46. • 10. Demosthenes, *Public Orations*. • 11. Barbara Everett, writing about the flowering of Elizabethan literature, commented: 'There is always an element of the random in the historical which demands respect.' Everett also quoted the poet Marianne Moore: 'We prove, we do not explain our birth.' *London Review of Books*, 19 August 2010, p. 32. • 12. In *The Laws*, written in his old age, Plato has a character called the Athenian argue for a combination of democracy and monarchy, but within this system everyone lives a life minutely prescribed by the state. • 13. For writings attributed to, and descriptive of,

Protagoras and Democritus, see Barnes, Chs 5 and 21 respectively; also Cartledge. • **14**. In 1957 Ralf Dahrendorf wrote: 'Totalitarian monism is founded on the idea that conflict can and should be eliminated, that a homogenous and uniform social and political order is the desirable state of affairs. This idea is no less dangerous for the fact that it is mistaken in its sociological premises.' Quoted in Arblaster, p. 423. • **15**. Livy's *The Early History of Rome*, for example, was written in the first and second decades AD. R. M. Ogilvie suspects that the coincidence of dates of the expulsion of tyrants from Rome and Athens – both around 507 BC – is due to Livy's copying of this and other stories from Greek history. See Introduction to Livy, p. 8. • **16**. Valerius Maximus Anecdotes 7, *Memorable Deeds and Sayings: One Thousand Tales from Ancient Rome*, related in Beard & Crawford, p. 64. • **17**. Suetonius, 'Julius Caesar', p. 76.

2 *Parliaments and Things*

1. Quoted in Cantor, p. 301. • **2**. See Monaghan and Just for an excellent introduction to this subject. • **3**. Herodotus, Book 3, 80. • **4**. Walbank, p 88. • **5**. Tacitus, *Germania*, I, 11. • **6**. For more on Scandinavian assemblies see Sawyer. • **7**. See Bartlett for a convincing analysis of this takeover of Europe. • **8**. Marongui, p. 20. • **9**. Keane, p. 155. • **10**. Ibid., pp. 169–88. • **11**. Quoted in Mundy, p. 407. • **12**. Henry III came to the throne as a child. In his minority, the barons of England effectively ruled, and when he grew old enough to take control there was a violent power struggle between monarch and nobility. Simon de Montfort led his forces to victory over Henry III at Lewes in 1264. • **13**. The account of the Good Parliament was recorded in the Anonimallie Chronicle; see Galbraith. • **14**. Marongui, p. 29. • **15**. See Uckelman. • **16**. Roman towns in western Europe had been administrative rather than trading centres. Arguably medieval towns were a revival of Celtic craft-based settlements, but these had not existed for nearly 1,000 years. • **17**. Charter of King John to Wells, Somerset, 1201, quoted in Anderson and Bellenger, p. 262. • **18**. The annual Mayor Making is still held in most English and many European towns. In a ceremony dating back to the seventeenth century the mayor of High Wycombe is weighed in public at the start and end of her term of office to see whether she has taken advantage of her position. • **19**. Bailey, Transcripts from the Archives of Winchester. • **20**. Magna Carta full text is at www.bl.uk/treasures/magnacarta.

3 Medieval Towns and City Republics

1. Englander et al. (eds), p. 276. • 2. Mak, p.11. • 3. Ibid, p 1. • 4. Bristol was granted its charter by the king of England; Mainz by its bishop; Rouen by the duke of Normandy; Lübeck by the count of Schaumburg and Holstein; Gdansk by the duke of Pomerania. • 5. Guicciardini, *Description des touts les Pais-Bas*, Antwerp, 1567, quoted in Englander et al. (eds), p. 127 et seq. • 6. Rembrandt's *The Night Watch* depicts an Amsterdam militia company. • 7. Hajo Brugmans, quoted in Mak, p. 75. • 8. Martines, p 7. • 9. Cipolla, pp. 25–71. • 10. Schevill, p. 43. • 11. Waley (1998), p. 10. • 12. Ibid., p 36, source: *Statuti Pisa*. • 13. *Boni homines* was also a name adopted by different monastic orders within the medieval Catholic Church. • 14. Schevill, p. 55. • 15. Mundy, p. 433, from P. M. Viollet (1901) 'Les communes au moyen âge', *Memoires de l'Academie des Inscriptions et Belles-Lettres*, pp. xxxvi, ii, 436.While Italian cities and those, like Marseilles, in marginal areas had claimed their right to govern, in other areas, such as east Saxony and Gascony, princes founded new towns for strategic and financial gain and provided rights and freedoms as incentives for people to settle in them. Other commune-type governments included Rouen where, in the late twelfth century, the group of One Hundred Peers annually chose a mayor and twenty-four *jurati* from among themselves; in Freiburg twenty-four consuls were selected from the Richterzeche (patrician association) and served for life; in Ghent there were three groups each of thirteen who served in rotation as the governors of the city. In Cologne the Richterzeche was a permanent element in the city government, though in 1216 participation in the city council was widened. See Jeep. • 16. Waley (1998), p. 41, source: *Annali Genovese*. • 17. Ibid., p. 145. • 18. Schevill, p. 148. • 19. Waley (1998), pp. 59–60. • 20. Elsewhere in Europe the guilds took power from the nobility in similar ways. In towns in Swabia, Burgundy and Alsace the post of Captain of the People appeared. In Freiburg in 1293 the council was chosen from eighteen guilds; in Liège sixty governors chosen from the guilds sat alongside the burgomasters, and from 1313 a general assembly brought in regulations that made the consent of the people a condition of raising taxes. • 21. Waley (1998), p. 140, source: *Statuti Modena*. • 22. Martines' book is a prolonged and persuasive argument for this interpretation. See also Shaw. • 23. Waley (1998), p. 132, source: *Statuti Spoleto*. • 24. Ibid., p. 131, source: *Statuti del commune di Padova*. • 25. See Shaw. • 26. *Cronica de Giovanni Villani*, quoted in Anderson and Bellenger, p. 277. • 27. Master Valesio, quoted in Shaw, p. 8.

4 *Democracy in the High Alps*

1. The state carried the full title of the 'Free state of the Three Leagues in Old Upper Rhaetia' having been formed by the amalgamation of three leagues, or groups of communes. • 2. Quoted in Head, p. 87. • 3. For the workings of Graubünden institutions, including referendums, see Barber, Ch. 7. • 4. Head, p. 84. • 5. Barber, p. 176. • 6. Head, p. 78. • 7. Barber, p. 173. • 8. Head, p. 1. • 9. Barber, p. 198.

5 *The English Revolution*

1. See Keegan, Ch. 5 and Bobbitt for more on the link between weaponry and the emergence of monarchies. • 2. Quoted in Wootton, p. 99 et seq. • 3. The quote is from the 1649 pamphlet, *True Levellers Standard Advanced*, though similar words had previously been used by Edward Sexby, indicating that it was a fairly common if not widespread belief. • 4. Marchamont Needham or Nedham gained a reputation by attacking Charles I in print, then became a royalist supporter during the civil war. Once the Commonwealth was established under Cromwell he wrote a tract defending republican government. See *Dictionary of National Biography*, Oxford, 2004. • 5. For Richard Overton's views on this subject see 'An Appeal to the Commons from the Free People' (1647), quoted in Woodhouse, pp. 323–38. • 6. Gentles, p. 158. • 7. Ibid, p. 179. • 8. Royal supporter John Evelyn returned from France 'and on 10th [October] to Hampton Court, where I had the honour to kisse his Majesty's hand . . . he being now in the power of those execrable villains'. Evelyn diary, entry for 5 October 1647. • 9. Notes of two days of the debates were taken by William Clark, and preserved, unpublished, until the late nineteenth century, when democracy became a goal rather than a threat to British politics. Transcripts can be found in Woodhouse, and extracts in Wootton, pp. 285–317. • 10. His name is variously transcribed as Rainborough, Rainborowe and Rainsborough. • 11. Hill, p. 362. • 12. Quoted in Kellner, p. 120. • 13. Binns, pp. 153–63.

6 *Democracy in America*

1. Indentured servants had to work for seven years for their master, after which they were free to work as they wished. • 2. Joshua Miller. p. 27. • 3. William Ames (1638) *The Marrow of Sacred Divinity*, p. 136. • 4. De Tocqueville, Book 1, Ch. 19. • 5. Williamson, p. 9. • 6. Figures from US Census Series Z-19. • 7. Brogan, Chs 4, 7, 13. • 8. Franklin, p. 226. • 9. Originally appearing under the name 'The Federalist' but now usually referred to as the 'Federalist Papers',

see Hamilton et al. • **10**. Letter to Jean-Baptiste Leroy, 1789. • **11**. See Farrand for a full record of the Convention. • **12**. 'Federalist Paper' No.10, see Hamilton et al. • **13**. *The Life of Elias Smith, written by Himself*, 1816, quoted in Dunn (ed.) Ch. 6. • **14**. Library of Congress archive at www.loc.gov/rr/program/bib/presidents/jefferson • **15**. From 'For Those Who Would Want To Remove To America', Franklin, pp. 240–1. • **16**. The members of each electoral college numbered the same as the number of senators and representatives in Congress and were, under the Constitution, appointed by each state. The assumption was that they would be chosen in the same way as members of Congress, though no member of Congress could be a member of the electoral college. • **17**. There are now legal sanctions against so-called 'faithless electors' – those members of an electoral college who do not follow the popular vote. • **18**. Brogan, p. 267. • **19**. De Tocqueville Book 2, Ch. 5. De Tocqueville believed democracy would spread to Europe and was fascinated by the different outcomes of the French and American Revolutions: 'A democratic republic exists in the United States and the principal object of this book is to explain the cause of its existence.' • **20**. *Fraser's Magazine*, April 1832.

7 *France 1789–95*

1. See Jonathan Israel for an analysis of the different strands of thinking circulating at this time. • **2**. See McPhee. • **3**. Quoted in McPhee, p. 37. • **4**. Jefferson, Journal entry for 12 July 1789. • **5**. Rousseau, *The Social Contract*, pp. 1, 15. • **6**. Bernard Crick has written: 'Think what you like of the argument, Rousseau for the first time provides a moral justification for democracy.' Crick, p. 54. But Rousseau also stated : 'If there were a nation of gods, it would be governed democratically. So perfect a government is unsuited to men.' *The Social Contract*, Book 3, Ch. 2. • **7**. De Tocqueville, *L'Ancien regime et la revolution*, p. 96. • **8**. Quoted in Carey (ed.), pp. 248–50. • **9**. Quoted in McPhee, p. 98. • **10**. Rousseau, *The Social Contract*, Book 3 Ch. 15. • **11**. Walzer, pp. 121–30. • **12**. With the Jacobins firmly in control, the sans-culotte practice of voting by openly declaring your choice in front of an audience was revoked, and replaced by the ballot. Historians such as Albert Soboul argue that the ballot was favoured by the bourgeoisie of every political persuasion. • **13**. Robespierre, *Textes Choisis*, iii, 112–15. Editions Sociales, Paris, 1974. • **14**. Campbell, p. 57.

8 *Republics in Latin America*

1. The 1536 settlement at Buenos Aires was abandoned in 1541; a permanent settlement was established in 1580. • **2**. Quoted in Harvey, p. 3. • **3**. As Harvey writes: 'The vibrant yet decadent heart of the whole system was the Viceroyalty of Peru where the silver mines had created a glittering city, Lima, of idle rich alongside a teeming and wretched Indian underclass' (p. 3). • **4**. For quotes from Bolívar, see Bushnell pp. 1–62, except where other sources given. • **5**. Circular letter to Colombia, 3 August 1826, quoted in Lynch (1983), p. 17. • **6**. Bushnell, pp. 1–62. • **7**. Letter to General Juan Jose Flores, 9 November 1830, see Bolívar, *Obras Completas*. • **8**. Quoted in Hale, p. 197 • **9**. Quoted in Williamson, p. 242. • **10**. See, for example, Camacho, Ch. 5 'Obstacles To Progress'. • **11**. Colonel J. P. Hamilton, *Travels Through South America* (1827), quoted in Camacho, p. 85. • **12**. Bethell, p. 231. • **13**. Victor Fidel López, *Revista del Río de la Plata* (1871–7).

9 *Europe in the Nineteenth Century*

1. St John, pp. 72–84. • **2**. Flaubert, pp. 310-11. • **3**. Victor Hugo 'The History of a Crime', trans. T. H. Joyce and Arthur Locker, 1886. • **4**. The first description of economic cycles in which expansion is always followed by a certain degree of retraction came in 1819, but economic theory did not produce political understanding in this area for many decades. • **5**. The complexities of the Schleswig Holstein affair led Lord Palmerston, the British Foreign Secretary, reputedly to contend: 'There are only three people in the world who understand the Schleswig Holstein question and I am one of them.' • **6**. Quoted in Cunningham, p. 32. • **7**. See Mack Smith, Ch. 3 'Cavour and Parliament'. • **8**. Quoted in Morrogh, p. 102. • **9**. Gildea, p. 218.

10 *Embrace and Retreat*

1. Examples from Britain include the *Sunday Chronicle*, the *Yorkshire Factory Times*, the *Cotton Factory Times*, the *Workman's Times* and the *Clarion*. • **2**. Jürgen Kocka argues that this was an essential part of the structure of society: 'For bourgeois culture a specific ideal of family life was essential . . . Dominated by the husband and father, it was an inner sanctum protected from the world of competition and materialism . . . the availability of serv-ants appears to be central. Bourgeois culture cannot flourish without plenty of space . . . and time for cultural activities and leisure.' *Bourgeoise Society in Nineteenth-Century Europe*, pp. 6–7. • **3**. I outlined some of the different mean-ings of the word 'socialism' in a previous book: see Osborne, pp. 358–9. • **4**. See Mann and Tillett, p. 3. • **5**. Leo Chiozza (1905) *Riches and Poverty*, Methuen. • **6**. Lenin, *Theses on Bourgeois Democracy and the Dictatorship of the Proletariat*, 1909. • **7**. In July 1918 Colonel Max Bauer wrote to Ludendorff: 'The war is not yet won. We will win it if the homeland no longer stabs the Army in the back.' Hindenberg told a Reichstag committee of inquiry in 1919: 'As an English general has very truly said, "The German Army was stabbed in the back".' The general was probably Frederick Maurice. See Feldman, p. 502. • **8.** Shirer, p. 56. • **9.** Henig, p. 27. • **10.** See, for example, Spengler. • **11.** Feuchtwanger, pp. 330, 331. • **12.** Quoted in Kaes et al. (eds), p. 115. • **13.** Bullock, p. 283. • **14.** Quoted in Noakes and Pridham, pp. 127–8, 135. • **15.** Quoted in Carey (ed), p. 507. • **16.** Hobsbawm, p. 111.

11 *India*

1. Quoted in Stokes, p. 34. • **2.** Letter to Rajendra Prasad, quoted in Brown (1999), p. 72. • **3.** The words 'socialist secular' were added after 'sovereign' in 1976. • **4.** Quoted in Brown (1999), p. 79. • **5.** Chandra, pp. 174–5. • **6.** Pakistan was originally made up of two separate territories. When East Pakistan broke away and declared Bangladesh independent, forces from West Pakistan invaded. Amid terrible scenes of brutality and starvation, India intervened in defiance of the United States.

12 *The Postwar West*

1. See Chapter 15 for a discussion of democracy indexes. • **2.** Just as one example, social housing bodies in Denmark are actually owned by their tenants, with decisions on rents and budgets taken by the residents' assembly or *beboermødet*. • **3.** Churchill had many things to say about democracy, which he called 'The worst form of government, except for all those other forms that have been tried from time to time.' His feelings about elections were nicely contradictory, in temper if not in fact: 'No part of the education of a politician is more indispensable than the fighting of elections.' 'The best argument against democracy is a five-minute conversation with the average voter.' • **4.** A constitutional change in 1962 brought direct elections for the presidency, and in 2000 the presidential term was reduced to five years. • **5.** D. S. Delmer, *Daily Express*, 23 October 1956. • **6.** Trumbo, p. 50 et seq. • **7.** In 1953 Sarah Louise Keys, a private in the Womens' Army Corps, took out a complaint against the Carolina Trailways bus company for discriminating against black travellers on buses that crossed state lines. The Supreme Court ruled in her favour days before the protest by Rosa Parks.

13 *Democracy and Decolonisation*

1. This constitution was later amended, bringing into being a two-chamber parliament and a multi-party system in 1971. However, Egyptian democracy remained highly restricted: an emergency law, in which civil rights were suspended, demonstrations banned and police powers extended, was first introduced in 1967, and had been in force continuously from 1981 until the forced resignation of Hosni Mubarak in 2011. • **2.** Quoted in Jones, p. 29. • **3.** Birmingham, p. 10. • **4.** Quotes from de Gaulle, see Smith.

14 *The Collapse of Communism in Europe*

1. David Gow, *Guardian*, 1 October 1990. • **2.** Visit: Centre Virtuel de la Connaissance sur l'Europe. • **3.** Previously suppressed novels and factual books began to see the light of day, including Vasily Grossman's *Life and Fate*, written in 1961 but only published in 1988; Vladimir Dudintsev's *White Coats*, about the Lysenko affair; Varlam Shalamov's *Kolyma*, an exposure of the infamous labour camp; and Anatolii Rybakov's *Children of the Arbat*. • **4.** Soviet forces and agents attempted to retake control of the Baltic States in January 1991; full independence came after the failed coup attempt in Moscow in August 1991. Estonia had effectively declared itself an independent republic through the Congress of Estonia, which was elected in February 1990, though a formal referendum on independence was held in March 1991. • **5.** The full text of Yeltsin's speech is at: web.viu.ca/davies/H102/Yeltsin.speech.1991.htm reform • **6.** Milosevic was arrested in March 2001, his trial in The Hague began in 2002 and he died in his cell in 2006 from a heart attack. • **7.** Quoted in Gray, p. 376. • **8.** A series of papers detailing conversations among the ruling group at the time of the crisis was published in the West in 2001, titled *The Tiananmen Papers*. See Zhang Liang. • **9.** The report by the mayor of Beijing, Chen Xitong, was reproduced in translation in *China Quarterly* 120. See Gray, p. 428.

15 *Democracy since 1989*

1. Speech to the Chicago Economic Club, 24 April 1999. • **2.** De Waal. • **3.** *Observer* Film Review, December 2009. • **4.** Mills, p. 14. • **5.** Visit www.eiu. com. • **6.** Keane, p. 697 et seq. • **7.** See Mair.

REFERENCES AND FURTHER READING

Note: the place of publication is London, unless stated otherwise.

Chapter 1: Athens and the Ancient World

Aeschylus, *Prometheus Unbound and Other Plays*, Penguin, 2001

Aristophanes, *Lysistrata and Other Plays*, Penguin, 2003

Aristophanes, *The Birds and Other Plays*, Penguin, 2003

Aristotle, *The Politics and The Constitution of Athens*, CUP, Cambridge, 1996

Jonathan Barnes (1987) *Early Greek Philosophy*, Penguin

Mary Beard and Michael Crawford (2000) *Rome in the Late Republic*, Duckworth

Cicero, *On the Good Life*, Penguin, 1971

Paul Cartledge (1999) *Democritus*, Routledge

Ralf Dahrendorf (1957) 'Colourful, Creative Conflict' in Antony Arblaster and
    Steven Lukes (1971) *The Good Society: A Book of Readings*, Methuen

Demosthenes, *Public Orations*, 2 vols, Echo Press, 2008

Cynthia Farrar (1992) Chapter 2, 'Ancient Political Theory as a Response to
    Democracy' in John Dunn (ed.) *Democracy: The Unfinished Journey*, OUP,
    Oxford

Mogen Herman Hansen (1999) *The Athenian Democracy in the Age of
    Demosthenes*, Bristol Classical Press

Simon Hornblower (1992) Chapter 1, 'Creation and Development of
    Democratic Institutions in Ancient Greece' in John Dunn (ed.) *Democracy:
    The Unfinished Journey*, OUP, Oxford

Herodotus, *The Histories*, Penguin, 1996

Livy, *The Early History of Rome*, Penguin, 2002

Christian Meier (1999) *Athens: Portrait of a City in its Golden Age*, John Murray

Plato, *The Laws*, Penguin, 1970

Plato, *The Republic*, Penguin, 1974

Karl Popper (1946) *The Open Society and its Enemies*, 2 vols, Routledge

Sophocles, *The Three Theban Plays*, Penguin, 1984

John Thorley (2004) *Athenian Democracy*, 2nd edn, Routledge

Thucydides, *History of the Peloponnesian War*, Penguin, 1972

Chapter 2: Parliaments and Things

Roberta Andersen and Dominic Aidan Bellenger (2003) *Medieval Worlds: A Sourcebook*, Routledge

Robert Bartlett (1993) *The Making of Europe: Conquest, Colonisation and Cultural Change, 950 to 1350*, Allen Lane

Norman Davies (1996) *Europe: A History*, OUP, Oxford

V. H. Galbraith (ed.) (1927) *The Anonimalle Chronicle 1333 to 1381*, University of Manchester, Manchester

Antonia Gransden (1982) *Historical Writing in England Vol 2*, Routledge

Charles A. Gross (1898) 'The Early History of the Ballot in England' in *American Historical Review*, III, pp. 456–63

Kirsten Hastrup (1985) *Culture and History in Medieval Iceland: An Anthropological Analysis of Structure and Change*, OUP, Oxford

Albert Hourani (2005) *A History of the Arabs*, 2nd edn, Faber and Faber

John Keane (2009) *The Rise and Fall of Democracy*, Simon and Schuster

Jennifer Loach (1991) *Parliament under the Tudors*, Clarendon Press, Oxford

Antonio Marongiu (1968) *Medieval Parliaments: A Comparative Study*, Eyre & Spottiswoode

John Monaghan and Peter Just (2000) *Social and Cultural Anthropology*, OUP, Oxford

John Mundy (1973) *Europe in the High Middle Ages, 1150 to 1309*, Longman, Harlow

Birgit and Peter Sawyer (1993) *Medieval Scandinavia*, University of Minnesota, Minneapolis

Joseph R. Strayer (1980) *The Reign of Philip the Fair*, Princeton University Press, Princeton

Tacitus, *Germania*, OUP, Oxford, 1999

Sarah Uckelman and Joel Uckelman, *Strategy and Manipulation in Medieval Elections*, ILLC Pre-Publication Series, pp. 2010–22, University of Amsterdam, Amsterdam

F. W. Walbank (1992) *The Hellenistic World*, Fontana

Chapter 3: Medieval Towns and City Republics

Roberta Andersen and Dominic Aidan Bellenger (2003) *Medieval Worlds: A Sourcebook*, Routledge

William M. Bowsky (1981) *A Medieval Italian Commune: Siena under the Nine, 1287–1355*, University of California, Berkeley

Gene Brucker (1998) *Florence: The Golden Age, 1138 to 1737*, University of California, Berkeley

Leonardo Bruni, *The Humanism of Leonardo Bruni*, Selected Texts, State University of New York, Binghampton, 1987

Carlo M. Cipolla (ed.) (1972) *The Economic History of Europe, Vol. I: The Middle Ages*, Collins, Glasgow

Daniel Englander et al. (eds) (1990) *Culture and Belief in Europe 1450 to 1600*, Blackwell, Oxford

J. K. Hyde (1973) *Society and Politics in Medieval Italy, 1000 to 1350*, Macmillan

John M. Jeep (2001) *Medieval Germany: An Encyclopedia*, Routledge

Niccolo Machiavelli, *The Discourses*, Penguin, 2000

Niccolo Machiavelli, *The Prince*, OUP, Oxford, 2008

Geert Mak (2008) *Amsterdam: A Brief Life of the City*, 2nd edn, Vintage

Marsilius of Padua, *The Defender of the Peace*, CUP, Cambridge, 2005

Lauro Martines (1979) *Power and Imagination: City-States in Renaissance Italy*, Knopf, New York

Lewis Mumford (1938) *The Culture of Cities*, Harcourt Brace & Company, New York

John Mundy (1973) *Europe in the High Middle Ages, 1150 to 1309*, Longman, Harlow

J. M. Najemy (1982) *Corporatism and Consensus in Florentine Politics 1280 to 1400*, University of North Carolina, Chapel Hill

Geoffrey Parker (1985) *The Dutch Revolt*, rev. edn, Penguin

Ferdinand Schevill (1909) *The History of a Mediaeval Commune*, Harper & Row, New York

Christine Shaw (2006) *Popular Government and Oligarchy in Renaissance Italy*, Brill, Leiden

Quentin Skinner (1992) Chapter 4, 'The Italian City Republics' in John Dunn (ed.) *Democracy: The Unfinished Journey*, OUP, Oxford

Daniel Waley (1988) *The Italian City Republics*, 3rd edn, Longman, Harlow

Daniel Waley (1991) *Siena and the Sienese in the Thirteenth Century*, CUP, Cambridge

Chapter 4: Democracy in the High Alps

Benjamin R. Barber (1974) *The Death of Communal Liberty: A History of Freedom in a Swiss Mountain Canton*, Princeton University Press, Princeton

Randolph Head (1995) *Early Modern Democracy in the Grisons*, CUP, Cambridge

Henry Lloyd (1907) *A Sovereign People: A Study of Swiss Democracy*, Doubleday, New York; reissued 2001, Adamant, Boston

Jonathan Steinberg (1996) *Why Switzerland?*, 2nd edn, CUP, Cambridge

Chapter 5: The English Revolution

Jack Binns (2001) *A History of Scarborough*, Blackthorn Press, Pickering

T. C. W. Blanning (2000) *The Eighteenth Century: Europe 1688 to 1815*, OUP, Oxford

Philip Bobbitt (2002) *The Shield of Achilles: War, Peace and the Course of History*, Knopf, New York

John Evelyn (2006) *The Diary of John Evelyn*, Everyman

Ian Gentles (1992) *The New Model Army in England, Ireland and Scotland, 1645 to 1653*, Blackwell, Oxford

Christopher Hill (1972) *The World Turned Upside Down: Radical Ideas During the English Revolution*, Penguin

Thomas Hobbes, *Leviathan*, OUP, Oxford, 2008

John Keegan (1993) *A History of Warfare*, Pimlico

Peter Kellner (2009) *Democracy: 1,000 Years In Pursuit of British Liberty*, Mainstream

John Locke (1993) *Two Treatises of Government*, Everyman

Lewis Namier (1962) *Crossroads of Power: Essays on Eighteenth Century England*, Hamish Hamilton

A. S. P. Woodhouse (1938) *Puritanism and Liberty, Being the Army Debates (1647–49) from the Clarke Manuscripts*, Dent

David Wootton (ed.) (1986) *Divine Right and Democracy: An Anthology of Political Writing in Stuart England*, Penguin

For a bibliography of the Civil Wars visit: www.british-civil-wars.co.uk/bibliography.htm

Chapter 6: Democracy in America

John H. Aldrich (1995) *Why Parties?: The Origin and Transformation of Political Parties in America*, University of Chicago Press, Chicago

Hugh Brogan (1999) *The Penguin History of the USA*, 2nd edn, Penguin

William Nesbit Chambers and Walter Dean Burnham (eds) (1967) *The American Party Systems: Stages of Political Development*, OUP, New York

John Dunn (ed.) (1992) *Democracy: The Unfinished Journey*, OUP, Oxford

Max Farrand (ed.) (1911–1937) *Papers of the Federal Convention of 1787*, 4 vols, New Haven

Benjamin Franklin (1840), *The Works of Benjamin Franklin*, Boston

Benjamin Franklin, *The Autobiography and Other Writings*, ed. Kenneth Silverman, Penguin, 1986

Alexander Hamilton et al., *The Federalist Papers*, OUP, Oxford, 2008

John F. Hoadley (1986) *Origins of American Political Parties, 1789–1803*, University Press of Kentucky, Louisville

Thomas Jefferson, *The Works of Thomas Jefferson*, 12 vols, G. P. Putnam's Sons, New York and London, 1904–5

Thomas Jefferson, *The Portable Thomas Jefferson*, ed. Merrill D. Petersen, Viking, New York, 1975

Joshua Miller (1991) *The Rise and Fall of Democracy in Early America, 1630–1789*, Pennsylvania State University Press

Thomas Paine, *Common Sense*, Dover, New York, 1997

J. F. Sly (1930) *Town Government in Massachusetts, 1620 to 1930*, Harvard University Press, Cambridge, Mass

Alexis de Tocqueville, *Democracy in America*, Wordsworth, 1998

George Washington (1860) *The Diary of George Washington, 1789 to 1791*, New York

Harry L. Watson (1990) Liberty *and Power: The Politics of Jacksonian America*, Farrar, Straus and Giroux, New York

Steve Wiegand (2001) *United States History*, IDG, Foster City

C. Williamson (1960) *American Suffrage From Property to Democracy, 1760 to 1860*, Princeton University Press, Princeton

Chapter 7: France 1789–95

Peter Campbell (1958) *French Electoral Systems and Elections since 1789*, Faber and Faber

John Carey (ed.) (1987) *The Faber Book of Reportage*, Faber and Faber

Bernard Crick (2002) *Democracy: A Very Short Introduction*, OUP, Oxford

Malcolm Crook (1996) *Elections in the French Revolution: An Apprenticeship in democracy*, CUP, Cambridge

William Doyle (1989) *Oxford History of the French Revolution*, OUP, Oxford

Jonathan Israel (2009) *A Revolution of the Mind: Radical Enlightenment and the Intellectual Origins of Modern Democracy*, Princeton University Press, Princeton

Thomas Jefferson, *The Essential Jefferson*, Collier, New York, 1963

Peter McPhee (2001) *The French Revolution*, OUP, Oxford

Jean-Jacques Rousseau, *The Social Contract*, Wordsworth, 1998

Albert Soboul (1988) *Understanding the French Revolution*, trans. April Knutson, International Publishers, New York

Michael Walzer (ed.) (1974) *Regicide and Revolution*, CUP, Cambridge

Chapter 8: Republics in Latin America

L. Bethell (ed.) (1984–95) *Cambridge History of Latin America*, CUP, Cambridge

Simón Bolívar (1950) *Obras Completas*, ed Vicente Lecuna, 2nd edn, Editorial Lex, Havana

David Bushnell (ed.) (1970) *The Liberator: Simón Bolívar*, Knopf, New York

George Camacho (1993) *Latin America: A Short History*, Allen Lane

Felipe Fernández-Armesto (2003) *The Americas: History of a Hemisphere*, Weidenfeld & Nicolson

Charles Hale (1968) *Mexican Liberalism in the Age of Mora*, Yale University Press, New Haven

Robert Harvey (2000) *Liberators: South America's Savage Wars of Freedom 1810–30*, John Murray

Kris E. Lane (1998) *Pillaging the Empire: Piracy in the Americas, 1500–1750*, Sharp, New York

Daniel K. Lewis (2001) *The History of Argentina*, Greenwood Press, Westport

John Lynch (1973) *The South American Revolutions*, Weidenfeld & Nicolson

John Lynch (1983) *Simón Bolívar and the Age of Revolution*, London University

John Lynch (2006) *Simón Bolívar: A Life*, Yale University Press, New Haven

Eduardo Posada-Carbó (1996) *Elections before Democracy: The History of Elections in Europe and Latin America*, Macmillan Press

Edwin Williamson (2003) *The Penguin History of Latin America*, Penguin

Chapter 9: Europe in the Nineteenth Century

Hugh Cunningham (2001) *The Challenge of Democracy: Britain 1832–1918*, Longman, Harlow

Erich Eyck (1964) *Bismarck and the German Empire*, Norton, New York

E. J. Feuchtwanger (2002) *Bismarck*, Routledge

Gustave Flaubert, *A Sentimental Education*, OUP, Oxford, 2000

Robert Gildea (2003) *Barricades and Borders, Europe 1800–1914*, 3rd edn, OUP, Oxford

Peter Jones (1991) *The 1848 Revolutions*, 2nd edn, Longman, Harlow

John Stuart Mill, 'On Representative Government' in *On Liberty and Other Essays*, OUP, Oxford, 2008

Denis Mack Smith (1971) *The Italian Risorgimento*, OUP, London

Michael Morrogh (1991) *The Unification of Italy: Documents and Debates*, Macmillan, Basingstoke

Jonathan Sperber (1994) *The European Revolutions, 1848–1851*, CUP, Cambridge

Percy B. St John (1848) *The French Revolution of 1848: The Three Days of February, 1848*, New York

A. J. P. Taylor (1980) *Revolutions and Revolutionaries*, OUP, Oxford

Chapter 10: Embrace and Retreat

Alan Bullock (1991) *Hitler and Stalin: Parallel lives*, Harper Collins

John Carey (ed.) (1987) *The Faber Book of Reportage*, Faber and Faber

Gerald D. Feldman (1966) *Army, Industry and Labor in Germany, 1914–18*, Princeton University Press, Princeton

E. J. Feuchtwanger (1995) *From Weimar to Hitler: Germany 1918–33*, 2nd edn, Macmillan

Paul Hayes (ed.) (1992) *Themes in Modern European History 1890–1945*, Routledge

Ruth Henig (1998) *The Weimar Republic 1919–1933*, Routledge

Eric Hobsbawm (1994) *The Age of Extremes*, Michael Joseph

Eric Hopkins (2000) *Industrialisation and Society: A Social History, 1830–1951*, Routledge

Anton Kaes et al. (1994) *The Weimar Republic Sourcebook*, University of California Press, Berkeley

Ian Kershaw (1998) *Hitler, 1889–1936: Hubris*, Allen Lane

Tom Mann and Ben Tillett (1890) *The 'New' Trades Unionism*, Green and McAllan

J. Noakes and G. Pridham (eds) (1983) *Nazism 1919–1945, Vol. 1: The Rise to Power 1919–1934, A Documentary Reader*, Exeter University Press, Exeter

Roger Osborne (2006) *Civilization: A New History of the Western World*, Jonathan Cape

Laurence Rees (1997) *The Nazis, A Warning from History*, BBC

William Shirer (1960) *The Rise and Fall of the Third Reich*, Simon and Schuster, New York

Otto Spengler (1926) *The Decline of the West*, 2 vols, Knopf, New York

Norman Stone (1983) *Europe Transformed, 1878–1919*, 2nd edn, Blackwell, Oxford

Heinrich August Winkler (2006) *Germany: The Long Road West, Vol. 1: 1789 to 1933*, OUP, Oxford

Chapter 11: India

Judith M. Brown (1994) *Modern India: The Origins of an Asian Democracy*, OUP, Oxford

Judith M. Brown (1999) *Nehru: Profile In Power*, Pearson, Harlow

Bipan Chandra, Mridula Mukherjee and Aditya Mukherjee (1999) *India after Independence*, Penguin, New Delhi

Ramachandra Guha (2008) *India after Gandhi: The History of the World's Largest Democracy*, Pan

John Keay (2010) *India: A History*, rev. edn, Harper

Atul Kohli (ed.) (2001) *The Success of India's Democracy*, CUP, Cambridge

Eric Stokes (1959) *The English Utilitarians and India*, OUP, Oxford

Chapter 12: The Postwar West

Hugh Brogan (1999) *The Penguin History of the USA*, 2nd edn, Penguin

Norman Davies (1996) *Europe: A History*, OUP, Oxford

Andrew J. Dunar (2006) *America in the Fifties*, Syracuse University Press, Syracuse

Economist Democracy Index (2008) www.eiu.com

Neil C. M. Elder (1982) *The Consensual Democracies? The Government and Politics of the Scandinavian States*, Robertson, Oxford

Ronald Irving (2002) *Adenauer*, Longman, Harlow

Tony Judt (2005) *Postwar: A History of Europe Since 1945*, Heinemann

Franklin D. Scott (1977) *Sweden: The Nation's History*, University of Minnesota Press, Minneapolis

Dalton Trumbo (1970) *Additional Dialogue: Letters of Dalton Trumbo, 1942–1962*, Ed. Helen Manfull, M. Evans, New York

Chapter 13: Democracy and Decolonisation

Guy Arnold (2005) *Africa: A Modern History*, Atlantic, New York

J.-F. Bayart, S. Ellis and B. Hibou (1999) *The Criminalisation of the State in Africa*, Indiana University Press, Bloomington

David Birmingham (1995) *The Decolonization of Africa*, Routledge

Paul Collier (2007) *The Bottom Billion: Why the Poorest Countries Are Failing and What Can Be Done about It*, OUP, Oxford

Paul Collier (2009) *Wars, Guns and Votes*, Bodley Head

Trevor Jones (1976) *Ghana's First Republic, 1960–1966*, Methuen

Patrick Manning (1988) *Francophone Sub-Saharan 1880–1985*, CUP, Cambridge

Stephen W. Smith (2010) 'Nodding and Winking', *London Review of Books*, Vol. 32, No. 3

Allister Sparks (1990) *The Mind of South Africa*, Heinemann

Chapter 14: The Collapse of Communism in Europe

Archie Brown (2007) *Seven Years that Changed the World: Perestroika in Perspective*, OUP, Oxford

Archie Brown (2009) *The Rise and Fall of Communism*, Bodley Head

Timothy Garton Ash (1999) *We The People: The Revolution of '89 Witnessed in Warsaw, Budapest, Berlin and Prague*, rev. edn, Granta

Jack Gray (2002) *Rebellions and Revolutions: China from the 1800s to 2000*, 2nd edn, OUP, Oxford

Tony Judt (2005) *Postwar: A History of Europe Since 1945*, Heinemann

Zhang Liang (2001) *The Tiananmen Papers*, eds Andrew Nathan and Perry Link, Abacus, New York

Jerzy Lukowski and Hubert Zawadzki (2001) *A Concise History of Poland*, CUP, Cambridge

Richard McGregor (2010) *The Party: The Secret Word of China's Communist Rulers*, Allen Lane

Victor Sebestyen (2009) *Revolution 1989: The Fall of the Soviet Empire*, Weidenfeld & Nicholson

J. N. Westwood (2002) *Endurance and Endeavour: Russian History 1812–2001*, 5th edn, OUP, Oxford

Chapter 15: Democracy since 1989

Ali Allawi (2008) *The Occupation of Iraq*, Yale University Press, New Haven
Tony Blair (2010) *A Journey*, Hutchinson
Paul Collier (2009) *Wars, Guns and Votes*, Bodley Head
Simon Jenkins (1995) *Accountable to No One*, Hamish Hamilton
John Keane (2009) *The Life and Death of Democracy*, Simon and Schuster
Peter Mair (2010) 'The Parliamentary Peloton', *London Review of Books*, Vol. 32, No. 4
Greg Mills (2010) *Why Africa is Poor*, Penguin
Rory Stewart (2006) *Occupational Hazards: My Time Governing in Iraq*, Picador
Alex de Waal (2010) 'Dollarised', *London Review of Books*, Vol. 32, No. 12

PICTURE CREDITS

Greek amphitheatre, Epidaurus (*Slow Images/Getty Images*).
Piazza del Campo and Palazzo Publico, Siena (*Buena Vista Images/Getty Images*).
The Tennis Court Oath, 20 June 1789 (*Universal History Archive/Getty Images*).
Simón Bolívar (*Hulton Archive/Getty Images*).
Fighting at a barricade in Berlin, 1848 (*Hulton Archive/Getty Images*).
The great Chartist meeting on Kennington Common, 10 April 1848 (*Rischgitz/ Getty Images*).
First Presbyterian Church members voting on decisions (*Allan Grant/Time & Life Pictures/Getty Images*).
Woman voting during the first post-war elections in Japan, 1946 (*Carl Mydans/ Time & Life Pictures/Getty Images*).
Women voting at the British general election, 1964 (*Keystone/Getty Images*).
South African voters, 2007 (*Andy Hall/Getty Images*).
Voters in Kashmir, 2011 (*Tauseef Mustafa/AFP/Getty Images*).
German Chancellor Franz von Papen at the ballot box, 1932 (*Imagno/Getty Images*).
US President Harry Truman in the voting booth, 1950 (*George Skadding/Time & Life Images/Getty Images*).
John F. Kennedy and Richard Nixon at a TV studio for the first ever televised debate between US presidential candidates, 1960 (*Ernst Haas/Hulton Archive/Getty Images*).
Soviet President Mikhail Gorbachev and Russian President Boris Yeltsin in the Russian parliament after the failure of the coup, August 1991 (*PIKO/ AFP/Getty Images*).
US President Barack Obama shakes hands with visitors at the Lincoln memorial in Washington, 2011 (*Jewel Samad/AFP/Getty Images*).
Government and opposition face each other in the British House of Commons, eighteenth century (*Fine Art Photographic/Getty Images*).
Voting in the European Parliament, 2011 (*Frederick Florin/AFP/Getty Images*).

INDEX

Aachen 33, 161
Acheson, Dean 231
Adams, John 98, 111
Adams, John Quincy 113
Adenauer, Konrad 221–2
advertising 202
Aeschylus 19
Afghanistan 258, 277–8, 279, 283
Africa 143, 182, 199, 208, 238, 239–50,
  253–4, 280, 281–2
  Britain's Government Colleges 245
  ethnic party lines 245
  see also individual countries
Ahmed, Fakhruddin Ali 215–16
Ai Weiwei 274
Akbar the Great 206
Alexander II of Russia 177, 187
Alexander III of Macedonia ('the
  Great') 21, 24, 31
Alexander III, Pope 44
Aleyn, Joseph 92
Alfonso IX of Léon 35
Alfonso X of Castile 35
Algeria 166, 224, 249
al-Jaafari, Ibrahim 278
Alkmaeonid family 14
Allende, Salvador 235
al-Maliki, Nouri 278, 279
Alsace 191, 229
Ames, William 100

Amphipolis 31
Amsterdam 47–51, 53
  charter 50
anarchism 186
Andagoya, Pascual de 142
Andropov, Yuri 259
Angers 123
Angola 247
Anthony, Susan B. 184
Antigone (Sophocles) 19
Antwerp 46
Aragon 34, 43
Archanians, The (Aristophanes) 18–19
archons 11, 13
Arezzo 57, 58, 60
  Bishop of 56
Argentina 143, 144, 149, 150, 152, 153,
  155, 182–3, 200, 280
Arginusae 19
Aristophanes 18–19
Aristotle 11, 12, 13, 22–3, 24, 101
Armado, Gen. Alfonso 228
Armas, Castillo 234
Asgar 32
Asia 182, 199, 218, 238, 280
  East, communism 233
  South-East 250–2
  see also individual countries
Asti 57
Asunción 143

Athenian Empire (Delian League) 18,
31
Athens 7–24, 29, 30, 148
  Acropolis 7, 18
  agora 7–8
  Areopagus 7, 8, 13, 17
  as centre of Greek world 18
  Council of 400 13, 14
  Council of 500 8, 9, 14–15, 17
  declining power 20
  democracy, development of, the
    how 12–15
  democracy, development of, the
    why 21
  democracy, duration of 9
  democracy, end of 24
  democracy, most highly developed
    5
  Dipylon vase 10
  ekklesia 8, 13
  emerges as wealthiest, most
    powerful state 16
  expansionary foreign policy 18
  Graubünden's similarity to 74
  Hill of Nymphs 8
  open meetings 8
  openness and transparency 9
  Parthenon 7, 18
  and Peloponnesian War 19–20
  Persian fleet defeated 16
  Persians burn 16
  Pnyx 8
  political divide emerges 17
  public projects 18
  seventh-century BC, sharing and
    rotation of power 11
  system of ostracism 9
  temple of Apollo 7
  see also Greece
Attica 7, 11, 13
Attlee, Clement 211
Aung San 251
Aung San Suu Kyi 251
Aurangzeb, Emperor 207

Australia 184
Austria 71, 132, 136, 158, 161, 162, 163,
  166–8, 173, 176, 177, 191, 221, 222
  bill of rights 183
  and First World War 188–9
  Germany absorbs 200
  People's Party 222
  Social Democrats 222
  US seeks to stabilise 220
  women's voting rights 184
Austro–Prussian War 158
Aztec Empire 142

Baader, Andreas 227
Bailly, Jean-Sylvain 127, 132
Balkans 166
Barbarossa, Frederick 36, 58–9
Barcelona 35
Barnstaple 41
Battle of the Golden Spurs 49–50
Bayle, Pierre 129
Beaumont-en-Argonne 59
Beijing 272–4
Belém 143
Belgium 33, 161–2, 184, 191, 193
  literacy 96
Bengal 207–8
Benjamin of Tudela 57
Bentovoglios 66
Bergamo 64
Berlin 2, 158, 256
  riots in 169
Berlin Wall 255, 256, 263, 264
Bern 53
Béthune 49
Bible 54, 78
Biko, Steve 248
Binns, Jack 95
Birka 32
Birmingham, David 249
Bismarck, Otto von 176–7, 179, 182,
  192
Björkö 32
Black Death 42, 56

Blair, Tony 277
Blum, Léon 201, 224
Bogotá 152
Bohemia 79, 166
Bolívar, Simón 145–6, 146–7, 147–8,
    153
Bolivia 144, 148, 154, 236, 280
Bologna 57, 61, 62, 63, 228
Bonaparte, Joseph 146
Bonaparte, Napoleon 27, 139, 146, 159,
    163
    exile 157
boni homines 58
Booth, Charles 185
Bordeaux 121
Borgia, Cesare 66
Bosnia–Herzegovina 266
Boston 103
Botha, P. W. 248
Bourbons 75, 127, 163
Brabant, Duke of 51
Bradshaw, John 93
Brandt, Willy 225, 257
Brazil 142, 143, 144, 147, 183, 200, 280,
    287
Brecht, Bertolt 231
Bretonne, Restif de la 133
Brezhnev, Leonid 259
Brisson, Henri 179
Brissot, Jacques-Pierre 134
Bristol 50, 121
Britain 170–2, 199
    America apes tripartite constitu-
        tion 108
    Blackshirts 200–1
    census introduced 158
    Chartists 171–2, 174
    and colonisation/decolonisation
        see Africa; Asia; *individual states*
    Combination Laws 159
    Corn Laws 170–1
    democracy suppressed 45
    demonstrations 227
    divides up Europe 219
    and Dutch Republic 54
    and early American settlers *see*
        North America; United States
        of America
    eighteenth-century, nepotism 95
    and European year of revolution
        161
    and First World War 189, 191
    Independent Labour Party 181–2
    Indian rule *see* India
    and Iran 234
    and Iraq 278, 284
    Labour Party 223
    Liberal Party 180
    minimum wages 181
    Municipal Corporation Act 161
    nepotism in electoral policy 95
    newspapers 96
    Peterloo Massacre 158
    Poor Law 158–9, 161
    Reform Act 95, 158, 171, 174
    school meals 180
    Second World War, major change
        after 223
    small elite shape politics 96
    social divide 179–80
    and Latin America *see* Latin
        America
    strikes 181, 182
    and Suez 240
    Tolpuddle Martyrs 159
    town vs country dwellers 159
    and War of 1812 112
    wealth distribution 184
    welfare provisions 223
    women's voting rights 184
    working hours limited 181
    see also England
British Empire 151
Brogan, Hugh 101
Bruges 49
Brugmans, Hajo 53
Bruni, Leonardo 66–7
Brüning, Heinrich 196

Brutus, Lucius Junius 25
Buenos Aires 143, 150, 151, 152, 153
Bulgaria 255, 265
Burgoyne, Gen. John 105
Burgundy 55
Burma 251–2, 281
Burr, Aaron 111
Bush, George H. W. 276
Bush, George W. 277
Byzantine Empire 33

Cadiz 144
Caesar, Augustus 139
Caesar, Julius 27
Caetano, Marcelo 228
California 154, 233
Callimachus 16
Calvin, Jean 52–3, 81
Calvinism 52–4, 78, 100
Cambodia 252
Cambridge 100
Cameron, David 1
Canada 199
Canning, George 152
Cape Verde 143
Capetian dynasty 36–7
capitalism 162, 202
Caracas 144, 154
Carcassonne 120
Carnot, Sadi 187
Carthage 30
Cassandreia 31
Castile 35
Castilla, Marshal Ramón 153–4
Catalonia 35
Catholicism 52–3, 78–9
    Anglo- 78
    in France 120
    in Ireland 79
    James I's repudiation of 77
    in South America 150
caudillos 152
Cavour, Count 173, 174
Ceauşescu, Nicolae 265–6

Central America see Latin America
Chalcis 10
Champagne 55
Charlemagne 33
Charles I of England 77–80, 81, 85–7
    entry into Commons chamber
        78–9
    escape 91
    house arrest 83, 84
    personal rule 77–8
    seizure 85
    trial and execution 93
Charles II of England 94, 207
Charles X of France 159, 164
Chartists 171–2, 174
Chávez, Hugo 280
Chen Erjin 272
Chenier, André 138
Chernenko, Konstantin 259
Chilcot, John 284
Chile 144, 146, 150, 151, 155, 235–6, 280
China 183, 200, 232, 233, 242, 251,
        269–75, 287–8
    and collapse of communism see
        under communism
    Communist Party 270, 273, 274–5
    Cultural Revolution 271
    Democracy Wall 272
    Democratic Party 274
    Falun Gong 274
    Great Leap Forward 270
    Tiananmen Square protests 272–4
Christian IV of Denmark 71
Churchill, Winston 223, 224–5
Cicero 26
Cimon 17
city republics and medieval towns,
    democracy in see towns and cities
Cleisthenes 14, 15–16, 17
Clinton, Bill 276
Clive, Robert 207
Cold War 236, 247, 248, 251, 279
Cologne 169
Colombia 144, 150, 151, 152, 199, 236

communism 190, 196, 197, 199, 200
    in China 269–72
    conformity 255
    collapse of 4, 255–75
    as major threat 220
    and USA see under USA
    see also Soviet Union
Como 57
Confederation of the Rhine 158
Congregationalism 100
conservatism 147, 159, 165, 172, 173,
    176, 180
Constance, treaty of 59
Constantine of Greece 229
Constitution of Athens (Aristotle) 12
consumerism 202–3
contado 55–6
Coolidge, Calvin 202
Corbières 120
Corinth 10, 11, 13
Cornwallis, Gen. Charles 105
Cortez, Hernan 142
Costa Rica 199
Council of Europe 230
Crassus 26
Cremona 57, 61
Crimean War 158
Crispi, Francesco 188
Cromwell, Oliver 80, 81, 83, 85, 91,
    92, 93–4, 207
    Protectorate 94
    and Putney Debates 87, 90, 97
Cromwell, Richard 94
Cuba 144
Curcio, Renato 227
Cylon 11, 12
Czech Republic 166
Czechoslovakia 233, 235, 255, 264
    Prague Spring 256–7
Czolgosz, Leon 187

Daily Mail 179
Daily Mirror 179
Daladier, Eduard 201

Dallas County 238
Danton (d'Anton), Georges 122, 137
Danube 55
Darius 30
Davison, Emily 184
Dawes, William 104
de Klerk, F. W. 248
Dean, Howard 284
del Valle, Cecilio José 153
Delhi 2, 207, 211
Delian League see Athenian Empire
Democracy in America (Tocqueville)
    115–16
democracy
    arguments over meaning of 3
    as concept 2
    in continual state of adaptation
        2–3
    and corporations' interests 236–7
    and decolonisation 239–54
    vs democracies 5
    EIU Index 282, 285, 286, 287
    etymology 9
    first modern declaration 68
    and globalisation 279–80
    as historical rarity 203
    locations of see individual cities,
        peoples, states
    media's influence on 226
    in medieval towns and city repub-
        lics 46–67; see also individual
        cities, towns; towns
    in parliaments see parliaments
    and Protestantism 52
    Puritan model 99–101
    restriction of access 185–6
    society's symbiotic relationship
        with 3
    attacks on 186
    US-imposed 204
    US a major factor in its history
        233, 235
    as victim of East–West stand-off
        236

Western life infused by 286
and women 26, 42, 129, 131, 150,
    175, 180, 184
and young people 285
Democritus 23–4, 74
Demosthenes 20–1
Deng Xiaoping 271–2, 273
Denmark 32, 37, 158, 170, 176, 183, 222
    Nazis invade 199
Desai, Morarji 216
Descartes, René 54
Description of the city of Antwerp
    (Guicciardini) 51
Desmoulins, Camille 131, 137
Díaz, Porfirio 154
Diderot, Denis 119
Dien Bien Phu 252
Disraeli, Benjamin 174
Dmytryk, Edward 231
Dubček, Alexander 256–7, 264
Dulles, Alan 234
Dulles, John Foster 234
Dürer, Albrecht 46
Dutch Republic *see* Netherlands
Dutch Revolt 52
Dutschke, Rudi 227

East India Company 103, 207–9
East Indies 250
Ebert, Friedrich 189–90
Economist Intelligence Unit (EIU)
    282, 285, 286, 287
Ecuador 144
Eden, Anthony 240
Edward I of England 29, 36
Egypt 239–40, 281
    bloodless coup 240
    invades Sinai 240
    Suez Canal 240
Eisenhower, Dwight 233, 240
Eisner, Kurt 190
El Dorado 142, 151
El Salvador 236
Elizabeth I of England 76, 207

England 32, 35–6, 37, 39, 75–97
    Act of Succession (1701–2) 94
    army occupies capital 86
    Bill of Rights (1689) 94
    constitutional monarchy 94
    Council of the Army 84, 85
    declares war on Spain 77
    Enclosures Acts 102
    first formal parliament 36
    invasion of Parliament 86
    Levellers 81–4, 90–1, 92, 93, 96, 106
    Long Parliament 79, 117
    Magna Carta 43
    monarchy restored 94
    New Model Army 80–1, 82–4, 85,
        86, 92
    Norman Conquest 33, 82
    as obstacle to Philip II's ambition 52
    Peasants' Revolt 42
    Petition of Right 77
    Procedures of Parliament 42
    Putney Debates 87–90
    Rump Parliament 81, 93, 94
    Self-Denying Ordinance 80
    strengthening of monarchy 53
    towns 40
    Triennial Act (1694) 94
    see also Britain; *under* parliaments
English ('Glorious') Revolution 54, 94
    prelude 75–94
English Civil War 4, 76, 80–1
    declared 80
    'Second' 92–3
Ensslin, Gudrun 227
Ephialtes 17
Eretria 10
Essex, Earl of 80
Establishments of King Louis 43
Estonia 42, 200
Ethiopia 249
Eupen 191
Euripides 18
Europe, nineteenth-century 157–77,
    253

central, profound changes 157
classic liberalism 172, 177
country-to-town migration 162
growing population 159, 162
income tax 180
moves towards industrial society
   159
newspapers 159–60
policy of national democracy 157
rural poor 162
urban middle class 159
Vienna Congress 157, 158, 163
worsening living conditions 163
year of revolutions 160–1
see also individual cities, states
Europe, twentieth-century
   eastern 225; *see also* communism,
      collapse of
   post-Second World War division
      219
   US economic support 220
   western, increasing prosperity 225
   western, rebuilding democracy 220
   see also individual cities, states
European Economic Community
   (EEC) 230
European Union (EU) 224, 230, 269,
   287
Everard, Robert 87–8

Fairfax, Sir Thomas 80, 84, 85, 86, 87,
   91, 92, 93
Farouk of Egypt 240
Farthings 32
fascism 196, 199
Faure, Edgar 250
Ferdinand I of Austria 166–7
Ferdinand II, Emperor 71
Ferdinand VII of Spain 146
feudalism 33, 34, 39, 40, 49, 56, 73, 167
   French National Assembly
      abolishes 127
   monarch's place 34
Findley, William 110

Finland 199, 200, 222
Flanders 42, 44, 49–50, 55
   French claim 49
Flaubert, Gustave 165
Florence 55, 57, 58, 59, 60, 62, 63
Florida 238
Floris of Holland, Count 48
Foccart, Jacques 250
Foulon, Joseph-François 120
France 33, 36–7, 42, 102, 118–41, 146,
   157, 158, 160, 162, 163–6, 173, 174–5,
   176, 187, 191, 223–4, 226–7, 228–9
   Action Française 201
   and American War of
      Independence *see under* North
      America
   artisans 121
   August decrees 127, 129
   Bastille stormed 120, 126; *see also*
      French Revolution
   campagne des banquets 164–5
   Catholic religion 120, 122–3, 130
   census introduced 158
   Charter of 1814 163
   Charter of 1830 164
   church lands nationalised 130
   civil war 136
   and colonisation/decolonisation
      see Africa; *individual states*
   Communist Party 224
   constitutions 131, 133, 137, 139,
      163–4, 166, 175, 183, 223
   Declaration of Rights 127–8, 129,
      137
   declining wages 161
   demonstrations 226–7
   desperate pre-Revolution poverty
      120
   Estates General 123–5
   failing *ancien régime* 123
   feudal system abolished 127
   Fifth Republic 224
   First Republic 135
   and First World War 188–9, 191

and Flanders 49–50
Fourth Republic 223–4, 250
Girondins 134, 136
as great military, economic,
    cultural power 119
guillotine introduced 130
Jacobins 130, 132, 133, 134, 135, 136,
    137, 138
July ordinances 164
Legislative Assembly 131, 132–4
legislative chambers 139
liberté, egalité, fraternité 129, 139
literacy 96
Lombardy invaded by 59
mass conscription 136
as militarised nation 136–7
monarchy dominates nobility 77
Napoleon declares himself
    emperor 139
National Assembly 125–7, 129, 130,
    131–2, 159
National Bloc 201
National Convention 133–5, 137,
    139, 140
Nazis invade 199, 201
newspapers suppressed 96
Oath of the Tennis Court 125, 132
parlements 121, 123
polarised pre-Revolution society
    119
political clubs 130
political factions 114
Popular Front 201
post-Revolution elections 131–2
pre-Revolution land ownership 122
pre-Revolution life expectancy 122
Prussian invasion 175
public demonstrations banned 164
Radical Party 201
rising pre-Revolution population
    122
Ruhr occupied by 193
Second Empire 166
Second Republic 165

Socialist Party 224
strengthening of monarchy 53
and Suez 240
Terror 118, 137, 138–9, 141; see also
    French Revolution
Third Republic 183, 223
trade guilds abolished 130
uprisings 136
Vendée rebellion 136
Vichy government 201
voting qualifications 164
voting records 140
Workers' Party 224
see also French Revolution; Paris
Franche-Comté 55
Franco, Gen. Francisco 228, 229
Franco–Prussian War 158
Franklin, Benjamin 103, 106, 108, 110
Franks 33–4
Franz Josef of Austria 168, 179
Frederick III of Sicily 37
Frederick William III of Prussia 159,
    168
Frederick William IV of Prussia 168,
    169, 170
Frei Montalva, Eduardo 235
French and Indian War see Seven
    Years War
French Revolution 4, 93, 96, 118, 120,
    126–41, 160
    lost sense of purpose 137–8
    process of European national
        democracy begun by 157
Fribourg 53

Gage, Gen. Thomas 104
Gandhi, Indira 215–16
Gandhi, Mohandas 210, 211, 212, 213,
    217, 218
    death of 215
Gandhi, Rajiv 216
Gandhi, Sanjay 216
Garibaldi, Giuseppe 173–4
Gaulle, Charles de 224, 226, 227, 250

Gbagbo, Laurent 282
Gdansk 50
Gemeinarbeit (common work) 73
Gemeinnutz (common good) 72
Geneva 53
    Accord 252
Genoa 55, 57
George IV of Britain 168
Georgia 261, 269
Georgia, USA 102
Germany 33, 36, 37, 69, 96, 157, 158,
    168–70, 173, 176–7, 185, 188–99,
    229–30
    Austria absorbed into 200
    Bismarck's social welfare 176–7
    Centre Party 190, 192, 196, 198
    Communist Party 196, 197
    declared a democratic republic 189
    Democrat Party 192
    East (GDR) 255, 256
    East, West opened to 264
    falling wages 161
    and First World War 188
    Freedom Party 196
    Freikorps 192–3
    'grand coalition' government 196
    hyperinflation 193
    idealisation of race 196
    Jews 196
    Nazis 196–8
    People's Party 193, 195, 196
    Reich myth 192–3, 198
    Reichstag fire 198
    reparation payments 191, 194
    Social Democratic Workers' Party
        182
    SPD 182, 185, 189–90, 192, 198
    united, appeal of 169
    US seeks to stabilise 220
    Weimar constitution 190, 192, 194,
        196
    West 220, 221–2, 227
    West, Baader–Meinhof Gang 227
    West, Christian Democrats 221–2

West, demonstrations 227
West, East opened to 264
West, SPD 221
women's voting rights 184
Gettysburg Address 116–17
Ghana 239, 241–6, 249
    British exploitation 245
    CPP 242, 244
    military coup 244
    Nkrumah's rule 243
    president's powers 243
Ghent 49
Gierek, Edward 257
Giotto 64
Gironde 130
Gladstone, William 174, 179
globalisation 269, 276–7, 279–80
Glorious Revolution *see* English
    ('Glorious') Revolution
Goebbels, Joseph 194
Gold Coast *see* Ghana
Gomułka, Władysław 257
Gonzaga, Ludovico 66
Gonzagas 55
Gorbachev, Mikhail 258–9, 260–1,
    262–3, 267, 273
Gouge, Olympe de 137
Gran Colombia 146, 148
Granby, Lord 95
Grant, Charles 208
Graubünden 68–74
    federal assembly (Bundestag) 69
    peasants as political actors 72
    referendums 69
Graubündnerische Handlungen 72
Gravensteen 49
Great Chain of History 27
Great Depression 203
Greece 229, 249
    cities' democracies 30
    city-states gain in prosperity 10
    Colonels' rule 229
    Dark Ages 10
    myths 9–10

Olympus, gods of 10
and Peloponnesian War 19–20
Phoenician alphabet extended and
    developed 10, 30
Phoenician traders' constant
    contact with 30
theory of politics 21
Troy, siege of 10
twelfth-century BC migrations 10
United Democratic Left 229
see also Athens; *individual cities*
Grey, Earl 171
Grósz, Károly 263
Guatemala 144, 234–5
Guicciardini, Ludovico 51
guilds 44, 50, 61–3, 64
    diminished political influence 65
    France abolishes 130
Guizot, François 164, 165
Gujarat 216, 217
Guzmán, Jacobo Arbenz 234, 235

Haarlem 47, 53
Habsburgs 35, 54, 75, 167
Hall, Basil 144
Hamilton, Alexander 106, 109, 111
Harding, Warren 202
Harrison, Col. Thomas 92
Haryana 217
Havel, Václav 264–5
Hayes, Rutherford 237
Head, Randolph 70
hektemoriori 11
Henig, Ruth 192
Henrietta Maria, Queen 78
Henry III of England 35, 36
Henry IV, Emperor 58
Henry V, Emperor 36
Henry VIII of England 78
Herodotus 13, 30
Hesdin 49
Hill, Christopher 90
Hindenburg, Paul von 189, 194, 196,
    197, 198

Hippias 14
Hiss, Alger 232
Hitler, Adolf 193, 197–8, 200, 201,
    202
Ho Chi Minh 252
Hobbes, Thomas 93
Hobsbawm, Eric 199, 200
Holbach, Baron d' 129
Holland *see* Netherlands
Holstein 170
Holy Roman Empire 36, 48, 54, 68,
    70, 157–8
    newspapers 96
    Peasants' War 42
Honecker, Erich 264
Hoover, Herbert 202
Horn, Gyula 263
Howe, Gen. William 104, 105
Hu Jintao 274
Hu Yaobang 272
Hua Guofeng 271–2
Hugo, Victor 166
Hungary 37, 166, 167, 177, 200, 235,
    240, 255, 256, 263
Husák, Gustáv 264
Hyderabad 207

Iberia 33, 147
Ijsselmeer 47
Inca Empire 143
Independent Journal 106
India 205–18, 287
    Battle of Plassey 208
    becomes British colony 209
    becomes democratic republic 212
    BJS/BJP party 214–15, 216
    British rule 207–11; *see also* East
        India Company
    Congress (I) 215
    Congress Party 209–16 *passim*, 217,
        218
    constitution 212–13
    Councils Act 209
    Deccan wars 207

Government of India Act 210–11
increased literacy 211
inter-communal violence 211, 212
Janata Party 216
Muslim League 209, 211
Mutiny 208–9
National Front 216
partition 212; *see also* Pakistan
religions 206
satyagraha 210
socialist and communist parties
   214
state of emergency 215–16
Swatantra Party 215
Indochina 252
Indonesia 251, 281, 287
Industrial Revolution 25, 95
Innocent III, Pope 39
Institutes of the Christian Religion, The
   (Calvin) 53
International Monetary Fund 267,
   268, 280
International Security Assistance
   Force 277–8
Iran 234, 253, 278
Iraq 253, 276, 278–9, 283, 284
Ireland 76, 79, 84, 93, 162–3, 199
   potato famine 162
Ireton, Henry 83, 85, 87, 88, 89, 93
Isle of Man 32
Israel, Jonathan 128
Italy 71, 157, 166, 227–8, 249
   Christian Democrats 221
   Communist Party 220–1
   constitution 173
   fascism 196
   Fascist Party 200
   internal divisions 220
   monarchy abolished 220
   Normans invade 33
   north of, city government 55–67
   north of, larger cities dominate 65
   Popolo system 61–5
   Red Brigades 227–8

Renaissance 55
ruling class 59
Socialist Party 220–1
unification 173–4
US seeks to stabilise 220
Ivory Coast 282

Jackson, Andrew 113
Jacquarie rebellion 42
James I of England 76–7
James II of England 94
Jamestown 99
Japan 183, 200, 251
Jauja 143
Jay, John 106
Jefferson, Thomas 5, 98, 104, 106,
   110–11, 126
   on political parties 112
Jiang Zemin 274
Jinnah, Muhammad Ali 211, 212
John of England 43
Jonathan, Goodluck 282
Jones, Trevor 244
Jordan 278
Joyce, Cornet George 85
Juan Carlos of Spain 228
Juárez, Benito 154
Justinian Codex 36, 39

Kádár, János 263
Kennedy, John F. 225, 226, 256
Kenya 246–7, 281, 282
Kenyatta, Jomo 246
Keynes, John Maynard 203
Kibaki, Mwai 281
King, Martin Luther 237, 241
Knights, The (Aristophanes) 18
Knox, John 81
Korean War 233
Kortrijk 49
Krenz, Egon 264
Kryuchkov, Vladimir 262
Kuwait 276

La Plata 144
Lafayette, Gen. 126
Lancaster 41
   Languedoc 55, 120
Laos 252
Lardner, Ring Jr 231
Latin America 142–56, 280–1
   anti-Spanish rebellions 145–6
   Britain's involvement 155
   Britain's importance 152
   Catholic Church's role 150
   criollos 144
   estancieros 145
   military dictatorships 236
   US recognises nations of 151
   viceroyalties established 144
   wars within 152
   see also individual countries
Latour, Count 168
Latvia 200, 261
Laud, William 78–9
   execution 79
Launay, Gov. de 120
Lavoisier, Antoine 138
Lebanon 30, 253
Legnano 58
Leiden 53, 54
Leipzig 161
Lenin, Vladimir 187–8
Léon 35
Leopold II, Emperor 132
Levellers 81–4, 90–1, 92, 93, 96, 106
Leviathan (Hobbes) 93
Lévi-Strauss, Claude 30
Li Peng 273
liberalism 140, 147, 156, 159, 160 161,
   168, 170, 172, 174, 193
   classic 172, 177, 180
Libya 281
Liebknecht, Karl 190
Liège 50
Life and Labour of the People of London
   (Booth) 185
Lilburne, Robert 92

Lille 121, 161
Lima 143, 144
Limoux 120
Lincoln, Abraham 114, 116–17
Lippmann, Walter 202, 203
Lithuania 200, 261
Liverpool Post 159
Locke, John 54, 93, 129
Lombardy 55, 56, 58–9, 161, 166, 173
London 41
   army occupies 86
   militias 83, 86
   see also Britain; England
López, Vicente Fidel 156
Loris-Melikov, Gen. 177
Lorraine 55, 191, 229
Louis Philippe of France 159, 164,
   169
   abdication 166
Louis V of France 36
Louis XVI of France 120, 123, 125–7,
   129, 130–1, 132–3, 135
   execution 136
   flight and capture 131
   treason charges 135–6
Louis XVII of France 163
Louis XVIII of France 163
Louis-Napoleon see Napoleon III of
   France
Low Countries 47, 50, 52, 53, 55, 157
   Nazis invade 199
Lübeck 50
Lucca 57, 58, 61
Ludendorff, Erich 189
Ludwig of Bavaria 169
Lueger, Karl 188
Lukanov, Andrey 265
Luther, Martin 52, 81
Luxemburg, Rosa 190
Lymington 41
Lynn 100
Lyons 121, 136, 161
Lysimachus, archonship of 8

Maastricht Treaty 230
McCarthy, Joseph 232
Machiavelli 66, 77, 138–9
McKinley, William 187
Macmillan, Harold 239, 240, 248
Madagascar 249
Madison, James 106, 108, 109
Magna Carta 43
magnati 64
Maharastra 217
Mainz 50
Mak, Geert 47–8
Malawi 247
Malaya 250
Malaysia 251, 281
Malmedy 191
Manchester
    Peterloo Massacre 158
Manchester, Earl of 80
Manchester Guardian 159
Manchuria 200
Mandela, Nelson 241, 248
Mann, Tom 181
Manners, George 95
Mao Zedong 232, 269–71
Maratha Empire 208
Marathon 16
Marcos, Ferdinand 252, 280–1
Marcy, William E. 114
Mare, Peter de la 36
Marlborough 100
Marseilles 10, 55, 59, 121
Marshall, George 231
Marshall Plan 220, 231
Martel, Charles 33
Marx, Karl 186
Marxism 182, 186, 270
Mary, Queen 81
Massachusetts 99, 100, 101
Maurya Empire 206
Mayawati 216
Mbeki, Tabo 248–9
Medfield 100
Medicis 55, 66

Meinhof, Ulrike 227
Melos 20
Mendoza 150
Mesopotamia 30
Metternich, Klemens von 157, 158,
    167, 169
Mexico 142, 144, 150, 151, 152, 154–5, 280
Michels, Roberto 188
Mier, Servando Teresa de 149
Milan 55, 57, 58, 60, 62
Mill, John Stuart 116, 174, 283
Milosevic, Slobodan 266
Milton, John 82, 90
Mirabeau, comte de 124
Miranda, Francisco de 146
Modena 57, 63
Mollet, Guy 240
Money, Leo Chiozza 185
Monroe, James 113
Montesquieu 120, 129, 135
Montevideo 143
Montford, Simon de 35, 36
Montgomery 237
Morales, Evo 280
Moro, Aldo 228
Morris, Robert 110
Moscow 259–60, 262
Mosley, Oswald 200–1
Mossadegh, Mohammad 234
Mountbatten, Lord 211–12
Mozambique 247
Mugabe, Robert 247
Mughal Empire 206–7
Müller, Hermann 196
Mussolini, Benito 196, 199, 200
Mytilene 19

Nagy, Imre 263
Nairobi 246
Namier, Lewis 96
Nantes 121, 124
Naples 10, 173, 174
Napoleon III of France (Louis-
    Napoleon) 166, 174

deposed 175
Napoleonic Wars 157, 167
Narbonne 120
Nasica, Scipio 26
Nasser, Gamal 240
nationalism 140–1, 160, 167, 170, 172,
    173, 174, 195
    ultra- 186, 193
NATO countries 220
Nazism 196–8, 219; see also Germany
Ne Win 251
Necker, Jacques 122
Needham, Marchamont 81
Nehru, Jawaharlal 211–12, 213–14, 241
Nestor's cup 10
Netherlands 37, 47–51, 54–5, 184
    and American War of
        Independence see under North
        America
    and colonisation/decolonisation
        see individual states
    literacy 96
New Granada 144, 146
New Hampshire 102
New Jersey 105
New Mexico 154
New Model Army 80–1, 82–4, 85, 86,
    92
'New' Trades Unionism, The (Mann,
    Tillett) 181
New York Packet 106
New York State 105, 106, 107
New Zealand 184
newspapers 96, 113, 159–60, 179
Nice 59
Nicholas II of Russia 183
Nigeria 245, 249, 253–4, 281–2
9/11 277–8
Nixon, Richard 226
Nkrumah, Kwame 239, 241, 242, 243–5
Nonconformists 52, 54, 99–101, 102
Norman Conquest 33, 82
Normans 33–4, 82
North America

destruction of indigenous popula-
    tion 102
early colonies 54, 99–102
European settlement 102
farms as basis of rural society 102
manufactured-goods market 145
Mayflower voyage 54, 99
rivalry between European states
    102
settlers' ballots and town govern-
    ment 101
slavery 102
Stamp Act riots 103
Townshend Acts 103
War of Independence 100, 103–5
see also United States of America
North Carolina 102, 103, 113
North Korea 281
Norway 32, 183, 222
    Nazis invade 199
Norwich 41
Nuruddin Salim Jahangir 207

Obama, Barack 1, 285
Obasanjo, Olusegun 281–2
O'Connor, Fergus 171–2
Octavian (Augustus) 27
O'Higgins, Bernardo 146
Ollivier, Emile 175
Oration over the Athenian War Dead
    (Pericles) 19–20
organised labour 181
Ottoman Empire 177, 183, 253
Ouattara, Alassane 282–3
Oudh 207
Overton, Richard 82
Owusu, Victor 243

Padavino, Giovanni Battista 70–1
Padua 55, 60, 62, 65, 227
Paine, Thomas 104, 129
Pakistan 212
Palme, Olaf 225
Panama 142–3

Papen, Franz von 197
Paraguay 144, 153
Paramaribo 143
Pareto, Victor 188
Paris 2, 120, 121, 126, 129, 137, 169
  Bastille stormed 120, 126; see also
    French Revolution
  Commune 132–3, 175
  student demonstrations 226
  Tuileries Palace 165
  workers' uprising 166
  see also France
Park, Robert 102
Parker, John 104
Parks, Rosa 237
parliaments and legislative assemblies
    29–45 passim
  in Amphipolis 31
  Anglo-Saxon 32
  in Aragon 35
  in Athens see Athens
  in Austria 167, 177, 183
  in Barcelona 35
  and Capetian dynasty 36–7
  in Cassandreia 31
  in Castile 35
  in Catalonia 35
  in China 275
  in Catholic Church 44
  corruption in 188
  in Denmark 37
  in England/Britain 32, 35–6, 37, 39,
    42, 54, 76–8, 79–97 passim, 106,
    134, 182, 243
  English Long 79, 117
  English Rump 81, 93, 94
  European 230
  in France 35, 36–7, 121, 123, 125–7,
    129, 130, 131–5, 137, 139, 140, 159,
    162, 164, 166
  in Germany 31, 170, 176, 182, 185,
    190, 196–8
  in Ghana 242, 244
  and guilds 44, 50
  in Hungary 37
  in India 205, 209, 212, 214, 215, 217,
    224
  in Isle of Man 32
  in Italy 174
  in Holy Roman Empire 36
  in Léon 35
  in medieval Europe 32–45
  in Netherlands 37
  in Ottoman Empire 183
  outside government 44
  peasants excluded from 39
  in Philippi 31
  in Poland 37
  potential of, Britain's example to
    Europe 95
  in Prussia 168, 169
  restraining of monarchs by 38
  in Roncaglia 36
  in Russia 183, 187
  in Scandinavia 31–2
  in Scotland 37
  in Sicily 37
  Soviet 260
  in Spain 35, 37, 146, 228
  in Sweden 37
  in Thessalonica 31
  twin functions of counsel and
    consent 37
  in USA 27, 106, 107–8, 113
Parma 57
Patel, Vallabhbhai 214
Pavia 57
Peasants' Revolt 42
Pedro I of Brazil 147
Pedro II of Brazil 183
Peel, Robert 170
Peisistratus 13
Peloponnesian War 19–20
Peninsular War 146
Pennsylvania 99, 102, 105, 110
People's Republic of Congo 279
Pericles 17, 19–20
Perpignan 120

Persia 16, 18, 30
Peru 143, 144, 146–7, 150, 151, 153–4
Pétain, Philippe 201
Peterloo Massacre 158
Petition of Right 77
Petty, Maximilian 87, 88–9
Philadelphia 103, 105
Philip II of Macedonia 21, 24
Philip II of Spain 52
Philip IV of France 39, 49
Philippi 31, 252, 280–1
Phoenicia 30
   alphabet 10, 30
Piacenza 57, 62, 63
Pinochet, Augusto 236
Pisa 55, 57, 58, 60
Pizarro, Francisco 142–3
Plato 22, 23, 24, 128, 199
podestà 60–1, 64
Poland 37, 166, 184, 191, 200, 255,
   257–8, 269
   Solidarity union 257–8
Pompeius, Gnaeus (Pompey), 26, 27
Pompidou, Georges 226
Pontefract 41
popes
   recognition of monarchs 34
   rules for election 44
Popolo 61–5
Portugal 144, 228
   in Latin America *see* Latin
     America
Potsdam 219
Presbyterianism 80, 83–4
   as creed of established order 84
Princeton 105
printing 53, 78, 82, 119, 179
Protagoras 23
Protestantism 52, 78–9, 81
   English, schism in 78
   Nonconformist, in North America
     99
Provence 55, 59
Provisions of Oxford 35

Prussia 119, 132, 133, 135, 136, 157, 162,
   168, 169, 170, 176
   East 162, 191
   and First World War 188–9
   invades France 175
Prussian–Danish War 158
Punjab 211
Puritans 5, 99–101, 102
Putin, Vladimir 268

Quakers 100

Rainborough, Col. Thomas 87, 89, 92
Randolph, Edmund 108
Raspe, Jan-Carl 227
Rawlings, Jerry 246
referendums 69
Reformation 52–3, 78, 81
Relly, Gavin 248
republic (res publica), defined 25
Republic, The (Plato) 22, 199
Revere, Paul 104
Rhine, lower 55
Rhine Palatinate 79
Rhineland 191
Rhode Island 102, 106
Rhodes 10
Rhodesia 237, 247
Rhône 55
Rio de Janeiro 143, 147
Robespierre, Maximilien de 122, 124,
   132, 134, 138–9
   execution 139
Rodríguez de Francia, José Gaspar 153
Roe, Sir Thomas 207
Romania 200, 255, 265–6
Romanovs 75
Rome 57
   Henry VIII's split from 77
Rome, Ancient
   domination of Mediterranean
     world and western Europe 31
   political history 24–7
   Republic, collapse of 27

Republic, foundation of 25
  rise 24
Roncaglia 36
Roosevelt, Franklin D. 203, 231
Roosevelt, Theodore 184
Rosas, Juan Manuel de 153
Rouen 50, 121, 165
Rousseau, Jean-Jacques 93, 128, 134,
  139
Rudolf of Habsburg 36
Russia 75, 177, 183, 187–8, 242, 261–3,
  267–9, 270
  democracy curbed 268
  monarchy dominates nobility 77
  state of emergency 262
  votes to leave Soviet Union 261
  Yeltsin's economic reforms 267
  see also Soviet Union
Russian Revolution 187

Saarland 191
Saddam Hussein 278
Sagunto 10
St Augustine 73
St John, Percy 165
Saint-Just 135
Salamis 16, 18
Salazar, Antonio 228, 229
Salem 100
Salta 150
San Martin, José de 146–7
Santa Anna, Gen. Antonio López de
  150, 154
Santa Cruz, Andrés de 154
Santa Fe 150
Santiago 2, 144
Santiago del Estero 143
São Paulo 143
Saudi Arabia 278
Sauvigny, Gov. de 120
Scandinavia 31–2, 187, 222–3
Scarborough 95
Schleswig 170
Schuman, Robert 229–30

Scotland 37, 52, 76, 79, 83, 91–2, 94
  literacy 96
  strengthening of monarchy 53
Scott, Adrian 231
Scottish National Covenant 79
Seeckt, Gen. Hans von 193
Sentimental Education, A (Flaubert) 165
Seven Years War 102, 207
Seville 144, 146
Sexby, Col. Edward 87, 89
Sforza, Francesco 66
Sforza, Ludovico 66
Sforzas 55
Shastri, Lal Bahadur 215
Sicily 19, 33, 37, 173
Siena 55, 56–7, 58, 59, 60–1, 62, 63, 66
Sierra Leone 249
Siete partidas 35
Sieyès, Abbé 124
Singapore 250
Singh, V. P. 216
Sisulu, Walter 248
Slovakia 166
Smith, Elias 109
Social Contract, The (Rousseau) 128
socialism 176, 181, 186–7
Socrates 22
Solon 11, 12–13
Sophocles 18, 19
Sorel, Georges 188
South Africa 237, 247–9, 282
  ANC 248, 282
  Inkatha Freedom Party 248
  Sharpeville massacre 248
South and Central America see Latin
  America
South Korea 233
South Wales 182
Soviet Union 219, 220, 232, 233, 235,
  240–1, 251, 255–6, 258–63, 269–70, 273
  attempted coup (1991) 262
  and collapse of communism see
    under communism
  democracy 260

economic stagnation 258
Europe divided up by 219
formally dissolved 263
glasnost and *perestroika* 259
rigid conformity 255
Russia votes to leave 261
see also communism; Russia
Soweto 248
Spain 147, 200, 228–9
   and American War of
     Independence *see under* North
     America
   early development of parliaments
     35
   England declares war on 77
   Ferdinand supported by 71
   monarchy dominates nobility 77
   rebellion against French occupa-
     tion 146
   in Latin America *see* Latin
     America
   strengthening of monarchy 53
Sparta 14, 17, 20
Stalin, Joseph 233, 259, 270
Standard Oil Company 184
Strafford, Earl of 79
Stresemann, Gustav 193–4, 195
Stuarts 75, 76, 94
Sudan 249, 279
Suetonius 27
Suez Canal 240
Suharto, Gen. 251, 281
Sukarno 251
Sun Yat-sen 183
Suppliants, The (Aeschylus) 19
Swabia 55
Sweden 37, 183, 199, 222
   literacy 96
   strengthening of monarchy 54
Switzerland 68, 199
syndicalism 186
   anarcho- 187
Syria 253, 278, 281

Tacitus 31
Talabani, Jalal 278
Tambo, Oliver 248
Tamil Nadu 216
Tanzania 247, 249
Tejero, Lt. Col. Antonio 228
Telegraph 159
Texas 154
Thatcher, Margaret 259, 261
Thebes 11
Thessalonica 31
Thiers, Adolphe 175
Thingvelir 32
Third Lateran Council 44
Thirty Tyrants 20
Thirty Years War 71, 77, 79
Thucydides 19–20, 24
Tiananmen Square 272–4
Tibet 275
Tillett, Ben 181
Times, The 159
Tit-Bits 179
Tocqueville, Alexis de 101, 115–16, 129,
   283
Tokyo 2
Tolpuddle Martyrs 159
Toulouse 55, 121
towns and cities
   church structures 58
   civic pride 46
   defence 51–2
   diminishing power 66
   medieval democracy 46–67
   as new type of community 40
   organic growth 40
   as places of entertainment 179
   Popolo system 61–5
   religion 52
   see also individual cities, towns
trade unions 159, 174, 181–2
Treaty of Rome 230
Trenton 105
True Law of Free Monarchies, The 76
Truman, Harry 231, 232

Trumbo, Dalton 231–2
Tudors 75
Tunisia 281
Turkey 220, 253, 269
Tuscany 55, 56, 58
Twiss, Richard 133

Uganda 249
Ukraine 166, 269
Umberto I of Italy 187
United Nations 233
United Provinces see Netherlands
United States of America 98–117,
    183–3, 187, 191, 199, 201–3, 204,
    230–8, 241, 276–9
    and Afghanistan 277–8
    Albany Regency party 114
    anti-communism 231–2, 233, 235,
        252
    Articles of Confederation 105
    Bill of Rights 106
    British imperialism displeases 211
    CIA 233–4, 236
    Civil War 114, 183
    Congress 27, 106, 107–8
    Constitution 5, 106, 184, 238
    consumerism 202–3
    currency issues 105
    Declaration of Independence 29,
        104–6, 107, 112
    democracy in other countries
        promoted by 277
    Democrat-Republicans 111
    Democrats 113, 203, 231, 232
    early voting rights 107–8
    economic boom 230
    eighteenth-century population
        growth 102
    elections, growing turnout for 113
    Europe divided up by 219
    Federalists 106, 108, 111, 112
    and First World War 189
    House of Representatives 108, 113
    income tax 180
    investment in Germany 194, 195
    and Iraq 278–9
    Ku Klux Klan 201
    leisured landowners despised 110
    party politics takes hold 111–12,
        114
    and Philippines 252
    presidential elections 111, 113
    pre-USA see North America
    racial segregation 201–2, 231, 237–8
    Republicans 112–13, 116, 231
    right-wing groups 201
    rising population 112
    Senate 27, 108
    September 11 terrorist attacks
        277–8
    slavery 102, 115, 116
    as sole superpower 276
    South African racism embarrasses
        248
    new South American nations
        recognised by 150–1
    Supreme Court 106–7
    tripartite constitution 108
    TV debates 226
    Un-American Activities
        Committee in 231–2
    and Vietnam 252
    voting qualifications 115
    Voting Rights Act 283
    and War of 1812 112
    War of Independence 100, 103–5
    Whigs 113, 114
    women's voting rights 184
    see also individual states, cities,
        towns; North America
Urbino 55
Uruguay 144, 155, 199
US Steel 184

Valesio, Master 66
Valley Forge 105
Valliant, August 187
van Aemstels 48

van Buren, Martin 113, 114
Vargas, Getúlio 200
Vasa 75
Vendée 136, 139
Venetia 69, 161, 166
Venezuela 144, 148, 150, 154, 155, 280
Venice 55, 61
Veracruz 144
Vermont 106
Verona 55, 57
Versailles 119, 120, 125–6, 129
Versailles, Treaty of 191, 194, 219
Victor Emmanuel of Italy 174
Vienna 167, 168, 169
   Congress 157, 158, 163
Vietnam 252
Vijayanagara Empire 206
Villani, Giovanni 65
Virginia 102, 113
Visigoths 33
Voltaire 95, 119, 129

Wałęsa, Lech 257
Wall Street Crash 195
Walsingham, Thomas 36
Walwyn, William 82
Warsaw Pact 220
Washington, George 104, 105, 109
Waterloo, Battle of 157
Weber, Tim 264
Wei Jingsheng 272
Weizsäcker, Richard von 255
Wellington, Duke of 157
Weymouth 100
Wilcox County 238

Wildman, John 87, 89
Wilhelm I of Germany 176
Wilhelm II of Germany 176, 189
William I of England (the
   Conqueror) 32
William III of England (of Orange)
   54, 94
William of Pusterla 61
Wilson, Harold, 225
Wilson, Woodrow 189
Winchester 41
Winstanley, Gerard 81
Winthrop, John 99
Wojtyla, Karol (John Paul II) 257
Wollstonecraft, Mary 129
World Bank 267, 268, 280
World War
   First 188–9
   Second 219, 258

Xerxes 16

Yalta 219
Yar'Adua, Umaru 282
Yeltsin, Boris 260, 261–3, 267
Yemen 281
Yorktown 105
Young, Arthur 124
Yugoslavia 200, 266

Zaïre 247
Zambia 247
Zhao Ziyang 273
Zhivkov, Todor 265
Zuma, Jacob 249